4TH EDITION

Cochran's German Review Grammar

Revised and Edited by
JONATHAN B. CONANT
University of Minnesota
Duluth

PRENTICE HALL, Englewood Cliffs, New Jersey 07632

Library of Congress Cataloging-in-Publication Data

COCHRAN, EMORY ELLSWORTH.
  [German review grammar]
  Cochran's German review grammar / revised and edited by Jonathan
  B. Conant.—4th ed.
    p.   cm.
  Includes index.
  Summary: A reference and review grammar of German for second year
  students.
  ISBN 0-13-139965-9
  1. German language—Grammar—1950- [1. German language—
Grammar.] I. Conant, Jonathan B. (date). II. Title.
PF3112.C66 1991
438.2'421—dc20   90-43086 CIP
                         AC

Editorial/production supervision
  and interior design: F. Hubert
Cover design: Bruce Kenselaar
Prepress buyer: Herb Klein
Manufacturing buyer: David Dickey

Printed in the United States of America

10 9 8 7 6 5 4 3 2 1

ISBN   0-13-139965-9

PRENTICE-HALL INTERNATIONAL (UK) LIMITED, *London*
PRENTICE-HALL OF AUSTRALIA PTY. LIMITED, *Sydney*
PRENTICE-HALL CANADA INC., *Toronto*
PRENTICE-HALL HISPANOAMERICANA, S.A., *Mexico*
PRENTICE-HALL OF INDIA PRIVATE LIMITED, *New Delhi*
PRENTICE-HALL OF JAPAN, INC., *Tokyo*
SIMON & SCHUSTER ASIA PTE. LTD., *Singapore*
EDITORA PRENTICE-HALL DO BRASIL, LTDA., *Rio de Janeiro*

Contents

Preface

In the 1930s, when Emory Cochran first published his grammar of German, foreign language learning was still dependent on the model of Latin. Languages were learned to be read, first of all. When I studied German as a teenager in Atlanta in the 1950s, and despite the experience of a juvenile year in Munich and an AFS summer in Göttingen, it was to me a school subject for analysis, memorization, and exercise, and not a living tool for real-life communication.

Any intermediate German text faces two sorts of tension. The first, suggested above, is between the language itself and the use to which the intended learners mean to put it. The introductory text enjoys the freedom of saying "This book is meant for graduate students who want to read Goethe" or "This book will teach you the German you need for everyday conversation with teenagers," and the teacher chooses the book which best matches the students' needs. Students who have graduated to the level of this book have several simultaneous needs. They will want to function without exciting criticism in both written and spoken German, and they will want to understand university lectures as well as the prose of Tieck, Droste-Hülshoff, Kafka, and Helga Novak. I have perserved most of Cochran's original, to meet the needs of this latter group, but added material to satisfy the expectations of the former. I have tried to strike a balance between the normative and the descriptive. Since I am inclined, as linguists are, to favor the descriptive, students will have to face the fact that there is often no single right answer to a question.

The other tension is between two general approaches to language teaching and learning. In Cochran's day and my youth, as remarked above, the Latin model was followed. Active use was not contemplated, so there was no reason not to work through the declensions and conjugations one at a time. Students only said and wrote what they were told to say and write. Now we know that language competence grows by enlargement from within, moving from a simple stick-figure sentence to a fully rounded expression; and that real language occurs within and is very much informed by a real context. A reference and review grammar needs to be sure that students can manage the little bits and pieces of German, and I have retained micromanagement exercises—fill in the blanks and translations—for that purpose. But I have also added wherever I could some open-ended exercises which ask students to blend the grammar items being learned with their own German competence and their own natural habitat. I advise teachers to encourage wit and humor in class when these exercises are done.

Many colleagues have responded over the years to requests for comments, and others have taken the initiative to send me suggestions for improvement, and to all of these kind people I am very grateful.

Adolph Wegener, Muhlenberg College
Linda DeMeritt, Allegheny College
David Dickson, Sierra College
Robert Elkin, West Virginia University
Ronald Wanner, Ball State University
Regula A. Meier, Old Dominion University
Roswitha Mueller, University of Wisconsin–Milwaukee
Jean M. Woods, University of Oregon
William G. Zell, Northwestern College
Charles J. Kenlan, Washington State University
Wallace Sue, Michigan State University
Robert Braff, Ely High School, Ely, Minnesota
T. C. Christy, University of Alabama–Huntsville
Clifton W. Hall, University of Colorado
Louise W. Kiefer, Baldwin-Wallace College
Juergen Eichhoff, University of Wisconsin–Madison

Six colleagues have reviewed parts of the fourth edition and sent numerous useful ideas:

Herbert Genzmer, University of California at Berkeley
Ingrid Walsoe-Engel, Yale University
Sonja Hedgepeth, Middle Tennessee State University
Herbert Rowland, Purdue University
Ralph H. Kaden, Yale University
Tiiu V. Laane, Texas A & M University

Gerhart Teuscher of McMaster University agreed to read the whole text of this edition and subjected it to a basilisk scrutiny, finding all manner of inconsistency, simple mistake, and forced idiom. The book is much improved by his dutiful effort.

The students who have used Cochran in advanced German here at UMD have been generous as well, offering more human-sounding variants for many examples and exercises.

It was the silver tongued Steve Debow, Acquisitions Editor at Prentice Hall, who talked me into undertaking a renewal of this old war horse. He has kept me hard at it, knowing best when to praise and when to urge. Thanks to him, and to Production Editor and Designer Frank Hubert, the profession has a bright and cheerful new Cochran. Herta Erville's copy editing has been meticulous, provocative, and challenging, and I am in her debt. We all hope this revision will continue unbroken the notable tradition of service to German language learning begun in 1934 with *A Practical German Review Grammar.*

Finally, my wife Gretchen and our son Diccon, by being untiringly fascinated by language, have maintained me in an environment where thinking about grammar is a noble occupation. I thank them both a lot.

JONATHAN B. CONANT
Duluth, Minnesota

Principles of Case

1

§1. CASE IN ENGLISH

Case shows the relationship which a noun phrase (NP) or a pronoun bears to other words in a sentence. This relationship is indicated in English by three cases: *nominative, possessive,* and *objective*. Except for the characteristic -'s and -s' of the possessive case, English noun phrases are not *marked*—made distinctive— to show their case and, thus, their function in the sentence. Only the pronoun sets *I-me, she-her, he-him, we-us,* and *they-them* are marked. Generally English relies on word order and sequencing to show which noun phrase is the subject, which the object, and so forth.

A. The nominative case. This case has three common uses:

    (1) As subject of a verb: *My **friend** is at home.*

    (2) As predicate noun: *He is **my friend**.*

    (3) As noun of address: *Please visit me, **Mr. Ryan**.*

B. The possessive case. As its name implies, this case denotes ownership. In English, but not in German, an apostrophe indicates the possessive case: *The **boy's** socks are on the floor.* Or with a plural possessive: *The **boys'** socks are on the floor.* The possessive is often replaced by a prepositional phrase (pP) using **of** followed by a noun phrase or a pronoun in the objective case: *The works **of our members** are not for sale.*

C. The objective case. The chief uses of this case are:

(1) As a direct object of a verb: *He loves **his son**.*

A transitive verb in the active voice requires a complement, which is called a "direct object." Only transitive verbs take direct objects. The complement which must follow such a verb indicates the target of the action. (In the preceding example the father's love is directed at the *son*.) Stated differently, a direct object denotes a thing or a person acted upon: *He pitched **the ball***. Here the ball was the thing acted upon.

(2) As indirect object of a verb: *He gave **his son** free tips.*

A noun phrase or pronoun denoting the person to whom or for whom something is done is called the "indirect object": the father gives the free tips, and he gives them to his son, or for his son's benefit. The indirect object is usually a person, but may be a thing as well: *He gave **the chair** a coat of paint*. English frequently expresses the indirect object by means of a prepositional phrase introduced by *to*:

> *She offered **the tourists** some good advice.*
>
> *She offered some good advice **to the tourists**.*

In both sentences *some good advice* is the direct object; the indirect object is expressed either as a noun phrase **the tourists** or a prepositional phrase **to the tourists**.

> *They showed **us** the city-plan.*
>
> *They showed the city-plan **to us**.*

Here the direct object is *the city-plan* while the indirect object is the pronoun *us* in the first sentence and the prepositional phrase *to us* in the second.

The verb usually suggests whether or not an object is needed to complete the idea of the sentence. *To be* allows no object, but anticipates a predicate noun or adjective; *to see* needs a direct object; *to give* is usually complemented by both a direct and an indirect object.

(3) As object of a preposition: *They chased **after him**.*

A preposition and its object is called a "prepositional phrase" (pP). Such phrases complement the verb (*He sells the car **to his buddy***) or—as adverbs of time, manner, or place—answer the questions *when?*, *how?*, or *where?*

§2. CASE IN GERMAN

There are four cases in German: *nominative, genitive, dative,* and *accusative.* One must distinguish carefully between transitive and intransitive verbs. Most verbs that are transitive in English are also transitive in German. An intransitive verb—e.g., **sein,** *to be,* and **gehen,** *to go*—is one that does not take an object.

A. The nominative case. The use of the German nominative matches that of the English nominative. Both generally *name* the subject in some way.

   (1) As the subject of the verb:

> **Mein Freund** ist nicht zu Hause.
> *My friend is not at home.*
> **Das Kind** wurde schnell müde.
> *The child got tired quickly.*

   (2) As a predicate noun, linked to the subject by a verb of equality like **sein, werden,** or **bleiben.**

> **Er** ist **mein bester Freund.**
> *He is my best friend.*
> **Sie** blieb **meine Freundin** durch dick und dünn.
> *She remained my friend through thick and thin.*

   (3) As a noun of address:

> Bitte, hören Sie damit auf, **Herr Bernotat!**
> *Please stop that, Mr. Bernotat.*

B. The genitive case. The genitive case corresponds to the English possessive case or to a prepositional phrase introduced by *of* to denote possession.

> Die Eltern **dieser Kinder** sind meistens weg.
> *The parents of these children are usually away.*
> Die Schultasche **des Jungen** liegt auf dem Pult.
> *The boy's bookbag is lying on the desk.*

   (1) With proper noun (i.e., names) German denotes possession simply by adding an **s** without an apostrophe. The only time an apostrophe is used is if the word ends in an "s" sound.

> **Goethes** Gedichte, *Goethe's poems*
> **Grass'** Romane, *Grass's novels*

   (2) In German the genitive noun phrase usually follows the noun phrase being possessed. An exception is shown above, where the genitive of proper nouns precedes the noun phrase being possessed.

   (3) German possessive determiners (all of which are **ein-** words, such as **mein, dein,** and **unser**) must not be confused with pronouns in the genitive case (which are, in any case, quite rare). The possessive determiner, like any

other **der**-word or **ein**-word, derives its ending from the gender, number, and case of the noun with which it is coupled.

C. **The dative case.** The dative is regularly used as the case of the indirect object.

(1) Wir haben **den Kindern** die Fotos geschickt.
*We sent **the children** the photos.*
*We sent the photos **to the children.***

(2) Sie zeigte **dem Polizisten** den Führerschein.
*She showed **the policeman** her driver's license.*

(3a) Ich werde *der Krankenschwester* den Zettel geben.
*I'll give **the nurse** the note.*

(3b) Ich werde ihn **der Krankenschwester** geben.
*I'll give it **to the nurse.***

(3c) Ich werde ihn **ihr** geben.
*I'll give it **to her.***

As shown in examples (3a), (3b), and (3c), the dative object precedes the accusative object, *unless* the accusative object is a pronoun. Whether the dative object is a noun or a pronoun is irrelevant.

D. **The accusative case.** The accusative is the case of most direct objects. Remember that only transitive verbs take direct objects.

Sie besucht **ihren Sohn.**
*She visits **her son.***

Wir haben **euch** schon gehört.
*We already heard **you.***

Ihr müßt **das lange Gedicht** auswendig lernen.
*You have to memorize **the long poem.***

E. **Other uses of the three objective cases.** The dative and accusative cases, and to a far lesser extent the genitive case, are used very productively in combination with prepositions, with some verbs, and even with adjectives. Indeed, any time the objective case is used in English, that use will have to be assigned to one of the three objective cases—the genitive, dative, or accusative—in German. This task will figure strongly in subsequent chapters.

F. **Appositives.** A noun standing in apposition to an earlier noun or pronoun is set off by commas and is in the same case.

Seine Freundin, **die Filmschauspielerin,** war wohlbekannt.
*His friend, **the movie actress,** was well known.*

Wir geben unsrem Freunde, **dem Rechtsanwalt,** die Akten.
*We give the documents to our friend, **the lawyer.***

E X E R C I S E S

A. Identify the subjects (S), predicate nouns (predN), predicate adjectives (predA), direct and indirect objects (dirO and indirO), and prepositional phrases (pP) in the following German sentences.

1. Mein Vetter ist Ministerpräsident.
2. Der Wienerwald ist wirklich fabelhaft.
3. Die meisten Touristen besuchen den Kaiser-Wilhelm-Turm.
4. Der Schirm meiner Tante liegt bestimmt nicht auf dem Tisch im Garten.
5. Der Taxifahrer gab dem Mann falsche Auskunft.
6. In der Zeitung liest man oft fürchterliche Nachrichten.
7. Kinder, begleitet ihr eure Lehrerin zum Tierpark?
8. Wir bieten dem Gastarbeiter einen besseren Job an.
9. Er gibt uns seine Antwort am folgenden Mittwoch.
10. Der Anfang eines Gedichtes ist immer bedeutsam.

B. Supply the missing endings. Sometimes no ending is required. Refer to the end vocabulary for the gender and number of unfamiliar words.

1. Er liest d＿＿ Kriminalroman.
2. Sie ist mein＿＿ Ärztin.
3. Ich werde d＿＿ Professor etwas Geld anbieten.
4. D＿＿ Eltern hatten d＿＿ Kind auf der Straße gesehen.
5. Er zeigt d＿＿ Frau＿＿ [*pl.*] d＿＿ Broschüren.
6. Habt ihr d＿＿ Kinder gehört?
7. Sie schenkte d＿＿ Verliebten ein＿＿ Ring.
8. Wo ist d＿＿ Mutter d＿＿ Mädchen＿＿ [*sing.*]?
9. D＿＿ Zahnarzt war gestern in d＿＿ Klinik.
10. Wer ist jetzt d＿＿ Lehrerin d＿＿ Jung＿＿ [*sing.*]?
11. Wie heißen d＿＿ Kinder dein＿＿ Frau?
12. Dies＿＿ Häuser sind altmodisch.
13. Ich wollte ein＿＿ Brief an [+acc.] mein＿＿ Freund, d＿＿ Jurist＿＿, schreiben.
14. Besuchen Sie m＿＿ bald, Herr Müller!
15. Hast du d＿＿ Deutsche Eck in Koblenz gesehen?

C. Translate the following sentences into idiomatic German.

1. She wants to visit the Prime Minister.
2. No one loves the lawyer.

3. We will show the customer the wristwatch.
4. My cousin the schoolteacher reads Kafka's works constantly.
5. This umbrella is green, not black.
6. The clinic lies near the Rhine Elbow.
7. Alois stayed my friend through thick and thin.
8. This VW is certainly old-fashioned.
9. A flight from Chicago to Frankfurt is very costly.
10. May this woman's children watch television now?

Principles of Tense

2

§3. TENSE IN ENGLISH

A verb—e.g., *write, wrote, written*—has six tenses. A "tense" is a category of verbal inflection which specifies the *time* of the action or state expressed by the verb. Other such categories are *voice, mood,* and *aspect*. Voice and mood will be discussed in due course. Aspect, which specifies *how* a verb's expressed action or state occurs, exists in English but not in German—and is thus a special source of difficulty in translating from either language into the other. The following sentences illustrate the use of the six tenses in English. Note the aspectual variation in the present and past.

A. **Present:** *I write the letter. I am writing the letter. I do write the letter.*

B. **Past:** *I wrote the letter. I was writing the letter. I did write the letter.*

C. **Present Perfect:** *I have written the letter.*

D. **Past Perfect:** *I had written the letter.*

E. **Future:** *I will write the letter.*

F. **Future Perfect:** *I will have written the letter.*

§4. TENSE IN GERMAN

The German verb also has six tenses. These are, however, less rich in forms than the English tenses and are somewhat differently named. As in English, each verb has three principal parts (or **Stammformen**)—e.g., **schreiben, schrieb, geschrieben.** A list of German strong and irregular verbs and their principal parts is included in most dictionaries and is to be found in the appendix to this book.

A. Present:

> **Ich schreibe** den Brief.
> *I write the letter.*
> *I am writing the letter.*
> *I do write the letter.*

B. Past (also called **Simple Past**):

> **Ich schrieb** den Brief.
> *I wrote the letter.*
> *I have written the letter.*
> *I was writing the letter.*
> *I did write the letter.*

C. Perfect (also called **Compound Past**):

> **Ich habe** den Brief **geschrieben.**
> *I wrote the letter.*
> *I have written the letter.*
> *I was writing the letter.*
> *I did write the letter.*

German cannot express aspectual nuances in its verb system, and there are thus no progressive or emphatic forms (e.g., *am writing, was writing, do write,* or *did write*). The English present tense, in whatever aspectual variation, can be translated in one way only: *he is playing, he does play,* and *he plays* are all equally **er spielt.** Similarly, *she was playing, she did play,* and *she played* are all equally **sie spielte** or **sie hat gespielt.** Great care must be taken to avoid falling into the trap laid by the English present and past progressive and emphatic forms. Usually an adverb of time or a flavoring particle must be added if the aspectual nuances are to be preserved—*He <u>did</u> write the letter* becomes **Er hat den Brief** *doch* **geschrieben.**

D. Past Perfect:

> **Ich hatte** den Brief **geschrieben.**
> *I had written the letter.*

E. **Future:**

>   **Ich werde** den Brief **schreiben.**
>   *I will write* the letter.

F. **Future Perfect:**

>   **Ich werde** den Brief **geschrieben haben.**
>   *I will have written* the letter.

§5. COMPARISON OF ENGLISH AND GERMAN TENSES

The following table shows the extent of correspondence between English and German tenses in their fundamental use. Special and idiomatic uses are explained in later chapters.

English	German	Tense
I write *I am writing* *I do write*	**ich schreibe**	PRESENT
I wrote *I have written* *I was writing* *I did write*	**ich schrieb** (SIMPLE) **ich habe geschrieben** (COMPOUND)	PAST
I had written	**ich hatte geschrieben**	PAST PERFECT
I will write	**ich werde schreiben**	FUTURE
I will have written	**ich werde geschrieben haben**	FUTURE PERFECT

A. German and English have inherited both simple and compound past formulations from their common ancestor. The difference between them in English is one of aspect: *they wrote* refers to a point in past time, while *they have written* stretches across past time. To highlight the difference between them, try inserting an adverb of precise time, like *yesterday at dinner,* into both formulations. The German simple past and compound past (or "perfect") tenses refer to the same time in the past and, since they lack the aspectual difference, are to a large extent interchangeable.

(1) The compound past is used in conversation, while the more economical simple past may be favored in the written language. Nearly exclusive use of the compound past is a dialect feature in Southern Germany and Austria.

(2) In conversation the compound past is ordinarily used when referring to a single event that has taken place:

> Gestern **haben wir ferngesehen.**
> *We watched TV yesterday.*
>
> Wann **habt ihr ferngesehen?**
> *When did you watch TV?*

(3) For simplicity's sake the simple past is regularly used to express two or more acts that occurred at the same time in the past, especially in the same sentence:

> Sie **spielte** Ball, während ihr Bruder seine Hausaufgabe **machte.**
> *She played ball while her brother did his homework.*

(4) In the written language the simple past is regularly used for narrating and describing past events, especially when such events are related as *a chain of facts:*

> Er kam, er sah, er siegte.
> *He came, he saw, he conquered.*
>
> Die Mutter ging in die Stadt, kaufte uns eine neue Kaffeemühle und kam um vier Uhr wieder nach Hause.
> *Mother went to town, bought us a new coffee grinder, and came home again at four o'clock.*

B. The German past perfect corresponds in use and meaning to the English past perfect. Its purpose is to set the stage for another, more important, event in the past, and so it seldom exists in an isolated sentence:

> **Wir hatten** ihn schon **besucht,** bevor er krank wurde.
> *We had already visited him before he got sick.*

C. The future tense is used chiefly as in English:

> Mein Freund **wird** bestimmt **anrufen.**
> *My friend will certainly call.*

But if an adverb of future time is included, the present tense is used in preference to the future—**Mein Freund ruft bestimmt** *morgen* **an** renders English *My friend will certainly call* **tomorrow.**

D. The future perfect tense in its literal sense is as rare in German as it is in English. Its function is to establish a context for a future event: "No, we haven't read the book yet, but before our report is due next Wednesday...

...**werden** wir das Buch schon **gelesen haben.**"
*...we **will have read** the book.*"

EXERCISES

A. Change the following present tense sentences into (a) the simple past, (b) the compound past, and (c) the future. Refer to the list of strong and irregular verbs in the appendix, and be sure to note whether the past-making auxiliary is **haben** or **sein**.

1. Meine Eltern lesen die Tageszeitung jeden Tag.
2. Anita schreibt eine Postkarte an den Abgeordneten.
3. Besucht ihr den Elefanten im Tierpark?
4. Onkel Leo spielt Skat in der Kneipe.
5. Du kommst mit dem letzten Zug an.
6. Ich studiere Pflanzenkunde auf der Uni.
7. Kaufen Sie sich ein Los für die Lotterie?
8. Es dauert nicht lange bis zur nächsten Sendung.
9. Im Herbst helfen wir bei der Ernte mit.
10. Sprichst du gern Französisch?

B. Answer the following questions negatively, first in either of the past tenses and then in the future tense. Be sure to use a sensible subject pronoun in each answer, and to add adverbs of time as appropriate.

Example: *Siehst du dir den Film heute an?*

Answers: Nein, ich habe mir den Film schon gestern angesehen.
Nein, aber ich werde mir den Film morgen ansehen.

1. Besuchst du die Kneipe?
2. Lesen Sie Bücher von Helga Novak?
3. Steigen sie in der Stadtmitte um?
4. Eßt ihr Torte am Sonntag?
5. Verliebst du dich in Filmpersönlichkeiten?
6. Geht ihr jeden Tag in die Kirche?
7. Trägst du einen Regenmantel bei diesem Wetter?
8. Lernen wir jetzt die deutschen Verbformen?
9. Fährt er mit dem alten Wagen nach Köln?
10. Bekomme ich ein Stück Kuchen, Inge?

C. Translate into German.

1. Earlier he had written a letter.
2. Did you read it aloud?
3. The students are playing tennis.
4. When will we learn the poem by heart?
5. She helped the children with their homework.
6. We took a hike in the country, sang folksongs, and ate too much.
7. Karl and Erik, you will arrive very early.
8. Did we buy the book in Cologne or in Munich?
9. She had visited friends in town and returned home at ten o'clock.
10. It is raining now outside.

3

Determiners
and
Negation

§6. DETERMINERS: USES OF THE DEFINITE ARTICLE (*DER*) AND THE INDEFINITE ARTICLE (*EIN*)

Determiners as a class of function words serve to introduce and identify the nouns which they precede without actually describing them. The task of describing nouns belongs to adjectives. German determiners are grouped together under two headings, **der-**words and **ein-**words. The **ein-**words—**ein**, its negative **kein**, and the possessives **mein, dein, ihr, sein, unser, euer,** and **Ihr**—are so called because they follow the paradigm of **ein**, the *indefinite article*. The other determiners, such as **dies-, solch-, jed-, all-** and **welch-**, are declined according to the paradigm of the *definite article,* **der**.

The first section of this chapter deals largely with the use of the two articles in German, their similarities to and differences from English usage. Review the tables in §§93–97 of Appendix II.

A. **Geographical names.** As in English, the names of countries, states, and cities are generally used without a definite article. This applies almost invariably if the name of a country is neuter (as most are, e.g., Deutschland, Frankreich, Spanien, England, Kanada).

Sind Sie je in **Deutschland** oder **Frankreich** gewesen?
*Were you ever in **Germany** or **France**?*

Er wurde in **Niedersachsen** geboren. Ja, in **Friedland**.
*He was born in **Lower Saxony**. Yes, in **Friedland**.*

Here are the most common exceptions:

(1) The definite article (here in the dative case) is required if the name of the country is feminine or plural:

Sie war Bankbeamtin in **der Schweiz.**
*She was a bank clerk in **Switzerland.***

Wir knipsten viele Windmühlen in **den Niederlanden.**
*We took snapshots of many windmills in **the Netherlands.***

Other examples are die Türkei, die Tschechoslowakei, die Normandie, die Pfalz, die Niederlande, and (of course) die Vereinigten Staaten.

(2) The definite article is always required if the name of the country is preceded by an adjective:

Wart ihr schon in dem verregneten **England?**
*Have you already been in rainy **England?***

(3) Certain masculine and some neuter names of countries require or permit the use of the definite article: **der Balkan, der Sudan, das Elsaß, der Irak, der Iran.**

B. **Parts of the body: Clothing.** Instead of using possessive determiners as English does with parts of the body or items of clothing, German uses the definite article—always assuming there is no doubt whose body or clothing is being discussed.

Er setzt sich **den** Hut auf.
*He puts **his** hat on.*

Was hat sie in **der** Hand?
*What has she got in **her** hand?*

C. **Seasons, months, and days.** The definite article is used with the names of the seasons, the months of the year, and the days of the week. Frequently the article is contracted with a preceding preposition.

Der Winter ist mir doch zu kalt!
Winter is really too cold for me!

Im Juli und **im** August arbeiten wir beim Rettungsdienst.
In July and August we work as lifeguards.

D. **Church and school.** German requires the article in such phrases as: *to go to school, to church; to be in school, in church;* and *after school.*

Seit ihr in **der** Schule?—*Are you in school?*

Wir gehen in **die** Schule.—*We go to school.*

Er ist in **der** Kirche.—*He's in church.*

Sie geht in **die** Kirche.—*She goes to church.*

Nach **der** Schule gehen wir nach Hause.—*After school we go home.*

E. Price, frequency, rate. Where English uses the indefinite article in the sense of *per*, German idiom requires the definite article.

> Es kostet zwei Mark fünfzig **das** Pfund.
> *It costs two marks fifty **a** pound.*

F. Names of streets. German often includes the definite article with the names of streets. In addresses, however, the article is left out.

> Sie wohnt in **der Giselastraße.**
> *She lives in **Gisela Street.***
>
> Ihre Adresse ist: **Giselastraße 64.**
> *Her address is: 64 **Gisela Street.***

G. General statements. The definite article is frequently used before nouns in general statements and trite-sounding proclamations. But it is often omitted in canonical proverbs.

> **Das** Leben ist kurz, aber **die** Kunst ist lang.
> *Life is short, but art is long.*
>
> **Der** Mensch ist sterblich.
> *Man is mortal.*
>
> Not bricht Eisen.
> *Necessity knows no law. (lit. Necessity breaks iron.)*

H. Infinitives used as nouns. Nouns adopted from the present infinitives of verbs are simply capitalized and used with the neuter form of the definite article. This is a very productive source of nouns.

> **Das** Übersetzen aus der deutschen Sprache ist anstrengend.
> *Translating from German is exhausting.*

I. Nouns in series. German usage requires that nouns in a series each have a definite article if they are of different genders. The same applies, of course, to other determiners and to adjectives. To do otherwise would suggest an erroneous gender for the second and subsequent nouns in the series.

> **Die** Mutter und **der** Vater sind in den Ruhestand getreten.
> *Mother and father have retired (i.e., from business).*
>
> **Die** Katze und **der** Hund sind beliebte Haustiere.
> *The cat and dog are beloved house pets.*

J. **Vocation.** Where English uses the indefinite article as a determiner before a predicate noun denoting vocation, rank, or nationality, German idiom requires that the article be omitted. This is a source of repeated difficulty for English-speaking learners of German.

> Meine Schwägerin ist Ärztin.
> *My sister-in-law is a physician.*
>
> Ich bin Berliner.
> *I am a citizen of Berlin.*

But if such a noun is preceded by an adjective, the indefinite article must be used to introduce the noun phrase.

> Er ist **ein begabter** Student.
> *He is **a gifted** student.*

K. **Meals.** German idiom requires the definite article before the names of meals. Where possible, contractions with preceding prepositions are favored, as in the first example below.

> Man hat Kaffee und Brötchen **zum Frühstück.**
> *We have coffee and rolls **for breakfast.***
>
> **Das Mittagessen** ist schon fertig.
> ***Dinner** is ready.*
>
> **Nach dem Abendessen** helfen wir beim Abwaschen.
> ***After supper** we help with the washing up.*

L. The superlative **meist-** must be preceded by the definite article.

> **Die meisten** Fußballspieler führen ein gesundes Leben.
> ***Most** football players lead a healthy life.*

M. **Some idioms.** A few common expressions that use the indefinite article in English use instead the definite article in German. As with many of the items in this section, these resist reduction to a rule and must simply be memorized.

> **In der Regel** bleibt er vormittags zu Hause.
> ***As a rule** he stays home in the morning.*
>
> **Zur Abwechslung** fahren wir heute mit dem Bus.
> ***For a change** we're taking the bus today.*
>
> Sie wurde krank und verlor **zur Folge** ihre Stellung.
> *She got sick and **as a result** lost her job.*

N. **What a, what kind of a, such a.** In expressions of this sort the indefinite article is used in both German and English, and there are a number of variations possible.

(1) **Welch ein** Erfolg!
What a success!

Welch eine Stadt!
What a city!

Welch (the uninflected form of **welcher**) followed by **ein** occurs in exclamations; the **ein** takes its ending from the following noun.

(2) Mit **was für einem** Computer arbeiten Sie?
What kind of computer do you work with?
What kind of a computer do you work with?

The interrogative phrase **was für ein** is best treated as a simple **ein**-word, since the **für** has lost any prepositional force and has nothing to do with the case of the following noun.

(3a) **Eine solche** Hitze habe ich nie erlebt.
(3b) **Solch eine** Hitze habe ich nie erlebt.
(3c) **So eine** Hitze habe ich nie erlebt.
*I have never experienced **such** heat.*

Such a may be translated in three ways: (3a) by **solch-** following the indefinite article and declined as an adjective; (3b) by **solch** preceding the indefinite article and remaining undeclined; (3c) by **so** followed by the indefinite article.

An alternative is to use **solch-** itself as a determiner, in which case it is a **der**-word and is inflected like **der** or **dies-**: **Solche** Hitze habe ich nie erlebt.

O. Unlike English, German uses no determiner in the following instances:

(1) Ich habe **hundert** Bücher gekauft.
*I bought **a** hundred books.*

Es sind **tausend** Jahre her.
***A** thousand years have passed.*

(2) Hast du **Kopfweh?** . . . **Magenweh?**
*Do you have **a** headache? . . . **a** stomach ache?*

Sie hat **Halsweh.** . . . **Zahnweh.**
*She has **a** sore throat. . . . **a** toothache.*

P. The idiom **machen zu** requires the definite article in German where none is present in English.

Man machte ihn **zum** Torwart.
He was made goalie. (They made him goalie.)

Here are some common phrases that use the definite article in German but not in English. Notice again that contractions with preceding prepositions are favored wherever possible.

zum Beispiel (z.B.), *for example (e.g.)*

zum Nachtisch, *for dessert*

zum Schluß, *in conclusion, finally*

zum Teil, *partly, to some extent*

mit der Post schicken, *to send by mail*

mit der Bahn, *by train*

in der Nacht, *at night*

in der Tat, *in fact, in reality, indeed*

im Bett, *in bed*

beim Namen nennen, *to call by name*

These and similar set phrases are to be found in any modern dictionary large enough to include usage notes. Check the Eng > Ger section under "dessert" and find an entry like: "for—, *zum Nachtisch*" to see how the usage notes work.

Q. Personal names are not normally preceded by the definite article. Demands of style may cause exceptions (colloquial: "Da kommt der Leo!"). Here are some more common exceptions and the difficulties they pose.

(1) Personal names modified, either attributively (as in *a*) or by apposition (as in *b*), almost always have the definite article.

(a) **Die** kleine Marie lernte schnell das Klavier.
   Little Mary quickly learned to play the piano.

(b) Karl **der** Große hat viele Klöster bauen lassen.
   Charlemagne built many monasteries.

(2) Where the name is followed by both the article and an adjective, all elements of the phrase are normally inflected. Where the name is preceded by a title without article, only the name is inflected. Where the name is preceded by a title with article, only the title and article are inflected.

Voltaire lebte am Hofe Friedrich**s des Groß**en.
Voltaire lived at the court of Frederick the Great.

König Friedrich**s** Schloß war in Potsdam.
Das Schloß **des** Königs Friedrich war in Potsdam.
King Frederick's castle was in Potsdam.

(3) **Herr** as a title is regularly inflected when it precedes a name.

Herr**n** Wagners Vertrag, *Mr. Wagner's contract*

ein Brief an Herr**n** Wagner, *a letter to Mr. Wagner*

R. Kein, the negative form of **ein,** is used to convey *not a, not any.*

Das ist **kein** übler Einfall.
*That's **not a** bad idea.*

Ich habe leider **keinen** Fernsehapparat.
*Unfortunately I haven't **any** TV.*

§7. NEGATION WITH *NICHT, NIE, NIEMALS*

If a message is to be negated entirely, German provides a location for the negating elements **nicht, nie,** or **niemals** which has the desired sweeping effect. This neutral location is *after* the subject, the finite (inflected) verb, adverbial expressions of time, indirect and direct objects; and *before* adverbial expressions of manner and place, predicate adjectives and nouns, and verbal complements (separable prefixes, infinitives, and past participles). (See illustrations **A** through **H** below.)

An alternative approach is to accept a wider definition of verbal complements to include not only separable prefixes, infinitives, and past participles, but also predicate adjectives and nouns and adverbial expressions of manner and place. Then one might say that the negation follows everything but verbal complements. Either approach works well with routine, neutral sentences.

But if an item in the message is singled out for negation, the negating element immediately precedes it, and a contrastive phrase or clause introduced by **sondern** (*but rather, on the other hand*) is added by way of correction. (See illustration **I** below.)

The negating element may always be intensified by preceding it directly with the adverb **gar.** (See illustration **J** below.)

A. After the subject, finite verb, and objects

Wir gehen gern zelten. Er **nicht.**
*We like to go camping in tents. He **doesn't.***

Das Feuer brennt **nicht.**
*The fire **doesn't** burn.*

Ihr kauft euch den Kassettenrekorder **nicht.**
*You **don't** buy yourselves the tape recorder.*

Note, however, that if the object is preceded by a form of **ein** or by no determiner at all, it is negated by a corresponding form of **kein.**

Ihr kauft euch **einen** Kassettenrekorder.
Ihr kauft euch **keinen** Kassettenrekorder.

Ich habe Zeit dafür. *I have the time for it.*
Ich habe **keine** Zeit dafür. *I have **no** time for it.*

Diese Limonade enthält Zucker.
This soft drink contains sugar.

Jene Limonade enthält **keinen** Zucker.
*That soft drink contains **no** sugar.*

B. Before a separable prefix

Sie sieht ihn **nicht** an.
*She **doesn't** look at him.*

Wir lernten unsre Schulkameraden **nicht** kennen.
*We **didn't** get to know our classmates.*

C. Before a complementary infinitive

Wir werden es ihm **nicht** geben.
*We **won't** give it to him.*

Er ließ sich das Haar **nie** waschen.
*He **never** had his hair washed.*

Wir brauchen die Tür **niemals** aufzumachen.
*We **never** need to open the door.*

D. Before a past participle

Er hat die Batterie **nicht** aufgeladen.
*He **didn't** charge the battery.*

Wir haben die Rechnung **nie** erhalten.
*We've **never** gotten the bill.*

Sie haben es ihr **niemals** geschickt.
*They **never** sent it to her.*

E. Before a predicate adjective

Er ist **nicht** schläfrig.
*He **isn't** sleepy.*

Ihr seid **niemals** bereit.
*You're **never** ready.*

F. Before a predicate noun

Sie ist **nicht** Stenotypistin. (or: Sie ist **keine** Stenotypistin.)
*She is **not** a stenotypist.*

Er war **nie** Sportredakteur.
*He was **never** a sports editor.*

G. After adverbial expressions of time

Sie kommen heute morgen **nicht.**
*They're **not** coming this morning.*

Wir arbeiten während des Wintersemesters **nicht.**
*We **don't** work during the winter semester.*

H. Before adverbial expressions of manner and place

Ich spiele Golf **nicht** gern.
*I **don't** like to play golf.*

Er zieht sich **niemals** einen Pelzmantel an.
*He **never** gets dressed in a fur coat.*

Sie ist **nicht** zu Hause.
*She is **not** at home.*

Du darfst **nicht** nach Europa fliegen.
*You may **not** fly to Europe.*

I. Specific negation in contrastive situations

Sie hat **nicht** das Bargeld, **sondern** einen Reisescheck.
*She **hasn't** got cash, **but rather** a traveler's check.*

Er kommt **nicht** heute morgen, **sondern** morgen.
*He's **not** coming this morning, **but** tomorrow **instead**.*

J. Negation intensified with *gar*

Er versteht es **gar nicht.**
*He **doesn't** understand it **at all**.*

Er hat **gar nichts.**
*He has **nothing at all**.*

E X E R C I S E S

A. Complete the following sentences. (A few are correct without any additions.)

1. Zürich und Luzern sind Städte in _____ Schweiz.

2. Lezten Sommer war ich in _____ Deutschland.

3. Warst du jemals in _____ Türkei oder in _____ Tschechoslowakei?

4. Meine beiden Vettern waren nie in _____ Vereinigten Staaten.

5. _____ Kunst ist lang, _____ Leben ist kurz.

6. _____ Mensch denkt, _____ Gott lenkt.

7. _____ Schreiben fällt meinem kleinen Bruder sehr schwer.

8. Sie setzt sich _____ Hut auf.

9. Er wohnt in _____ Weendestraße.

10. Dieses faule Mädchen kommt immer zu spät in _____ Schule.

11. Sein älterer Bruder war schon in _____ Schule.

12. Nach _____ Schule laufen wir schnell nach Hause.

13. _____ (In the) Winter spielt sie Eishockey.

14. _____ (In) Juli ist das Wasser in den Seen ziemlich warm.

15. _____ (On) Montag werde ich zur Disko gehen.

16. Ich besuchte ihn immer dreimal _____ (a/per) Monat.

17. Die Rasierklingen kosten sechs Mark _____ (per) Zehnerpackung.

18. _____ Bruder und _____ Schwester waren beide zu Hause.

19. Ist Ihre Schulfreundin jetzt _____ Ärztin oder _____ Rechtsanwältin?

20. Ich bin _____ _____ (a good) Arzt/Ärztin.

21. _____ solch____ Gewitter habe ich noch nie erlebt.

22. Solch _____ Gewitter haben wir noch nie erlebt.

23. Solch ein____ Stadt hat viele Sehenswürdigkeiten.

24. Heute haben wir Obst _____ (for) Frühstück.

25. _____ meisten jungen Leute gehen gern schwimmen.

26. _____ _____ (As a) Regel spielt Katrine nach der Schule Tennis.

27. Man machte ihn _____ Präsidenten.

28. _____ klein____ Karl wollte keine Hausaufgaben machen.

29. Karl d____ Groß____ vermißte Roland, seinen besten Ritter.

30. Als wir in Potsdam waren, besuchten wir die Bibliothek Friedrich____ d____ Groß____.

31. König Friedrich____ Schloß hieß Sanssouci.

32. Viele Bekannte d____ König____ Friedrich____ waren Künstler.

B. Give sensible and correct answers to the following questions, using complete German sentences. Follow the cues where given.

1. Ist die Schweiz eine Republik oder eine Monarchie?

2. Warst du je in Deutschland? (No, but in Switzerland)

3. Wie zieht sich der ältere Mann im Winter an?

4. Was ist leichter, das Lesen oder das Schreiben?

5. Welche Jahreszeit haben Sie jetzt?

6. In welchem Monat haben Sie Geburtstag?

7. Wieviel kostet ein Pfund Kaffee?

8. Du siehst krank aus. Was fehlt dir?

9. Wie habt ihr gewußt, daß das Kind schon weg wollte? (His hat)

10. Was für einen Zahnarzt/eine Zahnärztin haben Sie?

C. Answer the following questions in the negative.

1. Wird dein guter Freund kommen?
2. Ist der Kunde jetzt zufrieden?
3. Ist der reiche Mann da Professor?
4. Sind die Kindergärtner im Wald gewandert?
5. Ging sie dann nach Hause?
6. Dieses Bilderbuch hier, wird sie es ansehen?
7. Wann möchtest du mit ihm sprechen?
8. Fährt der Zug heute ab? Wenn nicht heute, dann wann?

D. Translate into complete German sentences.

1. Last summer my brother was in Turkey and Iran.
2. Man is mortal.
3. She had already put on her warm winter hat.
4. What has that little man got in his pocket?
5. Winter is finally past.
6. In February most people leave this town.
7. At what time do you go to school?
8. After school I often visit my friends.
9. What a big building!
10. Is dinner ready?
11. As a rule I study in the library.
12. Many French people lived at the court of Peter the Great.
13. He is never at home.
14. Unfortunately we have no book for you.
15. No, we don't have this book.
16. Benno is never sick.
17. She will not see him.
18. We were not in school today.
19. The train doesn't leave today, but tomorrow.
20. She's no dentist, she's a professor.

Adjective Declension

4

§8. GENERAL NOTE ON ADJECTIVE ENDINGS: THE WEAK DECLENSION

Noun phrases in German must be marked for number, gender, and function (i.e., case) to the extent allowable by the system of endings. In Latin, in comparison, the endings are added directly to the noun. In English, in contrast, only a few pronouns allow this marking to occur—*she* vs. *her,* for example, where function-as-subject is distinct from function-as-object.

In German, the pronouns have a fairly complete set of distinctive forms, and the determiners (**der**-words and **ein**-words) do a good job of marking the nouns they introduce. If a noun is preceded by an adjective, that adjective must have an ending too, and the ending chosen is either "strong" or "weak".

As applied to German adjective declension, the terms "strong" and "weak" identify inflectional endings as, respectively, distinctive or nondistinctive. A distinctive ending or form is one which shows the number, gender, and case of the noun following. The Brothers Grimm, who coined this terminology, appear to have thought that an ending which was informative was strong, while one that was neutral and uninformative was weak.

Remembering that noun phrases must be marked wherever possible, but that marking once is enough, we can state the following rules:

1. Adjectives preceded by **der**-words and inflected **ein**-words (i.e., distinctive forms) have *weak* (i.e., nondistinctive) endings.

2. Adjectives either unpreceded by a determiner, or preceded by uninflected **ein**-words, have *strong* endings. Of course, the strong endings are virtually identical to those which would otherwise have been attached to a **der**-word.

An alternative approach, adopted by this book among many, is to establish three paradigms: one of weak endings for adjectives following **der**-words; one of strong endings for adjectives not preceded by either **der**- or **ein**-words; and a mixed declension for adjectives preceded by **ein**-words. These three paradigms are available in tabular form in the Appendix, *§99*.

This section focuses on the weak declension of adjective endings, which are by far the most commonly encountered. Keep in mind that the **der**-words are: **der** (the definite article), **dieser** (*this*), **jener** (*that*), **jeder** (*each* or *every*), **mancher** (*many a*), **solcher** (*such* or *such a*), **welcher** (*which* or *what*), and **alle** (except for set phrases like **alles Gute**, this is used chiefly in the plural and means *all*). Below are some examples of their use with the weak adjective endings.

A. Singular number.

(1) The nominative case:

Der deutsche Rhein entspringt in der Schweiz.
The German Rhine has its source in Switzerland.

Die alte Stadt Wetzlar liegt an der Lahn.
The old city of Wetzlar is situated on the Lahn.

Dieses progressive Buch gefällt mir.
I like this liberal book.

(2) The genitive case:

Die Rede **des** neuen Abgeordneten war merkwürdig.
The speech of the new delegate was peculiar.

Die Straßen **jener** alten **Stadt** sind sehr eng und steil.
The streets of that old city are very narrow and steep.

Die Eltern **dieses** traurigen Kindes sind auf dem Land.
The parents of this sad child are in the country.

(3) The dative case:

Sie gibt **jedem** ausländischen Besucher einen Stadtplan.
She gives every foreign visitor a city map.

Der Mercedes gehört **dieser** reichen Autorin.
The Mercedes belongs to this rich author.

Wir wohnen in **jenem** eleganten Hochhaus.
We live in that elegant highrise building.

(4) The accusative case:

Welchen französischen Film habt ihr gesehen?
Which French film did you see?

Sie besuchen **jede** teuere Konditorei.
They visit every expensive pastry shop.

Ich verkaufte ihr **das** farbige Bilderbuch.
I sold her the colorful picturebook.

B. Plural number.

(1) The nominative case:

Die besten Fernseher (Uhren, Autos) sind preiswert.
The best TV sets (clocks, cars) are a good value.

Alle süßen Torten schmecken mir.
All sweet cakes taste good to me.

(2) The genitive case:

Die Eltern **der** fleißigen Schüler (Schülerinnen, Kinder) sind außerordent-
lich zufrieden.
*The parents of the hardworking schoolboys (schoolgirls, children) are exceptionally
satisfied.*

Aller guten Dinge sind drei.
All good things come in threes. (Literally, There are three of all good things.)

(3) The dative case:

Wir werden selbst **den** schläfrigsten Schülern (Schülerinnen, Kindern) die
Grammatik beibringen.
We'll teach even the sleepiest schoolboys (schoolgirls, children) grammar.

In **allen** deutschen Städten hat er Bekannte.
He has friends in all German cities.

(4) The accusative case:

Sie hat **die** schönsten Koffer (Blumen, Bücher) gebracht.
She brought the prettiest suitcases (flowers, books).

Er liest **alle** importierten Zeitschriften.
He reads all imported magazines.

Note: If another determiner follows **alle,** that determiner is inflected.

Alle diese Bücher sind kostspielig.
All these books are high-priced.

§9. THE STRONG ADJECTIVE DECLENSION

The sentences below illustrate how the "strong" endings are used on adjectives which are not preceded by any determiner. These endings are available in tabular form in the Appendix. Note that they are identical to the endings used with **dieser** and other **der**-words, with the trivial exception that the masculine and neuter genitive singular have **-en** instead of the expected **-es.** Since there is no determiner present to mark the noun phrase for number, gender, or case, the adjective must do the work and uses the same endings the determiner would have used.

A. Singular number.

    (1) The nominative case:

Arm**er** Mann, was fehlt Ihnen?
Poor man, what's the matter?

Lieb**e** Mutter, bitte schicke mir etwas Geld!
Dear Mother, please send me some money.

Lieb**es** Kind, wo ist dein älterer Bruder?
Dear child, where is your older brother?

    (2) The genitive case was used years ago to express a thing measured or contained, as in the following examples. Now the thing measured or contained is in the same case as the unit of measurement or the container—that is, it's an appositive—as illustrated here in parentheses:

Sie bestellte ein Glas rot**en** Weine**s** (or: rot**en** Wein).
She ordered a glass of red wine.

Das ist ein Beweis gut**en** Geschmack**s.**
That is proof of good taste.

Er trank ein Glas erfrischend**er** (or: erfrischend**e**) Limonade.
He drank a glass of refreshing lemonade.

Das ist das Ergebnis gut**er** Zusammenarbeit.
That is the result of fine collaboration.

Gib mir ein Glas sauber**en** Wasser**s** (or: sauber**es** Wasser)!
Give me a glass of clean water.

Das ist eine Reihe interessant**er** Projekte.
That's a lot of interesting projects.

    (3) The dative case:

Da steht ein groß**er** Dom mit hoh**em** Turm.
There stands a great cathedral with a high spire.

Er schreibt mit grün**er** Tinte.
He writes with green ink.

Das ist ein Buch **von** groß**em** wert.
That book is worth a lot.

(4) The accusative case is frequently heard in greetings, where a verb of wishing is implied (*I wish you a good morning*):

Gut**en** Morgen!   Gut**e** Nacht!
Good morning.   *Good night.*

Er hatte groß**en** Erfolg.
He was tremendously successful.

B. Plural number.

All cases:

Alt**e** Freunde sind gut**e** Freunde.
Old friends are good friends.

Er kaufte sich vier Paar feinst**er** Handschuhe.
He bought four pairs of the finest gloves.

Der schwere Wagen wurde von kräftig**en** Ochsen gezogen.
The heavy wagon was pulled by powerful oxen.

Sie las kurz**e** Gedichte am liebsten.
She liked best of all to read short poems.

Cardinal numbers other than **ein** require the following adjective to have strong endings.

Der Dom hatte drei hoh**e** Türme.
The cathedral had three tall spires.

§10. THE MIXED ADJECTIVE DECLENSION

The sentences below illustrate the endings employed when the adjective is preceded by an **ein**-word. They are displayed in tabular form in the Appendix. The **ein**-words are **ein** (the indefinite article), **kein** (the negated indefinite article), and the possessive determiners **mein** (*my*), **dein** (*your*), **sein** (*his* or *its*), **ihr** (*her* or *their*), **unser** (*our*), **euer** (your, plural informal), and **Ihr** (*your*, singular and plural polite). Where the **ein**-word has no ending, the following adjective has a strong ending; sentences which show this are highlighted with an asterisk. Otherwise, the adjectives have weak endings.

Singular and Plural Numbers

(1) The nominative case:

> **Ein** fleißiger Student besteht jede Prüfung.
> *A diligent student passes every exam.*

> Augsburg ist **eine** schöne Stadt.
> *Augsburg is a pretty city.*

> **Ein** interessant**es** Buch liegt auf dem Tisch.
> *An interesting book lies on the table.*

> **Deine** neu**en** Schuhe sind aber häßlich.
> *My, but your new shoes are ugly.*

(2) The genitive case:

> Das ist der Rat **eines** gut**en** Arztes.
> *That's the advice of a good doctor.*

> Hier ist das Ferienhaus **einer** berühmt**en** Sängerin.
> *Here is the vacation home of a famous singer.*

> Der Anfang **eines** philosophisch**en** Buches ist schwer.
> *The beginning of a philosophical book is difficult.*

> Die Zeichnungen **seiner** talentiert**en** Töchter sind vielversprechend.
> *The drawings of his talented daughters are promising.*

(3) The dative case:

> Sie machte einen Spaziergang mit **ihrem** alt**en** Freund.
> *She took a walk with her old friend.*

> Er gab **seiner** geliebt**en** Frau einen Ring.
> *He gave his beloved wife a ring.*

> Wir übernachteten in **einem** malerisch**en** Dorf.
> *We spent the night in a picturesque village.*

> Sie wird **unseren** krank**en** Kindern helfen.
> *She'll help our sick children.*

(4) The accusative case:

> Ich kaufe mir **einen** bissig**en** Hund.
> *I'm buying a dog that bites.*

> Wir haben da **keine** gemütlich**e** Bierstube gesehen.
> *We didn't see any cosy tavern there.*

> **Hast du heute **ein** blau**es** Heft gefunden?
> *Did you find a blue notebook today?*

> Nein, ich habe heute **keine** blau**en** Hefte gefunden.
> *No, I haven't found any blue notebooks today.*

Do not confuse **unser** and **euer** with the **der**-words just because they happen to end in **-er.** The endings of the "mixed" declension are added to **unser** and **euer**; when an ending is added, **unser** often and **euer** regularly lose the middle **-e-**:

Nom.	**unser** lie**ber** Freund, *our dear friend*
Acc.	**unseren** (or: **unsern**) lie**ben** Freund
Nom.	**euer** lie**ber** Freund, *your dear friend*
Acc.	**euren** lie**ben** Freund

§11. ADJECTIVES IN A SERIES; DERIVED FROM NAMES OF TOWNS; USED AS NOUNS

A. Adjectives in a series have the same ending:

ein gro**ßer**, grau**er**, alt**er** Dom = *a big, gray, old cathedral*

der gro**ße**, grau**e**, alt**e** Dom = *the big, gray, old cathedral*

B. Adjectives are formed from the names of towns by adding **-er.** Such adjectives are capitalized and have no additional endings:

eine Hamburg**er** Zeitung = *a Hamburg newspaper*

das Heidelberg**er** Schlo**ß** = *Heidelberg Castle*

C. Adjectives used as nouns are capitalized but keep their regular adjective endings:

die **Reichen** und die **Armen** = *the rich and the poor*

die **Reiche** = *the rich woman*

der **Reiche** = *the rich man*

eine **Arme** = *a poor woman*

ein **Armer** = *a poor man*

§12. USE OF *MANCH, WELCH, SOLCH*

Manch-, in the sense of *many a*, is used chiefly in the singular; one may say either:

manch**er** liebe Freund = *many a dear friend*

manch lieber Freund = *many a dear friend*

Similarly:

welch**es** schöne Haus = *what a beautiful house*
welch schön**es** Haus = *what a beautiful house*

solch**es** gute Wetter = *such good weather*
solch gut**es** Wetter = *such good weather*

When used in the plural **manch** means *some*.

In **manchen** Fällen = *in some cases*
Manche Leute = *some people*

E X E R C I S E S

A. Review this list of adjectives:

alt	arm	beid-
bequem	berühmt	best-
deutsch	ehrlich	erst
freundlich	frisch	ganz
groß	gut	hoch (hoh-)
klein	klug	kurz
lang	Leipziger	lieb
link	Münchner	neu
recht	reich	schön
schwer	treu	trocken
wenig	wichtig	wild

Use adjectives from this list to enlarge the following sentences; be sure to make good sense and to use the correct endings.

1. Haben Sie die Zeitung gelesen?
2. Der Wolf ist ein Tier.
3. Morgen! Wie geht's? Nacht! Schlaf wohl!
4. Das ist ein Witz.
5. Die Frau und der Mann hatten kein Geld.
6. Er gibt mir immer Rat.
7. Kind, was fehlt dir?
8. Ihr Freund war leider nicht zu Hause.
9. Im Klassenzimmer hing eine Wandkarte von der DDR.
10. Er ist ein Rockstar mit Haar.
11. Sagen Sie mir die Wahrheit!

12. Die Kinder dürfen nicht auf der Straße spielen.

13. Wir hatten nur ein Stück Brot.

14. Dieser Mann ist mein Freund.

15. Sie hat drei Bücher.

16. Der Präsident besaß ein Vermögen.

17. Euer Onkel wird euch bald besuchen.

18. Jene Gasse ist plötzlich dunkel geworden.

19. Wir verpassten den Zug nach Bad Kissingen.

20. Wo liegt die Vaterstadt der Freunde?

21. Was habt ihr solchen Leuten gegeben?

22. Sie hat einen Wagen und ein Boot.

23. Das war doch ein Unglück.

24. Er trägt einen Überrock.

25. Die Aktentasche liegt im Büro auf dem Schreibtisch.

26. Was hast du in der Tasche?

27. Der Rhein ist ein Fluß.

28. Ursula ist ein Mädchen.

29. Haben Sie die Messe besucht?

30. Sie hat alle Zeitungen gelesen.

31. Ich lasse alle Freunde grüßen.

32. Er hat viele Freunde.

33. Jenes Buch gehört dem Jungen.

34. Ihr solltet die Stadt Rothenburg besuchen.

35. Die Schulaufgaben des Jungen sind immer noch unbefriedigend.

36. Habt ihr Brot mitgebracht?

37. Er hat mehrere Dinge vergessen.

38. Unser Arzt hat eine Zeitung gekauft.

39. Wenige Leute würden das tun.

40. Das ist bestimmt ein Haus.

41. Kinder, wo ist euer Onkel?

42. Die Eltern haben viele Freunde.

43. Er hat alles, was zu einem Leben gehört.

44. Sie kaufte sich ein Taschenbuch und das Arbeitsheft.

45. Die Schauspielerin ißt in der Gastwirtschaft zu Mittag.

B. Translate the following sentences into German.

1. Our dear colleague was in the country this week.
2. Yesterday I visited my best friend.
3. Paris is the largest city in France.
4. The policeman is carrying an old-fashioned key.
5. This song needs a powerful voice.
6. Here boys and girls go to the same school.
7. When we were young we were never in the same school.
8. Have you seen the new discount stores in the suburbs?
9. She is a famous Austrian racecar driver.
10. He is wearing a new, light blue raincoat.
11. I always get good advice from her.
12. She has to pass this easy examination.
13. Oxen are domesticated animals.
14. I gave him many good reasons.
15. My younger sister is a famous physician.
16. If you don't understand, raise your right hand.
17. We learned many a German poem by heart.
18. Did you buy a Berlin newspaper?
19. Now we have to write about the Leipzig fair.
20. Please write with black ink.
21. Good morning. We have beautiful weather for a hike.
22. To whom do these expensive things belong?
23. All big buildings are together in the new part of the city.
24. I wish you all the best.
25. Several interesting facts became clear to me.

Nouns

5

§13. STRONG, WEAK, AND IRREGULAR NOUNS

The terms "weak" and "strong" as applied to German nouns identify plural formation as, respectively, uniform (ending in -**n** or -**en** for all weak nouns) or differentiated (various combinations of umlaut or no umlaut plus endings in -, -**e**, or -**er**). All originally German nouns have -**n** in the dative plural. Some nouns are classified as "mixed" because they have strong singular but weak plural forms, while others are called "irregular" because they deviate from the expected pattern. While it is possible to predict that nouns of certain shapes and contents will be weak, generally it is best to memorize the plural along with the gender for each noun learned.

A. Strong nouns fall into three classes according to their plural formation: (1) no ending, with frequent umlaut; (2) -**e**, with frequent umlaut; and (3) -**er**, with umlaut wherever possible. Strong masculines and neuters add -**s** or -**es** in the genitive singular. There are very few strong feminine nouns. Consult the tables of the strong nouns in the Appendix.

(1) Mein Onkel besucht mich.
My uncle is visiting me.

Das Haus meines Onkel**s** liegt an einem Fluß.
My uncle's house is situated on a river.

Meine Onkel haben je zwei Töchter.
My uncles each have two daughters.

Der Garten gehört der Gemeinde.
The garden belongs to the community.

Innerhalb des Gartens steht ein Häuschen.
Inside the garden stands a little house.

Unsre Gärten haben ständige Pflege nötig.
Our gardens need constant attention.

(2) Mein Freund ist nicht zu Hause.
My friend isn't at home.

Der Wagen meines Freundes hat wieder eine Panne.
My friend's car has a flat tire again.

Meine Freunde gehen nicht einmal ins Kino.
My friends don't even go to the movies.

Der Flug beginnt am linken Ufer.
The flight begins on the left bank.

Während des Fluges schlief ich ein.
During the flight I fell asleep.

Alle Flüge sind aber total ausgebucht.
All flights are, however, booked solid.

(3) Das Kind spielt Ball auf dem Hof.
The child is playing ball in the courtyard.

Die Schuhe des Kindes sind schmutzig.
The child's shoes are dirty.

Meine Kinder müssen ihr Zimmer selber aufräumen.
My children have to clean up their room themselves.

Dieses moderne Fahrrad hat zwölf Gänge.
This modern bicycle has twelve gears.

Der Sitz des Fahrrads ist nicht sehr bequem.
The bicycle seat is not very comfortable.

Fahrräder darf man nicht in die Bibliothek bringen.
Bringing bicycles into the library is not permitted.

B. Weak nouns. Most feminine nouns belong to the weak declension; they have no endings in the singular, and form their plural with **-n** or **-en**. There are no neuter weak nouns.

Many masculine nouns are weak, especially those naming people or animals and following one of two patterns: two syllables, of which the second is **-e**, such as **Junge** and **Löwe**; two or more syllables with the stress on the last syllable, as in **Advokat** and **Student**. These masculine weak nouns have **-n** or **-en** in all forms except the nominative singular. A glance at the paradigms in the Appendix will suggest why these nouns are now generally called "N-nouns".

(1) Der Junge heißt Alois.
The boy is named Alois.

Der Sport dieses Jung**en** ist Fußball.
This boy's sport is soccer.

Der Löwe im Tierpark hat Hunger.
The lion in the zoo is hungry.

Wir geben dem Löw**en** Rindfleisch zu fressen.
We give the lion beef to eat.

Der Elefant hat auch Hunger.
The elephant is hungry too.

Wir sehen den Elefant**en** etwas Stroh fressen.
We see the elephant eat some straw.

Mancher Student lernt Tippen nicht gern.
Many a student doesn't like to learn typing.

Viele Student**en** schreiben jetzt mit dem Computer.
Many students now write on the computer.

(2) Diese Wohnung gefällt mir sehr.
This apartment pleases me very much.

Selbst der Plan der Wohnung ist vielversprechend.
Even the layout of the apartment is promising.

Die Wohnung**en** in diesem Hochhaus sind aber teuer.
My, but the apartments in this highrise are expensive.

Ich kaufe mir eine dieser Wohnung**en**.
I'll buy myself one of these apartments.

C. **Mixed nouns** are those relatively few masculine and neuter nouns whose singular has the **-s** genitive of a strong noun but whose plural is formed with **-n** or **-en** like a weak noun. Members of this class are described along with irregular nouns in the Appendix, and they themselves possess occasional irregularities.

(1) Mein Vetter ist Lehrer.
My cousin is a teacher.

Die Frau meines Vetter**s** ist Ärztin.
My cousin's wife is a physician.

Meine anderen Vetter**n** sind Politiker.
My other cousins are politicians.

(2) Das Museum ist am Montag geschlossen.
The museum is closed on Monday.

Die Ausstellungen des Museum**s** sind beachtlich.
The exhibits of the museum are noteworthy.

Andere städtische Muse**en** sind am Montag geschlossen.
Other municipal museums are closed on Monday.

B. **Irregular nouns.** These deviate from one of the standard patterns enough that they must be treated as special cases. A few masculine examples behave like weak nouns, but have as well the genitive **-s** of the strong nouns. The only neuter example, **das Herz,** follows the masculine format but has no ending in the accusative singular. Foreign loanwords with a plural in **-s** are also classed as irregular.

  (1) Mein Name ist Huber.
     My name is Huber.

     Die Stammsilbe meines Nam**ens** hat keinen Umlaut.
     There is no umlaut in the root syllable of my name.

     Man buchstabiert meinen Nam**en** ohne "ü".
     You spell my name without "u-umlaut".

  (2) Er sprach aus dem Grunde des Herz**ens**.
     He spoke from the bottom of his heart.

     Und er hat doch ein gutes Herz.
     And he really has a good heart.

  (3) Dieses Hotel ist sehr elegant.
     This hotel is very elegant.

     Viele deutsche Hotel**s** haben keinen Parkplatz.
     Many German hotels have no parking lot.

     In vielen deutschen Hotel**s** findet man keinen Fernseher.
     In many German hotels there is no TV set.

E. **Agent nouns** whose masculine version ends in **-er** create a feminine version by adding **-in**. These in turn form a plural by adding **-nen**. The stress shifts in the plural to the **-in-** syllable.

     Mein Lehr**er** hatte eine deutschsprachige Frau.
     My teacher had a German-speaking wife.

     Sie war eine sehr beliebte Lehrer**in**.
     She was a much loved teacher.

     Habt ihr noch heute solche Lehrer**innen?**
     Do you still have such teachers today?

F. **Nouns ending in -nis** double the **-s** before an ending.

     Das war ein interessantes Erleb**nis**.
     That was an interesting experience.

Sie schrieb über ihre Erleb**nisse** während des Krieges.
She wrote about her experiences during the war.

G. Masculine and neuter monosyllables sometimes take an **-e** in the dative singular. In some noun phrases the extra **-e** has become usual and expected.

Sie half dem Mann**e** (or: dem Mann).
She helped the man.

Wir bleiben jetzt zu Haus**e**.
Now we stay home.

E X E R C I S E S

A. Rewrite the following sentences in the singular, making sure to change all verbs, adjectives and pronouns as needed to make sense.

1. Die Dienstmädchen werden die großen Zimmer reinigen.
2. Die Kellnerinnen haben ein gutes Trinkgeld verdient.
3. Die Arbeiter spitzen ihre stumpfen Bleistifte.
4. Siehst du die neuen Gebäude in den deutschen Städten?
5. Wir haben die alten Schlösser in den Bergen bewundert.
6. Meine Onkel haben mir diese Handwerkzeuge geschenkt.
7. Die kleinen Vögel singen romantisch in den Bäumen.
8. Die Polizisten haben den Männern geholfen.
9. Katzen fangen gerne Mäuse.
10. Wie heißen eure Nachbarinnen?

B. Rewrite the following sentences in the plural, making sure to change all verbs, adjectives and pronouns as needed to make sense.

1. Die Bibliothek hat das deutsche Buch bestellt.
2. Der Dieb hat meinen Goldring gestohlen!
3. Die Studentin antwortet auf jede Frage.
4. Hast du den kleinen Garten in der Vorstadt gesehen?
5. Der Ochse hat diesen schweren Wagen nach oben gezogen.
6. Die moderne Schallplatte gefällt meiner Tochter.
7. Die Mutter hat ihrem Sohn das Autofahren beigebracht.
8. Wo hat der Herr diesen altmodischen Hut gekauft?
9. Der Ausdruck ist mir nicht bekannt.
10. Ludwig ließ sich den allerschönsten Hof bauen.

11. Das Museum besitzt ein merkwürdiges Auto.

12. Der kleine Hund hat ein schlechtes Gedächtnis.

13. Unsere Freundin schreibt uns bestimmt eine Postkarte.

14. In dem grünen Tal steht eine wichtige Barockkirche.

15. Das Foto an der Wand paßt nicht.

    C. Translate the following sentences into German.

1. The Germans are very proud of their forests and gardens.

2. Here is the prettiest city in the state.

3. This boy wants to buy some larger buttons.

4. I'll sell the boy these used buttons.

5. It is only one folksong among many good folksongs.

6. I saw that student in a tavern with his girlfriend.

7. German highschools are said to be very strict.

8. The beginning of the experience was the worst.

9. In the zoo I like the lion and the elephant best of all.

10. The monkey reminds me of my German teacher.

11. Peter sold his shadow to a stranger.

12. Long walks are good for the health.

13. She was one of my professors at the university.

14. Mothers and daughters, fathers and sons, please enter!

15. Many other movie theaters cost too much money, too.

6

Verbs; Auxiliaries

§14. WEAK VERBS

The terms "weak" and "strong" as applied to German verbs identify tense formation as, respectively, regular (by suffix) or irregular (by internal vowel alternation). Thus, German weak verbs correspond to English "regular" verbs:

PRESENT INFINITIVE	PAST	PAST PARTICIPLE
hören *to hear*	**hörte** *heard*	**gehört** *heard*

The following sentences illustrate the German weak verb in all six active tenses. Before proceeding to study them be sure to know the conjugation of the auxiliary verbs **haben, sein,** and **werden** (Appendix §102) and of the weak verb **lernen** (Appendix §103).

A.

Sie liebt ihn.
She loves him.

Sie lieb**te** ihn.
She loved him.

Sie hat ihn geliebt.
She (has) loved him.

Sie hatte ihn geliebt.
She had loved him.

Sie wird ihn lieben.
She will love him.

Sie wird ihn geliebt haben.
She will have loved him.

The stem of a verb is found by dropping final -en from the present infinitive: for **lieben** the stem is **lieb**-. To this stem are added (subject to some variation):

1. For the present tense, the present tense endings -e, -st, -t, -en, -t, -en.

2. For the simple past tense, the past suffix -t- and the past tense endings -e, -est, -e, -en, -et, -en.

3. For the past participle (used in forming the compound past, past perfect, and future perfect tenses), the participial prefix **ge**- and the suffix -t.

B.

Er wartet auf mich.	Er hatte auf mich gewart**et**.
He is waiting for me.	*He had waited for me.*
Er wart**ete** auf mich.	Er wird auf mich warten.
He was waiting for me.	*He will wait for me.*
Er hat auf mich gewart**et**.	Er wird auf mich gewart**et** haben.
He (has) waited for me.	*He will have waited for me.*

The past tense suffix is -**et**- instead of -**t**- if the stem of a verb ends in **t** or **d** (e.g., **reden, redete,** *to speak*) or if the stem ends in **m** or **n** preceded by a consonant other than **l** or **r** (e.g., **atmen, atmete,** *to breathe;* but **warnen, warnte,** *to warn*). In the same cases the past participle ending is -**et** instead of -**t**.

C.

Ich studiere die Aufgabe.	Ich hatte die Aufgabe studier**t**.
I am studying the lesson.	*I had studied the lesson.*
Ich studier**te** die Aufgabe.	Ich werde die Aufgabe studieren.
I was studying the lesson.	*I shall study the lesson.*
Ich habe die Aufgabe studier**t**.	Ich werde die Aufgabe studiert haben.
I (have) studied the lesson.	*I shall have studied the lesson.*

Verbs ending in -**ieren** are weak and do not take the participial prefix **ge**-. A few of the more common verbs in -**ieren** (usually of foreign origin) are: **regieren** (*to govern*), **probieren** (*to try*), **buchstabieren** (*to spell*), **telefonieren** (*to telephone*), **telegrafieren** (*to telegraph*), **operieren** (*to operate*), **sich amüsieren** (*to have a good time*), **spazieren** (*to walk*), **studieren** (*to study*), and **sich interessieren für** (*to be interested in*).

D.

Er beantwortet die Frage.	Er hatte die Frage beantwort**et**.
He answers the question.	*He had answered the question.*
Er beantwort**ete** die Frage.	Er wird die Frage beantworten.
He answered the question.	*He will answer the question.*
Er hat die Frage beantwort**et**.	Er wird die Frage beantwort**et** haben.
He (has) answered the question.	*He will have answered the question.*

Verbs (both weak and strong) with the inseparable prefixes **be-**, **emp-**, **ent-**, **er-**, **ge-**, **ver-**, **zer-**, and sometimes **miß-** take no prefix in the past participle.

E.

Ich mache die Tür zu.	Ich hatte die Tür zu**ge**macht.
I am closing (or *close*) *the door.*	*I had closed the door.*
Ich mach**te** die Tür zu.	Ich werde die Tür zumachen.
I was closing (or *closed*) *the door.*	*I shall close the door.*
Ich habe die Tür zu**ge**macht.	Ich werde die Tür zu**ge**macht
I (have) closed the door.	haben.
	I shall have closed the door.

Verbs (both weak and strong) with separable prefixes have the participial prefix **ge-** between prefix and verb.

§15. STRONG VERBS

German strong verbs correspond to English "irregular" verbs:

PRESENT INFINITIVE	PAST	PAST PARTICIPLE
singen	**sang**	**gesungen**
to sing	*sang*	*sung*

The sentences below indicate that the characteristics of strong verbs are: a change in the stem vowel of the present infinitive in the past and usually in the past participle, and the past participle ending in **-en**.

The best way to learn a verb is to memorize its principal parts and form sentences in the various tenses. Since many strong verbs change their stem vowels in the second and third persons singular of the present indicative, as well as in the past and often in the past participle, the present indicative should be learned together with the principal parts of a verb, e.g.,

sprechen, sprach, hat gesprochen, er spricht

For a complete conjugation of strong verbs, see Appendix II, §104. The principal parts of strong and irregular verbs are listed in §111.

A. Classes. Grammarians have divided strong verbs into seven classes (the ablaut series) according to the vowel changes which characterize each group. The details of this division are given below; they will not replace memorization, but may aid it.

(I) Wir bl**ei**ben zu Hause.
We stay at home.

Wir bl**ie**ben zu Hause.
We stayed at home.

Wir sind zu Hause gebl**ie**ben.
We (have) stayed at home.

Wir waren zu Hause gebl**ie**ben.
We had stayed at home.

Wir werden zu Hause bl**ei**ben.
We shall stay at home.

Wir werden zu Hause gebl**ie**ben sein.
We shall have stayed at home.

Class I: **ei—ie—ie** or **ei—i—i**: bleiben, blieb, geblieben; schneiden, schnitt, geschnitten.

(II) Er g**ie**ßt das Wasser ins Glas.
He pours the water into the glass.

Er g**o**ß das Wasser ins Glas.
He poured the water into the glass.

Er hat das Wasser ins Glas geg**o**ssen.
He (has) poured the water into the glass.

Class II: **ie—o—o**. The **o** may be short or long: gießen, goß, gegossen; ziehen, zog, gezogen.

(III) Sie s**i**ngt das Lied.
She sings the song.

Sie s**a**ng das Lied.
She sang the song.

Sie hat das Lied ges**u**ngen.
She has sung the song.

(IV) Er spr**i**cht zu schnell.
He speaks too rapidly.

Er spr**a**ch zu schnell.
He spoke too rapidly.

Er hat zu schnell gespr**o**chen.
He has spoken too rapidly.

Class III: **i—a—u**. These vowels are short: singen, sang, gesungen.

Class IV: **e—a—o**. The **e** and **o** of this class are sometimes long and sometimes short; short **e** becomes **i** and long **e**, **ie** in the second and third persons singular of the present indicative and in the singular familiar imperative:

sprechen, sprach, hat gesprochen, er spricht, sprich!

stehlen, stahl, hat gestohlen, er stiehlt, stiehl!

(V) Sie l**ie**st das Buch.
She is reading the book.

Sie l**a**s das Buch.
She was reading the book.

Sie hat das Buch gel**e**sen.
She (has) read the book.

(VI) Er schl**ä**gt den Hund.
He strikes the dog.

Er schl**u**g den Hund.
He struck the dog.

Er hat den Hund geschl**a**gen.
He (has) struck the dog.

Class V: **e—a—e**. The **a** is regularly long but the **e** varies both in the infinitive and in the participle; vowel changes in the present indicative and singular familiar imperative are the same as for Class IV:

lesen, las, hat gelesen, er liest, lies!

essen, aß, hat gegessen, er ißt, iß!

Class VI: **a—u—a.** The **u** is regularly long but the **a** varies in both cases; in the second and third persons singular of the present indicative the latter becomes **ä,** but not in the singular imperative:

schlagen, schlug, hat geschlagen, er schlägt, schlag(e)!

wachsen, wuchs, ist gewachsen, er wächst, wachs(e)!

(VII) Er läuft nach Hause.   Er lief nach Hause.
He runs home.   *He ran home.*

Er ist nach Hause gel**aufen.**
He has run home.

Class VII: All verbs of this class have **ie** or **i** in the past; the vowel of the past participle is always the same as that of the present infinitive; **a** changes to **ä** in the present indicative, but not in the singular familiar imperative (just as in Class VI):

laufen, lief, ist gelaufen, er läuft, lauf(e)!

fangen, fing, hat gefangen, er fängt, fang(e)!

Rufen (*to call*) is the only verb in this class with **u** as the stem vowel. The vowel is not modified.

rufen, rief, hat gerufen, **er ruft, ruf(e)!**

Heißen [(tr.) *to bid, call; (intr.) to be called*] is the only verb with **ei** in the present infinitive which does not belong to Class I:

heißen, hieß, hat geh**eiß**en, er heißt, heiß(e)!

B. Imperatives. The singular familiar imperative of strong verbs has no vowel ending if **e** is the stem vowel of the infinitive:

sprechen, **sprich!**

lesen, **lies!**

Karl, sprich nicht zu schnell!   Lies das Buch!
Carl, don't talk too fast.   *Read the book.*

A few verbs, however, such as **gehen, stehen,** and **heben,** which do not change the stem vowel in the present indicative, may have singular familiar imperative forms in -**e: geh(e)! steh(e)! heb(e)!**

All other strong verbs, including those with the stem vowel **a,** may or may not have a final **e** in the imperative. In conversation this **e** is usually omitted:

Schlag(e) den Hund nicht.
Don't hit the dog.

Komm schnell nach Hause!
Hurry home.

The present infinitive is often used as an imperative, particularly in giving commands to children and directions to the general public:

Mund **halten**! *Hold your tongue.*

Schweigen, bitte! *Please be quiet.*

Alles umsteigen! *Everyone change cars.*

The past participle is used with the force of an imperative in giving sharp commands and warnings:

Zugefaßt! *Help yourself. Help yourselves.*

Aufgestanden! *Get up.*

Aufgepaßt! *Pay attention.*

§16. IRREGULAR WEAK VERBS

A. Certain weak verbs have a stem vowel change:

Kennen Sie ihn?
Do you know him?

Das Feuer brennt.
The fire is burning.

Ich **kannte** ihn.
I knew him.

Es **brannte**.
It was burning.

Ich habe ihn **gekannt**.
I knew him.

Es hat **gebrannt**.
It (has) burned.

Sie denkt an mich.
She is thinking of me.

Sie **dachte** an mich.
She was thinking of me.

Sie hat an mich **gedacht**.
She (has) thought of me.

This change was occasioned by mutation of the present infinitive stem vowel and not by vowel gradation (ablaut); these irregular weak verbs are in no way related to strong verbs.

In the table below, note particularly that the present Subjunctive II of the first six verbs keeps the stem vowel of the present infinitive.

PRESENT INFINITIVE	PAST	PERFECT	PRESENT SUBJUNCTIVE II	
brennen	brannte	hat gebrannt	brennte	*to burn*
kennen	kannte	hat gekannt	kennte	*to know*
nennen	nannte	hat genannt	nennte	*to name*
rennen	rannte	ist gerannt	rennte	*to run*
senden	sandte (sendete)	hat gesandt (gesendet)	sendete	*to send*
wenden	wandte (wendete)	hat gewandt (gewendet)	wendete	*to turn*
bringen	brachte	hat gebracht	brächte	*to bring*
denken	dachte	hat gedacht	dächte	*to think*

The verb **wissen,** *to know,* and the modal auxiliaries (treated in Chapter 24) show similar stem vowel changes, but have a different historical origin and are therefore not listed here.

B. There are three German verbs meaning *to know:* **kennen, wissen,** and **können,** but they are used in different contexts:

(1) **Kennen** means *to know* in the sense of *to be acquainted with,* and may refer either to persons or to things.

Kennen Sie den Mann?   Er **kennt** Goethes Werke.
*Do you **know** the man?*   *He **knows** Goethe's works.*

(2) **Wissen** means *to know a fact.*

Ich **weiß,** daß er recht hat.   Ich **weiß** es.
*I **know** that he is right.*   *I **know** it.*

(3) **Können** (which means *to be able to, can*), like some other modal auxiliaries, is frequently followed by an object which leaves the complementary infinitive too obvious to be stated. In these cases the infinitive is "understood", i.e. omitted, and the sentence is translated with *know.*

Er **kann** Deutsch.   Sie **kann** ihre Aufgabe nicht.
*He **knows** German.*   *She does not **know** her lesson.*

Wir **können** das Gedicht.
*We **know** the poem.*

§17. THE AUXILIARIES *HABEN* AND *SEIN*

A.

Er **hat** den Brief geschrieben.
He has written (or wrote) the letter.

Er **hatte** den Brief geschrieben.
He had written the letter.

Sie **hat** das Lied gesungen.
She has sung (or sang) the song.

Sie **hatte** das Lied gesungen.
She had sung the song.

Er **hat** die Tür zugemacht.
He (has) closed the door.

Ich **hatte** eine Geschichte erzählt.
I had told a story.

The sentences above indicate that all transitive verbs require the auxiliary **haben** to form their perfect tenses. The same holds true for the rare future perfect:

Er wird den Brief geschrieben **haben.**
He will have written the letter.

B.

Er **ist** aufgestanden.
He got up.

Sie **waren** gekommen.
They had come.

Er **ist** nach Hause gegangen.
He has gone home.

Sie **war** nach Hause gegangen.
She had gone home.

Er **ist** gekommen.
He has come (or came).

Er **war** aufgestanden.
He had gotten up.

These sentences indicate that intransitive verbs require the auxiliary **sein** to form their perfect tenses, provided they denote a change of place. The same holds true for the rare future perfect:

Er wird gekommen **sein.**
He will have come.

Haben is used as an auxiliary when the action itself is emphasized rather than the goal toward which the action is directed:

Haben Sie lange geschwommen?
Did you swim long?

Here the *action* of swimming is important.

Ich **bin** über den Fluß geschwommen.
I swam across the river.

In this sentence the *goal*—the other side of the river—is implied.

C.

Sie **ist** eingeschlafen.
She has fallen (or fell) asleep.

Sie **war** eingeschlafen.
She had fallen asleep.

Es **ist** kalt geworden.
It has become (or became) cold.

Es **war** kalt geworden.
It had become cold.

These sentences indicate that intransitive verbs require the auxiliary **sein**, provided they denote a change of condition.

D.   Hier **hat** er gestanden.   Er **hat** nicht geschlafen.
Here he (has) stood.   *He has not slept (or did not sleep).*

Er **hatte** gestanden.   Er **hatte** nicht geschlafen.
He had stood.   *He had not slept.*

These sentences indicate that intransitive verbs are conjugated with **haben**, provided they do not denote a change of place or condition.

E. The following verbs are also conjugated with **sein**:

bleiben	blieb	ist geblieben	*to remain*
geschehen	geschah	ist geschehen	*to happen*
sein	war	ist gewesen	*to be*
gelingen	gelang	ist gelungen	*to succeed*
glücken	glückte	ist geglückt	*to succeed*

Geschehen, gelingen, and **glücken** are impersonal verbs:

Es ist ihm noch nicht gelungen, den Bleistift zu finden.
He has not yet succeeded in finding his pencil.

E X E R C I S E S

A. Here is a narration told in the compound past, as if it were part of a larger conversation. Restate the text in the simple past, which is more suitable for a written history of past events.

Dann habe ich auf meinen lieben Freund gewartet. Er hat nämlich zu Hause studiert, aber jetzt haben wir in der Bibliothek studieren müssen. Fritz—mein Freund hat "Fritz" geheißen—hat die Familie sehr geliebt und hat immer bei der Familie leben und lernen wollen, aber unser Professor hat die notwendigen Bücher in der Bibliothek im deutschen Seminarzimmer für uns reserviert. Ich habe lange vor seiner Tür gestanden und mich auf das Ende des Frühjahrssemesters gefreut. Endlich hat die Mutter die Tür aufgemacht, und Fritz ist mit mir gekommen. Wir haben unterwegs über das Leben zu Hause gesprochen. Er hat nicht gern von der Familie geredet, und er hat nichts Gutes über sie gesagt. Wir sind dann mit der Straßenbahn zur Uni gefahren, und da in dem Seminar haben wir drei Stunden lang gesessen und gelesen.

B. Here the narration continues in the present tense. Rewrite this also in the simple past tense.

Ich erfahre bei unsrem Gespräch, daß Fritz der Mutter in allen Bereichen des Lebens gehorcht. Er vermißt zum Beispiel seine Schulkameraden, aber sie meint, daß er sich jetzt wie ein Universitätsstudent benehmen muß. Er fährt um sieben Uhr von zu Hause ab, er kommt um halb neun in der Uni an, er trägt eine Aktenmappe anstatt einer Büchertasche, er denkt immer nur an das Studium, und er wendet seinen ehemaligen Schulfreunden den Rücken zu—all das, weil es ihm die Mutter sagt. Aber das gefällt ihm nicht. Er will Fußball spielen. Er ißt Eis lieber als Butterbrot und trinkt Cola lieber als Bier. Er geht gern ins Kino. Er liest alte Romane, schreibt Referate, und hält sehr ungern Reden vor der Klasse.

C. The narration continues, this time in the simple past tense. Rewrite it in the future tense, as if it were a prediction of Fritz's future.

Er blieb noch drei Jahre auf der Uni. Er bestand alle seine Prüfungen. Er schrieb eine längere Doktorarbeit und wurde selbst Lehrer. Wir mieteten eine Wohnung zusammen und lernten neue Freunde kennen. Sie fuhren jeden Sommer zum Strand, und Fritz und ich besuchten sie in ihrem Ferienhaus. Einer dieser Freunde hatte eine begabte Schwester. Sie war Fernsehansagerin. Sie hieß Inge. Inge verliebte sich natürlich in ihn und eine kleine Weile später heirateten sie. Ich mußte aus unserer Wohnung ausziehen—es war dort nicht genug Platz für drei.

D. Translate into German. Remember that German has no progressive or emphatic forms (review §4B), and that the difference between simple and compound past is in their use, not their time (review §5A).

1. He did not hear me.
2. We are answering (= *beantworten*) the second question.
3. Our parents were traveling through Switzerland.
4. Heidi studied mathematics.
5. She had never really loved him, but she wrote him a nice letter.
6. I was home—when did you telephone me?
7. They will certainly have a good time.
8. Why didn't you open the door?
9. When did Inge buy herself that new car?
10. Rolf sat down on the sofa.
11. How long had you stayed in the country before you became sick?

12. Those little children looked very tired.

13. He had already written two long letters to his parents by then.

14. She changes her coat every evening before work.

15. When does school begin?

16. He always arrived late.

17. Were they singing while they marched?

18. Grandmother had given me money before, but not this time.

19. The elephant was lying happily in the street.

20. She was too late—they had gone home before she arrived.

21. Do you know German?

22. Yes, I know German, but I certainly don't know you.

23. I know you, but I don't know where you live.

24. I don't know if (=*ob*) you know German.

25. How long did you stay in Turkey?

26. I was thinking of her when I turned my back on you.

27. We brought three bottles of wine and cooked a good meal.

28. Is she there? She surely will have arrived already.

29. I have not yet succeeded in selling my old car.

30. When it became too cold she feel asleep.

Numerals

7

§18. CARDINAL NUMERALS

A. Zählen Sie von **eins** bis **ein**undzwanzig!

   Count from 1 to 21.

The forms **eins** is used in counting, except where **und** follows.

B.   (1) **Ein** Bleistift liegt auf dem Tisch.
           There is a (one) pencil on the table.

   (2) Wie viele Bleistifte liegen darauf?   (a) **Einer.**
           How many pencils are there on it?   *One.*

   (3) **Ein** Buch gehört mir.   (a) **Ein(e)s** gehört mir nicht.
           One book belongs to me.   *One does not belong to me.*

   (4) Haben Sie **ein** Buch?   (a) Ja, ich habe **ein(e)s.**
           Do you have a book?   *Yes, I have one.*

   When followed by a noun the numeral **ein** is declined like the indefinite article (examples (1), (3), and (4) above). If **ein** stands alone (i.e., as a pronoun) it has the endings of a **der**-word (examples (2a), (3a), and (4a) above).

C.   **Der eine** Sohn war in der Stadt, der andere war auf dem Land.
           (The) one son was in the city, the other was in the country.

   After a **der**-word **ein** has the weak endings, functioning as an adjective.

D.   **Sein einer** Sohn war in der Schule.
His only son was in school.

After an **ein**-word, **ein** takes the customary endings of a descriptive adjective.

E.   Vor dem zweiten Weltkrieg hatte Berlin über vier **Millionen** Einwohner.
Before World War II Berlin had more than four million inhabitants.

Million and **Milliarde** are weak feminine nouns and are always inflected.

F.   (1) Es waren **hundert** Menschen da.
*There were **a hundred** people there.*

Ich habe viele **H**undert**e** gesehen.
I saw many hundreds.

(2) Es waren **tausend** Menschen da.
*There were **a thousand** people there.*

Ich habe viele **T**ausend**e** gesehen.
I saw many thousands.

A *hundred* and **a** *thousand* are rendered by **hundert** and **tausend**, which are capitalized when used as nouns: Hundert, Tausend. Observe the plurals **H**undert**e** and **T**ausend**e**.

G.   Das ist **eine Fünf.**   Er ist **eine Null.**
That is a (figure) five.   *He is a nobody* (lit. *a zero*).

Cardinal numbers are feminine when used as nouns.

H.   Es ist **ein** Uhr (*or* **eins**).   Es ist ein**e Uhr.**
It is one o'clock.   *It is a watch.*

Ein takes no ending in the time phrase **ein Uhr,** *one o'clock.*

I. Cardinal numbers rarely take endings in modern German, except, occasionally, the numbers two to twelve:

durch **zweier** (*gen. pl.*) Zeugen Mund, *by mouth of two witnesses*
auf allen **vieren,** *on all fours*

J.   (1) Ihre **beiden** Brüder spielen Schach.
*Her **two** (or both her) brothers are playing chess.*

(2) Keiner von den **beiden** interessiert sich für Musik.
*Neither of the **two** is interested in music.*

(3) Welches von den **beiden** Häusern haben Sie verkauft?
*Which of the **two** houses did you sell?*

(4) Meine **beiden** Schwestern sind musikalisch.
Both of my sisters are musically gifted.

When referring to but two of a kind, English *two* (or *both*) is usually translated by German **beide** (with adjective inflection). Instead of **die beiden Männer** one may also say **beide Männer** without change of meaning.

K. The cardinals.

0 = Null	11 = elf	30 = dreißig
1 = ein(s)	12 = zwölf	31 = einunddreißig
2 = zwei	13 = dreizehn	40 = vierzig
3 = drei	14 = vierzehn	50 = fünfzig
4 = vier	15 = fünfzehn	60 = sechzig
5 = fünf	16 = sechzehn	70 = siebzig
6 = sechs	17 = siebzehn	80 = achtzig
7 = sieben	18 = achtzehn	90 = neunzig
8 = acht	19 = neunzehn	100 = hundert
9 = neun	20 = zwanzig	101 = hundert(und)eins
10 = zehn	21 = einundzwanzig	200 = zweihundert

1000 = tausend	1.000.000 = eine Million
100.000 = hunderttausend	1.000.000.000 = eine Milliarde

1989 = neunzehnhundertneunundachtzig

Note: All multiples of ten except *dreißig*, end in **-zig**.

§19. ORDINAL NUMERALS

Ordinal numerals are declined like adjectives.

A.   Das ist der **zweite** Fehler.
That is the second mistake.

Heute fehlt der **fünfte** Schüler in der **vierten** Reihe.
The fifth pupil in the fourth row is absent today.

Mein Geburtstag ist am **sechsten** Oktober.
Der **sechste** Oktober ist mein Geburtstag.
October 6th is my birthday.

Mein Freund wird am **achtzehnten** (18**ten** or 18.) oder am **neunzehnten** (19**ten** or 19.) dieses Monats abreisen.
My friend will leave on the 18th or 19th of this month.

Ordinals up to *nineteenth* (except *first, third, eighth,* and *seventh*) are formed by adding the suffix **-t** to the corresponding cardinals.

B.   Heute ist der **erste** Schnee gefallen.
The first snow fell today.

Das ist das **dritte** Buch, das er verloren hat.
That is the third book (that) he has lost.

The ordinals *first* and *third* are irregular.

C.   Heute ist der **zwanzigste** Juni.
Heute haben wir den **zwanzigsten** Juni.
Today is June 20.

Goethe wurde am **achtundzwanzigsten** August siebzehnhundert-
neunundvierzig geboren.
Goethe was born August 28, 1749.

Was ist der Inhalt des **dreiunddreißigsten** Kapitels?
What are the contents of the thirty-third chapter?

Ordinals from *twentieth* upward are formed by adding **-st** to the corresponding cardinals.

D. When used in dates, titles, etc., ordinals are usually abbreviated to number and
a period:

Heute ist der 20. Juni. *Today is June 20.*

die zweite Hälfte des 18. Jahrhunderts, *the second half of the 18th century*

die 3. Ausgabe, *the third edition*

Wilhelm I. (*read:* der Erste), *William I (the First)*

E. The ordinals. Some ordinals are listed below; irregular forms are in boldface:

1. = (der, die, das) **erste**, *first*

2. = (der, die, das) zweite, *second*

3. = (der, die, das) **dritte,** *third*

4. = (der, die, das) vierte, *fourth*

7. = (der, die, das) siebente or **siebte,** *seventh*

8. = (der, die, das) **achte,** *eighth*

19. = (der, die, das) neunzehnte, *nineteenth*

20. = (der, die, das) zwanzigste, *twentieth*

21. = (der, die, das) einundzwanzigste, *twenty-first*

30. = (der, die, das) dreißigste, *thirtieth*

100. = (der, die, das) hunderste, *hundredth*

1000. = (der, die, das) tausendste, *thousandth*

§20. DERIVATIVES FROM NUMERALS

A. Forms in -*mal*. The indeclinable forms **einmal** (*once*), **zweimal** (*twice*), **dreimal** (*three times*), etc. are formed regularly by adding -**mal** to the corresponding cardinals:

> Wir haben Deutsch **fünfmal** die Woche.
> *We have German five times a week.*

B. Forms in -*erlei*. The indeclinable forms **einerlei** (*one kind of*), **zweierlei** (*two kinds of*), **dreierlei** (*three kinds of*), **wievielerlei** (*how many kinds of*), etc. are formed regularly by adding -**erlei** to the corresponding cardinals:

> **Wievielerlei** Fragen stellt die Prüfung? **Dreierlei.**
> *How many types of questions does the test ask? Three types.*

C. Forms in -*ens*. The adverbial forms **erstens** (*first, in the first place*), **zweitens** (*secondly*), **drittens** (*thirdly*), etc. are formed by adding -**ens** to the stem of the corresponding ordinals:

> Sie konnte mich nicht besuchen: **erstens** war sie beschäftigt, **zweitens** hatte sie kein Reisegeld.
>
> *She could not visit me: in the first place, she was busy; secondly, she had no money for traveling.*

D. Forms in -*fach*. The declinable adjectives **dreifach** (*triple, threefold*), **vierfach** (*fourfold*), etc. are formed by adding -**fach** to the corresponding cardinals:

> Er trägt eine **dreifache** Krone.
> *He wears a triple crown.*

Similarly with forms in -**stufig**, e.g., **dreistufig** (*with three steps*). For *double* or *twofold* one may say **doppelt, zweifach,** or **zwiefach**.

E. Fractions. The fractions **ein Drittel** (*a third*), **ein Viertel** (*a fourth*), **ein Zwanzigstel** (*a twentieth*) etc. are neuter nouns formed by adding -**el** to the stem of the corresponding ordinals:

> **Zwei Drittel** von einundzwanzig ist vierzehn.
> *Two thirds of twenty-one is fourteen.*

The preceding explanation is a simple and practical one for the formation of fractions. What actually happens, however, is that the suffix -**tel** (from

Teil, *part*) is added to the stem of an ordinal, which drops the final **t**; thus **dritt-** plus **-tel** (literally *third part*) becomes **Drittel**.

F. *Halb* **and combinations with** *halb.*

(1) **Halb** is the adjective for *half*:

Er hat einen **halben** Apfel gegessen.
He ate half an apple.

(2) Die **Hälfte** is the noun for *half*:

Die andere **Hälfte** hat er der Schwester gegeben.
He gave his sister the other half.

The form **anderthalb**, *one and a half*, takes no ending and is followed by a plural noun:

Ich wartete **anderthalb** Stunden.
I waited an hour and a half.

The same applies to the forms **zwei(und)einhalb**, *two and a half*, **sechs(und)einhalb**, *six and a half*, etc.

In **acht(und)einhalb** Jahren kehrt er zurück.
In eight and a half years he will return.

EXERCISES

A. Give numerical data about yourself. While writing out cardinal numbers is unusual, do it for the purposes of this exercise. There is no need to tell the truth, of course, but at least tell reasonable fibs. By "numerical data" is meant your age, date of birth, date of marriage, number and kinds of siblings, number and kinds of pets, zip code (*die Postleitzahl*), telephone number, intended date of graduation (*der Studienabschluß*), street address and apartment number, and anything else you can think of that involves numbers.

B. Here are vital statistics about two famous German-speaking people of the past. Use these data to write capsule biographies. Pertinent extra vocabulary is included, and don't forget to consult the glossary at the end of the book for added help. By the way, for the English *in 1941* you may choose German **im Jahre 1941** or simply **1941.**

1. Immanuel Kant, German philosopher (*der Philosoph, -en, -en*). Born April 22, 1724, Königsberg, Prussia. Father died 1746. Became professor of poetry in 1762, next year librarian (*der Bibliothekar, -s, -e*). Professor of logic (*die Logik*) when he was 46. Greatest work, *Die Kritik der reinen Ver-*

nunft, appeared in 1781. Retired (*in den Ruhestand treten*) in 1797 and died on February 12, 1804.

2. Clemens Wenzel Nepomuk Lothar, Prinz Metternich, Austrian politician (*der Diplomat, -en, -en*). Born May 15, 1773, in Koblenz. Married a wealthy Austrian woman in 1795 and became ambassador (*der Botschafter, -s, -*) to Dresden, Berlin, and—in 1806—Paris. Formed an alliance (*das Bündnis schließ*en) with Napoleon in 1813, and in 1814 another alliance against France. Was frequently Chancellor of Austria thereafter. Left Austria at the time of the revolution in 1848, returned in 1851 from England, and died in Vienna on June 11, 1859.

C. The German word for *plus* is **plus**, for *minus* is **minus**, for *times* is **mal**, for *divided by* is **durch**, and for *equals* is **ist. . .gleich**. Perform the computations below and state the process and the result in written German.

1. $3 + 2 =$
2. $4 - 2 =$
3. $3 \times 2 =$
4. $4 \div 2 =$
5. $12 + 8 =$
6. $27 - 4 =$
7. $15 \times 3 =$
8. $52 \div 4 =$
9. $12 \times 12 =$
10. $36 \div 9 =$

D. Translate into German. You need not write out the years.

1. Today is the 30th of January.
2. Washington was born on February 22, 1732.
3. The 22nd of February is therefore his birthday.
4. This morning there were a thousand cars on the expressway between Köln and Bonn.
5. Hundreds of (*von*) people were late for work.
6. A vacation trip to Spain costs a thousand marks.
7. In 1989 West Berlin had almost two million inhabitants and East Berlin had a little more than one million.
8. One son will go to the country, but one will stay in the city.
9. I don't want to clean my car today: in the first place, I'm too tired; and in the second place, it's raining.
10. I had to ring at your place three times.

11. Please give me half a pound of cheese.

12. It is a quarter past twelve and we have to arrive at one o'clock.

13. I baked her a cake, and she ate half of it (*davon*).

14. After an hour and a half we left the movie theater.

15. Which one of the two sisters studied physics?

8

Comparison of Adjectives and Adverbs

§21. USES OF THE COMPARATIVE AND SUPERLATIVE

In German as in English, adjectives have three degrees of comparison: positive, comparative, and superlative:[1]

spät, spät**er,** spät**est**e (am spät**est**en)

late, later, latest

As illustrated below, the comparative is formed by adding **-er** to the stem (i.e., the uninflected form) of an adjective; the superlative, by adding **-(e)st**. This closely parallels the procedure in English: *faster, fastest.* But note that German does not use *more* and *most* in comparisons: *more interesting* = **interessanter;** *most interesting* = **am interessantesten.**

A.

Das Eisen ist schwer.
Iron is heavy.

Das Blei ist schwer**er.**
Lead is heavier.

Welches Metall ist am schwer**sten**?
Which metal is heaviest?

Bier ist stark.
Beer is strong.

Korn ist stärker.
Corn whiskey is stronger.

Akvavit ist am stärksten.
Aquavit is strongest.

---

[1]Certain adjectives have no comparatives because of their meaning: **halb** (*half*), **mündlich** (*oral*), **neunfach** (*ninefold*), etc.

Der Mond ist groß.
The moon is large.

Die Erde ist grö**ßer**.
The earth is larger.

Die Sonne ist am grö**ßten**.
The sun is largest.

(1) Adjectives of one syllable with the vowels **a, o,** or **u** usually take umlaut in the comparative and superlative degrees: **alt, älter,** der **älteste** (am **ältesten**).

The following are the most common adjectives that take umlaut in forming the comparative and superlative degrees: **alt, arm, dumm, grob, groß, hart, hoch, jung, kalt, klug, krank, kurz, lang, nah(e), scharf, schwach, schwarz, stark, warm.** The comparative of **rot** may be either **röter** or **roter**.

(2) The superlative form with **am,** known as the "adverbial superlative," is used either as a predicate adjective or as an adverb: Er singt **am lautesten** = *He sings **loudest**.*

The English equivalent of the adverbial superlative does not have the definite article (**am** = **an dem**), wherein it differs from the "relative superlative" (explained in **B**).

B. (1) Die Lahn ist ein starker Fluß.
The Lahn is a strong river.

Die Weser ist ein stärk**erer** Fluß.
The Weser is a stronger river.

Der Rhein ist der stärkste Fluß.
The Rhine is the strongest river.

Der Rhein ist der stärk**ste**.
The Rhine is the strongest.

(2) Er schreibt einen kurzen Satz.
He writes a short sentence.

Er schreibt einen kürz**eren** Satz.
He writes a shorter sentence.

Er schreibt den kürz**esten** Satz.
He writes the shortest sentence.

The superlative with the definite article, known as the "relative superlative," is used both when a noun is expressed and when it is understood.

C. Es war eine dunkle Nacht.   Es war eine dunk**lere** Nacht.
It was a dark night.   *It was a darker night.*

Es war die dunkel**ste** nacht.
It was the darkest night.

Adjectives and adverbs of more than one syllable do not take umlaut.

D. Es wird immer heißer.　　　　　Es wurde immer schlimmer.
　　　It is getting hotter and hotter.　　*It was getting worse and worse.*

Immer followed by the comparative is used to express continuous increase in the quality denoted by the adjective. Two comparatives, as in English, may also be used: Es wurde **schlimmer** und **schlimmer.**

E. Er ist **stolz.**　　　　　　Er geht **stolz** davon.
　　　He is proud.　　　　*He walks away proudly.*

Many German adjectives may, without change of form, be used as adverbs. The comparative of adverbs must always end in **-er** and the superlative (unless used absolutely) must use the invariable **am**-form:

　　Er geht langsam.　　　　　Er geht langsam**er.**
　　He walks slowly.　　　*He walks more slowly.*

　　Er geht am langsam**sten.**
　　He walks most slowly.

F. (1) Sie sang aufs schön**ste.**
　　　　She sang most beautifully.

　　　　Das Rauchen ist aufs streng**ste** (*or* streng**stens**) verboten.
　　　　Smoking is very strictly forbidden.

　　(2) Das ist höch**st** interessant.
　　　　That is extremely interesting.

　　　　Die Reise war äußer**st** gefährlich.
　　　　The trip was exceedingly dangerous.

The superlative adverb in **aufs,** known as the "absolute superlative," denotes merely a very high degree without any actual comparison.

Another form of the absolute superlative is **höchst** or **äußerst**—or some similar word in the sense of *very*—followed by the positive degree.

Note that, while both the adverbial and relative superlatives express real comparison, the absolute superlative does not.

G. Sie ist die allerschön**ste** auf　　　Sie tanzt am allerbe**sten.**
　　　　der Welt.　　　　　　　　*She dances best of all.*
　　　She is the most beautiful in the world.

　　　Sie ist die schön**ste** von allen.　　Sie schreibt am allerschön**sten.**
　　　She is the most beautiful of all.　　*She writes most beautifully of all.*

　　　Das ist das allerbe**ste.**
　　　That is the best of all.

Aller (gen. pl. of **all**) may be used to strengthen the superlative adjective or the superlative adverb. It is then invariable and serves for all cases and genders.

H. Die Reise war **mehr** anstrengend als interessant.
The trip was more strenuous than interesting.

Mehr followed by the positive degree is used when two qualities of the same individual or thing are compared; *than* = **als.**

I. Wir besuchen eine **ältere** Dame.
We visit an elderly lady.

Sie wohnt hier seit **längerer** Zeit.
She has lived here for some time.

The comparative degree may be used absolutely, without any idea of comparison.

Note that endings are added to the stem of the comparative and superlative, just as they are to the uninflected form of an adjective in the positive degree: ein arm**er** Mann, ein ärmer**er** Mann, der ärmst**e** Mann.

J. The use of *als* and *wie* in comparisons.

(1) **Als** is used after the comparative degree:

Sie ist **fleißiger als** ihr Bruder.
She is more industrious than her brother.

(2) **Wie** is used after the positive degree (affirmative or negative):

Sie ist ebenso **fleißig wie** ihr Bruder.
She is just as industrious as her brother.

Sie ist nicht so **fleißig wie** ihr Bruder.
She is not as industrious as her brother.

§22. IRREGULAR FORMATIONS OF THE COMPARATIVE AND SUPERLATIVE

A. Adjectives ending in **-d, -t**, or an *s* sound (written **s, z, ß**, or **sch**) add **-est** to form the superlative: kurz, kürzer, der kürz**est**e, am kürz**est**en.

Present participles used as adjectives do not insert **e** before the superlative ending: **reizend** (*charming*), der reizend**ste** (*the most charming*).

B. Adjectives ending in **-e** drop it before a comparative ending: **weise** (*wise*), **weiser** (*wiser*).

C. Adjectives ending in -el, -en, and -er usually drop the **e** before a comparative ending: **dunkel, dunkler, der dunkelste, am dunkelsten** (*dark*). The **e** is also frequently dropped before an ending in the positive degree:

> eine **dunkle** Nacht, *a dark night*

D. Adjectives that never or sometimes take umlaut. Although the general rule is that adjectives of one syllable take umlaut in the comparative and superlative degrees, there are exceptions.

(1) Adjectives that never take umlaut: **klar, rasch, voll, froh, lahm, rund, starr, schlank,** and all **au**-stems: **laut, blau, schlau,** etc.

(2) Adjectives that sometimes take umlaut, although occurring also without it: **blaß, glatt, karg, naß, rot, schmal, fromm.**

E. Irregular comparison of adjectives and adverbs.

(1) The following adjectives have irregular comparisons:

groß (*large*)	größer	der größte	am größten
gut (*good*)	besser	der beste	am besten
hoch (*high*)	höher	der höchste	am höchsten
nah (*near*)	näher	der nächste	am nächsten
viel (*much*)	mehr	der meiste	am meisten

When **hoch** in the positive takes an ending, the -c- is dropped:

> ein **hoher** Berg, *a high mountain*

(2) The following adverbs are irregular in their comparison:

bald (*soon*)	eher	am ehesten
gern (*gladly*)	lieber	am liebsten

Früher (*sooner*) is quite frequently used instead of **eher**; it is also very often used in the sense of *formerly*.

Gern is used idiomatically with **haben** to translate the English verb *to like*, provided what is liked is the direct object of the verb:

Ich **habe** Tee **gern.**
I like tea.

Ich **habe** Limonade **lieber.**
I prefer soda.

Ich **habe** Bier **am liebsten.**
I like beer best.

If the action of the subject of a sentence is the point of comparison, merely add **gern**:

Er spricht **gern.**
*He **likes to** talk.*

Er spricht **lieber.**
*He **prefers to** talk.*

Er spricht **am liebsten.**
*He **likes best to** talk.*

Here the act of talking is the point of comparison.

E X E R C I S E S

A. Form sentences according to the following model:

Die Lahn, die Weser, der Rhein; *stark* sein.

Die Lahn ist **stark**. Die Weser ist **stärker**. Der Rhein ist **am stärksten**.

1. Schloß Berlepsch, Schloß Lindau, Schloß Neuschwanstein; *eindrucksvoll* sein.
2. Die Stunde, die Minute, die Sekunde; *kurz* sein.
3. Das Haus, die Kirche, der Berg; *hoch* sein.
4. Der Personenzug, der D-Zug, der Inter-City-Zug; *schnell* fahren.
5. Der italienische Wein, der deutsche Wein, der Wein aus Kalifornien; *gut* schmecken.
6. Das Bier, der Kaffee, der Tee; *warm* sein.
7. Hans, Arnold, Monika; *gern* radfahren.
8. Ein Einfamilienhaus auf dem Lande, eine Wohnung in München, ein Ferienhaus in Amalfi; *kostspielig* sein.
9. Ein Löwe, das Flußpferd, der Elefant; *groß* sein.
10. Der Nachmittag, der Abend, die Nacht; *dunkel* sein.
11. Die Teetasse, das Bierglas, die Weinflasche; *voll* sein.
12. Schlagball, Korbball, Tennis; *anstrengend* sein.

B. Make sentences of the model *X is faster than Y* or *X is (just) as fast as Y,* using nouns and adjectives suggested by the two lists below. It's more realistic to use people you know.

Klassenkollegen X, Y, und Z

Klassenkolleginnen A, B, und C

der Deutschlehrer, die Deutschlehrerin, oder Lehrer im allgemeinen

der Polizeibeamte, oder die Polizeibeamtin

der/die Football-/Fußball-/Korbball-/Hockey-Trainer oder Trainerin

der Briefträger oder die Briefträgerin

schnell	langsam
grob	höflich

einsilbig	mehrsilbig
stark	schwach
pflichtmäßig	nachlässig
zuverlässig	unzuverlässig
entgegenkommend	zurückhaltend
fleißig	faul
laut	ruhig
konservativ	progressiv

C. Supply comparative and superlative forms according to the model:

Hansi ist ein bissiger Hund. Schatzi ist ein **bissigerer** Hund. Golem ist aber der **bissigste** Hund.

1. Heute haben wir einen kalten Tag. Gestern hatten wir einen _____ Tag. Vorgestern hatten wir aber den _____ Tag des ganzen Winters.

2. Das war ein harter Schlag. Doch es kam noch ein _____ Schlag. Aber der _____ Schlag war für ihn der Verlust seines Vermögens.

3. Ein langer Weg liegt vor mir. Ein _____ Weg liegt vor dir. Aber der _____ Weg liegt vor der Person, die zu Hause bleiben will.

4. Das ist ein scharfes Messer. Das da ist aber ein _____ Messer. Und das ist das _____ Messer, das ich je schleifen mußte.

D. Complete the sentences as indicated in parentheses.

1. Ich wurde _____ (weaker and weaker)

2. Die Nacht wird _____ (darker and darker)

3. Der Vogel sang _____ (most beautifully)

4. Von allen Vögeln sang die Nachtigall _____ (most beautifully)

5. Der Adler war _____ (the most noble of all)

6. _____ (The most beautiful) Vogel war der Adler.

E. Translate into German.

1. He works most diligently when he is alone.

2. She likes to watch TV. She prefers to talk. She likes best of all to read a book.

3. Gießen is a charming city. Wetzlar is more charming. Marburg is the most charming city in central Germany.

4. He likes Coca-Cola. (use *gern*) She prefers mineral water. But we all like coffee best of all at breakfast.

5. July was the warmest month, but which was the coldest?

6. Have you ever driven a faster car?

7. We will certainly visit the most expensive cities in Germany.
8. Oh yes, Professor Heimbach, that is extremely interesting.
9. The Lahn is one of the quietest rivers in Europe.
10. This week we are supposed to have warmer weather.
11. She always speaks more clearly than her younger sister.
12. Most girls like to play tennis.
13. My roommate likes most of all to travel alone.
14. The bakery is pretty near, but the supermarket is much nearer.
15. I speak German well, but I speak English better.

Expressions of Time and Date

§23. THE DAYS, MONTHS, AND SEASONS

The days of the week, the months, and the seasons are all masculine. The seasons regularly have the definite article; the days of the week and the months have the definite article when they are used with a preposition. Contraction of preposition and definite article is usual: **in dem** becomes **im, an dem** becomes **am**.

A. The days of the week.

(1) Es war **am** Dienstag, dem 21. Juni.
It was on Tuesday, June 21.

In phrases such as *on Monday(s), on Tuesday(s), etc.,* English omits, but German requires, the definite article after the preposition. In German **an + dem** becomes **am**. The preposition, however, may be omitted both in English and German:

Montag (acc.) war ich beschäftigt.
I was busy (on) Monday.

(2) **Letzten** Donnerstag war ich bei meinem Freund.
Last Thursday I was at my friend's house.

Nächsten Sonntag wird er mich besuchen.
He will visit me next Sunday.

Jeden Freitag gehe ich ins Theater.
Every Friday I go to the theater.

As illustrated by **letzten, nächsten,** and **jeden** in the sentences above, the *accusative* denotes *definite* time.

Instead of **jeden Freitag** (Montag, Dienstag, etc.) one may also say **freitags, des Freitags,** or **alle Freitage.**

Freitags bin ich immer zu Hause.
I'm always home on Fridays.

(3) **Eines** Sonntags war ich auf dem Lande.
One Sunday I was in the country.

The *genitive* case is used to denote *indefinite* time or *habitual action.*

B. The months.

(1) Es war **im** März (Dezember).
It was in March (December).

Sein Geburstag ist **am** 17. Oktober.
His birthday is on October 17.

(2) As the heading of a letter:
den 22. Mai, *May 22nd.*

The date in the heading of a letter is in the accusative case.

C. The seasons.

(1) **Im Frühling** singen die Vögel.
The birds sing in spring.

(2) **Jeden Sommer** macht er eine Reise.
He takes a trip every summer.

Letzten Herbst war sie in der Schweiz.
She was in Switzerland last fall.

Nächsten Winter werden wir zu Hause bleiben.
We shall stay at home next winter.

§24. HOURS, MINUTES, AND IDIOMATIC TIME EXPRESSIONS

A. Hours.

Wieviel Uhr ist es?
or: Wie spät ist es?
What time is it?

Es ist ein Uhr.
or: Es ist eins.
It is one o'clock.

Es ist halb vier.
It is half past three.

Es ist Viertel nach zwölf.
or: Es ist Viertel eins.
It is a quarter after twelve.

Es ist Viertel vor elf.
or: Es ist drei Viertel elf.
It is a quarter to eleven.

B. Minutes

Es ist zehn Minuten nach acht.
It's ten minutes after eight.

Es ist sieben Minuten vor zwei.
It's seven minutes of two.

Just as one can relate a number of minutes to the nearest hour, as in the two examples above, one may relate up to five or ten minutes to the half hour, as in the examples below. Such expressions are colloquial, and are frequently shortened in speech.

Es ist fünf Minuten vor halb sechs.
or: Es ist fünf vor halb sechs.
It's five twenty-five.

Es ist fünf nach halb sechs.
It's five thirty-five.

C. Idiomatic time expressions.

Er wird **um** sieben Uhr kommen.
*He will come **at** seven o'clock.*

Er wird **ungefähr um** sieben Uhr kommen.
*He will come **at about** seven o'clock.*

Der wievielte **ist** heute?
or: **Den** wievielten **haben** wir heute?
What is today's date?

Heute ist der 25. Januar.
or: Heute haben wir den 25. Januar.
Today is the 25th of January.

Der wievielte ist morgen?
What is tomorrow's date?

Morgen ist der 26. Januar.
Tomorrow is January 26.

Vor zwei Stunden ⎫   ⎧ *two hours ago.*
Vor acht Tagen ⎬ erhielt ich den Brief. ⎨ *a week ago.*
Vor einem Monat ⎬ *I received the letter* ⎨ *a month ago.*
Vor drei Jahren ⎭   ⎩ *three years ago.*

Heute **über acht Tage** wird er abreisen.
or: Heute **in acht Tagen** wird er abreisen.
*He'll leave **a week from** today.*

Heute **in vierzehn Tagen** kommt er wieder zurück.
*He'll be back again **two weeks from** today.*

Sie geht **auf** einen Monat aufs Land.
*She's going to the country **for** a month.*

§25. PERIODS OF THE DAY IN TIME EXPRESSIONS

A. Adverbial phrases denoting time.

(1) am Morgen (morgens *or* des Morgens), *in the morning*
am Vormittag (vormittags *or* des Vormittags), *in the forenoon*
am Mittag (mittags *or* des Mittags), *at noon*
Wir essen zu Mittag. *We are having lunch.*
am Nachmittag (nachmitags *or* des Nachmittags), *in the afternoon*
am Abend (abends *or* des Abends), *in the evening*
Wir essen zu Abend. *We eat supper.*
am Tage, *in the daytime*

The forms in parentheses are particularly common when denoting some customary or habitual action:

Vormittags bin ich immer zu Hause.
I am always at home in the forenoon.

Nachmittags macht der Großvater ein Schläfchen.
In the afternoon grandfather takes a nap.

(2) in der Nachts, *at night*

(3) gegen Abend, *toward evening*
gegen Morgen, *toward morning*

B. The accusative denotes definite time and duration of time.

Jeden Abend (Morgen, Freitag, etc.) mache ich einen Spaziergang.
I take a walk every evening (morning, Friday, etc.).

Er arbeitete **den ganzen** Morgen (**die ganze** Nacht).
He worked all morning (all night).

C. Combinations with *heute, morgen, gestern*. In combinations with these words, such time expressions as **morgen, vormittag, mittag,** etc. are not capitalized, since they function as adverbs:

heute morgen, *this morning*

heute vormittag, *this forenoon*

heute mittag, *this noon*

heute nachmittag, *this afternoon*

heute abend, *this evening, tonight*

heute nacht, *tonight*

gestern morgen, *yesterday morning*

gestern vormittag, *yesterday forenoon*

gestern mittag, *yesterday noon*

gestern nachmittag, *yesterday afternoon*

gestern abend, *yesterday evening, last night*

gestern nacht, *last night*

vorige Nacht, *last night*

vorgestern, *day before yesterday*

morgen früh, *tomorrow morning*

frühmorgens, *early in the morning*

morgen vormittag, *tomorrow forenoon* or *tomorrow morning*

morgen mittag, *tomorrow noon*

morgen nachmittag, *tomorrow afternoon*

morgen abend, *tomorrow evening* (or *night*)

morgen nacht, *tomorrow night*

übermorgen, *day after tomorrow*

E X E R C I S E S

A. Fill in the blanks.

1. Letzt____ Jahr war ich in Deutschland.
2. Nächst____ Sommer werde ich nach Europa fahren.
3. Vorig____ Woche bin ich ins Theater gegangen.

4. Sie ist a____ 15. Mai 1905 geboren.

5. Ein____ Morgen____ erhielt ich einen längeren Brief von ihr.

6. "D____ 18. Juni" stand oben auf der ersten Seite des Briefes.

7. Nächst____ Montag muß ich eine Antwort diktieren.

8. D____ wie____ ist heute?

9. D____ wie____ haben wir heute?

10. Es ist _____ (*half past ten*).

11. Es ist _____ (*three twenty-five*).

12. Es ist _____ (*a quarter past seven*).

13. Der D-Zug sollte _____ (*at*) vierzehn Uhr drei ankommen.

14. _____ (*Tomorrow morning*) geht es wieder los.

15. _____ (*Last evening*) haben wir zuviel geschwätzt.

16. _____ (*This morning*) gibt es noch Arbeit zu tun.

17. _____ (*In the*) Winter sind diese Straßen gefährlich glatt.

18. D____ ganz____ Sommer habe ich mich herrlich amüsiert.

19. _____ Tage arbeiten wir. Arbeitet ihr d____ ganz____ Tag?

20. _____ (*At*) Nacht kann man die Gassen nicht mehr finden.

21. Der Sturm ließ _____ (*towards*) morgen nach.

22. Heute _____ vierzehn Tag____ kommt der Film bestimmt.

23. _____ acht Tag____ (*A week ago*) schickten wir den Film ein.

B. Many disagreements, even between friends, stem from misunderstandings about times, dates, and numbers. Here is a series of mild or even outraged complaints. Say something by way of explanation or excuse in return. If you're writing your answer, please write the numbers out, as in the example.

Example: *Aber du sagtest doch Straßenbahn Linie dreiundzwanzig.*

Your response: *Nein, umgekehrt, ich sagte zweiunddreißig.*

1. Aber du sagtest doch fünf vor halb sechs.

2. Ich dachte, wir wollten uns jeden Freitag treffen, oder?

3. Noch nicht da? Du sagtest bestimmt Montag in acht Tagen.

4. Wollte er nicht um drei viertel sieben anfangen?

5. Hast du im Sommer nicht Urlaub gemacht?

6. Sagte der Lautsprecher eben Gleis zwei oder Gleis drei?

7. Habt ihr nicht gegen Abend warm gegessen?

8. Heute ist der wievielte? Nicht der achte?

9. Spät? Wieso spät? Der Zug fährt erst um sieben, oder?

10. Es *ist* aber drei Uhr. Wie kann das Schiff schon vor zwölf Stunden abgefahren sein?

C. Write out as many versions of each of the times given below as you can think of. Remember that morning or afternoon is implied by some contexts and lacking in others, and that some events require more precise information than others.

1. 1:15
2. 2:30
3. 12:00
4. 4:55
5. 7:35
6. 9:45
7. 3:05
8. 8:22

D. Translate into German.

1. Every Saturday I go to the movies.
2. Last Saturday I saw my little brother there.
3. Next week I believe I'll see him again.
4. Goethe died on March 22, 1832. He said: "More light!"
5. This morning we're walking to school.
6. Next week we'll go by bike.
7. She'll arrive tomorrow morning at seven.
8. Last evening she called me up.
9. The day before yesterday she was in Switzerland.
10. The day after tomorrow she'll be in Austria.
11. What is tomorrow's date?
12. We usually have a study group in the late morning.
13. Some day I'll learn these endings.
14. Children get tired towards noon.
15. The class was already over two hours ago.

Prepositions 10

English prepositions are followed by noun and pronoun objects in the objective case. This is only visible and audible with certain of the pronouns, where subjective/objective contrasts are preserved (*I/me, she/her, he/him, we/us,* and *they/them*). Otherwise only the adjacent word order links an English preposition with its object. German, on the other hand, has three objective cases, and allocates the prepositions among them. And, because of the preserved richness of the endings, noun or pronoun objects are almost always obviously in one or another objective case.

§26. PREPOSITIONS WITH THE ACCUSATIVE

The following seven prepositions, as illustrated below, govern the accusative case: **bis** (*to, until, as far as*), **durch** (*through, by means of*), **für** (*for*), **gegen** (*against*), **ohne** (*without*), **um** (*around*), and **wider** (*against*).

A. Bis:

Er hat **bis** zehn Uhr gewartet.
*He waited **until** ten o'clock.*

Er hat mich **bis** München begleitet.
*He accompanied me **to** (= **as far as**) Munich.*

Er ging **bis an** die Tür.
*He went **up to** (= **as far as**) the door.*

Er hat mich **bis auf** den Tod gequält.
He worried (lit. *tortured*) *me **almost to** death.*

Er war **bis vor wenigen** Jahren gesund.
*Until a few years **ago**, he was well.*

Bis is usually followed by another preposition which determines the case of the following noun. If the noun is preceded by an article, a second preposition *must* be used with **bis.**

B. Durch:

Er ging **durch das** Zimmer.
*He went **through** the room.*

Der Löwe wurde **durch einen** Schuß getötet.
*The lion was killed **by** a shot.*

By usually becomes **von** with a passive verb to denote the *personal agent.* **Durch,** however, is often used to denote the means or instrument.

C. Für:

Die Mutter kaufte ein Geschenk **für die** Tochter.
*The mother bought a gift **for** her daughter.*

Wir lernen nicht **für die** Schule, sondern **fürs** Leben.
*We do not learn **for** school but **for** life.*

Er ist **für einen Tag** weggefahren.
*He is away **for one day**.*

Wir brauchen Wein **für nächsten Sonntag.**
*We need wine **for next Sunday**.*

D. Gegen:

Was haben Sie **gegen ihn?**
*What have you got **against** him?*

Es war **gegen den** Wunsch seines Vaters.
*It was **contrary to** his father's wish(es).*

Gegen Morgen sind sie weggefahren.
*They left **toward** morning.*

E. Ohne:

Ohne dich kann ich nicht leben.
*I cannot live **without** you.*

Ohne Freunde ist das Leben traurig.
*Life is dreary **without** friends.*

F. Um:

Der Gärtner baute einen Zaun **um den** Garten.
*The gardener built a fence **around** the garden.*

Kümmern Sie sich nicht **um mich!**
*Don't worry **about** me.*

G. Wider:

Er tat es **wider seinen** Willen.
*He did it **against** his will.*

Do not confuse the adverb **wieder** (*again*) with the preposition **wider**
(*against*).

§27. USES OF *OHNE, UM,* AND *ANSTATT* WITH INFINITIVES

When followed by nouns or pronouns, **ohne** and **um** govern the accusative
case, **anstatt** (or simply **statt**) the genitive. But when followed by an infinitive
with **zu** they have these meanings:

A. Ohne:

Er sprach **ohne aufzustehen.**
*He spoke **without getting up.***

B. Um:

Um das alles **zu verstehen,** muß man aufpassen.
In order to understand *all that, one must pay attention.*

C. (An)statt:

(An)statt mit mir **zu kommen,** ging er mit Reinhard.
Instead of coming *with me, he went with Reinhard.*

§28. PREPOSITIONS WITH THE DATIVE

The following nine prepositions, as illustrated below, govern the dative
case: **aus** (*out of, of, from*), **außer** (*except, besides*), **bei** (*near, with, at, at the house of*),
mit (*with*), **nach** (*to, toward, after, according to*), **seit** (*since*), **von** (*of, from, by*), **zu** (*to*),
and **gegenüber** (*opposite*).

A. Aus:

Er kommt **aus dem** Haus heraus.
*He comes **out of** the house.*

Was ist **aus ihm** geworden?
*What has become **of him?***

Der Tisch ist **aus** Holz.
*The table is (made) **of** wood.*

B. Außer:

Außer meinem Bruder war niemand da.
*Nobody was there **but** (or **except**) my brother.*

Ich war **außer mir** vor Freude.
*I was **beside** myself with joy.*

C. Bei:

Das Haus steht **bei der** Kirche.
*The house is **near** the church.*

Bei wem wohnt er?
***With whom** (or At whose house) does he live?*

Ich habe kein Geld **bei mir.**
*I have no money **on me** (or **with me**).*

D. Mit:

Sie reiste **mit der** Mutter.   Man ißt die Suppe **mit einem** Löffel.
*She traveled **with her** mother.*   *One eats soup **with a** spoon.*

E. Nach:

Nach dem Frühstück geht er in die Schule.
***After** breakfast he goes to school.*

Morgen fährt er **nach** Berlin.
*Tomorrow he will go **to** Berlin.*

In der Klasse sitzen die Schüler **nach dem Alphabet.**
*In class the pupils are seated alphabetically (**according to the alphabet**).*

Nach der Schule gehen sie **nach Hause.**
After** school they go **home.

Der Sage nach ist Rübezahl Herrscher über das Riesengebirge.
***According to the legend,** Ruebezahl rules over the Riesengebirge (Giants'
    Mountains).*

In the sense of *according to,* **nach** frequently follows its noun.

F. Seit:

(1) **Seit dem Krieg** habe ich ihn nicht gesehen.
*I have not seen him **since the war.***

(2) **Seit vier Monaten** wohne ich in diesem Haus.
*I have been living in this house **for four months.***

(3) **Seit wann** sind Sie hier?
***How long** have you been here?*

Examples (2) and (3) illustrate the use of **seit** with the *present tense* for an action begun in the past and continuing in the present.

G. Von:

Der Zug kommt **von** Hamburg.
*The train comes **from** Hamburg.*

Das ist ein Gedicht **von** Goethe.
*That is a poem **by** Goethe.*

Was will er **von mir**?
*What does he want **from me**?*

Der Löwe wurde **vom** Jäger getötet.
*The lion was killed **by** the hunter.*

H. Zu:

(1) Ich gehe **zu meinem** Bruder.
*I am going **to** my brother's (house).*

Following verbs of going, **zu** renders English *to,* when the action is directed toward a person, and in such phrases as **zur Kirche** and **zur Schule.**[1] Before the names of cities or countries, *to* is rendered by **nach:**

Er reist **nach** Deutschland.   Er ging **nach** Berlin.
*He is traveling **to** Germany*   *He went **to** Berlin.*

(2) Er sagte **zu mir**: „Ich werde Sie **zu Weihnachten** besuchen."
*He said **to me**: "I shall visit you **at Christmas."***

The preposition **zu** is required, following **sagen,** to introduce a direct quotation. In an indirect quotation the preposition is omitted:

Er sagte mir, er würde mich zu Weihnachten besuchen.
He told me that he would visit me at Christmas.

---

[1]**zur Schule gehen** means *to attend school;* **zur Kirche gehen** implies regular attendance at church. *To enter the school (church)* is **in die Schule (Kirche) gehen.** One also hears **zum Bahnhof** (*to the train station*), **zum Fest** (*to the festival*), etc., where **zu** functions as neutrally as English *to.*

(3) Er war nicht **zu Hause.**
*He was not **at home.***

I. Gegenüber:

Wir haben Verpflichtungen **gegenüber** dem Staat und der Gesellschaft.
We have responsibilities to the country and to society.

Er saß **mir gegenüber.**   Unser Haus liegt **dem Park gegenüber.**
*He sat **opposite** me.*   *Our house is **opposite** the park.*

Gegenüber often follows the word it governs.

§29. PREPOSITIONS WITH THE DATIVE OR ACCUSATIVE

The following prepositions, as illustrated below, may govern either the dative or accusative: **an** (*at, on, to*), **auf** (*on, upon*), **hinter** (*behind*), **in** (*in, into*), **neben** (*beside, next to*), **über** (*over, about, across*), **unter** (*under, beneath, below, among*), **vor** (*before, in front of, ago*), and **zwischen** (*between*).

The dative case is used in answer to the question *where?* or *when?*—i.e., when the verb is one of *rest*. The accusative answers the question *whither?*—i.e., when the verb denotes *motion toward some goal.*

A. An:

Er steht **an der** Tafel.   Er geht **an die** Tafel.
*He is standing **at** the board.*   *He is going **to** the board.*

Am Sonntag brauchen wir nicht in die Schule zu gehen.
***On** Sundays we do not have* (lit. *need*) *to go to school.*

B. Auf:

Das Buch liegt **auf dem** Tisch.   Er legt das Buch **auf den** Tisch.
*The book lies **on** the table:*   *He puts the book **on** the table.*

Sie ist **auf dem** Land.   Sie geht **aufs** (= **auf das**) Land.
*She is **in** the country.*   *She is going **to** the country.*

C. Hinter:

Der Hund liegt **hinter der** Tür.   Der Hund läuft **hinter die** Tür.
*The dog is lying **behind** the door.*   *The dog runs **behind** the door.*

D. In:

Sie ist **im** (= **in dem**) Zimmer.

She is in the room.

Sie kommt **ins** (= **in das**) Zimmer.
She comes into the room.

Im Winter sind die Nächte lang.
In winter the nights are long.

Er geht **im** Zimmer auf und ab.
He is walking up and down in the room.

E. Neben:

Ich saß **neben** ihm.   Ich setzte mich **neben ihn.**
I sat beside him.   *I sat down beside him.*

F. Über:

Eine Lampe hängt **über dem** Tisch.
A lamp hangs over the table.

Hängen Sie die Lampe **über den** Tisch!
Hang the lamp over the table.

Er sprach **über den** Krieg.
He spoke about the war.

Er wundert sich **über die** Schnelligkeit des Flugzeugs.
He marvels at the speed of the airplane.

G. Unter:

Er schlief **unter dem** Baum.   Er lief **unter den** Baum.
He was sleeping under the tree.   *He ran under the tree.*

Unter meinen Papieren habe ich diesen Brief gefunden.
I found this letter among my papers.

Sie hält es für **unter ihrer** Würde.
She considers it beneath her dignity.

Das bleibt **unter uns.**
That is between us.

H. Vor:

Er steht *vor der* Klasse.   Er tritt **vor die** Klasse.
He stands before the class.   *He steps before the class.*

Vor kurzer Zeit wurde das Gesetz aufgehoben.
A short time ago the law was repealed.

I. **Zwischen:**

Er saß **zwischen mir** und **meinem** Bruder.
*He was sitting **between** me and my brother.*

Er setzte sich **zwischen mich** und **meinen** Bruder.
*He sat down **between** me and my brother.*

Note: Certain of the prepositions listed above may be used in set phrases, and in such situations the case is dictated and invariable. For example:

(1) **über** meaning *about* or *concerning* requires the accusative.

(2) **sich wundern über** always takes accusative.

(3) **vor** meaning *ago* requires the dative and must precede the noun it governs.

§30. *WO-* AND *DA-*FORMS

When a thing is referred to, interrogative and relative pronouns may be replaced by the prefix **wo-**, personal pronouns by **da-**, as objects of prepositions governing the dative or accusative cases. Pronouns referring to people cannot be so replaced. If the preposition begins with a vowel, the prefixes are **wor-** and **dar-**.

A. **Womit, wodurch, woraus, wovon, woran,** etc.

(1) **Womit** schreibt er?   **Wovon** spricht sie?
What is he writing with?   *What is she talking **about**?*

Worüber wird die Geschichte handeln?
*What will the story be **about**?*

(2) Die Feder, **womit** [= mit der (*or* welcher)] ich schreibe, gehört meiner Schwester.
*The pen **with which** I am writing belongs to my sister.*

Die Bücher, **wovon** [= von denen (*or* welchen)] er sprach, gefallen mir.
*I like the books **of which** he was speaking.*

B. **Damit, dadurch, daraus, davon, daran,** etc.

Er schreibt **damit.**   Sie spricht **davon** (or **darüber**).
*He is writing **with it**.*   *She is talking **about it**.*

Das Kind hat viele Spielsachen.   Es spielt **damit.**
The child has many playthings. *It is playing **with them**.*

§31. CONTRACTIONS

A. Common contractions. The following are the most common contractions of prepositions with the definite article:

am	(= an dem)	**im**	(= in dem)
ans	(= an das)	**ins**	(= in das)
aufs	(= auf das)	**vom**	(= von dem)
beim	(= bei dem)	**zum**	(= zu dem)
fürs	(= für das)	**zur**	(= zu der)

B. Other contractions. Contractions other than those listed above are readily intelligible, provided one remembers that final -m stands for **dem** and final -s for **das: durchs** (= durch das), **ums** (= um das), **hinterm** (= hinter dem), etc.

§32. PREPOSITIONS WITH THE GENITIVE

The genitive case is often replaced by the dative in older writing and in casual conversation, especially when the object is plural (the dative plural of many nouns is more distinctive than the genitive plural); or when the prepositional phrase abuts another genitive (such as a proper noun), in order to avoid clusters of genitives. One should not be surprised to read *während Pauls langem Gespräch* instead of *während Pauls langen Gesprächs*, or *während Pauls Gesprächen* instead of *während Pauls Gespräche*.

The following prepositions, as illustrated below, govern the genitive case: **während** (*during*), **wegen** (*on account of*), **trotz** (*in spite of*), **(an)statt** (*instead of*), **diesseits** (*on this side of*), **jenseits** (*on that side of*), **oberhalb** (*above*), **unterhalb** (*below*), **außerhalb** (*outside of*), **innerhalb** (*inside of* or *within*), and **um . . . willen** (*for the sake of*).

A. Während:

> **Während der Nacht** regnete es.   **Während des Tages** arbeiten wir.
> *During the night it rained.*   *During the day we work.*

B. Wegen:

> **Wegen des schlechten Wetters** blieb er zu Hause.
> **Des schlechten Wetters wegen** blieb er zu Hause.
> *He stayed at home **on account of the bad weather.***

(1) **Wegen** may precede or follow the noun it governs.

(2) **Wegen** must follow when used with personal pronouns, which assume a

form in -t: meinetwegen (*on my account*), deinetwegen [*on your* (sing. fam.) *account*], seinetwegen (*on his account*), ihretwegen [*on her* (*their*) *account*], unsertwegen (*on our account*), euretwegen [*on your* (pl. fam.) *account*], Ihretwegen (*on your account*).

Tun Sie es nicht meinetwegen!
Do not do it on my account.

(3) **Meinetwegen** may also mean *for all I care.*

Meinetwegen darf er das tun.
He may do that for all I care.

C. Trotz:

Trotz des kalten Wetters machte er einen Spaziergang.
He took a walk in spite of the cold weather.

D. (An)statt:

(An)statt des Vaters kam die Mutter.
Mother came instead of father.

(An)statt des baren Geldes gab ich ihm einen Scheck.
I gave him a check instead of cash.

E. Diesseits:

Der Dom ist **diesseits des Flusses.**
The cathedral is on this side of the river.

F. Jenseits:

Das Rathaus ist **jenseits des Flusses.**
The town hall is on that side of the river.

G. Oberhalb:

Oberhalb des Dorfes ist eine kleine Kirche.
Above the village there is a small church.

H. Unterhalb:

Unterhalb der Kirche ist eine schöne Wiese.
There is a beautiful meadow below the church.

I. Außerhalb:

Er wohnt **außerhalb der Stadt.**
He lives outside of the city.

J. Innerhalb:

Innerhalb einer Stunde muß ich fertig sein.
I must be ready within an hour.

K. Um . . . willen:

Um Gottes (or **Himmels**) **willen!**
For heaven's sake!

Tun Sie es **um meinetwillen!**
Do it for my sake.

Note: **Other uses and meanings of common prepositions.** Only the most common prepositions have been included in this chapter. There are many others—chiefly with the genitive and dative—which occur, for the most part, in the written language. The common prepositions have many other uses and meanings than those given above, particularly in idiomatic expressions and with certain reflexive verbs. The simplest conversation is apt to involve idioms with prepositions—e.g., the common phrase *in other words* = **mit** anderen Worten. The following sentences, which might be multiplied indefinitely, show that the same English preposition may have numerous German equivalents:

I thank you for the book.
Ich danke Ihnen **für** das Buch.

I ask you for the book.
Ich bitte Sie **um** das Buch.

He hopes for good weather.
Er hofft **auf** gutes Wetter.

She longs for her friends.
Sie sehnt sich **nach** ihren Freundinnen.

For what reason did he do that?
Aus welchem Grunde hat er das getan?

For what price?
Zu welchem Preise?

She has been here for two months.
Sie ist **seit** zwei Monaten hier.

He is looking for me.
Er sucht mich.

Cologne is famous for its cathedral.
Köln ist **durch** den Dom (or **wegen** des Domes) berühmt.

E X E R C I S E S

A. Fill in the blanks in the following sentences.

1. Ein kleiner Vogel ist auf d____ hoh____ Baum geflogen.
2. Hagen ging sofort an d____ Fenster.
3. Er stand eine Weile an dies____ Fenster.

4. Er blickte auf d____ Hof und sah Siegfried auf d____ Pferd.

5. Während d____ Sommer____ war er in Dänemark.

6. Er wohnte bei sein____ Mutter und sein____ Vater.

7. Er bereitete sich auf sein____ groß____ Reise vor.

8. Er sah Kriemhild und sehnte sich nicht nach d____ Heimat.

9. "Helfen Sie mir! Tun Sie es mein____ Schwester wegen!"

10. "____wegen (*On her account*) mache ich das gerne."

11. Siegfried ging mit d____ Brüder____ auf die Jagd.

12. Wir müssen uns aber um____ (*him*) kümmern.

13. Der graue Mann stieß dem Helden den Speer in d____ Rücken.

14. Die Weltraumforscher warten auf günstig____ Wetter.

15. Der lustige Hund ist dreimal um d____ Haus gerannt.

16. Trotz d____ Sonntagspause arbeitet sie auf d____ Acker.

17. Marburg und Wetzlar liegen an d____ Lahn, einem schönen, ruhigen Fluß.

18. Warum bist du nach____ (*me*) gelaufen?

19. Der Boxer kämpft vergebens gegen d____ Weltmeister.

20. Man trinkt Kaffee aus ein____ Kaffeetasse.

21. Der Polizeibeamte steht neben d____ Café.

22. Außer d____ Trainerin kam niemand zum Tennisplatz.

23. Statt ein____ Diktatur hat das Land jetzt einen Präsidenten.

24. Ich bin schon seit ein____ Woche krank.

25. Das Foto liegt da auf d____ Pult.

26. Wer hat denn dieses Foto auf d____ Pult gelegt?

27. Bolzano liegt in Norditalien, jenseits d____ Alpen.

28. Bayern liegt in Deutschland, diesseits d____ Alpen.

29. Der Empfangschef begleitet jeden Kunden bis an d____ Tür.

30. Was hast du gegen m____ (*me*)?

31. Der Kanzler bleibt bis z____ nächst____ Monat in Bonn.

32. Ich denke oft an d____ Höhe der alten Mauer in Berlin.

33. Das Protestlied ist von dies____ jung____ Radikalen [*pl.*].

34. Innerhalb ein____ Jahr____ kommen wir bestimmt wieder.

35. Früher durfte der Politiker außerhalb d____ Stadt wohnen.

36. Diese demokratische Jugendbewegung ist gegen d____ Wunsch der heutigen Regierung.

37. Benno hat eine Rede für d____ Sportklub gehalten.

38. Wir wanderten lange durch d____ naß____ Wald.

39. Wer nicht für m____ ist, ist gegen m____ (*me, me*).

40. Der Gast verschwand dann in sein____ Zimmer in d____ teuren Hotel.

41. Ohne d____ Brille erkenne ich dich nicht.

42. Die beste Apotheke steht gegenüber d____ Rathaus.

43. Sie geht zu jed____ Ostern zu ihr____ Bruder.

44. Jetzt muß der Politiker direkt in d____ Stadt wohnen.

45. Früher ist er jeden morgen in d____ Stadt gefahren.

46. "Ohne ein____ Straßenbahnlinie ist mir das tägliche Hin- und Herreisen zu umständlich," sagte sie zu m____ (*me*).

47. Nur hartnäckige Leute schwimmen gegen d____ Strom.

48. Darf ich jetzt über eur____ Zukunft reden, Kinder?

49. Ich weiß nicht, was aus d____ (*you*) werden wird.

50. Der Politiker reiste unter falsch____ Namen.

B. Conclude the second sentence in each set below in a way suggested by the first sentence.

1. Sie lernt Deutsch. Sie geht zur Schule, um . . .

2. Ich ziehe mich um. Ich gehe in die Kirche, ohne . . .

3. Wir gehen ins Kino. Wir besuchen die Stadtmitte, anstatt . . .

4. Du übst das Überholen. Du gehst zur Fahrschule, um . . .

5. Ich rauche meine Pfeife. Ich kann mich ja ausruhen, ohne . . .

6. Du gehst zu oft zu deinem Bruder. Komme zu mir, statt . . . !

C. Many prepositions have locational function—they help tell where something is located. In our three dimensional world, things are surrounded by other things in front, in back, to either side, above, and below. Here is a selection of things you probably have in your own world. Locate them as fully as you can, even if it sounds a little silly.

1. Ihr Arbeitstisch zu Hause oder in Ihrer Studentenbude.

2. Das beste Pizzarestaurant in Ihrer Nachbarschaft.

3. Ihr Schließfach. Wenn Sie jetzt keins haben, dann das Schließfach im Gymnasium oder in der Turnhalle.

4. Ihr Lieblingstier im zoologischen Garten.

D. Rewrite the following sentences twice, once as questions using a **wo-**form and once as simple statements using a **da-**form. Here is a model:

Sie spielt **mit der Puppe. Womit** spielte sie? Sie spielt **damit.**

1. Der Philosoph dachte an die Vergangenheit.

2. Die Theaterkarten liegen da auf dem Tisch.

3. Wir lesen nicht gern über das letzte Jahrhundert.
4. Wir haben ihm für die Hilfe gedankt.

E. Translate into German:

1. He came to town without visiting me.
2. The river runs between two villages.
3. When we're in New York we live with our grandparents.
4. Anna always travels by streetcar, never by car.
5. After school the children have to travel to Duderstadt, in order to go shopping.
6. I have been here for two weeks, and only now do I hear from you!
7. Elke and her friends go quickly through the museum.
8. They are not interested in art.
9. Bärbel comes from Switzerland, where she lives opposite a famous bank.
10. Without a tie you get no service in a good restaurant.
11. I understand everything in school except the philosophers.
12. I have nothing against the philosophers, but they're not very clear.
13. She worries a lot about art, but not about science.
14. Two years ago I bought a car instead of making a trip to Germany.
15. The chancellor stood behind his desk and gave a speech about the economy.
16. Let's go to the new school next year.
17. "I'm only thinking about your future," she said to her son.
18. We look forward with pleasure to our vacation.
19. We found the mouse under the table, near a piece of cheese.
20. Go to the window and look out at the parking lot.

11

Absolute Uses of the Genitive, Dative, and Accusative Cases

Languages with a diversified noun case ending system, such as Latin, Greek, and German, can use the case endings to link nouns directly with verbs or adjectives to make verb or adjective phrases. Nouns so linked are said to be used *absolutely,* that is, without the need for a linking agent such as a preposition. In English, which has virtually no case endings, nouns in comparable settings are frequently linked to other elements in a sentence with prepositions.

§33. USES OF THE GENITIVE CASE

A. **The genitive to denote indefinite time.** The genitive case is frequently used to denote indefinite time:

> **Eines Tages (eines Morgens, eines Abends)** besuchte er mich.
> *One day (one morning, one evening) he visited me.*

Similarly with the adverbial forms **morgens** (*in the morning*), **abends** (*in the evening*), etc.

B. **The genitive with certain verbs.** A clue that the genitive may be expected with certain verbs and adjectives (C below) is that the English equivalents of such phrases frequently include the preposition *of:* Er ist sich meiner Hilfe bewußt— *He is conscious of my help.*

(1) A few verbs may take a genitive as sole object. These verbs should be noted in order to develop reading facility. In modern German, however, many such verbs are felt to be poetic, choice, pedantic or archaic. It is generally advisable to use other constructions in writing and conversation. Such alternative constructions are given in the examples that follow.

(*a*) **bedürfen:**

> Ich bedarf **Ihrer Hilfe.**
> Ich brauche Ihre Hilfe.
> *I need your help.*

(*b*) **denken:**

> Ich denke **seiner.**
> Ich denke an ihn.
> *I think* (or *am thinking*) *of him.*

(*c*) **gedenken:**

> Gedenke **deines Eides!**
> Erinnere dich an deinen Eid!
> *Remember your oath.*

(2) A number of reflexive verbs may govern the genitive case, although other constructions are often possible:

(*a*) **sich erbarmen:**

> Erbarmen Sie sich **meiner!**
> Erbarmen Sie sich über mich!
> Haben Sie Mitleid mit **mir!**
> (*Have*) *pity* (*on*) *me.*

(*b*) **sich bedienen:**

> Ich bediente mich **seiner Güte.**
> Ich machte von seiner Güte Gebrauch.
> *I availed myself* (or *made use*) *of his kindness.*

(*c*) **sich bemächtigen:**

> Er hat sich **unseres Eigentums** bemächtigt.
> Er hat unser Eigentum in Besitz genommen.
> *He took possession of our property.*

(*d*) **sich erinnern:**

> Er erinnert sich **des Vorfalls.**
> Er erinnert sich an den Vorfall.
> *He remembers the incident.*

(*e*) **sich rühmen:**

> Er rühmt sich **seines Erfolgs.**

Er prahlt mit seinem Erfolg.
*He boasts of **his success.***

(*f*) **sich schämen:**

Schämt er sich **seiner Armut?**
Schämt er sich über seine Armut?
*Is he ashamed of **his poverty?***

(3) Verbs of "judicial action" (e.g., **anklagen** and **beschuldigen,** *to accuse*) and certain verbs of separation or deprivation (e.g., **berauben,** *to rob*) take the genitive of the *thing* (that of which one is accused or from which one is separated) but the accusative of the *person:*

(*a*) **anklagen:**

Man hat **ihn des Diebstahls** angeklagt.
Er wurde **des Diebstahls** angeklagt.
He was accused of theft.

(*b*) **beschuldigen:**

Hast du **ihn der Unehrlichkeit** beschuldigt?
*Did you accuse **him of dishonesty?***

(*c*) **berauben:**

Er hat **mich meines ganzen Geldes** beraubt.
*He robbed **me of all my money.***

Rauben, however, takes the dative of the person and the accusative of the thing:

Man hat **ihm alles** geraubt.
*They robbed **him of everything.***

C. The genitive with certain adjectives.
Certain adjectives govern the genitive case, usually following the nouns they modify. Some of the common ones are:

(1) **bedürftig** (*in need of*):

Sie ist **meines Trostes** bedürftig.
*She is in need **of my consolation.***

(2) **bewußt** (*conscious*):

Ich bin mir **keines Unrechts** bewußt.
*I am **not** conscious **of any injustice.***

(3) **fähig** (*capable*):

Er ist **einer solchen Tat** fähig.
*He is capable **of such a deed.***

(4) **froh** (*happy*):

Sie wird **ihrer hohen Stellung** nicht froh.

*She is not happy **in her high position.***

Er ist froh über **den langen** Urlaub.
He is happy about the long vacation.

The adjective **froh** with the genitive and **werden** usually means *happy in.* To be *happy about* is **froh sein über,** which, like the verbal idiom **sich freuen über,** is followed by the accusative. The adjective may either precede or follow the prepositional phrase.

(5) **gewahr werden** (*become aware of, perceive*):

Er wurde **seines Irrtums** gewahr.
*He perceived (or became aware of) **his mistake.***

Gewahr is used only with **werden;** it sometimes takes the accusative.

(6) **gewiß** (*certain*):

Er ist **seiner Sache** gewiß.
*He is sure **of his case.***

(7) **mächtig** (*master or in control of*):

Er war **seiner Sinne** nicht mächtig.
*He was not in (control of) **his senses.***

(8) **müde** (*tired*):

Ich bin **dieses Treibens** müde.
*I am tired **of this activity.***

Müde (*tired*) and los (*free, rid of*) very often govern the accusative in modern German:

Ich bin **es** müde.   Ich bin **es** los.
*I am tired **of it.***   *I am rid **of it.***

This is due to the fact that this **es** was genitive in the older language but came to be felt as accusative—a use of the accusative which spread to forms other than **es:**

Ich bin **ihn** los.
*I am rid **of him.***

(9) **sicher** (*sure*):
Sie sind **meines Beistands** sicher.
*You are sure **of my assistance.***

(10) **wert** (*worth*): In modern German this adjective usually governs the accusative but in a few idiomatic expressions it governs the genitive:

Es ist nicht **der Mühe** wert.   Es ist nicht **der Rede** wert.
It is not worthwhile.   *It is not worth talking about.*
It is not worth the trouble.

(11) **würdig** (*worthy*):

Die Angelegenheit ist **Ihrer Unterstützung** würdig.
The affair deserves your support.
The affair is worthy of your support.

D. The genitive in idiomatic expressions:

Ich fahre **zweiter Klasse.**   Er ist **derselben Meinung.**
I travel second class.   *He is of the same opinion.*

Leichten (schweren) Herzens ging er an die Arbeit.
With a light (heavy) heart he went to work.

Sie ist **guter Laune** [or **guten Mut(e)s**].
She is in (a) good humor.

Meines Wissens verhalten sich die Tatsachen anders.
As far as I know, the facts are different.

Laß ihn **seines Weges** ziehen!
Let him go his way.

Many adverbs preserve traces of the genitive:

meinerseits, *on my part;* **glücklicherweise,** *fortunately;* **jedenfalls,** *in any event* (or *case*); **keineswegs,** *by no means;* **gewissermaßen,** *in a certain sense;* **links** (**rechts**), *on* (*at* or *to*) *the left* (*right*); etc.

E. When the genitive is not used. (1) Proper names used in apposition after, and names of months preceded by *of* are *not* in the genitive but in the same case as nouns preceding them:

die Stadt **München,** *the city of Munich*

im Monat **Mai,** *in the month of May*

den 25. **Juni,** *the 25th of June* (as the heading of a letter)

(2) Nouns of number, weight, measure, and kind are *not* followed by the genitive:

drei Pfund **Butter,** *three pounds of butter*

zwei Glas **Bier,** *two glasses of beer*

eine neue Art **Teppich,** *a new kind of carpet*

Masculine and neuter nouns denoting measurement are usually in the singular, provided they follow a numeral: **drei** Pfund, **zwei** Glas, *etc.* Feminine nouns ending in **-e,** however, require the plural form:

drei Tassen Tee, *three cups of tea*

Die Mark always has the singular form:

zwanzig **Mark,** *twenty marks*

If the thing weighed or measured is modified by an adjective, the genitive *may* be used:

ein Glas kalt**en** Wasser**s,** *a glass of cold water*

drei Pfund frisch**en** Fleisch**es,** *three pounds of fresh meat*

In ordinary speech, however, the thing measured is in the same case as the preceding noun: ein Glas kalt**es** Wasser, drei Pfund frisch**es** Fleisch, etc.

§34. USES OF THE DATIVE CASE

The dative is traditionally the case used with verbs and adjectives taking persons as complements. English equivalents of dative verb and adjective phrases frequently contain the prepositions *to* or *for:* Das warme Wetter ist **mir** sehr angenehm—*The warm weather is very pleasant **to me.*** Notice in **A-17** that one believes a person in the dative case but a thing in the accusative case, and that the other dative-taking verbs under **A** are most plausible with people (and not things) as objects.

A. **The dative with certain verbs.** The following are a few of the more common verbs that govern the dative case:

(1) **antworten** (*to answer*):

Antworten Sie **mir!**
*Answer **me.***

(a) **Antworten** takes the dative of the person. Observe, however, its idiomatic use with **auf** and the accusative:

Antworten Sie **auf die Frage!**
*Answer **the question.***

(b) **Beantworten,** on the other hand, takes a direct object:

Beantworten Sie **die Frage!**
*Answer **the question.***

(2) **befehlen** (*to command, order*):

Der Herr befahl **dem Diener,** bald zurückzukommen.
*The master ordered **the servant** to return soon.*

(3) **begegnen** (*to meet*):

Er ist **mir** auf der Straße begegnet.
*He met **me** on the street.*

(4) **danken** (*to thank*):

Er wird **ihnen** danken.
*He will thank **them.***

(5) **dienen** (*to serve*):

Er hat **seinem König** treu gedient.
*He has served **his king** faithfully.*

(6) **drohen** (*to threaten*):

Er drohte **ihm** mit Schlägen.
*He threatened **him** with blows.*

(7) **einfallen** (*to occur to, come to mind*):

Das war **mir** nie eingefallen.
*That had never occurred **to me.***

Was fällt **Ihnen** denn ein?
*What do you **mean?***

(8) **fehlen** (*to be the matter with, lack*):

Was fehlt **Ihnen?**   **Mir** fehlen zwei Bücher.
*What is the matter **with you?***   *I am short two books.*

(9) **folgen** (*to follow*):

Er wird **den Männern** folgen.
*He will follow **the men.***

   (*a*) In the sense of *follow,* **folgen** must be conjugated with **sein:**

     Er war **mir** gefolgt.
     *He had followed **me.***

   (*b*) In the sense of *obey,* **folgen** is conjugated with **haben:**

     Er hat **mir** gefolgt.
     *He obeyed **me.***

(10) **gefallen** (*to please*):

Wie gefällt **Ihnen** das neue Buch?
How do you like the new book?
(lit.: How does the new book appeal *to you?*)

What one likes is the subject of the verb. This is a serious translation problem.

(11) **gehorchen** (*to obey*):

Das Kind gehorcht **der Mutter.**
*The child obeys **its mother.***

(12) **gehören** (*to belong*):

Es gehört **mir.**
It belongs to me.

The preposition **zu** is not used with gehören if the verb denotes owner-ship; it is required if the verb is used in the sense of *to be a part of:*

Das Haus gehört **zum** (= **zu dem**) Gut.
The house belongs to (i.e., is a part of) the estate.

(13) **gelingen** and **glücken** (*to succeed*):

Es ist **ihm** nicht gelungen (*or* geglückt), das zu tun.
He has not succeeded in doing that.

Both of these verbs are conjugated with **sein,** and both are impersonal. A thing may be the subject:

Dieser Plan ist mir nicht gelungen.
This plan did not turn out well for me.

(14) **genügen** (*to suffice, satisfy*):

Es genügt **ihm** nicht ganz.
He is not quite satisfied with it.
It isn't enough for him.

(15) **geschehen** (*to happen;* used only impersonally, see §62):

Es geschieht **ihm** recht.
It serves him right.

(16) **gleichen** (*to resemble*):

Er gleicht **der Mutter.**
He resembles his mother.

(17) **glauben** (*to believe*):

Ich glaube **Ihnen.**   Ich glaube **es** nicht.
I believe *you.*   *I don't believe it.*

Glauben takes the dative of the *person* but the accusative of the *thing.*

(18) **gratulieren** (*to congratulate*):

Ich gratuliere **Ihnen** zu Ihrem Erfolg.
I congratulate you on your success.

(19) **helfen** (*to help*):

Helfen Sie **dem armen Mann!**
Help the poor man.

(20) **sich nähern** (*to approach*):

Ich näherte mich **der Stadt.**
*I approached **the city.***

(21) **nützen** (*to be of use, benefit*):

Was nützt **ihm** das?
*Of what use is that **to him?***

(22) **passen** (*to fit, be convenient, suit*):

Der Rock paßt **mir** nicht.
*The skirt does not fit **me.***

Es paßte **mir** nicht, heute aufs Land zu gehen.
*It was not convenient **for me** to go to the country today.*

(23) **raten** (*to advise*):

Wozu raten Sie **mir?**
*What do you advise **me** to do?*

But, **raten,** *to guess (at)* and **erraten,** *to guess (correctly)* both take the accusative:

Er kann raten, aber er wird es niemals erraten.
He can guess at it, but he will never succeed in guessing it.

(24) **schaden** (*to harm, hurt*):

Das wird **Ihrer Gesundheit** schaden.
*That will harm **your health.***

(25) **schmeicheln** (*to flatter*):

Der Maler hat **dem Diplomaten** auf diesem Bild geschmeichelt.
*The artist flattered **the diplomat** in this picture.*

(26) **trauen** (*to trust, believe in*):

Ich traue **ihm** nicht.
*I don't trust **him.***

(27) **vergeben** (*to forgive*):

Vergeben Sie **ihnen!**
*Forgive **them.***

(28) **widersprechen** (*to contradict*):

Widersprechen Sie **mir** nicht!
*Don't contradict **me.***

B. **Verbs governing both dative and accusative.** There is a group of very common "exchange verbs" which describe a three-sided activity. Typically, one person gives a thing to another person. The person doing the giving is the subject; the thing being given is the direct object; and the third participant, the person receiving the thing, is the so-called indirect object. The indirect, or "person", object is in the dative case, while the direct, or "thing", object is in the accusative case.

Ich werde es ihm geben.
I shall give it to him.

Er wird mir das Bild zeigen.
He will show me the picture.

Sagen Sie mir die ganze Wahrheit!
Tell me the whole truth.

C. **Verbs of taking and stealing.** Most verbs of taking and stealing have the thing stolen in the accusative but the person from whom it was taken in the dative:

Der Dieb hat **mir** die Uhr gestohlen.
The thief stole my watch.
*The thief has stolen the watch **from me.***

D. **The dative with certain adjectives.** The adjectives listed below usually follow the nouns they modify.

(1) **ähnlich** (*similar, resembling*):

Der Sohn ist **der Mutter** ähnlich.
*The son resembles **his mother.***

(2) **angenehm** (*pleasant, agreeable*):

Das warme Wetter ist **mir** sehr angenehm.
I find the warm weather very agreeable.

(3) **bekannt** (*known*):

Das Gedicht war **ihm** nicht bekannt.
Er kannte das Gedicht nicht.
He did not know the poem.

(4) **bequem** (*comfortable*):

Mach es **dir** bequem!
Make yourself at home.

(5) **böse** (*angry*):

Seien Sie **mir** nicht böse!
Seien Sie nicht böse auf mich!
*Don't be angry **with me.***

(6) **dankbar** (*grateful*):

Er war **seinen Eltern** stets dankbar.
*He was always grateful **to his parents**.*

(7) **feindlich** (**gesinnt**) (*hostile*):

Ich bin **Ihnen** nicht feindlich gesinnt.
*I am not hostile **towards you**.*

(8) **fremd** (*strange, unknown*):

Er ist **mir** fremd.
*He is a stranger **to me**.*

(9) **freundlich** (*friendly*):

Seien Sie **ihm** freundlich!
Seien Sie freundlich gegen ihn! or: . . .zu ihm!
Be friendly to (or toward) him.

(10) **gelegen** (*opportune*):

Das kommt **mir** recht gelegen.
*That comes quite opportunely **for me**.*

(11) **gleich** (*like, the same*):

Die Gestalten gingen **Gespenstern** gleich an uns vorüber.
*Like **ghosts** the figures passed us.*

Es ist **mir** ganz gleich.
*It is all the same **to me**.*

(12) **leicht** (*easy*):

Es war **dem Schüler** leicht, die Prüfung zu bestehen.
*It was easy **for the pupil** to pass the examination.*

(13) **lieb** (*dear, charming*):

Es ist **ihm** sehr lieb.
He likes it very much.
*It is very dear **to him**.*

Lieb is frequently used in the impersonal construction to express liking for; it may be followed by a **daß**-clause:

Es ist **mir** lieb, daß Sie das sagen.
I am pleased to hear you say that.

(14) **nah(e)** (*near*):

Das Dorf liegt **unserer Stadt** nahe.

*The village is near **our city**.*

Near is more frequently rendered by **in der Nähe**:

Er wohnt **in meiner Nähe**.
He lives near me.

(15) **nützlich** (*useful*):

Der Beamte ist **dem Lande** nützlich.
*The official is useful **to the country**.*

(16) **schwer** (*difficult*):

Diese Arbeit fällt **den kleinen Kindern** schwer.
*This work is hard **for the little children**.*

(17) **treu** (*true, faithful*):

Werden Sie **mir** treu bleiben?
Will you be (or *remain*) *true **to me?***

(18) **willkommen** (*welcome*):

Sie sind **uns** jederzeit willkommen.
You are welcome at any time.

E. The dative of possession. English denotes possession with reference to parts of the body or to articles of clothing by the possessive determiner. *I wash my hands;* the German idiom, however, ordinarily uses the *definite article* combined with a dative case expression of the possessor, provided there is no doubt as to the possessor.

Ich wasche **mir die** Hände.
*I wash **my** hands.*

Er setzt (**sich**) **den** Hut auf.
*He puts on **his** hat.*

Ich wasche **dem Kind die** Hände.
*I wash **the child's** hands.*

Er setzt **dem Jungen den** Hut auf.
*He puts **the** hat on **the boy's** head.*

F. The dative of reference. The dative is often used to denote the person concerned in a statement, or the person with reference to whom the statement holds good:

Schreiben Sie **mir** diese Aufgabe ab!
*Copy this exercise **for me**.*

Es war **ihm** ein Rätsel.
*It was a riddle **to him**.*

Notice that English does not always express such a dative:

Zu Hause nahm ich **mir** nur Zeit, mich anzuziehen und zu frühstücken.
At home I only took time to dress and to have breakfast.

§35. USES OF THE ACCUSATIVE CASE

A. The accusative to denote definite time.

> **Letzten Monat** war ich bei ihm.
> *Last month I was at his house.*

> **Nächsten Sommer** wird er mich besuchen.
> *He will visit me next summer.*

B. The accusative to denote duration of time.

> Wir arbeiteten **den ganzen Tag.**
> *We worked all day.*

> **Den ganzen Morgen** spielte sie Ball.
> *She played ball all morning.*

C. The accusative to denote extent.
The accusative case is used to denote extent, especially with such adjectives as **breit, dick, hoch, lang,** and **tief**:

einen Zoll **breit,** *an inch wide*	eine Meile **lang,** *a mile long*
einen Fuß **hoch,** *a foot high*	einen Ton **tiefer,** *a tone lower*
einen Fuß **dick,** *a foot thick*	einen Kopf **größer,** *a head taller*
zwei kilometer **weiter,** *two kilometers further*	

D. The double accusative.
Certain verbs such as **lehren** (*to teach*), **nennen** and **heißen** (*to call*), and **schelten** and **schimpfen** (*to call names*) take two accusative objects:

> Sie lehrte **ihn das Lied.**   Er nannte (*or* hieß) **mich seinen Freund.**
> *She taught him the song.*   *He called me his friend.*

> Sie hat **ihn einen Narren** geschimpft (*or* gescholten).
> *She called him a fool.*

The verb **kosten** (*to cost*) may take either the accusative or dative of the person, but always the accusative of the thing:

> Es kostete **ihn** (*or* ihm) ein**en** Dollar.
> *It cost him a dollar.*

> Das Buch kostete **mich** (*or* mir) zehn Mark.
> *The book cost me ten marks.*

E. The cognate accusative.
The cognate accusative repeats the idea contained in a verb:

> Gar schöne **Spiele** spiel' ich mit dir. (Goethe)
> *I shall play very beautiful games with you.*

Er starb **einen sanften Tod** (*or* eines sanften Todes).
He died an easy death.

The optional form indicates that **sterben** is sometimes followed by the genitive.

F. **The absolute accusative.** The accusative case is often used absolutely with some such word as *having* understood:

Den Stock unter dem Arm, ging er in den Wald.
*With (i.e., **having**) **his cane** under his arm, he went into the forest.*

G. **The accusative in salutations.** Such expressions as **guten Morgen! guten Abend! guten Tag!** etc., are in the accusative case because they imply a verb of wishing: *I wish you a good morning (evening, day, etc.).*

H. **The accusative with *gewohnt, wert* and *entlang*.** The accusative is used with **gewohnt** (*accustomed*), **wert** (*worth*), and **entlang** (*along*):

Er ist **schwere Arbeit** gewohnt.
He has experience with hard work.

Er ist **an** schwere Arbeit gewöhnt.
He is used to hard work.

Es ist **einen Dollar** wert.   Er ging **das Ufer** entlang.
It is worth a dollar.   *He walked along the shore.*

(1) The construction with **an** plus accusative and the past participle **gewöhnt** is more common.

(2) **Entlang** governs the dative occasionally and the genitive still less frequently. It sometimes precedes the noun it governs.

I. **Compounds from intransitive verbs.** Many intransitive verbs become transitive when compounded:

(1) Er folgte mir.   Er **be**folgte mein**en** Rat.
He followed me.   *He followed my advice.*

Er **ver**folgte **mich.**   Ich wohne in diesem Haus.
He pursued me.   Ich **be**wohne dies**es** Haus.
I live in this house.

Er steigt auf den Berg.
Er **be**steigt **den** Berg.
He climbs the mountain.

(2) Similarly:

Er redete **mich** an.   Sie haben **den** alten Mann fast **über**fahren.
He addressed me.   *You almost ran over the old man.*

J. Causatives. Causative verbs, which require a direct object, must not be confused with intransitive verbs of similar spelling. Causative verbs are regularly weak.

(1) Die Bäume **fallen** im Sturm. (intr.)
The trees fall in the storm.

Die Holzhacker **fällen** die Bäume.
The woodcutters fell the trees (i.e., cause to fall, cut down)

(2) Die Männer **ertrinken.** (intr.)
The men are drowning.

Sie **ertränken** ihren Kummer im Wein.
They drown their sorrow in wine.

INTRANSITIVE	CAUSATIVE
fallen, *to fall*	fällen, *to cause to fall*
ertrinken, *to drown*	ertränken, *to drown*
liegen, *to lie*	legen, *to lay*
sitzen, *to sit*	setzen, *to set*
versinken, *to sink*	versenken, *to sink*
erschrecken, *to be frightened*	erschrecken, *to frighten*
verschwinden, *to disappear*	verschwenden, *to squander*

In fact, the causative version in each of the pairs above is derived from the intransitive member of the pair. Note that the intransitive version is always a strong verb, and therefore the more ancient of the two, while the causative version is always a weak verb and therefore more modern. (The strong verb family has fewer than 150 members and is fixed: any new processes need to be described with weak verb coinages, some of which are like these causatives in being based on strong verb originals.)

E X E R C I S E S

A. In the sentences below some of the noun phrases have not been marked for case. Each such noun phrase is used absolutely—without a preposition linkage—and should be in the genitive, dative, or accusative case. Please mark them accordingly by filling in the blanks. Note that some blanks require nothing. As you master this material please remember that the genitive absolutes are a feature of the written language and are either avoided or replaced in *spoken* German.

1. Ein____ Morgen____ begegnete sie mir auf der Straße.

2. Antworten Sie d____ Polizist____!

3. Wir werden d____ ganz____ Sommer in der Schweiz sein.

4. Sie hat m____ ihr____ best____ Freund____ genannt.

5. Jed____ Mittwoch gehen wir zum Sportklub.

6. Dieser VW ist mein____ VW ähnlich.

7. Wir waren uns unsr____ Schuld bewußt.

8. Die Handlung dieses Films ist m____ gar nicht bekannt.

9. Ein____ Tag____ wurde ich sehr krank.

10. Das Band war ein____ Finger breit.

11. Ich singe d____ gerne d____ neuest____ Lied vor.

12. W____ seid ihr im Café begegnet?

13. Sie ist ihr____ Sache ganz gewiß.

14. Dann bestellte ich zehn Glas____ Bier____.

15. Ich bestellte nur dunkles Bier, und er wollte ein Glas hell____
    Bier____. (*There are two ways to do this.*)

16. Ist er ein____ solch____ Tat fähig?

17. Erst jetzt werde ich mein____ Irrtum____ gewahr.

18. Die Schloßmauer war ein____ Meter dick.

19. Das Buch kostete uns ein____ Dollar.

20. Endlich bin ich dies____ Sache los.

21. Es ist m____ noch nicht gelungen, diesen Plan auszuführen.

22. Seien Sie____ (*him*) nicht böse!

23. Mein____ Wissen____ ist sie immer noch bei der Arbeit.

24. "Ich bedarf ein____ stark____ alkoholisch____ Getränk____," rief der
    normalerweise nüchterne Lehrer.

25. Ich werde es m____ bequem machen.

26. Wie gefällt _____ (*you*) dieses preiswerte Fertighaus?

27. Das Essen aus dem Bio-Laden kann dein____ Gesundheit nicht schaden,
    obwohl es dir nicht schmeckt.

28. Der Protestzug ging langsam d____ Straße entlang.

29. Die Seminararbeit kostete m____ viele Mühe.

30. Er sieht _____ (*for himself*) das neue rote Honda an.

31. Es ist m____ ganz gleich, was du da sagst.

32. Ihr Büro steht ihr____ Haus nahe.

33. Habt ihr d____ Kind mit der Hausarbeit geholfen?

34. Wir geben d____ Schaffner unsr____ Fahrkarten.

35. Eine Tasse Kaffee nach dem Essen ist _____ (*to her*) immer willkommen.

B. Translate into German.

1. How do you like this new necktie?
2. I believe you. But I don't believe your story.
3. With the flowers in his hand he went to visit his aunt on Sunday.
4. The city of Hamburg lies on the Elbe.
5. She is by no means satisfied.
6. We need a physician.
7. Now, to whom does this gun belong?
8. That serves her right!
9. Why didn't you answer my question?
10. The lion frightened me; were you frightened too?
11. Is this short test hard for the students? (*not* Studenten)
12. Yesterday we encountered the American tourists.
13. I have to get rid of it quickly.
14. They squandered our money and then they disappeared.
15. The delegate never travels second class.
16. Are you in a good mood today?
17. What's the matter with you?
18. I'll show them a new way into the forest.
19. Very slowly he approached the bank of the river.
20. One morning I saw an elephant near my house.

12

Idiomatic Uses of Tense

§36. IDIOMATIC USE OF THE PRESENT FOR THE ENGLISH PRESENT PERFECT

German uses the present tense to denote an action begun in the past and still continuing in the present. This construction, used where English uses a present perfect, must contain an adverbial expression of time (**schon, seit** plus the dative, **erst, zwei Monate, wie lange,** etc.).

Er **ist** schon zwei Monate hier.
*He **has been** here for two months.*
   (i.e., he came here two months ago and is still here.)

Wie lange **lernen Sie** schon Deutsch?
*How long **have you been studying** German?*
   (i.e., the person addressed began the study of German some time ago and is still studying it.)

Wir **arbeiten** schon einen Monat.
*We **have been working** for a month.*
   (i.e., we began to work a month ago and are still working.)

Sie ist (schon) **seit drei Jahren** in dieser Stadt.
Sie ist **schon drei Jahre** in dieser Stadt.
*She has been in this city **for three years.***
   (i.e., she came three years ago and is still in the city.)

Seit wann wohnen Sie in dieser Stadt?
Since when have you been living in this city?
   (i.e., the person addressed is still living in the city.)

Ich wohne **erst seit** zwei Monaten hier.
I have been living here for only two months.
   (i.e., I began living here two months ago and am still living here.)

§37. USE OF THE PRESENT FOR THE FUTURE

The present tense is often used instead of the future, particularly when accompanying adverbs of time—such as **bald** and **morgen**—clearly show futurity. If the future indicative occurs in the main clause of a conditional sentence, the present indicative is ordinarily employed in the **wenn**-clause (just as in English). The present tense is also used for the future in other types of sentences where there can be no chronological ambiguity.

Bald sind wir da.   Morgen reist mein Freund ab.
We shall soon be there.   *My friend will leave (is leaving) tomorrow.*

Wenn Sie sich beeilen, so werden Sie ihn noch einholen.
If you hurry, you will still catch (up with) him.

§38. IDIOMATIC USES OF THE PAST

A. **The use of the past for the English past perfect.** The German simple past is often used to denote an action begun at some previous time and continuing up to the time referred to in the past. This past context may be supplied by a verbal phrase or an adverbial phrase (usually **schon,** or **seit** plus dative, or both).

Er **wartete** schon anderthalb Stunden auf mich, als ich kam.
He had been waiting an hour and a half for me when I came.
   (i.e., he began to wait for me at some time in the past and was still waiting for me when I came.)

Er **kannte** mich schon seit vielen Jahren.
He had known me for many years.

Wir **waren** schon lange Freunde.
We had been friends for a long time.

B. **The use of the past to denote a customary occurrence in the past.** The simple past in German, usually reinforced by such adverbs as **früher, immer,** and **gewöhnlich,** may be used to express a recurring or habitual action.

Früher **rauchte** er viel.
*Formerly he **used to smoke** (or he smoked) a great deal.*

Er **stand gewöhnlich** um sieben Uhr auf.
*He **used to get up** (or he usually got up) at seven o'clock.*

Wenn er bei mir war, **sprach** er immer über seine Zukunftspläne.
*Whenever he was at my house, he **would talk** (or he always talked) about his plans for the future.*

Pflegen (*to be accustomed* or *used to*) with a dependent infinitive is a common equivalent of the above construction:

Er pflegte viel zu rauchen.

Er pflegte um sieben Uhr aufzustehen.

Er pflegte über seine Zukunftspläne zu sprechen.

§39. IDIOMATIC USE OF THE FUTURE AND FUTURE PERFECT WITH *WOHL*

A. The German future tense, usually with **wohl,** and with **schon** may be used to express *present probability.*

Er wird es **schon** verstehen.
Er wird es **wohl** verstehen.
He doubtless understands it.
He'll understand it.

Sie wird **wohl** wissen, was das bedeutet.
She probably knows what that means.
She'll know what it means.

B. The German future perfect is chiefly used, generally with **wohl,** and with **wahrscheinlich** to express *past probability.*

Mein Freund wird **wahrscheinlich** krank gewesen sein.
Mein Freund wird **wohl** krank gewesen sein.
My friend was probably sick.

Er wird **wohl** zu viel gegessen haben.
He probably ate too much.

E X E R C I S E S

A. Translate into idiomatic English.

1. Wie lange ist Herr Schmidt schon in Amerika?

2. Wir waren schon eine Viertelstunde im Hotel, als er kam.

3. Sie wartet schon seit einer Stunde auf mich.

4. Du wirst wohl wissen, warum ich so spät komme.

5. Seit wann singt der Rockstar in Bad Kissingen?

6. Ihr werdet wohl gewußt haben, warum ich euch letztes Jahr zu Weihnachten nicht besuchen konnte.

7. Ich wohne erst seit zwei Wochen in dieser Studentenbude.

8. Der Winter ist bald da (= *here*).

9. Wenn du dich nicht warm anziehst, so wirst du dich bestimmt erkälten.

10. Du hast keinen Hunger mehr? Du wirst wohl zu viel gegessen haben.

11. Die zwei Nobelpreisträger waren schon lange Freunde.

12. Sie pflegte jeden Morgen zehn Kilometer zu laufen.

13. Kant ging gewöhnlich nachmittags spazieren.

14. Morgen früh müssen wir nach Berlin.

15. Wie lange spielst du schon Gitarre?

B. Here is a series of activities. Ask your classmates at large if anyone does a particular activity, and then ask the classmate who admits to it: "Wie lange?" or "Seit wann?" It is then up to the classmate to answer using a time expression and the appropriate verb tense. Try to vary the format of the time expressions.

1. Wer spielt hier Tennis? Eishockey? Tischtennis? Fußball?

2. Wer ringt? Wer hebt Gewichte? Wer macht Langstreckenlauf?

3. Wer kauft täglich eine Zeitung? Wer sieht täglich fern?

4. Wer wohnt zu Hause bei den Eltern? Wer wohnt in einer Studentenbude?

5. Wer fährt hier Auto? Wer fährt mit dem Fahrrad? Mit dem Motorrad? Mit dem Motorfahrrad?

C. Each item in the following series contains an assertion about the past or present which can be explained by an obviously possible past or present circumstance. See A-10 above for an example. Using the idioms for past or present probability in complete German sentences, try to react to the conditions described.

1. Du hast keinen Durst mehr?

2. Ihr seid vollständig ausgeruht?

3. Helge spricht eben mit dem jungen Studenten da.

4. Du kannst Deutsch? Ich erzähle dir eine deutsche Geschichte.

5. Deine Eltern wollen den neuen Film nicht sehen?

6. Die Radiosendung über Raumschiffe interessiert euch nicht mehr?

D. Translate into German, being careful to consider the tense.

1. Since when has the retired postal official lived in this village?
2. She no doubt knows why I study physics.
3. We've been waiting here for an hour and a half.
4. She had been there for half an hour when I came.
5. How long have you lived in your present apartment?
6. My notebooks are probably in my locker at school.
7. Otherwise I probably misplaced them.
8. He used to shave every day.
9. We probably studied too hard for the test.
10. Formerly he used to smoke too much.

Personal Pronouns

13

Pronouns replace nouns, usually to keep from over-naming people, places, and things, and to avoid belaboring the obvious. The first person pronouns *I* and *we* replace the name(s) of the speaker(s) or writer(s). The second person pronouns *you* and *you* replace, similarly, the name(s) of the person(s) being addressed. The third person pronouns *he, she, it,* and the plural *they* replace the names of persons, places, and things being talked or written about.

Any pronoun stands in the place of a noun phrase, and must therefore be able to do much of what a noun phrase can do—whether it be the subject or object of a sentence, or the object of a preposition, or the complement of a verb or adjective.

There are many kinds of pronouns: personal, relative, interrogative, reflexive, reciprocal, indefinite, demonstrative, even possessive (although these are usually grouped with the **ein**-words). Of these, the personal pronouns are the most commonly encountered.

A pronoun must agree as best it can with the noun it replaces—its "antecedent"—in gender and number; agreement of gender is only possible with the third person singular *he, she,* and *it.* Its case will come naturally from the use to which it is put in its own sentence.

§40. FORMS OF THE PERSONAL PRONOUNS

Listed below are the personal pronouns, singular and plural, for all cases. Personal pronouns cannot possess—the possessive **ein**-words perform that function—and the genitive case is rarely used in modern German to express an object or a complement; for this reason the genitive forms are in brackets, and many elementary texts omit them entirely.

	SINGULAR					
	FIRST PERSON	SECOND PERSON		THIRD PERSON		
Nominative	*ich*	*du*	*Sie*	*er*	*sie*	*es*
Genitive	*[meiner]*	*[deiner]*	*[Ihrer]*	*[seiner]*	*[ihrer]*	*[seiner]*
Dative	*mir*	*dir*	*Ihnen*	*ihm*	*ihr*	*ihm*
Accusative	*mich*	*dich*	*Sie*	*ihn*	*sie*	*es*
	PLURAL					
Nominative	*wir*	*ihr*	*Sie*		*sie*	
Genitive	*[unser]*	*[euer]*	*[Ihrer]*		*[ihrer]*	
Dative	*uns*	*euch*	*Ihnen*		*ihnen*	
Accusative	*uns*	*euch*	*Sie*		*sie*	

§41. THIRD PERSON AGREEMENT, *DU* VS. *SIE*, THE INDEFINITE

A. Since German preserves grammatical gender, the pronouns of the third person singular will not always be directly translated into English; rather, sensible idiomatic equivalents must be sought.

Wo ist der Computer?
Where's the computer?

Er ist wieder in Reparatur.
It's being repaired again.

Wo ist die Angelrute?
Where's the fishing pole?

Sie ist ins Wasser gefallen.
It fell in the water.

Wo ist das Hotelverzeichnis?
Where's the hotel listing?

Es ist noch unter der Theke.
It's still under the counter.

Occasionally one finds that the antecedent is biologically male or female but grammatically neuter. Nowadays in the written language the pronoun agrees with the grammatical gender, consistent with the rule:

Ich sah **ein** Mädchen.
I saw a girl.

Es stand an der Tür.
She stood at the door.

In older writing, and even today in the spoken language, biology asserts itself:

Ich sah **ein** Mädchen.

Sie stand an der Tür.

And even in written German, if the pronoun is removed some distance from the antecedent, it is as if the force field of grammatical gender is weakened and biological gender takes over.

B. There are four pronouns for the second person. **Sie,** singular and plural, was adopted from the third plural **sie,** *they,* to provide generally urban and educated speakers with a conventionally polite form of address. All its forms are capitalized.

Frau Zipf, was schreiben **Sie?**	Meine Herren, was wollen **Sie?**
*Ms. Zipf, what are **you** writing?*	*Gentlemen, what do **you** want?*

The historical forms, **du** and **ihr,** are more informal, and are used in urban and educated speech and writing with children, parents, close friends, animals, and God. The strictness of this usage today is hard to measure. The familiar plural **ihr** has always been used in addressing even a stranger as a representative rather than an individual: Wie macht ihr das in Amerika? *How do you Americans do that?* People in villages use the informal forms, as do young people everywhere, and each year the popularity of **Sie** is reduced.

Karl, was schreibst **du?**	Kinder, was schreibt **ihr?**
*Carl, what are **you** writing?*	*Children, what are **you** writing?*

C. The indefinite pronoun **es** is used idiomatically in the following common constructions (note that the verb ignores the **es** and agrees with the other noun or pronoun):

Es sind dreißig Schüler in der Klasse.
***There are** thirty pupils in this grade.*

Es waren meine Freunde.
***They** were my friends.*

Ich bin **es.**	Ist er **es?**
It's me.	*Is **it** him?*

§42. THE GENITIVE OF PERSONAL PRONOUNS

A. With certain verbs, adjectives, and numerals. The genitive form of the personal pronouns, though rare in modern German, is found as a complement to certain verbs, adjective, and numerals. There is an alternative construction using the accusative noted in (2).

(1) Schone **meiner!**	Erbarmen Sie sich **ihrer.**
*Spare **me!***	*Pity **her!***

    (2) Gedenke **ihrer**!
        Erinnere dich **ihrer**!
        Erinnere dich **an sie**!
        Remember her! (or: *them*)

    (3) Er wurde **meiner** gewahr.   Wir waren **unser** drei.
        He became aware of me.   *There were three of us.*

B. With certain prepositions. The genitive of the personal pronouns is also found with some prepositions governing the genitive case. This is particularly true with certain combinations, when the pronoun ends in **-t** instead of **-r**.

    meinetwegen, *on my account*   um meinetwillen, *for my sake*
    seinetwegen, *on his account*   Ihrethalben, *on your account*

Meinetwegen! is often encountered with the sense of *I don't mind!*

§43. PERSONAL PRONOUNS OF ADDRESS IN LETTERS

In letters all pronouns of direct address, and all of their forms and corresponding possessives, are capitalized.

    Meine liebe Rose!

    Schon lange habe ich nichts mehr von **Dir** gehört. Vielleicht is **Dein** letzter Brief verlorengegangen. . . .

                Herzliche Grüße
                Dein **Dich** liebender Alois.

E X E R C I S E S

A. Complete the following sentences by filling in the blanks. If the second person "you" is requested, repeat the sentence with any German equivalent of "you" that makes sense.

    1. Bitte, reichen Sie _____ (*me*) das Hotelverzeichnis!

    2. Wird sie _____ (*you*) heute besuchen?

    3. Sie hat _____ (*me*) heute vor der Sporthalle gesehen.

    4. Das wird _____ (*you*) nicht schaden.

    5. Ich habe _____ (*him*) nicht verstanden.

    6. Ursula und Kurt! Kann ich _____ (*you*) helfen?

    7. Ich gab _____ (*her*) den Scheck.

8. Werdet ihr _____ (*him*) nächste Woche zu uns mitbringen?

9. Der Polizeibeamte hat _____ (*us*) hoffentlich nicht erkannt.

10. Gefällt _____ (*you*) das neue Sofakissen?

11. Es ist _____ (*us*) gelungen, den alten Stadtteil zu finden.

12. Wir begegneten _____ (*them*) unten vor dem Hotel.

13. Was fehlt _____ (*you*)?

14. Ich kannte _____ (*them*).

15. Er folgte _____ (*me*) in die Stadt.

16. Wir haben _____ (*her*) dann ins Kino geführt.

17. Gehört die Aktenmappe _____ (*her*) oder _____ (*him*)?

18. So laut waren wir nicht. Du hörtest _____ (*us*) sicher nicht.

19. Sie hat _____ (*me*) befohlen, sofort aufzustehen.

20. So bissig ist der Hund nicht. Der wird _____ (*you*) nicht beißen.

21. Das sollst du _____ (*on my account*) machen.

22. Sie waren da _____ (*of them*) sieben.

23. Fräulein Zipf, man muß _____ (*you*) loben.

24. Herr und Frau Zipf, man muß _____ (*you*) loben.

25. Die Karte ist nicht im Handschuhkasten. _____ (*It*) ist leer.

26. Diese Prüfung ist nicht lang. _____ (*It*) ist aber schwer.

27. Das ist doch mein Gepäck. _____ (*It*) gehört mir.

28. Es war einmal ein kleines Mädchen. _____ (*She*) hieß Gretel und ging mit dem Bruder in den dunklen Wald.

29. Die Mutter wollte mit ihrem lieben Hänschen telefonieren, aber _____ (*he*) war noch nicht zu Hause.

30. Bitte, gedenken Sie _____ (*me*) im Gebet.

B. Imagine that sentence groups A-20 and A-26 above had been spoken by two people, and that you were the second speaker, commenting on what your friend has just said. You use pronouns to avoid repeating obvious nouns. Here are several comments which invite your response. You may agree, disagree, support, answer, or illustrate each comment. But use complete sentences, and use pronouns.

1. Diese Theaterkarten sind sehr teuer.

2. Ich finde diese Vorlesung sehr langweilig.

3. Wir können keinen Mercedes mieten.

4. Warum siehst du mich so erstaunt an?

5. *Ich* würde sowas von ihnen nie erwarten!

6. Nun, was sollen wir jetzt tun?

7. Fritz und ich sind zu müde.

8. Ich habe das Hotelverzeichnis verloren.

9. Kennst du das Ehepaar da drüben?

10. Wem gehört der neue Farbfernseher?

C. Translate into German:

1. "Where is your trunk?" "It's still at the station."

2. Please give me the ballpoint. It's near the rubber stamp.

3. The conductor must count me and all travelers.

4. That city-plan will help me a lot.

5. Where is the city-plan? Have you forgotten it?

6. We're donating our old computer to them.

7. Which wristwatch do you like the best? (*use all versions of* you *that you think make sense*)

8. Father heard them but didn't believe them at all.

9. Don't forget the letter. You must thank her for it.

10. The professor recognized me and then I had to study hard.

11. That's our luggage. It belongs to us, not to them.

12. Inge and Josef! Take little Hans along; he wants to ride with you.

Interrogative Pronouns and Determiners

§44. WER, WAS, WO- FORMS; WELCHER AND WAS FÜR EIN

A. The interrogative pronouns **wer** and **was** have the following declension. This set of words is exceptional in that grammatical gender and number are ignored, with **wer** asking about male or female persons, singular or plural, and **was** asking about things, singular or plural and without regard to the gender of those things.

	MASCULINE AND FEMININE	NEUTER
Nom.	wer	was
Gen.	wessen	(wessen, wes) (*rare*)
Dat.	wem	——
Acc.	wen	was

Even though *wer* and *was* have no plural forms, they may be followed by a plural form of the verb *to be*:

Was **sind** das für Dinge?
*What **are** those things?*

Was is found almost exclusively in the nominative and accusative. The genitive is extremely rare and is confined chiefly to such adverbial combinations as **weshalb** and **weswegen** (*on account of what, why*).

The missing dative of **was** is supplied by **wo-** in such combinations as **womit, worauf.** The accusative **was** is quite rare after prepositions and is also usually replaced by **wo-**forms. **Um was** instead of **worum,** however, is quite common in such a sentence as:

Um was handelt es sich?
What is it (all) about?

The following sentences exemplify the use of these interrogative pronouns.

(1) The nominative case:

Wer ist die Dame?   **Wer** sind die Damen?
Who is the lady?   *Who are the ladies?*

Was ist das?
What is that?

(2) The genitive case:

Wessen Buch ist das?   **Wessen** Bücher sind das?
Whose book is that?   *Whose books are those?*

Weshalb (*or* **wes**wegen) haben Sie die Stadt verlassen?
Why did you leave the city?

(3) The dative case:

Wem haben Sie die Briefe gegeben?
To whom did you give the letters?

Mit **wem** hat er einen Spaziergang gemacht?
With whom did he take a walk?

Womit schreiben Sie?   Mit **wem** sprechen Sie?
With what are you writing?   *With whom are you speaking?*

(4) The accusative case:

Wen haben Sie heute gesehen?
Whom did you see today?

An **wen** denken Sie?
Of whom are you thinking?

Worauf warten Sie?   Auf **wen** warten Sie?
What are you waiting for?   *For whom are you waiting?*

Was hat er gefunden?
What did he find?

B. The interrogative determiner **welcher,** one of the **der-**words, and the phrase **was für ein,** basically an **ein-**word, are illustrated by the following examples: ·

> **Welcher** Mann ist zu Hause?
> *Which man is at home?*

> Mit **was für einem** Bleistift schreiben Sie?
> *With what kind of (a) pencil are you writing?*

Note that **für** in **was für ein** is not a preposition and does not determine the case of a following noun. The plural of **was für ein** is simply **was für:**

> **Was für** Bücher haben Sie?
> *What kind of books do you have?*

Was für ein is used in exclamations without interrogative force:

> **Was für ein** Unglück!   **Was für** Leute!
> *What a misfortune!*   *What people!*

Both **welcher** and **was für ein** may be used without following nouns, i.e., as interrogative pronouns:

> **Welcher** ist zu Hause, der Professor oder sein Sohn?
> *Which one* (pron.) *is at home, the professor or his son?*

> **Was für einen** haben Sie gekauft?
> *What kind* (of one) (used as pron.) *did you buy?*

E X E R C I S E S

A. Complete the following sentences by filling in the blanks.

1. _____ (*Whom*) hast du heute im Schnellimbiß gesehen?

2. _____ (*To whom*) hast du deinen alten Wagen verkauft?

3. _____ (*What*) hat er dir dafür gegeben?

4. _____ (*With what*) wirst du jetzt deine Miete bezahlen?

5. Mit _____ (*what kind of a*) Studium beschäftigt sie sich?

6. _____ (*What*) Teesorten kann man hier bestellen?

7. _____ (*Which*) Baum soll ich denn nun fällen?

8. _____ (*Which one*) fehlt euch heute? Nur die Hausaufgabe oder die ganze Schultasche?

9. _____ (*Whom*) hat der Lehrer geglaubt, dir oder mir?

10. _____ (*Whom*) habt ihr gestern da getroffen?

11. _____ (*Whose*) Auto hatte da eine Panne?

12. Er wollte wissen, _____ (*who*) gekommen wäre.

13. _____ (*Upon what*) bestehst du im Vertrag?

14. _____ (*Of what*) denkt ihr?

15. _____ (*Of whom*) denkt ihr?

16. _____ (*What kind of*) Jeans hast du neulich gekauft?

B. Make up questions to which the following sentences might provide plausible answers. Some answers allow more than one question. A-9 above supplies a way to deal with the first one.

1. Es tut mir leid, aber der Lehrer hat mir geglaubt.

2. Es handelt sich hier um unsre Zukunft.

3. Ich meine, Dr. Porsche baut die schnellsten Rennwagen.

4. Sie hat sich nur Beyer-Tabletten gekauft.

5. Ich ziehe meistens chinesische Teesorten vor.

6. Nein, nur das Ferienhaus wollte ich erben.

7. Das da ist mein Dollar!

8. Ich schreibe die Arbeit mit dem Computer.

9. Sie machte es wegen ihrer Schwester.

10. Wir alle freuen uns auf den kommenden Urlaub.

C. Translate into German.

1. With whom are you discussing your future?

2. With what do you intend to cover this table?

3. Who's there at the door?

4. The physician is here: which one is sick?

5. Which cathedral will we visit today?

6. Whose paintings are more difficult to find?

7. To whom did you rent your student room?

8. From whom did you rent your student room?

9. What are you thinking about?

10. What kind of a movie do we want to see tonight?

Relative
Pronouns

15

Relative pronouns and related constructions covered in this chapter are strategies for expanding noun phrases. There are three levels of expansion beyond the bare noun:

determiner plus noun (**die Kirche**) specifies a definite noun without describing it;

(determiner plus) adjective plus noun ([**die**] **alte Kirche**) specifies and provides a simple description of the noun; and

(determiner plus) (adjective plus) noun plus relative clause ([**die**][**alte**] **Kirche, die dem Dem gegenübersteht**) does all of the above *and* supplies further description than the class of German adjectives can alone provide.

However a noun phrase is expanded, it is important to remember that it is an integrated unit functioning like any noun—as subject, or object, or whatever.

§45. THE RELATIVES *DER* AND *WELCHER*

There are two common relative pronouns in German, **der** and **welcher**. Observe in the following paradigm that the declension of the relative **der** is (except for the forms in boldface) the same as that of the definite article; and that **welcher** has no genitive forms.

	SINGULAR			PLURAL
				ALL
	MASC.	FEM.	NEUT.	GENDERS
Nom.	der (welcher)	die (welche)	das (welches)	die (welche)
Gen.	**dessen**	**deren**	**dessen**	**deren**
Dat.	dem (welchem)	der (welcher)	dem (welchem)	**denen** (welchen)
Acc.	den (welchen)	die (welche)	das (welches)	die (welche)

The following sentences illustrate the use of the relatives **der** and **welcher**. The relative pronoun always agrees with its antecedent in *gender* and *number;* its *case* is determined by its use in the relative clause.

A. Singular number.

(1) The nominative case:

    (*a*) Der reiche Mann, **der** (or **welcher**) sein Geld verloren hatte, war unehrlich.
        *The rich man **who** had lost his money was dishonest.*

    (*b*) München ist eine Stadt, **die** (or **welche**) durch ihre Schönheit berühmt ist.
        *Munich is a city **which** is famous for its beauty.*

    (*c*) Das deutsche Buch, **das** (or **welches**) auf dem Tisch liegt, gehört meinem Bruder.
        *The German book **which** is lying on the table belongs to my brother.*

The relative **der** is used much more frequently than **welcher**, especially in conversation. **Welcher**, however, is often used to avoid a repetition of some form of **der**. In the following sentence **der** would occur successively in three forms—the demonstrative, the relative, and the definite article—if **welcher** were not used:

    Die Freude war groß, denn der, **welcher** der Familie am liebsten war, war heimgekehrt.
    *The joy was great, for the one **who** was dearest to the family had returned home.*

(2) The genitive case:

    (*a*) Ein Witwer ist ein Mann, **dessen** Frau gestorben ist.
        *A widower is a man **whose** wife is dead.*

    (*b*) Eine Witwe ist eine Frau, **deren** Mann gestorben ist.
        *A widow is a woman **whose** husband is dead.*

(c) Eine Waise ist ein Kind, **dessen** Eltern gestorben sind.
*An orphan is a child **whose** parents are dead.*

Whose is always genitive, but particular care must be taken to have it agree with its antecedent and *not* with the noun following:

Er ist der Mann, **dessen** Frau krank ist.
*He is the man **whose** wife is ill.*

Here **dessen** is masculine singular to agree with **Mann**.

(3) The dative case:

(a) Der Herr, **dem** (or **welchem**) ich das Buch gegeben habe, ist mein bester Freund.
*The gentleman **to whom** I gave the book is my best friend.*

(b) Leipzig ist eine Handelsstadt, **in der** (or **welcher**) jährliche Messen stattfinden.
*Leipzig is a commercial city **in which** annual fairs are held.*

(c) Das Haus, **in dem** (**in welchem** or **worin**) wir jetzt wohnen, gefällt mir nicht.
*I do not like the house **in which** we now live.*

A **wo**-form is frequently used instead of a preposition and a relative, provided the antecedent is a *thing*.

(4) The accusative case:

(a) Er ist der Mann, **den** (or **welchen**) ich gestern besucht habe.
*He is the man **whom** I visited yesterday.*

(b) Wo ist die Feder, **die** (or **welche**) ich heute gekauft habe?
*Where is the pen **(that)** I bought today?*

(c) Das ist das Buch, **das** (or **welches**) ich gestern gelesen habe.
*That is the book **(that)** I read yesterday.*

Contrary to English usage, *the relative pronoun is never omitted in German.*

B. Plural number.

(1) The nominative case:

Das sind die Männer (die Frauen, die Kinder), **die** (or **welche**) uns gegenüber wohnen.
*Those are the men (the women, the children) **who** live opposite us.*

(2) The genitive case:

Das sind die Männer (die Frauen, die Kinder), **deren** Bücher wir jetzt lesen.
*Those are the men (the women, the children) **whose** books we are now reading.*

(3) The dative case:

Das sind die Männer (die Frauen, die Kinder), **denen** (or **welchen**) wir das Geld gegeben haben.

Those are the men (the women, the children) **to whom** *we gave the money.*

(4) The accusative case:

Das sind die Männer (die Frauen, die Kinder), **die** (or **welche**) wir letztes Jahr besucht haben.

Those are the men (the women, the children) **whom** *we visited last year.*

Note:

(*a*) All relative clauses are set off by commas.

(*b*) Since all relative clauses are subordinated to the main clause of the sentence, their inflected verb must be moved to the end.

§46. THE RELATIVE *WAS*

The relative **was** is used, instead of **das** or **welches**, if the antecedent is (1) an indefinite neuter form such as **alles, nichts, vieles, etwas, manches,** or a neuter superlative; or (2) really the *thought* or *content* of the preceding clause. It may not be used if the antecedent is a noun (see example H).

A. **Alles, was** er sagt, ist wahr.
    All (that) he says is true.

B. **Nichts, was** sie tat, ist ihr gelungen.
    Nothing (that) she did turned out well for her.

C. Es gibt **vieles, was** mir fehlt.
    There is **much that** *I lack.*

D. Das ist **etwas, was** sie noch nicht weiß.
    That is **something** *(that) she does not yet know.*

E. Er hat **manches** vergessen, **was** er in der Schule gelernt hat.
    He has forgotten **much** *(or* **many a thing***)* **that** *he learned in school.*

F. **Das Beste, was** ich habe, gebe ich dir.
    I am giving you **the best** *(that) I have.*

G. Er sagte, **es gehe ihm gut, was** mich sehr freute.
    He said **he was well, which** *made me very happy.*

H.   Das ist **das Buch, das** (or **welches**) ich zweimal gelesen habe.
*That is **the book** (**that**) I read twice.*

§47. THE RELATIVE *WO*

Wo as a relative equivalent to *in which,* but often translated by *where,* requires the verb at the end of the clause:

Das ist **der Ort, wo** meine Wiege stand.
*That is **the place where** I was born* (*lit. where my cradle stood*).

Relative **wo** is not to be confused with interrogative **wo,** which requires the inverted word order:

Wo stand Ihre Wiege?
Where were you born?

At the time **when** is often rendered by **zur Zeit, als** (*or* da *or* wo) with the dependent word order:

Zur Zeit, **als** (*or* da *or* wo) er im Lande war, gab es keine Eisenbahnen.
There were no railroads (at the time) **when** *he was in the country.*

§48. THE GENERAL (OR INDEFINITE) RELATIVES *WER* AND *WAS*

The general or indefinite relatives **wer** and **was** (not to be confused with the interrogatives) *never have an antecedent.*

A.   **Wer** nicht für mich ist, (der) ist gegen mich.
***Whoever** is not for me is against me.*

B.   **Was** nicht gut ist, (das) ist schlecht.
***Whatever** is not good is bad.*

§49. THE EXTENDED MODIFIER vs. THE RELATIVE CLAUSE

In German the written language provides a participial (and, less frequently, adjectival) construction which may be substituted for a relative clause. Since English makes no equivalent provision, these *extended modifiers* must be rendered as relative clauses. The extended modifier is stylistically stuffy and may always be avoided in writing German. The following sentences illustrate this construction and show the corresponding relative clause in each case:

> **Ein** von allen Zeitungen gelobter **Sänger** ist heute angekommen.
> Ein Sänger, **den** alle Zeitungen gelobt haben, ist heute angekommen.
> *A singer whom all the newspapers have praised arrived today.*

> **Ein** alt**es**, ursprünglich nicht zu Schulzwecken bestimmt**es Gebäude** stand an der Ecke.
> Ein altes Gebäude, **das** ursprünglich nicht zu Schulzwecken bestimmt war, stand an der Ecke.
> *An old building, which was not originally intended for school purposes, stood on the corner.*

> Das Dach **des** schon seit dem Dreißigjährigen Kriege von der Familie Wagner bewohnt**en Hauses** ist neulich umgebaut worden.
> Das Dach des Hauses, **das** die Familie Wagner schon seit dem Dreißigjährigen Kriege bewohnt, ist neulich umgebaut worden.
> *The roof of the house that the Wagner family has occupied since the Thirty Years' War, has recently been rebuilt.*

The extended modifier is readily recognized, when encountered, by the break in syntax, the absurdity (from the point of view of a native speaker of English, who is used to reading from left to right) of an article followed by a preposition, an adverb, or an uninflected adjective.

The reader must learn to collect and reserve the information imparted in the modifier until the noun phrase is complete. If a written translation is required, this material will have to be presented as a relative clause: (1) If the last element in the extended modifier is a participle, it must be changed to a verb; (2) if the last element is an adjective, the verb *to be* must be added.

A simple variation of this use of the participle is to be found at the end of letters:

> Dein Dich liebender Vater, *your loving father*
> Deine Dich liebende Mutter, *your loving mother*

§50. PERSONAL PRONOUNS FOLLOWED BY A RELATIVE

The relative **der** follows a personal pronoun. If the antecedent is a personal pronoun of the first or second person, it is usually repeated after the relative. If the pronoun is not repeated, the verb of the relative clause is in the third person.

> **Ich, der ich** selber krank war, konnte nicht mitgehen.
> *I, **who** was ill myself, could not go along.*
> *Being ill myself, I could not go along.*

Wir, die wir selber krank waren, konnten nicht mitgehen.
We, who were ill ourselves, could not go along.

Du, der du selber krank warst, konntest nicht mitgehen.
You, who were ill yourself, could not go along.

Ich, der schon so viel gelitten hat, verlor noch mein Vermögen.
I, who have suffered so much already, lost my fortune besides.

§51. CONCESSIVE CLAUSES WITH *WER AUCH,* *WAS AUCH, WO AUCH,* ETC.

Normal word order is used in a clause following one of concessive force introduced by **wer auch** (*whoever*), **was auch** (*whatever*), **wo auch** (*wherever*), etc. The combinations with **auch** are used if *nevertheless* may be supplied as introducing the second clause.

A. wer auch (*whoever*):

Wer er **auch** sein mag, ich werde ihm helfen.
Whoever he may be, I will help him.

B. was auch (*whatever*):

Was sie **auch** tun mag, er wird sie lieben.
Whatever she may do, he will love her.

C. wo auch (*wherever*):

Wo er **auch** sein mag, man wird ihn finden.
Wherever he may be, he will be found.

E X E R C I S E S

A. Complete the following sentences by filling the blanks with the appropriate relative pronoun. Since the relative **welcher** is quite stilted, it would be best to use forms of **der** instead.

1. Der pensionierte Soldat, _____ wir eine Stellung angeboten haben, war damit zufrieden.

2. In dem Tante-Emma-Laden, _____ an der Ecke steht, wird man persönlicher bedient.

3. Die Studentin, _____ verlorenes Heft ich gefunden habe, wird bestimmt Angst haben.

4. Die schöne Stadt, _am Fluß_ _____ an der Isar liegt, heißt München.

5. Und die Stadt, _____ Dom weltbekannt ist, heißt Köln.

6. Die Frau, _____ ich des Buches beraubt habe, ist Bibliothekarin.

7. Eine Kaffeemühle ist ein Gerät, _____ man Kaffee mahlt.

8. Die Bude, _____ wir gemietet haben, hat keinen Kühlschrank.

9. Das Hotel, _____ Eingang am Park ist, heißt *The Plaza*.

10. Der Computer, _____ ich jetzt schreibe, kommt aus Kalifornien in den U.S.A.

11. Die Getränke, _____ er Alkohol zugesetzt hat, sind uns zu stark.

12. Die Freunde, _____ wir besuchen wollten, waren leider nicht zu Hause.

13. Die Kinder, _____ sich auf der Straße amüsieren, sind in Gafahr.

14. Die Schüler, _____ ich Deutsch beibringen will, sind nicht sehr fleißig.

15. _____ reich ist, (der) ist nicht immer glücklich.

16. _____ ihr versprecht, (das) vergeßt ihr immer.

17. Sie meinte, ich hätte den Preis gewonnen, _____ mich sehr freute.

18. Die Herren, mit _____ ich sprach, waren Ausländer.

19. Alles, _____ ich hatte, ist jetzt wieder weg.

20. Die Künstlerin, _____ Werke ich bewunderte, wird von dem Gemälde-händler in SoHo vertreten.

21. Nichts, _____ er sagt, ist zu glauben.

22. Der Zug, _mit_ _____ wir nach Hamburg fahren müssen, kommt immer pünktlich an.

23. _____ er auch sein mag, ich erkenne ihn nicht.

24. Die Abgeordneten, _____ politisch sehr progressiv sind, haben dieses Jahr nur schlechte Chancen.

25. Der Gründungstag, _____ die DDR-Bürger an die Gründung ihres Staates im Jahre 1949 erinnert, wird am siebten Oktober gefeiert.

B. It will be remembered that an extended modifier must be rethought as a noun plus relative clause before it can be translated into English. Here are some sentences in which one noun has been extended with a relative clause. Restate these sentences with extended modifiers.

1. Ich suche das Denkmal, das in der Kirche steht.

2. Ich suche die Kirche, die dem Dom gegenüber steht.

3. Das Denkmal, das sich in der dem Dom gegenüberstehenden Kirche befindet, stellt Walther von der Vogelweide dar.

4. Den Anweisungen der Aufsichtspersonen, die beim Spielplatz wohnen, ist Folge zu leisten.

5. Jeder Aufenthalt neben einem Bagger, der läuft, ist gefährlich.

6. Das ist ein Buch, das ich schon zweimal gelesen habe.

C. Here is a catalog of items you probably have in your bedroom.

das Bett	*bed*	das Kissen	*pillow*
der Spiegel	*mirror*	der Nachttisch	*bedside table*
das Radio	*radio*	die Garderobe	*closet*
das Poster	*poster*	das Bücherregal	*bookshelf*
der Schreibtisch	*desk*	der Sessel	*(easy) chair*
die Lampe	*light*	der Wecker	*alarm clock*

Using these words, suitable prepositions, adjectives, verbs like **stehen, liegen, lehnen** (*to lean*), and **sein,** and relative clauses, describe the items themselves, and their relationship to each other. Example: **Ich habe ein Bett, das neben dem Fenster steht.**

D. Translate into German.

1. The people in whose house I lived have moved.

2. The little girl from whom I have to buy the cookies is my sister.

3. That's the soccer player whose shirt was ripped.

4. I have here a letter which consists of four pages.

5. Certainly you don't believe the story which he told his mother.

6. She gave me everything she had.

7. At the time when I visited him he was very sick.

8. Whatever you may say, I will help you.

9. We were usually late with the rent, which pleased him not at all.

10. A coffeegrinder is an implement with which one grinds coffee.

16

Possessives;
Demonstratives;
Indefinite Pronouns
and Adjectives

§52. POSSESSIVE DETERMINERS

The possessive determiners, sometimes called possessive adjectives despite the fact that they do not describe the nouns with which they are paired, have the same endings as the indefinite article and are therefore classed among the **ein**-words. The sentences under **A** below simply illustrate these possessives, while the sentences under **B** show them with their corresponding personal pronouns. Review the forms in §96 of Appendix II.

A. (1) **Mein** lieber Bruder ist zu Hause.
   My dear brother is at home.

   (2) **Dein** alter Vater hat eine lange Reise gemacht.
   Your old father took a long trip.

   (3) **Sein** jüngster Sohn ist aufs Land gegangen.
   His youngest son has gone to the country.

   (4) **Ihr** reicher Onkel ist auf dem Lande.
   Her rich uncle is in the country.

   (5) **Unser** bester Freund hatte ihn gesehen.
   Our best friend had seen him.

   (6) Kinder, wo ist **euer** kleiner Hund?
   *Children, where is **your** little dog?*

   (7) Wo ist **ihr** lieber Vater?
   *Where is **their** dear father?*

(8) Wo ist **Ihr** neues Buch?
Where is your new book?

B.   (1) Ich habe **meinen** Bleistift verloren.
I have lost my pencil.

(2) Du hast **deinen** Bleistift verloren.
You have lost your pencil.

(3) Er hat **seinen** Bleistift verloren.
He has lost his pencil.

(4) Sie hat **ihren** Bleistift verloren.
She has lost her pencil.

(5) Es (*e.g.,* das Kind) hat **seinen** Bleistift verloren.
It has lost its pencil.

(6) Wir haben **unsere** Freunde besucht.
We have visited our friends.

(7) Ihr habt **eure** Freunde besucht.
You have visited your friends.

(8) Sie haben **ihre** Freunde besucht.
They have visited their friends.

(9) Sie haben **Ihre** Freunde besucht.
You have visited your friends.

There are numerous duplications in the forms of the possessives in German. For example, **ihr** may mean either *her* or *their;* and when it refers to an inanimate object or to an abstract noun which is grammatically feminine, **ihr** must be translated by *its:*

Die Sache hat **ihre** gute Seite.
The affair has its good (or *bright*) *side.*

Sein may be translated as either *his* or *its,* depending upon whether it refers to a masculine or neuter noun. In a few instances it must be translated by *her,* if the noun is feminine in English:

Das **Mädchen** hat **sein** Buch.
The girl has her book.

As implied above, the German equivalent of *its* may be either **sein** or **ihr**:

Jeder Staat hat **seine** Vorzüge.
Each state has its advantages.

Die Stadt ist durch **ihre** Museen berühmt.
The city is famous for its museums.

Das Kind liebt **seinen** Vater.
The child loves its father.

§53. AGREEMENT OF THE POSSESSIVE DETERMINER

The possessive in German may be thought of as part pronoun and part adjective: choice of possessive is determined by the antecedent, while choice of ending is determined by the noun modified. Thus, in the phrase **seine kleine Schwester,** *his little sister,* **sein-** is chosen because the gender of the possessor is masculine, the ending **-e** because **Schwester** is nominative singular and feminine.

Ihr klein**er** Bruder liest das Buch.
Her little brother is reading the book.

Seine klein**e** Schwester lernt Deutsch.
His little sister is studying German.

Er hat **seine** Bücher.
He has his books.

§54. POSSESSIVE PRONOUNS

Possessive determiners are, as noted above, **ein-**words, i.e., they take the same endings as **ein** and **kein.** When an **ein-**word is used without a following noun it functions as a pronoun. An **ein-**word used as a pronoun takes **der-**word endings.

Mein Buch ist auf dem Tisch.
My book is on the table.

Wo ist **Ihres?**
Where is yours?

Mein Vater ist in der Stadt.
My father is in the city.

Seiner ist in Deutschland.
His is in Germany.

Wessen Bleistift ist das?
Whose pencil is that?

Es ist mein**er.**
It is mine.

Wessen Buch ist das?
Whose book is that?

Es ist mein**es.**
It is mine.

A possessive pronoun in the predicate, other than **ihr** and **Ihr,** may be found in older writing without an ending if the subject of the sentence is a noun.

Das Buch ist mein.
The book is mine.

Der Bleistift ist dein.
The pencil is yours.

Das Buch ist ihres.
The book is hers (or theirs).

Der Bleistift ist Ihrer.
The pencil is yours.

Instead of the verb *to be* followed by a possessive, **gehören** with the dative is commonly used:

Das Buch gehört mir.
Es ist mein**es.**
The book is mine (lit. *belongs to me*).

§55. POSSESSIVES WITH VARIOUS FORMS OF THE IMPERATIVE

The sentences below indicate that **dein** is used with the singular familiar imperative; **euer,** with the plural familiar; and **Ihr,** with the formal imperative. Observe that the plural familiar imperative has the same form as the second person plural of the present indicative (but without the personal pronoun).

Karl, lies **deine** Aufgabe!
Carl, read your lesson.

Kinder, lest **eure** Aufgabe!
Children, read your lesson.

Bitte, **lesen Sie Ihre** Aufgabe!
Please read your lesson.

§56. LONG FORMS OF THE POSSESSIVE PRONOUN

The so-called long forms of the possessive pronoun are:

	MASCULINE	FEMININE	NEUTER
Nom.	der meine	die meine	das meine
Gen.	des meinen, *etc.*	der meinen, *etc.*	des meinen, *etc.*
or			
Nom.	der meinige	die meinige	das meinige
Gen.	des meinigen, *etc.*	der meinigen, *etc.*	des meinigen, *etc.*

These long forms are met with chiefly in books and are to be avoided in conversation and composition. They cannot be used with nouns. The following, therefore, are the three possible translations of *Where is mine?* (referring to some masculine noun such as **der Bleistift**):

Wo ist **meiner?**

Wo ist **der meine?**

Wo ist **der meinige?**

§57. THE DEMONSTRATIVES *DIESER, JENER, DERSELBE,* AND *DERJENIGE*

A *demonstrative* is a word that points out, e.g., *this* or *that*. It may precede a noun: *This street is closed;* or it may stand alone: *No, this is mine and that is yours.*

The sentences under **A** and **B** show that **dieser** (*this*) and **jener** (*that*) are declined alike; the paradigm resembles that of the definite article **der,** i.e., **dieser** and **jener** are **der**-words.

A. Dieser (*this*):

(1) **Dieser** Junge ist mein Bruder, **jener** (*or* der andere da) ist mein Vetter.
   *This boy is my brother, **that one** is my cousin.*

(2) **Dieses** Buch gefällt mir.   **Diese** Bücher gefallen mir.
   *I like **this** book.*   *I like **these** books.*

B. Jener (*that*):

(1) **Jener** Berg (*or* der Berg da) ist der Brocken.
   ***That** mountain is the Brocken.*

(2) **Jene** Häuser (*or* die Häuser da) wurden im Mittelalter gebaut.
   ***Those** houses were built in the Middle Ages.*

In modern German **jener** is generally restricted in use to a specific contrast with **dieser.** In such contrastives **dieser** is often translated by *the latter* and **jener** by *the former.*

The demonstratives **derselbe** and **derjenige** are written as one word, but the first element is declined like the definite article while the second takes weak adjective endings:

Nom. Sing.	**der**selbe	**der**jenige
Gen. Sing.	**des**selben, *etc.*	**des**jenigen, *etc.*
Nom. Plur.	**die**selben, *etc.*	**die**jenigen, *etc.*

C. Derselbe (*the same*):

(1) Er ist **derselbe** Mann, den ich gestern gesehen habe.
   *He is **the same** man whom I saw yesterday.*

(2) Die beiden Schwestern sind an **demselben** Tag geboren.
   *The two (or Both) sisters were born on **the same** day.*

(3) Ich hatte **denselben** Lehrer, wie mein Bruder.
   *I had **the same** teacher as my brother.*

Derselbe (unstressed) is often used—particularly in the written language—instead of a personal pronoun:

Er hat viele Schulden, aber er will **dieselben** nicht bezahlen.
*He has many debts but he does not want to pay **them**.*

D. Derjenige (*that, the one*):

    (1) Das ist nicht mein Buch, sondern **dasjenige** meiner Schwester.
        *That is not my book but **my sister's.***
  lit.: *That is not my book but **that** of my sister.*

    (2) **Dasjenige** im roten Einband habe ich schon gelesen.
        *I have already read **the one** with a red cover.*

    (3) **Diejenigen,** die das nicht verstehen, sollen Fragen stellen.
        ***Those** who do not understand that are to ask questions.*

The three sentences above show how **derjenige** may precede a genitive construction (1), a prepositional phrase (2), or a relative clause (3). The plural as in (3) is the form most commonly heard.

§58. THE DEMONSTRATIVE *DER*

The demonstrative **der** may function as either a determiner or a pronoun, and is declined accordingly in two different ways.

A. The demonstrative **der** (which is much more common in conversation than **jener**) is stressed; in print, this stress is often indicated by spacing the letters: **d e r.**

    D e r Mann ist klug.
    ***That** man is clever.*

    D e r ist immer auf dem Lande.
    ***He** is always in the country.*

B. As a determiner, the demonstrative **der** is declined like the definite article. But when used as a pronoun, i.e., without a following noun, **der** is declined like the relative pronoun.

    Tut Gutes **denen,** die euch hassen!
    *Do good **to those** who hate you.*

C. The genitive plural of the demonstrative pronoun is **deren;** but, when the pronoun comes before the noun or pronoun upon which it depends, another form, **derer,** is employed.

    Nimm diese Äpfel, es gibt **deren** genug.
    *Take these apples; there are plenty **of them.***

    Das ist die Schuld **derer,** die nicht mitgeholfen haben.
    *This is the fault **of those** who did not help.*

D. The genitive singular **dessen** exists in combinations, of which the following are characteristic:

> **infolgedessen** (= deshalb), *consequently, as a result*
>
> **währenddessen** (= inzwischen), *in the meantime*
>
> **dessenungeachtet** (= trotzdem), *in spite of that*

§59. THE USE OF *SOLCHER*

If **solch** is uninflected, the following adjective takes strong endings, see **A(1)**. If **solch** has strong endings, the following adjective is weak (i.e., **solch,** when inflected, is a **der**-word), see **A(2)**.

A. (1) **Solch schönes** Wetter haben wir nicht im Winter.

(2) **Solches schöne** Wetter haben wir nicht im Winter.
*We do not have **such beautiful** weather in winter.*

B. Er ist **kein solcher** Narr.
*He is **no such** fool.*

No such is rendered by **kein solch**-. See also §6, **N** (3).

§60. INDEFINITE PRONOUNS AND ADJECTIVES

The indefinite pronouns **man** (*one, they, people, you*), **jemand** (*somebody, someone*), **jedermann** (*everybody*), **niemand** (*nobody, no one*), **etwas** (*something, some*), and **nichts** (*nothing*) occur only in the singular, and govern a third person singular verb.

A. (1) **Man** (sometimes **einer**) is used only in the nominative. The other cases are supplied by the forms **einem,** and **einen.**

> **Man** tut das nicht.   Es tut **einem** weh.
> *That isn't done.*   *It hurts **one**.*
> ***One** does not do that.*

(2) When **man** is used with reflexive verbs, **sich** is its reflexive pronoun:

> Damals konnte **man sich** (dat.) so etwas nicht leisten.
> *At that time one couldn't afford such a thing.*
>
> **Man** gewöhnt **sich** (acc.) endlich an alles.
> *One finally gets used to everything.*

(3) **Man** and **er** cannot be used interchangeably; if **man** is used, it must be retained throughout the sentence:

Wenn **man** etwas nicht weiß, soll **man** (not **er**) nichts sagen.
If one doesn't know, he should say nothing.

B.   **Jemand (niemand)** hat das gesagt.
Someone (nobody) said that.

Er hat **niemand** (or **keinen**) gesehen.
He saw no one.

Hat **irgend jemand** das Buch gefunden?
Did anyone find the book?

Haben Sie **jemand anders** (or **sonst jemand**) besucht?
Did you visit someone else?

(1) **Jemand** and **niemand** have a genitive in **-(e)s.** The dative and accusative of these pronouns usually occur without endings, although datives in **-em** and accusatives in **-en** are also found.

(2) **Keiner** is often used for **niemand.**

C.   **Jedermann** (or **jeder**) weiß das.   **Alle** geben es zu.
Everybody knows that.   *All admit it.*

(1) **Jedermann** has a genitive ending in **-s** but its dative and accusative are like the nominative.

(2) **Alle** is used as the plural of **jedermann.**

(3) **Jeder** is often used for **jedermann.**

D.   (1) Hat er **etwas** gesagt?
Did he say something?

Nichts, etwas, allerlei, and **ein paar** are indeclinable.

(2) Haben Sie **etwas** Interessant**es** gefunden?
Did you find something interesting?

(a) Neuter adjectives are capitalized when used as nouns following **etwas, nichts, viel, wenig,** and **allerlei.** The adjective has the strong ending **-es.** The word **anderes,** however, is not capitalized:

etwas anderes, *something else*

nichts anderes, *nothing else*

(b) **Alles** usually requires the following adjective to be capitalized. The adjective has the weak ending **-e.**

alles Gute, *everything good, all good things*

but: **alles mögliche,** *everything possible*

alles übrige, *all the rest*

alles andere, *all else*

(3) Sie hat **etwas** Brot gekauft.
*She bought **some** (not much) bread.*

Er hat **einige** Bücher mitgebracht.
*He brought **some** books along.*

Some is ordinarily rendered by **etwas** when followed by a singular noun; by **einige** when followed by a plural noun.

(4) Ich vermisse **irgend etwas.**
*I miss **something** (or other).*

Etwas can also mean *a little* or *a bit* when preceding an adjective.

(5) Der Rock ist **etwas** zu kurz.
*The skirt is **a bit** too short.*

(a) **Irgend** (*any, some,* etc.) is rarely used alone, but appears in various combinations:

irgend jemand, *anyone* (emphatic)

irgend etwas, *something or other*

irgendein (adj.), *some, other*

irgendeiner, *someone* (emphatic)

irgendwie, *somehow, anyhow*

irgendwo, *somewhere, anywhere*

(b) **Nirgend(s)** is the negative of **irgend**:
nirgendwo, *nowhere, not anywhere*

E. **Viel(e)** and **wenig(e)** have both singular and plural forms:

(1) Er hat **wenig** Geld bei sich.
*He has **little** money with him.*

Haben Sie **viel** Geld verloren?
*Did you lose **much** money?*

Distinguish between **klein,** *little* (in size), and **wenig,** *little* (in quantity):

ein **kleines** Geldstück, *a small coin*
wenig Geld, *little (i.e., not much) money*

(2) Er hat **wenige** Freunde.
*He has **few** friends.*

Ich habe **viele** Schulden.
*I have **many** debts.*

(3) Ich weiß **wenig** Gutes über ihn zu erzählen.
*I know **little** good to relate about him.*

Sie hat **viel G**utes getan.
*She has done **much** good.*

(4) Man kann **vieles** lernen und doch nicht viel wissen.
*One can learn **many things** and still not know much.*

The form **vieles** is very often equivalent to the English *many things.*

E X E R C I S E S

A. Complete the following sentences, supplying the correct form of the possessive determiner or possessive pronoun suggested in parentheses.

1. Die Mutter liebt _____ (*her*) Kind, und das Kind liebt _____ (*its*) Mutter.

2. Ist der Fernseher _____ (*hers*) oder _____ (*yours*)?

3. Mein Freund suchte _____ (*his*) Regenmantel.

4. Mein Mantel ist in der Garderobe. Wo ist _____ (*yours*)?

5. _____ (*His*) Lage ist sehr ernst, aber nicht hoffnungslos.

6. Gib mir _____ (*my*) Buch!

7. Dein Buch liegt da auf dem Bett. Wo ist aber _____ (*mine*)?

8. Er hat _____ (*his*) Enkeln den Bauernhof geschenkt.

9. _____ (*Her*) Bruder hat sie das Rad sicher nicht geliehen.

10. Bitte, zeigen Sie mir _____ (*your*) Fahrkarte!

11. Die Stadt Köln ist durch _____ (*its*) Dom berühmt.

12. Dieser Wecker ist nicht _____ (*mine*), sondern _____ (*his*).

13. _____ (*Her*) älterer Bruder ist Physiker.

14. _____ (*Our*) Hof ist viel schöner als _____ (*theirs*).

15. _____ (*Their*) Wohnung ist bequemer als _____ (*ours*).

B. Complete the following sentences using the demonstratives suggested in parentheses.

1. Diese kurze Hose gefällt mir, _____ (*that one*) aber nicht.

2. Ich finde dieses Haus preisgünstiger als _____ (*that one*).

3. Dieser Weihnachtsbaum ist nicht so schön geschmückt wie _____ (*that one*).

4. Wir lassen unser Ferienhaus auf dieser Insel bauen, nicht auf _____ (*that one*).

5. Das ist aber _____ (*the same*) Film, den wir gestern abend gesehen haben.

6. Es ist _____ (*the same*) Krawatte, die mein Zimmerkollege vier Jahre lang getragen hat.

7. Das Verkehrsamt hat _____ (*the same*) Touristen [*sing.*] heute schon zweimal geholfen.

8. _____ (*The same one* [*fem.*]) hat drei Fahrkarten am Schalter gekauft.

9. Er hat immer _____ (*the same*) Studenten schlechte Noten gegeben.

10. Im Herbst _____ (*of the same*) Jahres sind die zwei Brüder nach Amerika eingewandert.

11. _____ (*Those*), die den Satz nicht verstehen, sollen Fragen stellen.

12. Das sind die Namen _____ (*of those*), die mitgemacht haben.

13. Treue Freunde halten fest zusammen! Es gibt aber _____ (*of them*) nicht viele.

14. Groß war die Schadenfreude, denn _____ (*the one*), der auf seine Stärke sehr stolz gewesen war, hat verloren.

15. Karlheinz hatte _____ (*no such*) Erfolg.

16. Nun, wir werden _____ (*for that*) warten.

17. _____ (*Such*) Fragen wie _____ (*these*) wollte der Politiker nie beantworten.

18. _____ (*In spite of that*) werden wir später eine Rundfahrt durch die Altstadt machen.

19. Ich begegnete Herrn Hanson und Herrn Munger auf der Straße. _____ (*The former*) ist Physiker, und _____ (*the latter*) ist Arzt.

20. Vor dem Rennen hat es stark geregnet; _____ (*consequently*) ist die Rennbahn gefährlich glatt.

C. Translate into German.

1. Please bring my old coat along. Where is yours, at home?

2. We both got expensive fountain pens at Christmas. Here's mine, but where is hers?

3. Give me only some soup, thanks.

4. Oh, his lecture was about something boring.

5. No one may smoke in our classroom, not even your teacher.

6. My large suitcase probably holds more than that one.

7. We met the same American tourist twice this week.

8. Children, don't forget to do your homework!

9. The two professors say they wrote the same book.

10. Please believe us! We saw no one.

11. The policeman had little patience.

12. Here they understand everything.

13. She did everything possible.

14. When I was in Europe I saw many things.

15. In the meantime my best friend had to stay home.

Reflexive and Impersonal Verbs

§61. REFLEXIVE VERBS

Compare the sentences in the parallel columns below. In **A**, the direct objects (**Kind, Kleid,** etc.) do not refer to the subject of the sentence while in column **B** the direct objects (**mich, dich,** etc.) are pronouns referring to the subject. Such pronouns are called *reflexive pronouns;* verbs regularly used with such reflexives may be loosely termed *reflexive verbs.*

A. (1) Ich wasche das Kind.
   I wash the child.

   (2) Du wäschst das Kleid.
   You wash the dress.

   (3) Sie wäscht das Handtuch.
   She washes the towel.

   (4) Wir waschen die Strümpfe.
   We wash the stockings.

   (5) Ihr wascht die Kleider.
   You wash the clothes.

   (6) Sie waschen die
      Taschentücher.
   They wash the handkerchiefs.

B. (1) Ich wasche **mich.**
   I wash myself.

   (2) Du wäschst **dich.**
   You wash yourself.

   (3) Sie wäscht **sich.**
   She washes herself.

   (4) Wir waschen **uns.**
   We wash ourselves.

   (5) Ihr wascht **euch.**
   You wash yourselves.

   (6) Sie waschen **sich.**
   They wash themselves.

(7) Haben Sie die Tischtücher
    gewaschen?
Did you wash the tablecloths?

(7) Haben Sie **sich** gewaschen?
Did you wash yourself?

The form of the reflexive is the same as the personal pronoun in the first and second persons, singular or plural; for the third person, singular or plural, it is **sich.**

No verb is inherently reflexive. Many are used almost exclusively with reflexive pronouns, others rarely, and verbs conjugated with the auxiliary **sein** never.

C. Idiomatic expressions with reflexive verbs. Almost any transitive verb can be used reflexively with its literal meaning intact. If the object pronoun and the subject refer to the same real-life person or thing, the object reflects the subject like a mirror, and a reflexive pronoun is used. *He cuts the bread* is not reflexive, since the subject and object refer to different things; *While shaving he cut himself* is reflexive, since the person doing the cutting and the person being cut are the same.

But German has many verbs which, when used with reflexive pronouns, mean something different from what a literal translation into English would suggest. Furthermore, in many of these idiomatic usages the true object must be expressed by means of a prepositional phrase, since the object slot is occupied by a reflexive pronoun. If the preposition is one of those which can take either dative or accusative, the case must be specified since the ordinary location rule is of no help in idioms. Thus, the verb used in the first illustration below should be learned in this format: "sich fürchten vor + dative". The reflexive pronoun is usually in the accusative; if it is in the dative, this format should be used: "sich (dat.) Sorgen machen um".

Der Elefant fürchtet sich vor Mäusen.
The elephant is afraid of mice.

Interessiert ihr euch für Musik?
Are you interested in music?

Ich muß mir Sorgen um die Schlußprüfung machen.
I have to worry about the final exam.

D. Common reflexives. The verbs listed below are among those more commonly used idiomatically with reflexive pronouns. Frequently a preposition is part of the idiom.

sich **amusieren,** to have a good time

sich **ankleiden** (or **anziehen**), to get dressed

sich **ärgern über** + acc., to be angry about

sich **ausruhen,** to rest

sich **auskleiden** (or **ausziehen**), to get undressed

sich **beeilen,** to hurry

sich **befinden,** to be, to feel, to be located

sich **benehmen,** to behave

sich **bewegen,** to move, to be in motion

sich **bewerben um,** to apply for

sich (*dat.*) **denken, einbilden,** or **vorstellen,** to imagine

sich **entschließen,** to decide

sich **erholen von,** to recover from

sich **erinnern an** + acc., to remember

sich **erkälten,** to catch cold

sich **erkundigen nach,** to make inquiries about

sich **freuen,** to be glad;—**auf** + acc., to look forward to;—**über** + acc., to be happy about

sich **fühlen,** to feel (as in "I feel sad")

sich **fürchten vor** + dat., to be afraid of

sich **gewöhnen an** + acc., to get used to

sich **hüten vor** + dat., to guard against

sich **interessieren für,** to be interested in

sich **irren,** to be mistaken (may be also heard without *sich*)

sich **kümmern um,** to worry about

sich **legen** or **hinlegen,** to lie down

sich (*dat.*) **leisten,** to afford

sich **nähern** + dative object, to approach

sich **schämen über** + acc., to be ashamed of

sich **sehnen nach,** to long for

sich **setzen** or **hinsetzen,** to sit down

sich (*dat.*) **Sorgen machen um,** to worry about

sich **üben,** to practice

sich **verlassen auf** + acc., to rely upon, to depend on

sich **wundern über** + acc., to be surprised at

E. Reflexives instead of the passive. The passive voice is explained in Chapter 21. German frequently employs a verb used reflexively instead of the passive.

Das läßt sich machen.   Das läßt sich nicht machen.
That can be done.   *That can't be done.*

Es wird sich bald zeigen. . .
Time will tell. . .

Das versteht sich.
That's understood.

Alles hat sich aufgeklärt.
Everything has been cleared up.

So etwas lernt sich bald.
Such things are soon learned.

F. Dative reflexives. As noted above in **C** and **D,** certain verbs take a dative reflexive pronoun instead of an accusative.

So etwas hätte ich **mir** nie vorgestellt.
I would never have imagined such a thing.

Ich mache **mir** Sorgen um meine Zukunft.
I'm worried about my future.

Kannst du **dir** das leisten?
Can you afford that?

The dative forms of the reflexive pronouns are the same as the accusative except in the case of **ich** and **du,** which have **mir** and **dir** as datives beside the accusatives **mich** and **dich.**

G. The intensives *selbst* and *selber.* In translating *myself, himself,* etc., one must distinguish carefully between reflexives and intensives. **Selbst** and **selber,** when used as intensives, follow (but not always immediately) the personal pronoun, reflexive pronoun, or noun which they emphasize:

(1) Ich setzte **mich** (refl.).
I sat down.
*I seated **myself**.*

Ich **selbst** (or **selber**) habe es gesehen.
Ich habe es **selbst** (intens.) gesehen.
*I saw it **myself**.*

Selbst and **selber** never change their forms.

(2) Sie lobt **sich selbst** (or **selber**).
*She praises **herself**.*

Here **selbst** strengthens the reflexive. The reflexive, however, cannot be omitted.

(3) Sie ist die Freundlichkeit **selbst.**
She is friendliness personified.
*She is friendliness **itself**.*

Here **selbst** emphasizes the noun.

(4) **Selbst** er hat das verstanden.
Even he understood that.

Selbst in the sense of *even* precedes a noun or pronoun.

(5) **Selbst** occurs in a number of compounds: **selbst**verständlich, *self-understood (it goes without saying);* **selbst**gebackenes Brot, *homemade bread;* das

Selbstgespräch, *monologue, soliloquy;* die **Selbst**steuerung, *automatic control;* etc.

H. The reciprocal pronoun *einander*. The reciprocal pronoun **einander** is often used for the dative and accusative plural of the reflexive pronouns—i.e., instead of **uns, euch,** and **sich. Einander** never changes its form.

(1) Wir sehen **einander** (*or* uns) bald wieder.
  We shall soon see each other again.

(2) Sie loben **einander** (*or* sich).
  They praise each other.

(3a) **Einander** occurs in combinations with prepositions: **an**einander, **auf**einander, **aus**einander, **bei**einander, **durch**einander, **mit**einander, **nach**einander, **neben**einander, **von**einander, and **zu**einander:

  Sie kümmern sich nicht **um**einander.
  They aren't concerned about each other.

(3b) These forms, whose meaning varies with that of the preposition, are in turn combined with numerous verbs: aneinander**binden,** *to tie together* (lit. *to tie to each other*); aufeinander**folgen,** *to follow each other;* etc.

§62. IMPERSONAL VERBS

Verbs that require impersonal **es** as their subject are known as *impersonal verbs.* They are used *only* in the third person singular and have neither passive nor imperative. Except for the type of verbs explained in **A** and **B** following, there are comparatively few German verbs that are *always* impersonal. Quite common, however, is the verb **geschehen** (*to happen*), which can only be used impersonally—i.e., it cannot have as subject a noun or pronoun referring to a person. It cannot, therefore, be used in such a sentence as:

  He happened to be at home.
  Er **war zufällig** zu Hause.
  Zufälligerweise war er zu Hause.

A. Impersonal verbs denoting natural phenomena. As in English, verbs denoting phenomena of nature are regularly impersonal.

Es regnet.	*It is raining.*	Es hagelt.	*It is hailing.*
Es schneit.	*It is snowing.*	Es friert.	*It is freezing.*
Es blitzt.	*It is lightning.*	Es tagt.	*It is dawning.*
Es donnert.	*It is thundering.*	Es dämmert.	*It is getting dark* (if dusk) or *light* (if dawn)

B. Impersonal verbs denoting mental or physical states. Some impersonal verbs denoting mental or physical states take the accusative, others the dative.

(1) **Ihn** schläfert.
Er ist schläfrig.
He is sleepy.

(2) **Mir** schwindelt.
Mir ist schwind(e)lig.
I am dizzy.

(3) **Mir** graut.
I shudder.

Impersonal **es** is the understood subject of the verb in the above examples. Impersonal verbs often omit the **es** in inverted word order: **Mir graut** for **Mir graut es** (or less commonly, **Es graut mir**).

C. Es gibt and **es ist** (pl. **es sind**).

(1) **Es gibt** weiße Mäuse.
There are *white mice.*
It is a fact that there are white mice.

Es gibt kein**en** Winter in jenem Land.
There is *no winter in that country.*

Es gibt is used in a general sense, is always singular, and must be followed by the accusative case.

(2) **Es sind** zwei weiße Mäuse in diesem Zimmer.
There are (not pointing) *two white mice in this room.*

Es ist (pl. **sind**) is more specific and definite than **es gibt.**

(3) **Da sind** zwei weiße Mäuse.
There (pointing) ***are*** *two white mice.*

Da serves as a demonstrative adverb.

D. Impersonal use of certain verbs in the passive. Note that the impersonal subject (**man**) of active sentences is omitted entirely in the corresponding passive sentences. Personal subjects (e.g., **er**) become agents (**von** + dative).

Active voice	*Passive voice*
(1) Man tanzt viel. *There is much dancing.*	Es wird viel getanzt. *There is much dancing.*
(2) Er hilft mir. *He helps me.*	Mir wird von ihm geholfen. *I am helped by him.*
(3) Man folgte ihnen nicht. *They* (lit. *one*) *did not follow them.*	Ihnen wurde nicht gefolgt. *They were not followed.*

(4) Der Arzt riet mir, in die Berge
   zu gehen.
   *The physician advised me to go to
   the mountains.*

Mir wurde vom Arzt geraten,
   in die Berge zu gehen.
   *I was advised by the physician to
   go to the mountains.*

All verbs that take the dative—e.g., **helfen, folgen, raten, glauben,** etc.—keep the dative in the passive voice and are used impersonally with **es,** expressed or understood. If inverted word order is used in this construction, **es** must be omitted; If **es** is expressed, it comes at the head of a sentence: **Es** wurde mir vom Arzt geraten, in die Berge zu gehen.

E X E R C I S E S

A. Here are some sentences based on transitive verbs, used as in Column **A** in §61. Write a reflexive version of each one, replacing its object. Add an intensifier if it seems desirable.

1. Ich wasche meinen Wagen.
2. Du siehst dein Gesicht im Spiegel.
3. Sie schlägt den Nagel in die Wand.
4. Das Kind malt ein Bild im Kindergarten.
5. Karl beschreibt die Landschaft in seinem Tagebuch.
6. Wir verteidigen unser Dorf im Krieg.
7. Ihr fragt mich zu oft nach philosophischen Ideen.
8. Bescheidene Leute stimmen nicht für ihre Verwandten.
9. Herr Professor, empfehlen Sie mich dem Präsidenten?
10. Ich kleide meine Puppe an.

B. Use the idiomatic reflexives in §61.D in complete sentences to comment on these scenes and situations.

1. Wir gehen gern ins Kino, und danach zur Bierstube.
2. Erst am Bahnhof vorbei, dann zwei Straßen geradeaus, dann links, dann rechts, and dann endlich stehst du vor unserer Schule.
3. Ich dachte, ich hätte den Scherz vergessen, aber jetzt...
4. Sie war drei Tage lang sehr krank, aber nun geht es ihr viel besser.
5. Die Schularbeiten sind schwer und langweilig, aber heute in vierzehn Tagen beginnen wir endlich die Ferien.
6. Immer wieder muß ich die Geige spielen, wenn ich im Konzert mitspielen will.
7. Zuerst stand sie da, dann lag sie auf der Wiese. Wie ist denn das möglich?

8. Er kann nicht denken, er kann nicht schlafen. Immer erscheint vor ihm ein Wunschbild vom Strand auf der Nordseeinsel Sylt.

9. Ich komme zu spät, viel zu spät. Was soll ich tun?

10. Das wäre bestimmt ein Beruf für Ulrike. Was soll sie tun?

11. Du siehst traurig aus. Du hältst Fotos von deinem neuen Wagen in der Hand. Der ist kaputt, ist eben beim Mechaniker. Was fehlt dir?

12. Das erste Mal ist das Wasser sehr kalt. Später wirst du die Kälte nicht so sehr spüren.

C. Complete the following sentences by filling in the blanks. You may need to use the end vocabulary for some of the verbs.

1. Erkundigen Sie sich _____ d___ Herrn!

2. Freuen Sie sich _____ d___ Reise nächsten Frühling?

3. Haben Sie sich _____ d___ Besuch heute bei Ihrem Freund gefreut?

4. Kann ich mich _____ dies___ einzig___ Jungen verlassen?

5. Er war sehr altmodisch und verbeugte sich _____ d___ Verlobten.

6. Sie hat sich _____ ihr___ zwei Feind___ gerächt.

7. Warum sollen wir uns _____ jen___ Mann hüten?

8. Haben Sie sich _____ all___ gewöhnt?

9. Letzte Woche bei dem Unwetter habe ich _____ stark erkältet.

10. Freunde, habt ihr _____ entschlossen, so eine lange Reise zu machen?

D. Translate into German sentences.

1. It was thundering and raining heavily.

2. Have you rested enough, Erik?

3. You may always rely on me, as you know.

4. Did you remember your old dad at Christmas?

5. And please believe me, we look forward with pleasure to your arrival, Mrs. Handschuhmacher.

6. I shudder when I think of that.

7. He is not believed.

8. We are dizzy on account of the height.

9. They love each other and there was a lot of dancing.

10. Are you interested in the German states? There are ten German states, you know.

11. Every winter it freezes hard, and one has to get used to it.

12. I can easily imagine such a thing.

Word Order

18

There are two imprecise ways of thinking about German word order. They are imprecise because each yields almost as many unnatural sounding results as natural ones. Nonetheless, they are presented here to provide an overview, a vantage point from which to organize the word order details contained in this chapter and elsewhere in this book. Both ways are represented in commonly used elementary text books, and will no doubt be familiar to students.

The first way is nearly mechanical. German word order is just like English word order, except that verb complexes—verbs made up of more than one word—are split up: the verb agreeing with the subject comes second, and the rest of the complex comes last, in (from an English point of view) reverse order. In subordinate clauses, the verb agreeing with the subject (the "finite verb") joins the others at the end. This approach works fairly well in helping the reading and translating process. One reads from left to right, as in English; if a clause is introduced by a subordinating element, such as a conjunction or a relative pronoun, one jumps to the end and reads backwards until all verbal elements have been exhausted; if there is no subordinating element, one continues reading from left to right, except that certain verbs (haben, sein, werden, modals) are so regularly part of a larger complex verb that one is advised to check the end of any clause containing them to see if there is more to the verb lurking there.

The second approach makes use of concepts like "topic", "comment", and "news value". The sentence is like a suspension bridge, with major supporting elements at the beginning and the end. The topic of the sentence comes first, and the rest of the sentence comments on the topic, with items in the comment having greater news value coming closer to the end. This leaves relatively secondary items of information in the middle. So, for example, the subject or an adverb of time might come first, being the information the speaker wants to talk about. The verb is attached directly to the topic, in second position. If the verb is in two or more parts, its other parts are clearly of great news value and so come at the end of the comment section. In subordinate word order the finite verb leaves one bridge buttress to become the most important element in the other buttress at the far end of the bridge. This approach provides a framework for building natural sounding sentences, and helps explain such niceties as, for example, the placement of unstressed pronoun objects in inverted word order (§66.C). It also explains why most arguments about word order focus on the middle area, where competing claims for greater news value need to be resolved.

It is well to emphasize that the rules in this chapter attempt to describe what German speakers do. If we knew exactly why they did it, then we could do it too. The topic-comment notion supplies a glimmer of insight into the sentence-making power of German speakers.

§63. NORMAL WORD ORDER

It is usual to differentiate *normal* from *inverted* word order. Both are used for independent (as opposed to dependent, i.e., subordinate) clauses, and both have the inflected verb in second position.

The sequence in normal word order is: (1) the complete subject, (2) the inflected verb, and (3) predicate modifiers and verbal elements.

A.   Die Sonne geht um sechs Uhr auf.
The sun rises at six o'clock.

B.   Der Apfel ist reif.
The apple is ripe.

C.   Mein Freund ist müde geworden.
My friend has become tired.

D.   Die Dame, die mich jetzt besucht, ist meine Freundin.
The lady who is visiting me now is my friend.

E.   Er arbeitet nie.   Sie spielt immer.
He never works.   *She always plays.*

Contrary to English usage, an adverb cannot come between subject and verb.

F. Coordinating conjunctions require normal word order. The most common are: **und** *(and)*, **aber** *(but)*, **oder** *(or)* and **sondern** *(but rather)*. **Denn** *(for, because)* is to be noted particularly, since it must not be confused with **dann** *(then)*, an adverb requiring inverted word order:

> Er ist nicht hier, **denn er ist** krank.
> *He is not here because he is sick.*

> **Dann ist er** zu Hause geblieben.
> *Then he stayed home.*

§64. INVERTED WORD ORDER

The sequence in inverted word order is: (1) any word or phrase except the subject or a conjunction, or (in the case of a direct question) nothing at all; (2) the inflected verb; (3) the subject; and (4) the rest of the clause. The introductory element which displaces the complete subject may be any of those shown in **A–J**. Even an infinitive or participle may take first position where (as in **E** and **G**) it gets added emphasis.

A. An interrogative.

> Wann **geht die Sonne auf**?
> *When does the sun rise?*

B. The inflected verb.

> **Ist der Apfel** reif?
> *Is the apple ripe?*

C. An adverb or adverbial phrase.

> Heute morgen **machte ich** einen Spaziergang.
> *This morning I took a walk.*

D. A prepositional phrase.

> Nach dem Spaziergang **ging ich** nach Hause.
> *After the walk, I went home.*

E. A direct object.

> Den Hut **hatte ich** vergessen.
> *I had forgotten my hat.*

F. An indirect object.

> Dem alten Mann **hatte er** die Bücher gegeben.
> *He had given the old man the books.*

G. A predicate adjective.

Schön **ist es** nicht.
*It's **not** beautiful.*

H. A direct quotation.

„Ich werde mitkommen,“ **sagte er.**
"I shall come along," he said.

I. A conjunctive adverb.

Er war krank, darum **ging er** zum Arzt.
He was ill; therefore he went to a doctor.

Dann **ging er** nach Hause.
Then he went home.

J. A dependent clause.

Als ich in die Schule ging, **regnete es.**
As I was going to school, it was raining.

Weil sie gestern nicht gearbeitet hat, **wird sie** heute doppelt so fleißig sein.
Because she didn't work yesterday, she'll be twice as industrious today.

The dependent clause is equivalent to an adverb or other part of speech. Even in the presence of an introductory dependent clause, the inverted independent clause may begin with an adverb:

Wenn er Zeit hat, **so** wird er bei uns ein Bier trinken.
If he has time he'll have a beer at our house.

K. Exceptions.

(1) The insertion of a comma after ordinal conjunctions derived from numerals removes the necessity for inverting subject and verb.

Zweitens, er bespricht alles sehr genau.
In the second place, he discusses everything in great detail.

(2) The insertion of a comma after **nun** has the same effect, and changes the meaning of **nun.**

Nun, wir werden doch fortfahren.
Well, we shall nevertheless continue.

Nun werden wir fortfahren.
Now we shall continue.

(3) A direct quotation is not inverted if preceded by an introductory clause (often called the "governing clause"). They are treated as separate sentences.

Er sagte: „Meine Freundin hat mich verlassen.“
He said, "My girlfriend left me."

Karl fragt: „Wann kommt sie zurück?“
Carl asks, "When is she coming back?"

§65. DEPENDENT (TRANSPOSED) WORD ORDER

A clause subordinated to (i.e., dependent upon) another has *the inflected verb in final position.* Such clauses are introduced by some subordinating element (e.g., a relative pronoun), and may come before, in the middle of, or after the independent clause.

A. Als ich in Deutschland **war,** besuchte ich meine Freunde.
When I was in Germany, I visited my friends.

B. Hunde, die viel **bellen,** beißen nicht.
Dogs that bark a great deal do not bite.

C. Wenn er die Tür **aufmacht,** wird es zu kühl im Zimmer sein.
If he opens the door, it will be too cool in the room.

Verbs with separable prefixes are not separated in dependent clauses.

D. Wenn ich Zeit gehabt **hätte,** so hätte ich ihn besucht.
If I had had time, I would have visited him.

The auxiliary, since it is the inflected verb in compound tenses, comes at the end of the dependent clause, displacing the past participle.

E. Das ist ein Rätsel, das sie nicht **hat** lösen können.
That is a riddle which she has been unable to solve.

In a dependent clause having the double infinitive construction, the inflected verb (the auxiliary) must *precede* that construction. This is an exception to the rule given in **D** immediately above. The double infinitive has overpowering news value.

F. **Je** mehr ich Goethe lese, **desto** mehr bewundere ich ihn.
The more I read Goethe, the more I admire him.

Je reicher er wird, **desto** unverschämter benimmt er sich.
The richer he becomes, the more insolently he behaves.

(1) Clauses with **je** and **desto,** both followed by a comparative, take dependent word order in the first clause and inverted word order in the second.

(2) **Um so** may be used instead of **desto:**

Je mehr er hat, **um so** mehr will er haben.
The more he has, the more he wants.

G.   Er fragte mich, ob ich ihn verstanden **hätte.**
He asked me whether I had understood him.

Ich fragte ihn, wer das gesagt **hätte.**
I asked him who had said that.

Sie fragte mich, wo ich gewesen **wäre.**
She asked me where I had been.

H. Subordinating conjunctions. Subordinating conjunctions are those which introduce subordinate (or dependent) clauses. The most common are: **als, als ob, bis, da, damit, daß, ehe** (or **bevor**), **falls, indem, nachdem, ob, obgleich, obwohl, obschon, seitdem, sobald, solange, sooft, während, weil, wenn.**

A preposition followed by a relative or interrogative pronoun may function as a subordinating conjunction to introduce a dependent clause.

Das ist das Haus, **in dem** sie früher **wohnte.**
That is the house in which she formerly lived.

Ich fragte ihn, **von wem** er das gehört **hätte.**
I asked him from whom he had heard that.

§66. SPECIAL POINTS ABOUT WORD ORDER

A. Omission of *daß.* If **daß** is omitted, the normal word order is required:

Er sagte, **er hätte** ihn gesehen.
Er sagte, daß er ihn gesehen hätte.
He said that he had seen him.

B. Omission of *wenn.* If **wenn** is omitted, the inverted word order is required:

Hätte ich Geld, so würde ich reisen.
Wenn ich Geld hätte, so würde ich reisen.
If I had money, I would travel.

C. Position of unemphatic pronoun objects. Unemphatic—i.e., unstressed—pronoun objects often come between verb and subject, contrary to the rule for inverted word order. The subject presumably has greater news value.

Heute **hat mich niemand** besucht.
Nobody called on me today.

Wann **gab dir dein reicher Onkel** das Segelboot?
When did your rich uncle give you the sailboat?

D. Position of adverbs of time, manner, and place. Adverbs (or adverbial phrases) of time precede adverbs of manner, and both precede adverbs of place:

Er geht jetzt nach Hause.
He is going home now.

Er fährt mit dem Zug nach Berlin.
He's going to Berlin by train.

Sie geht jeden Morgen langsam am Hotel vorbei.
Every morning she walks slowly past the hotel.

If there is more than one adverb or adverbial phrase of the same type in a clause, the general precedes the specific:

Jeden Nachmittag um drei treibt Ursula Gymnastik.
Every afternoon at three Ursula does gymnastics.

E. Position of direct and indirect object. Unless the direct object is a personal or reflexive pronoun, the indirect object precedes it:

Er zeigte dem Freund das Bild.　　Er zeigte es dem Freund.
He showed his friend the picture.　*He showed it to his friend.*

Er zeigte ihm das Bild.　　Er zeigte es ihm.
He showed him the picture.　*He showed it to him.*

Der König zeigte sich dem Volke.
The king showed himself to the people.

F. Position of pronoun objects. These precede adverbs:

Er hatte es gestern nicht.
He did not have it yesterday.

G. Negation. The position of negatives (**nicht, nie,** etc.) is fully explained in §7.

E X E R C I S E S

A. Combine the sentence pairs below into single sentences using the conjunction given in parentheses. Number 0 is provided as a model.

0. Sie war nicht hier. Sie war krank. (denn)
Sie war nicht hier, denn sie war krank.

1. Wir kamen ins Zimmer. Wir setzten uns. (und dann)

2. Gewöhnlich legt man sich hin. Man ist müde. (wenn)

3. Ich rief ihn an. Er kam zu spät zur Vorlesung. (als)

4. Sie mäht den Rasen. Es ist furchtbar heiß. (obwohl)

5. Die Frau bleibt nicht zu Hause. Sie arbeitet in der Stadt bei einem Computergeschäft. (sondern)

6. Ich blieb gestern im Bett liegen. Es regnete stark. (als)

7. Wir rufen den ADAC an. Wir brauchen Pannenhilfe. (denn)

8. Du brauchst die Polizei. Du bist in Gefahr. (weil)

9. Sie sollen nicht antworten. Er fragt Sie. (ehe)

10. Er erklärte die Wortstellung. Er schrieb ein Beispiel dafür an die Tafel. (und)

11. Wir verließen die Klinik. Wir hatten ihn besucht. (nachdem)

12. Er hat nichts von seiner Familie gehört. Er ist vor zwölf Jahren nach Amerika ausgewandert. (seitdem)

13. Ich sitze ruhig hier und trinke meinen Tee. Mein Klassenkollege kommt mit meinem Taschengeld. (bis)

14. Der Kellner will sofort wissen. Ich kann bezahlen. (ob)

15. Das Wetter in den Alpen ist im Sommer sehr angenehm. Im Winter schneit es täglich. (während)

B. Restate the following sentences with the dependent clause first. Note that the effect of this transformation is to make the dependent clause more important than it was originally, becoming basically the topic of the new sentence.

1. Es regnete stark, als er in der Schule war.

2. Sie antwortete nicht, obwohl ich sie zweimal fragte.

3. Er sagte nichts, bevor ich ihn unter das heiße Licht stellte.

4. Wir werden eine Seminararbeit über das Drama von Grabbe schreiben, wenn es nicht zu oberflächlich ist.

5. Ich mache die Rundfahrt um die Stadt Rothenburg nicht, weil ich keine Lust dazu habe.

C. Move each italicized item forward in its clause, thereby giving it more importance. You will have to move one or more other items to make room. Then write a brief statement or question to precede the one you have just restructured, justifying the restructuring. Number 0 provides an example.

0. Wir hatten *das Wetter da* gar nicht gern.
   Die Leute waren sehr nett. Aber das Wetter da hatten wir gar nicht gern.

1. Wir waschen *heute* unsren Wagen.

2. Ich gehe *nach dem Spaziergang* nach Hause.

3. Ich habe leider *den Hut* vergessen.

4. Dieser Hund ist nicht *sehr bissig.*

5. Wir wußten nicht, *daß er bei uns übernachten wollte.*

6. Der Apfel *ist* reif.

7. Der Rennfahrer kaufte sich *eine schnellere Maschine.*

8. Die erfolgreiche Verkäuferin zeigt es *dem interessierten Kunden.*

9. Er hat das Fahrrad absichtlich gegen die Mauer *gefahren.*

10. Meine Tante Elisabeth ist nicht *Zahnärztin.*

D. Translate into German.

1. The sun sets at half past seven.

2. Señora Gucci is not very happy, although she is probably very rich.

3. While they danced, we sat quietly and drank wine.

4. We never speak English in class, but rather German.

5. They will become very tired before the game is over.

6. I hope I won't fail, because I've studied very hard.

7. Every day a different customer is interested in our wares.

8. A babysitter must know that good children dress themselves quickly and well.

9. If we close the door and the windows it will be too warm for us.

10. Before she went on vacation she rented herself a room.

Conjunctions

19

§67. COORDINATING CONJUNCTIONS

Conjunctions which join clauses of equal rank, i.e., independent clauses, are termed *coordinating conjunctions*. Clauses so joined continue to have normal word order. The more common coordinating conjunctions, illustrated below, are: **und** (*and*), **aber** (*but*), **sondern** (*but*), **denn** (*for*), **oder** (*or*), **sowohl. . . als auch** (*both. . .and*), and other correlatives.

A. und:

Das Auto hält, **und** wir steigen ein.
*The auto stops **and** we get in.*

B. aber:

(1) Er sah mich, **aber** ich sah ihn nicht.
*He saw me, **but** I did not see him.*

(2) Er war nicht zu Hause, **aber** sein Bruder war da.
*He was not at home, **but** his brother was there.*

When **aber** is used in the sense of *however* not equivalent to *but*, it may not head a clause and is not set off by commas:

(3) Der alte Mann **aber** wollte es nicht zugeben.
*The old man, **however,** did not want to admit it.*

C. sondern:

Er ging nicht in die Stadt, **sondern** er blieb auf dem Lande.
*He did not go to the city **but** remained in the country.*

Sondern is used only after a negative, and means *on the contrary* when it connects two clauses having a common subject. Whereas **aber** merely modifies a previous statement, **sondern** introduces a statement which excludes or contradicts that of the preceding clause.

D. denn:

Sie konnte nicht kommen, **denn** sie hatte Besuch.
*She could not come, **for** she had guests.*

Denn must not be confused with **dann** (*then*), an adverbial of time, which causes inversion.

E. oder:

Tue deine Pflicht, **oder** du wirst es später bereuen!
*Do your duty, **or** you will regret it later.*

F. The combination **sowohl. . . als auch** (*both. . .and*) also requires normal word order:

Sowohl die Reichen **als auch** die Armen haben gelitten.
***Both** rich **and** poor suffered.*

G. Other correlatives:

(1) **Entweder** er **oder** sein Freund wird uns helfen.
***Either** he **or** his friend will help us.*

Entweder du bleibst, **oder ich** bleibe.
***Either** you stay, **or I** stay.*

(2) **Weder** er **noch** seine Frau konnte das Auto fahren.
***Neither** he **nor** his wife could drive the car.*

(3) **Nicht nur** die Kinder, **sondern auch** die Eltern wollten die Ausstellung besuchen.
***Not only** the children **but also** the parents wanted to visit the exposition.*

(a) Correlatives such as **entweder. . .oder** (*either. . .or*), **weder. . .noch** (*neither. . .nor*), and **nicht nur. . .sondern auch** (*not only. . .but also*) take normal word order when they connect different subjects of the same verb, or when the subjects are emphasized.

(b) These correlatives otherwise use inverted word order:
Weder kann **noch** will er es tun.
*He **neither** can, **nor** wants to do it.*

Inverted order may be avoided, however, by placing the emphatic word first:

Entweder **du** machst die Arbeit, oder ich rufe deine Mutter.
*Either **you** will do the work, or I'll call your mother.*

§68. SUBORDINATING CONJUNCTIONS

Conjunctions which subordinate one clause to another (i.e., make one clause dependent upon another for completion) are called *subordinating conjunctions*. Clauses introduced by such conjunctions will have verb-last (sometimes called *dependent* or *transposed*) word order.

Some of the more common subordinating conjunctions are illustrated below.

A. als:

Als wir gestern nach Hause kamen, regnete es.
***When** we came home yesterday, it was raining.*

When may be translated by **als, wann,** or **wenn,** with the following distinctions:

(1) **Als** refers to a single, definite past action.

(2) **Wann** is used only in questions, both direct and indirect:

Wann ist er nach Hause gekommen?
***When** did he come home?*

Ich fragte ihn, **wann** er nach Hause gekommen wäre.
*I asked him **when** he had come home.*

(3) **Wenn** is often used in the sense of *whenever* to express a customary or habitual action, either with the present or with the simple past tense:

Wenn ich ihn besuchte, war er immer beschäftigt.
***When (ever)** I visited him, he was always busy.*

Wenn is commonly rendered by *if* in conditional sentences (Chapter 23).

B. als ob:

(1) Er tat, **als ob** er krank **wäre.**
*He acted **as if** he were ill.*

(2) Sie sehen aus, **als ob** Sie nicht geschlafen hätten.
*You look **as if** you had not slept.*

Als ob may be shortened to **als**, causing *inverted* word order, without change of meaning.

> Er tat, **als** wäre er müde.
> Er tat, **als ob** er müde wäre.
> *He acted **as if** he were tired.*

C. bis:

> Er arbeitete, **bis** es dunkel wurde.
> *He worked **until** it became dark.*

D. da:

> Er konnte nicht arbeiten, **da** der Lärm zu groß war.
> *He could not work **because** the noise was too great.*

E. damit:

> Ich sage es dir, **damit** du es weißt.
> *I am telling you **so that** you'll know.*

(1) **Damit** is very often followed by the indicative in modern German:

> Er trägt das Geld auf die Bank, **damit** es Zinsen bringt.
> *He takes his money to the bank **so that** it may bear interest.*

(2) **Um zu** with the infinitive is often used instead of **damit** to denote purpose, provided there is no change of subject:

> Das Geld wird auf die Bank getragen, **um** Zinsen **zu** bringen.
> *Money is taken to the bank **in order that** it may bear interest.*

F. daß:

> Wir wissen, **daß** die Erde rund ist.
> *We know **that** the earth is round.*

G. ehe (or bevor):

> Er wird mich besuchen, **ehe** (or **bevor**) er nächsten Monat abreist.
> *He will visit me **before** he leaves next month.*

Note the distinction between **bevor, vor,** and **vorher,** all meaning *before:*

(1) **Bevor** (like **ehe**) is a conjunction.

(2) **Vor** is a preposition:

> Das ist **vor** Weihnachten geschehen.
> *That happened **before** Christmas.*

(3) **Vorher** is an adverb:

Das war **vorher** geschehen.
*That had happened **before**.*

H. falls:

Falls er kommen sollte, würden wir ihn freundlich empfangen.
In case he should come, we would welcome him cordially.

I. nachdem:

Nachdem er angekommen war, besuchte er seine Freunde.
After he had arrived, he visited his friends.

Note the distinction between **nachdem, nach,** and **nachher,** all meaning *after:*

(1) **Nachdem** is a conjunction.

(2) **Nach** is a preposition:

Nach dem Tanz gingen sie nach Hause.
After the dance, they went home.

(3) **Nachher** is an adverb:

Sie tanzten **nachher.**
They danced afterwards.

J. ob:

Er fragte mich, **ob** ich ihn verstanden hätte.
*He asked me **whether** I had understood him.*

K. obgleich (obwohl or obschon):

Er ist nicht glücklich, **obgleich** er reich ist.
Although he is rich, he is not happy.

L. seitdem (also abbreviated as seit):

Seitdem sie uns vor fünf Jahren besucht hat, haben wir sie nicht gesehen.
*We have not seen her **since** (the time that) she visited us five years ago.*

Note the distinction between **seitdem, seit,** and **seither:**

(1) As a subordinating conjunction **seitdem** calls for verb-last word order. **Seitdem** also serves as an adverb, calling for inversion.

Seitdem ist er krank.
*Since then (or **that time**) he has been sick.*

The conjunctions **da** and **seitdem**, both translating *since*, should not be confused; **da** is causative (= *because*), **seitdem** is temporal (= *ever since, since the time*).

(2) **Seit** is a preposition:

Er ist schon **seit** einem Monat hier.
*He has been here **for** a month.*

(3) **Seither** is an adverb (less commonly used than **seitdem**).

M. sobald:

Sobald sie angekommen war, ließ sie einen Arzt holen.
***As soon as** she had arrived, she sent for a doctor.*

N. solange:

Solange ich krank war, ist er bei mir geblieben.
*He stayed with me **as long as** I was sick.*

O. sooft:

Sooft Sie mich bitten, werde ich Ihnen helfen.
***As often as** you ask me, I shall help you.*

P. während (or **indem**):

(1) **Während** ich auf der Uni war, konnte ich nicht arbeiten.
*I could not work, **while** (during the time that) I was in college.*

(2) **Indem** sie das sagte, trat sie ins Zimmer herein.
***While** (as) she was saying that, she entered the room.*

Indem indicates simultaneous action in both clauses. The clause introduced with **indem** is often equivalent to the English present participle:

Er grüßte den König, **indem er sich tief verbeugte.**
***Bowing deeply**, he saluted the king.*

Q. weil:

Er trägt einen Überrock, **weil** es kalt ist.
*He wears an overcoat **because** it is cold.*

Do not confuse the conjunctions **weil** (= *because*) and **während** (= *while*).

R. wenn:

(1) **Wenn** ich Zeit habe, so werde ich ihn besuchen.
***If** I have time, I shall visit him.*

Note the distinction between **wenn** and **ob**, both translated by *if:*

(*a*) **Wenn** is commonly rendered by *if* in conditional sentences.

(*b*) **Ob** may be translated by *if*, but is used only in indirect questions in the sense of *whether*.

(2) **Wenn** man heutzutage reist, benutzt man das Flugzeug.
When(ever) one travels nowadays, one uses the airplane.

(3) **Wenn** er **auch** sehr schwer gearbeitet hat, so hat er doch nicht viel Geld gespart.
Even though he has worked very hard, he has nevertheless not saved much money.

The combination **wenn. . .auch** (*even though*) also requires the dependent word order.

S. Interrogatives such as **wann, seit wann, warum, wie, wo, woher, wohin, womit, worauf,** etc., take inverted word order in direct questions. But when used in indirect questions, they function as subordinating conjunctions and, therefore, require that the verb stand at the end of the dependent clause:

Direct:	„Woher wissen Sie das?"
	How do you know that?
Indirect:	Ich fragte ihn, woher er das wisse (*or* wüßte).
	I asked him how he knew that.
Direct:	„Warum haben Sie das getan?"
	Why did you do that?
Indirect:	Ich fragte ihn, warum er das getan hätte.
	I asked him why he had done that.

T. Two conjunctions may not come together in German as they may in English: *She said **that if** it had rained, she would not have come.* To avoid the juxtaposition of **daß** and **wenn,** translate in one of the following ways:

Sie sagte, daß sie nicht gekommen wäre, wenn es geregnet hätte.

Sie sagte, sie wäre nicht gekommen, wenn es geregnet hätte.

Sie sagte, wenn es geregnet hätte, wäre sie nicht gekommen.

U. *Da*-form + **daß-clause or infinitive phrase.** Attention has already been called to the three prepositions **ohne, um,** and **(an)statt,** which require **zu** with a dependent infinitive (see §27). Other prepositions in similar constructions require **da**-forms (dar**auf**, da**mit**, dar**an**, *etc.*), which serve to anticipate a **daß**-clause or an infinitive. A **daß**-clause is usually used when there is a change of subject (sentences 1–5 below); an infinitive, when there is no such change (sentences 6–8). An **ob**-clause (like a **daß**-clause) is shown in example (9). Note, too, that **da**-forms vary according to the idiom.

(1) Ich verlasse mich **darauf, daß** Sie mir helfen.
I count on your helping me.

(2) Ich habe nichts **dagegen, daß** Sie Klavier spielen.
I have no objection to your playing the piano.

(3) Er ist schuld **daran, daß** ich arm bin.
He is to blame for my being poor.

(4) Das kommt **davon, daß** Sie zu viel rauchen.
That comes from (your) smoking too much.

(5) Das Buch unterscheidet sich **darin, daß** es viele Beispiele enthält.
The book is distinguished by the fact that it contains many examples.

(6) Er besteht **darauf,** die beiden Fahrpreise **zu bezahlen.**
He insists on paying both fares.

(7) Er hat nie **daran** gedacht, so etwas **zu tun.**
He never thought of doing such a thing.

(8) **Daran** ist nicht **zu denken.**
That's out of the question.

(9) Es handelte sich **darum, ob** sie die erste gewesen war.
It was a question of whether she had been the first.

The sentences above illustrate the so-called "anticipatory **da**-compound". This is used when the verb of the main clause, e.g., **denken,** is complemented by a prepositional phrase based (here) on **an** + accusative. But suppose that the real object of **an** is not expressible in a single noun. Prepositions require nouns or pronouns as objects, and do not admit of whole clauses or infinitive phrases. German solves this puzzle by letting the prefix **da-** be the object of the preposition, serving as a dummy to let the listener know that the true object is coming up in a second in the form of a dependent clause or infinitive phrase. Thus, the **da**-compound anticipates the true object. English does much the same thing with the dummy object *the fact* in the illustration below.

Er dachte **an** seine Zukunft.
*He thought **about** his future.*

Er dachte **daran, daß** seine Zukunft vielversprechend war.
He reflected that his future was very promising.
*He thought **about the fact that** his future was very promising.*

EXERCISES

A. Combine the following pairs of sentences using the German equivalent of the conjunction shown in parentheses. You may reverse the order of the sentences in each pair, if you think the result will be more interesting.

1. Man nimmt den Hut ab. Man geht in die Kirche. *(when)*

2. Ich trage jetzt eine Brille. Ich muß besser sehen. (*because*)

3. Ich wollte ins Kino gehen. Der Film war als "Jugendverbot bis 18 Jahre" gekennzeichnet. (*aber*)

4. Man füllt einen Freiballon mit Helium. Es ist unverbrennbar und leichter als Luft. (*because*)

5. Wir konnten nicht denken. Der Lärm war zu groß. (*since*)

6. Sie konnte nicht mehr gut sehen. Sie ging zum Augenarzt. (*therefore*)

7. Nimm mich mit! Ich werde böse auf dich sein. (*or*)

8. Sprechen Sie bitte lauter! Wir alle können hören. (*so that*)

9. Ich durfte nicht früher anrufen. Ich war im Geschäft sehr beschäftigt. (*for*)

10. Die Inhaberin macht gerade Mittagspause. Der Prokurist soll uns informieren. (*but*)

11. Sie las uns den Brief vor. Sie schaute ihn zuerst einmal durch. (*after*)

12. Ich lernte die Geige spielen. Meine Schwester studierte Mathematik. (*while*)

13. Wir gehen nach Hause. Wir sind mit der Hausaufgabe fertig. (*as soon as*)

14. Ich wollte sofort wissen. Das Auto kostet mir zuviel. (*whether*)

15. Er besuchte die Familie. Er reiste um sechs Uhr ab. (*before*)

16. Das alles, was du sagst, ist sehr schön. Ich glaube es nicht. (*but*)

17. Ich sah, daß du unzufrieden warst. Du sagtest nichts. (*although*)

18. Jeden Tag mußten wir arbeiten. Es wurde dunkel. (*until*)

19. Du hattest vor, mich zu besuchen. (*when?*)

20. Mozart komponierte fünf Violinkonzerte im Jahre 1775. Er war erst neunzehn. (*when*)

21. Ich werde zig Jahre alt sein. Ich komponiere *ein* Violinkonzert. (*before*)

22. Ich amüsierte mich herrlich. Ich war im Juni bei meinen Eltern. (*as long as*)

23. Wir kaufen uns gute Zigarren aus Kuba. Wir sind in der Tschechoslowakei. (*as often as*)

24. Wir werden euch etwas geben. Ihr habt nichts zu essen. (*in case*)

25. Du bist nie zu Hause. Ich will bei dir vorbeikommen. (*when*)

26. Ich weiß nicht. Er sitzt noch im Gefängnis. (*whether*)

27. Du mietest dir ein Ferienhaus. (*when?*)

28. Der Freund spielte Klavier. Mozart spielte Geige. (*while*)

29. Ich habe keine Lust mehr dazu. Du bist weg. (*since*)

30. Ich machte es ihr sehr deutlich. Ich will den neuen Film nicht sehen. (*that*)

B. Review the correlatives in §67F and §67G, and notice that there are in each example two of something—two subjects, two verbs, or two complements. Below is a list of simple sentences, each one with an additional item in parentheses after it. Provide each with a correlative, as in the example.

0. Die Armen haben gelitten. (die Reichen)
   Weder die Reichen noch die Armen haben gelitten.

1. Seine Freundin wird uns helfen. (er)

2. Er will es tun. (können)

3. Der Lehrer will die Ausstellung besuchen. (die Schüler)

4. Ich bleibe. (du)

5. Ihr könnt das Auto fahren. (die Pritsche)

6. Die Königin begrüßte den Präsidenten. (der Kanzler)

7. Die Bedienung war langsam. (grob)

8. Ich darf mir ein Auto mieten. (ein Hotelzimmer reservieren)

C. Replace the object of the preposition in each sentence below with the contents of the clause or phrase in parentheses by using a suitable **da**-compound.

1. Ich erinnere mich an die Abfahrtzeit. (Der Zug kommt am Montag immer früh an.

2. Du sollst dich um die Schlußprüfung kümmern. (Die Schlußprüfung ist besonders lang und schwer.) [For a word order hint, see §68U(7).]

3. Wir schämen uns über unsere schlechten Noten. (Wir haben uns auf die mündliche Prüfung nicht genug vorbereitet.)

4. Ihr könnt euch auf mich verlassen. (Der Wagen startet im Winter immer sofort.)

5. Sie gewöhnen sich allmählich an unsere Sitten. (Wir essen warm zu Mittag.)

D. Translate into German.

1. If the weather is warm we shall take a long walk in the country.

2. That he would arrive tomorrow surprised us very much.

3. Yes, that happened before the party, but what had happened *before?*

4. She acted as if she were fine.

5. While it was raining this morning we had to go shopping.

6. The harder it rained, the wetter our clothes got.

7. I simply don't know. If I have the time, I'll come.

8. When will I be home? Do you really want to know when I'll be home today?

9. Before I go to work I always brush my teeth.

10. She always insists on paying for our vacation trip.

Verbal Prefixes: Inseparable and Separable

20

While the inventory of inseparable prefixes is tightly limited and capable of quick survey in §69, the number and variety of separable prefixes is virtually limitless, and can only be hinted at in §70. Separable prefixes are drawn from every category of words, from adverbs and prepositions, from nouns and even verbs, and one must be careful not to confuse (say) the preposition **aus** with the prefix **aus** in **Er brach aus dem Gefängnis heraus.**

§69. INSEPARABLE PREFIXES

The conjugation of verbs with inseparable prefixes is shown in the following table. Such verbs are stressed on the root syllable and only rarely take the **ge-** of the past participle (see **H**).

PRESENT

Er besucht mich.
He is visiting me.

SIMPLE PAST

Er besuchte mich.
He visited me.

FUTURE

Er wird mich besuchen.
He will visit me.

COMPOUND PAST

Er hat mich besucht.
He visited me.

PAST PERFECT

Er hatte mich besucht.
He had visited me.

FUTURE PERFECT

Er wird mich besucht haben.
He will have visited me.

The inseparable prefixes with examples of each are listed below. The meanings of these prefixes, and the effect they have on the verbs to which they are joined, are explained fully in §91 B.

A. be-:

Tiefer Schnee **be**deckte die Erde.
Deep snow covered the earth.

Ich bin ihm auf der Straße **be**gegnet.
I met him on the street.

Was **be**deutet das Wort?
What does the word mean?

Wo **be**fand er sich?
Where was he?

B. emp-:

Sie hat mich freundlich **emp**fangen.
She welcomed me cordially (or in a friendly fashion).

Er hatte mir diese Firma **emp**fohlen.
He had recommended this firm to me.

Ich habe es peinlich **emp**funden.
It pained me.

Er läßt sich Ihrem Herrn Vater **emp**fehlen.
He wants to be remembered to your father.

C. ent-:

Kolumbus hat Amerika **ent**deckt.
Columbus discovered America.

Er wird den unehrlichen Buchhalter **ent**lassen.
He will discharge the dishonest bookkeeper.

Der Rhein **ent**springt in der Schweiz.
The Rhine has its source in Switzerland.

Entschuldigen Sie mich!
Pardon (or excuse) me.

D. er-:

Erklären Sie die Aufgabe!
Explain the lesson.

Sie hatte mir diese Geschichte **er**zählt.
She had told me this story.

Der Sage nach ist Friedrich Barbarossa in einem Fluß **er**trunken.
According to legend, Friedrich Barbarossa drowned in a river.

Ich habe mich **er**kältet.
I have caught cold.

E. ge-:

Wie **ge**fällt Ihnen das Buch?
How do you like the book?

Es **ge**hört meiner Schwester.
It belongs to my sister.

Er mußte dem Vater **ge**horchen.
He had to obey his father.

Wir haben die schöne Musik **ge**nossen.
We enjoyed the beautiful music.

Es ist mir noch nicht **ge**lungen, meinen Plan auszuführen.
I have not yet succeeded in carrying out my plan.

F. ver-:

Er hatte sein Geld **ver**loren.
He had lost his money.

Ich **ver**misse meine alten Freunde.
I miss my old friends.

Er hat den ersten Zug **ver**paßt (*or* **ver**säumt).
He missed the first train.

Verstehen Sie diesen Satz?
Do you understand this sentence?

G. zer-:

Der Wolf **zer**fleischte ihn.
The wolf mangled him.

Er wurde in Stücke **zer**rissen.
He was torn to pieces.

Das Kind hatte seine Brille **zer**brochen.
The child had smashed its glasses.

Der Feind wird die Stadt **zer**stören.
The enemy will destroy the city.

H. miß-:

Sie haben mich **miß**verstanden.
You misunderstood me.

Man **miß**handelte ihn.
He was mistreated.

Es ist ihm völlig **miß**lungen.
He failed completely.

Es **miß**fällt mir.
I am not pleased with it.

Er **miß**deutete meine Worte.
He misconstrued my words.

(1) Although most inseparable prefix verbs do not form their past participle with ge-, common exceptions are **miß**gebildet and **miß**gestaltet (both meaning *misshapen* or *deformed*), and **miß**gestimmt (*discordant,* or fig., *depressed, in ill humor*).

(2) Certain verbs with the prefix **miß**- admit a participial form with ge-: **miß**handelt (*or* **ge**mißhandelt), *mistreated.* The prefix, however, is never written separately from the verb. Its accent varies—before an unaccented prefix it is stressed (*e.g.,* **miß**verstehen); in most other verbs it is either not at all, or just slightly, stressed.

I. Prefixes that are usually inseparable.

(1) **voll-**:

Der Bildhauer hat das große Werk **voll**bracht.
The sculptor has completed the great work.

Verbs compounded with the prefix **voll-** are inseparable when they denote completion: **voll**bringen, voll**enden,** voll**führen,** etc. When the literal meaning is preserved, the verb is separable: **voll**pfropfen and **voll**stopfen (*to stuff full*), **voll**machen (*to make full*), etc.

(2) **hinter-**:

Er hat seinen Kindern viel Geld **hinter**lassen.
He left (or *bequeathed*) *his children much money.*

(3) **wider-**:

Widersprechen Sie mir nicht!
Don't contradict me.

§70. SEPARABLE PREFIXES

The conjugation of verbs with separable prefixes is shown in the following table. Such a prefix is really separable only in independent clauses in the present, simple past, and imperative; otherwise it is prefixed to the verb, either directly or linked by the perfective **-ge-** or the infinitive marker **-zu-**. In separable prefix verbs, the prefix receives the stress.

PRESENT	PAST PERFECT
Ich stehe früh **auf**.	Ich war früh **auf**gestanden.
I rise early.	*I had risen early.*
SIMPLE PAST	FUTURE
Ich stand früh **auf**.	Ich werde früh **auf**stehen.
I rose early.	*I shall rise early.*
COMPOUND PAST	FUTURE PERFECT
Ich bin früh **auf**gestanden.	Ich werde früh **auf**gestanden sein.
I rose early.	*I shall have risen early.*

A. (1) Heute reist sie **ab**.   Sie kehrt bald **zurück**.
She's leaving today.   *She'll return soon.*

(2) Wenn ihr die Tür **zu**macht, wird es zu warm sein.
If you close the door it will be too warm.

B.   Er machte die Tür **zu**.
He closed the door.

C.   Wann bist du **an**gekommen?   Du warst früh **fort**gegangen.
When did you arrive?   *You had left early.*

D.   Sie wird das Buch auf Seite drei **auf**machen.
She'll open the book to page three.

E.   (1) Er will **fort**gehen.   (2) Er wünscht **fort**zugehen.
          He wants to go away.   *He wishes to go away.*

      Zu is omitted in (1) because the dependent infinitive complements a modal auxiliary (see §83B).

F.   Steht sofort **auf**, Kinder!   Dreh das Licht **an**, Ernst!
          Get up at once, children.   *Turn the light on, Ernest.*

      Drehen Sie das Wasser **ab**!
      Turn off the water.

G. Common separable prefixes. Most verbal prefixes not listed in §69 are separable. It is very important to sense the meaning of separable prefixes (which usually have the force of adverbs), since they are used to form a great number of German verbs. Some of the more common separable prefixes are listed below. Their meanings are by no means limited to those given here.

    ab, *off, down*: abnehmen, *to take off*; absteigen, *to come down from*

    an, *at, on*: ansehen, *to look at*; anziehen, *to put on*

    auf, *up*: aufstehen, *to get up*

    aus, *out*: ausführen, *to carry out, execute*

    bei, *by with*: beistehen, *to render aid, assist*

    ein, *into*: eintreten, *to enter*

    empor, *up*: emporsteigen, *to climb up*

    entzwei, *in two*: entzweibrechen, *to break in two*

    entgegen, *toward*: entgegeneilen, *to hasten toward*

    fort, *away*: fortgehen, *to go away*

    heim, *home*: heimgehen, *to go home*; heimkommen, *to come home*

    her, *here, hither*: herkommen, *to come hither* (toward the speaker)

In addition to being a separable prefix, **her** may also be used to indicate *past time*. It is often used with the present tense where the English idiom requires the past: Das **ist** schon lange **her** = *That **was** (a) long (time) ago.*

hin, *there, thither*: hingehen, *to go there* (away from the speaker)

los, *loose*: loslassen, *to release*

mit, *with, along*: mitbringen, *to bring along*

nach, *after*: nachlaufen, *to run after*

nieder, *down*: sich niederlegen, *to lie down*

um, *around:* umrechnen, *to convert* (implies change)

vor, *before*: vorgehen, *to precede; be fast* (of a clock)

weg, *away*: weggehen, *to go away*

zu, *to*: zuhören, *to listen to*

zurück, *back*: zurückkehren, *to turn* (or *come*) *back, return*

zusammen, *together*: zusammenbringen, *to bring together*

H. Verbs compounded with *her* and *hin*.

(1) Many verbs are compounded with the prefixes **her** and **hin**. These prefixes are always separable; if the verb already has a separable prefix, it becomes linked to **hin** or **her**:

herkommen:	Kommen Sie **her**!
	Come here.
herauskommen:	Kommen Sie **heraus**!
	Come out here.

In all such compounds **her** denotes *motion toward*, whereas **hin** denotes *motion away from* the speaker or observer. Therefore, it is highly important to determine *the observer's position*:

Der Hund springt zum Fenster **her**ein. (The observer is inside.)
Der Hund springt zum Fenster **hin**ein. (The observer is outside.)
The dog jumps (in) through the window.

Here the English translation is the same for both sentences, but fails to bring out the difference of viewpoint clearly indicated by **her**ein and **hin**ein.

(2) Verbs of motion with prepositional prefixes expressing locality—e.g., **aus**gehen, **auf**gehen, etc.—denote motion of a *general and indefinite* nature; when compounded with the prefixes **her** and **hin**, such verbs denote motion of a *definite* nature. In English the distinction is less strongly perceived than in German.

(*a*) Sie geht immer gern **aus**.　　　　Sie geht **hinaus**.
She always likes to go out.　　　　*She goes out.*

The first sentence is a general statement and indicates no direction of the motion; in the second, the motion is definitely away from the speaker or observer.

(*b*) Die Sonne geht **auf**.
The sun rises.

Er geht die Treppe **hinauf**.
He goes upstairs.

In the first sentence a general upward direction is indicated; in the second, definite motion away from the observer.

(*c*) Das kommt oft **vor**.
That often happens.

Er kam aus seinem Versteck **hervor**.
He came forth from his hiding place.

In the first sentence the verb **kommt** is used figuratively; in the second, **kam** is used literally to denote motion of a definite nature toward the speaker.

(*d*) Similarly: **unter**gehen, *to set* (of the sun and moon) and **hinunter**gehen, *to go down* (e.g., a mountain); **ein**kommen, *to come in, be collected* (e.g., of money) and **herein**kommen, *to come in, enter* (e.g., a room), etc.

§71. MIXED PREFIXES

Certain prefixes, of which the more common are illustrated below, may function as both separable and inseparable. Generally, when used in a *figurative* sense they are *inseparable*, with stress on the root syllable and no **ge-** in the past participle. When they are used in a *literal* sense they are *separable*, with stress on the prefix and interposed **-ge-** in the past participle.

A. durch:

(1) Ich fuhr **durch**.
I drove through.

(2) Der Blitz durch**fuhr** die Luft.
Lightning pierced the air.

B. um:

(1) Er hat sich **um**gekleidet.
He has changed clothes.

(2) Er hat seine Gedanken mit schönen Worten um**kleidet**.
He has clothed his thought(s) in beautiful language.

C. über:

(1) Er hat mich **über**gesetzt.
He ferried me across.

(2) Er hat den Satz über**setzt**.
He translated the sentence.

D. unter:

(1) Er stellt sich bei der Bushaltestelle **unter**.
He takes cover at the bus stop.

(2) Er unter**stellt** ihm eine Lüge.
He accuses him of a lie.

E. wieder:

(1) Holen Sie das Buch **wieder**!
Go get the book back.

(2) Wieder**holen** Sie den Satz!
Repeat the sentence.

E X E R C I S E S

A. Supply a proper form of the verbs in parentheses. Notice how the finite verb in complex (two-or-more part) verbs predicts the form that the verbal complement will take, infinitive or past participle.

1. Der Beamte hatte seine Aktentasche _____ . (*verlieren*)
2. Der Elefant hat viele Teller im Porzellanladen _____ . (*zerbrechen*)
3. Wie _____ dir das italienische Rennrad? (*gefallen*)
4. Gestern _____ er dir bestimmt auf der Straße _____ . (*begegnen*)
5. _____ _____ nicht! (*sich erkälten*)
6. Die Mutter wird uns heute abend das Märchen _____ . (*erzählen*)
7. Warum hat der Chef den Prokuristen _____ ? (*entlassen*)
8. Er hat alles _____ , was sie gesehen haben. (*beschreiben*)
9. Sie hat es schmerzlich _____ . (*empfinden*)
10. Wer sollte Amerika _____ haben? (*entdecken*)
11. Es tut mir leid—ich habe Sie _____ . (*mißverstehen*)
12. Gregor hat den früheren Zug _____ . (*verpassen*)

B. Make sentences with the following sets of words, using the advice in parentheses for each set. You need add no words of your own, unless you think the result would be interesting.

1. die Bankbeamtin / die geheime Tür / aufmachen (compound past tense)
2. die Gepäckträger / meine Koffer / forttragen (simple past)
3. die Volksschule / im September / anfangen (present tense)
4. der Postbote / die Treppe / hinaufgehen (simple past)
5. der Weihnachtsmann / die Kinder / einladen (add a simple past form of *wollen*)
6. der Athlet / drei Kilo / abnehmen (add a present tense form of *beginnen*— see §114B(2))
7. Gregor / immer um fünf Uhr / aufstehen (present tense)

8. die Schauspielerin / zwischen dem 2. und 3. Akt / schnell / sich umziehen (simple past tense)

9. der Student / während der Vorlesung / einschlafen (compound past tense)

10. wann / Sie / nach Oberniederböpp / zurückkehren (future perfect tense)

C. Complete the following sentences with the logical **hin-** and **her-** compounds.

1. Karla (*oben*) sagte zu Ingrid (*unten*): Komm ____auf!

2. Pia (*unten*) zu Fritz (*unten*): Geh mal ____auf!

3. Jörg (*unten*) zu Alois (*oben*): Komm ____unter!

4. Franz (*oben*) zu Renate (*oben*): Geh doch ____unter!

5. Willi (*vor der Tür*) zu Fred (*vor der Tür*): Geh ____ein!

6. David (*an der Tür*) zu Johann (*im Zimmer*): Komm ____aus!

7. Ignatz (*im Zimmer*) zum Postboten (*an der Tür*): Kommen Sie ____ein!

8. Helene (*im Zimmer*) zu Dimitri (*im Zimmer*): Geh ____aus!

D. Translate into German.

1. The sun rises at six o'clock.

2. Did you enjoy a German breakfast?

3. Do you wish to sit down in the hall?

4. She translated the third sentence elegantly.

5. She met her old friend by accident in the restaurant.

6. Repeat the last word, please. I misunderstood it.

7. I returned home very late last night.

8. If you open your books the test will be too easy.

9. The letter carrier brought the letter in immediately.

10. I fell asleep early but missed the train anyhow.

The Passive Voice

21

If a sentence is in the active voice, usually the subject is the topic and the verb flows from left to right, exerting the influence of the subject on the object. But there are times when the doer of a deed is not known, as in instructional manuals—"The engine is started by pressing lever B." And there are times when we would rather suppress the subject—"The window was broken late last night." The passive voice, by reversing the flow of the verb, allows us to disguise the object as a subject and place it in front, where the topic of a sentence is expected to be. Meanwhile the true subject, if stated at all, has very little news value and is therefore in the middle of the sentence in a prepositional phrase.

§72. ACTIVE AND PASSIVE FORMS

The sentences below show that the direct object of a verb used actively becomes the subject of the same verb used in the passive voice, and that *the past participle occurs in each tense of the passive voice.* Other characteristics of the passive in German are:

1. The auxiliary is **werden**.
2. **Worden** follows the past participle in the three perfect tenses.
3. The future tense ends in **werden**.
4. **Sein** is always used to form the three perfect tenses.
5. *By* becomes **von**, which is followed by the dative case.

A. *The active voice:*	**B. *The passive voice:***

(1)   PRESENT

Er lobt den Jungen.
He praises (is praising, does praise) the boy.

(1)   PRESENT

Der Junge **wird** von ihm **gelobt.**
The boy is (being) praised by him.

In forming B(1) the prepositional phrase **von ihm** supplies the real subject, and is optional, being of secondary news value. A colloquial translation of B(1) would be *The boy gets praised by him* or, omitting the agent, *The boy gets praised.*

(2)   SIMPLE PAST

Sie lobte den Jungen.
She praised (was praising) the boy.

(2)   SIMPLE PAST

Der Junge **wurde** von ihr **gelobt.**
The boy was (being) praised by her.

(3)   PERFECT (COMPOUND PAST)

Er hat den Jungen gelobt.
He (has) praised the boy.

(3)   PERFECT (COMPOUND PAST)

Der Junge **ist** von ihm **gelobt worden.**
The boy has been (or was) praised by him.

(4)   PAST PERFECT

Er hatte den Jungen gelobt.
He had praised the boy.

(4)   PAST PERFECT

Der Junge **war** von ihm **gelobt worden.**
The boy had been praised by him.

(5)   FUTURE

Sie wird den Jungen loben.
She will praise the boy.

(5)   FUTURE

Der Junge **wird** von ihr **gelobt werden.**
The boy will be praised by her.

(6)   FUTURE PERFECT

Sie wird den Jungen gelobt haben.
She will have praised the boy.

(6)   FUTURE PERFECT

Der Junge **wird** von ihr **gelobt worden sein.**
The boy will have been praised by her.

C. Additional examples of the passive voice.

Er wird von dem Friseur rasiert.
He gets shaved by the barber.

Das Bild wurde von dem Maler gemalt.
The picture was being painted by the artist.

Alles ist von dem Feind verwüstet worden.
Everything was (lit. has been) laid waste by the enemy.

Er war von seiner Tante erzogen worden.
He had been reared by his aunt.

Mein Auto wird morgen repariert werden.
My car will be repaired tomorrow.

§73. ACTIONAL AND STATAL PASSIVES

The *actional* (*real* or *true*) *passive,* formed with **werden** and the past participle, denotes an action that is going on at the time indicated by the tense of the verb.

The *statal* (or *apparent*) *passive,* formed with the verb *to be,* **sein,** and the past participle functioning as a predicate adjective, denotes a state or condition that has already resulted from some previous action.

A. The actional passive:	*B. The statal passive:*
(1) Die Tür **wird** zugemacht. *The door is being closed.*	(1) Die Tür **ist** zugemacht. *The door is closed.*
(2) Die Kleider **werden** gewaschen. *The clothes are being washed.*	(2) Die Kleider **sind** gewaschen. *The clothes are washed.*
(3) Das Haus **wird** grün angestrichen. *The house is being painted green.*	(3) Das Haus **ist** grün angestrichen. *The house is painted green.*
(4) Der Zaun **wurde** aus kleinen Brettern gemacht. *The fence was (being) made of small boards.*	(4) Der Zaun **war** aus kleinen Brettern gemacht. *The fense was made of small boards.*

§74. ADDITIONAL FEATURES OF THE PASSIVE

A. Customary occurrence. The passive voice is often used to denote a customary occurrence:

Die Tür **wird** um zehn Uhr **geschlossen.**
The door is closed (regularly) *at ten o'clock.*

Kaffee **wird** bei uns um fünf Uhr **getrunken.**
We have coffee (regularly) *at five o'clock.*

B. Wurde, ist geboren. To express *was born,* the passive **wurde geboren** is used for the dead; **ist geboren,** for the living:

Schiller **wurde** im Jahre 1759 **geboren.**
Schiller was born in 1759.

Wann **sind** Sie **geboren?**
When were you born?

C. Means or instrument. In the passive voice, means or instrument is usually expressed by **durch** with the accusative:

Die Bretter wurden **durch** einen Nagel zusammengehalten.
The boards were held together by a nail.

Der Löwe wurde **durch** einen Schuß getötet.
The lion was killed by a shot.

The **instrument** may also be expressed by **mit**:

Der Bericht wurde **mit** der Hand geschrieben.
The report was written by hand.

D. Intransitive verbs used impersonally in the passive. For the impersonal use of intransitive verbs in the passive, see §62 D.

E. The passive imperative. The passive imperative is usually formed with **sein** (as in examples 1, 2, and 3 below) but sometimes with **werden** (example 4). The present Subjunctive I is used for the third person; **lassen** with a dependent infinitive is a common equivalent to this construction in the second person (example 5).

(1) Es **sei** ferner erwähnt, daß endere Gründe vorliegen.
It is furthermore to be noted that there are other reasons.

(2) **Seien** Sie gegrüßt!
We salute you.

(3) Der Herr **sei** gelobt!
May the Lord be praised.

(4) Er **werde** hereingeführt!
Have him brought in.

(5) **Lassen** Sie sich nicht täuschen!
Don't be deceived.

§75. SUBSTITUTE CONSTRUCTIONS FOR THE PASSIVE

A. The active voice with *man*. A common equivalent of the passive voice is the active voice with **man**.

Man tut das nicht.
That is not done.

Man muß es tun.
It must be done.

Wie buchstabiert man das Wort?
How is that word spelled?

Man gab ihm die Gelegenheit.
He was given the opportunity.

In the last sentence, the subject *he* could not be rendered by **er**. But a passive verb might be used with **Gelegenheit** as subject:

Die Gelegenheit wurde ihm gegeben.
Ihm wurde die Gelegenheit gegeben.
The opportunity was given (to) him.

B. Reflexive verbs. For the common use of a reflexive verb instead of the passive, see §61 E.

C. The active infinitive preceded by *zu*. After the verb **sein**, the active infinitive preceded by **zu** is equivalent to the passive:

> Er ist telefonisch nicht zu erreichen.
> *He cannot be reached by telephone.*
> *He is not **to be reached** by telephone.*

D. Lassen with a dependent infinitive. The verb **lassen** with a dependent infinitive, while not equivalent to the passive in meaning, shares with the passive voice the fact that the secondary subject is deleted, as in this example where the cutter of hair is unstated:

> Ich habe mir das Haar schneiden lassen.
> *I had my hair cut.*

E. Verbs whose English equivalents are passive. The following German verbs, while not themselves passive or in many cases even transitive, have English equivalents which are passive: **dürfen** (*to be allowed to*), **sollen** (*to be said to*), **heißen** (*to be called*), **ertrinken** or **ersaufen** (*to be drowned*, i.e., *to drown* used intransitively), and **erschrecken** (the strong verb meaning *to be frightened*):

> Das Kind **darf nicht** auf der Straße spielen.
> *The child **is not allowed** to play on the street.*

> Er **soll** sehr klug sein.   Wie **heißt** es?
> *He **is said** to be very clever.*   *What **is** it **called**?*

> Er **ist ertrunken.**   Sie **erschrak.**
> *He **was drowned.***   *She **was frightened.***

E X E R C I S E S

A. Change the following sentences from the active to the passive voice. Be sure to retain the tense of the original verb. It will sometimes be more sensible to delete the original subject than to restate it as a prepositional phrase.

1. Man öffnet die Bierflasche mit der linken Hand.
2. Der Junge fotografierte den Löwen sehr früh am ersten Morgen der Jagd.
3. Der Kellner hat uns das belegte Brot mit Käse gebracht.
4. Bevor er zu uns kam, hatten wir unser schönstes Zimmer für ihn aufgeräumt.
5. Man wird für Montag den besten Platz reservieren.
6. Man wird den Film wohl zum Entwickeln geschickt haben.
7. Dann singen wir unser Lieblingslied.

8. Er wurde so böse, daß er die schönen Blumen zurück in die Mappe stieß.

9. Man versteigerte die wertvollen Briefmarken auf der Auktion.

10. Er wird den Regenschirm wohl in der feinen Stube gefunden haben.

11. Der Mechaniker reparierte den Luxuswagen der bekannten Sängerin.

12. Jeden Tag schließt man die Ladentür um halb vier.

13. Die Polizei verbietet uns strengstens die Übernachtung in jenem Hotel.

14. Die ältere Schwester verwöhnte den kleinen Jungen sehr.

15. Dieses Selbstporträt hat kein berühmter Maler gemalt.

16. Die Mutter wird die Tochter zum Tanzabend begleiten.

17. Auf diese Weise macht man die Tür auf.

18. Die Bauarbeiter pflastern die Straße immer sehr früh, weil die Berufstätigen täglich zur Arbeit fahren müssen.

19. Wir haben unsren freundlichen Postboten zum Weihnachtsfest eingeladen.

20. Schade! Wir haben das Fenster gebrochen.

B. Here are some sentences in the passive which can be restated using one or another of the passive avoidance strategies suggested in §75. This cannot be done entirely literally.

1. Das wird oft gesagt.

2. Warum wurde es den Kindern verboten, vor dem Haus zu spielen?

3. Was konnte da gesehen werden?

4. Es wird von ihm gemeint, er sei ein bekannter Politiker.

5. Er konnte nicht mehr gerettet werden.

6. Das wird leicht verstanden.

7. Es wird von diesen Reisebüchern gesagt, daß sie sehr interessant sind.

8. Nichts konnte in der dunklen Gasse gesehen werden.

C. Translate into German. Be careful to distinguish between actional and statal passives.

1. She was reared by her grandparents.

2. The German newspaper *Die Zeit* is now being printed in Canada.

3. Many comfortable houses had been built before the war.

4. Too much coffee is said to be drunk in America.

5. When I walked past at three o'clock the door was closed.

6. Our first president was called George Washington.

7. As a rule German nouns are capitalized.

8. I have been bitten by your small but terrible dog.

9. My new car is being repaired today.
10. Goethe was borne in 1749. When were you born?
11. Since I hurt myself I have been shaved by the barber.
12. Your notebooks will be returned tomorrow.
13. They were given the opportunity. (*Use* **man**)
14. That is easier to say than to do.
15. You are permitted to use the kitchen between seven and seven-thirty.
16. Then the flowers are laid on the grave by the chancellor.
17. The book was held together by three rubberbands.
18. The students are not allowed to smoke in the classroom.
19. These cellars are inhabited by many happy mice.
20. We are no longer visited as often as before.

The Subjunctive in Indirect Discourse and Independent Sentences

22

Enough modern grammars of English maintain that there is no English subjunctive that a cautionary note is warranted here. Except for *were* with a singular subject and a few oddities like *be* as a finite verb, English has no subjunctive forms. But it has a distinctly subjunctive usage: any past tense verb used with present tense meaning is in the present subjunctive mood; any past perfect tense verb used with ordinary past tense meaning is in the past subjunctive mood. To say that English has no subjunctive is to say that English speakers cannot dream or hope or wish, cannot report the statements of others, and cannot soften requests and demands. These are all necessary tasks of the subjunctive mood.

§76. INDIRECT STATEMENTS

Before examining the uses of the subjunctive, reference should be made to the paradigms in §§102–109 in the Appendix. It will be seen that although the indicative has six tenses, the subjunctive has only four: present, past, future, and future perfect. There are, however, two sets of subjunctive tenses, called Subjunctive I and Subjunctive II; the future and future perfect Subjunctive II forms are also called the Conditional.

While Subjunctive I forms are encountered in written German, modern usage favors Subjunctive II forms. With infrequent exceptions, the user may always employ Subjunctive II for indirect discourse (statements, questions, and commands).

Formation of the subjunctive is simply stated: To the stem of the present infinitive (for present Subjunctive I) and to the stem of the simple past (for present Subjunctive II), add the endings **-e, -est, -e, -en, -et, -en**. Strong verbs and modal auxiliaries (except **sollen** and **wollen**) are umlauted in Subjunctive II. The verb **sein** is normal except for the loss of final **-e** in the first and third persons singular: **ich sei, es sei**.

The following sentences illustrate the use of the subjunctive for indirect statements. Column **A** shows the original direct statement, Column **B** the indirect statement. Note that:

1. The Subjunctive II forms are given in parentheses.

2. If the indirect statement is introduced by the subordinating conjunction **daß**, the inflected verb is moved to final position; if not, normal word order prevails.

3. The tense of the indirect statement is always the same as that of the original direct statement, and is unaffected by the tense of the introductory (or governing) clause.

A. *Direct statement:*	B. *Indirect statement:*
(1) Er sagte: „Ich **habe** Glück." *He said: "I am lucky."*	(1) Er sagte, er **habe** (or **hätte**) Glück. Er sagte, daß er Glück **habe** (or **hätte**). *He said that he was lucky.*
(2) Er sagte: „Ich **hatte** Glück." *He said: "I was lucky."* Er sagte: „Ich **habe** Glück **gehabt**." *He said: "I have been lucky."* Er sagte: „Ich **hatte** Glück **gehabt**." *He said: "I had been lucky."*	(2) Er sagte, er **habe** (or **hätte**) Glück **gehabt**. Er sagte, daß er Glück **gehabt habe** (or **hätte**). *He said that he had been lucky.*
(3) Er sagte: „Ich **werde** Glück **haben**." *He said: "I shall be lucky."*	(3) Er sagte, er **werde** (or **würde**) Glück **haben**. Er sagte, daß er Glück **haben werde** (or **würde**). *He said that he would be lucky.*
(4) Er sagte: „Ich **werde** Glück **gehabt haben**." *He said: "I shall have been lucky."*	(4) Er sagte, er **werde** (or **würde**) Glück **gehabt haben**. *He said that he would have been lucky.*

C. **Changes of tense from direct to indirect statements.** In translating an English indirect statement into German it is best to return to the original direct statement, for from the tense of its verb the tense of the subjunctive verb is most easily determined:

1. A present indicative in the direct statement becomes a present Subjunctive I or II.

2. *Any* past indicative (past, perfect, or past perfect) becomes a past Subjunctive I or II.

3. A future indicative becomes a future Subjunctive I or a present Conditional.

4. A future perfect indicative becomes a future perfect Subjunctive I or a past Conditional.

It is usual to employ the Subjunctive I forms of **sein,** the three singular persons of the modals, the third person singular of **haben** and **werden,** and the third person singular of strong and weak verbs: these forms are all clearly distinct from the present indicative—**er sei, ich könne, er habe, er werde, er schlage, er lebe.** But otherwise Subjunctive II and the Conditional are used for indirect discourse.

D. **Verbs of knowing or averring followed by the indicative.** Verbs such as **wissen** (*to know*), **sehen** (*to see*), and phrases such as **es ist klar** (*it is clear*), **es ist nicht zu leugnen** (*it cannot be denied*) are followed by the indicative. This use of the indicative is particularly common after the first person present of such verbs as **wissen.** Verbs of knowing emphasize, support, or endorse the truth of what follows—thus giving to the sentence as a whole the force of a direct statement—and the indicative, as the mood of fact, is used to express this certainty:

Wir **wissen** alle, daß Sie recht **haben.**
We all know that you are right.

Ich **weiß,** daß sie morgen **abfährt.**
I know that she will leave tomorrow.

Es ist nicht zu leugnen, daß der Blitz manchmal **einschlägt.**
It cannot be denied that lightning sometimes strikes.

Similarly, verbs of averring such as **sagen,** particularly in the present tense, first person, are frequently followed by the indicative:

Ich **sage** Ihnen, daß der Mann unschuldig **ist.**
I tell you that the man is innocent.

Ich **sage** Ihnen nochmals, daß ich furchtbar müde **bin.**
I tell you again (or *repeat*) *that I am terribly tired.*

E. **Verbs that introduce indirect statements.** Indirect statements are introduced by verbs of saying, thinking, and feeling such as: **sagen** (*to say, tell*), **erzählen** (*to tell, relate*), **schreiben** (*to write*), **antworten** (*to answer*), **berichten** (*to report*), and **fürchten** (*to fear*):

> Er sagte, er würde mich um acht Uhr besuchen.
> *He said (that) he would call on me at eight o'clock.*
>
> Sie schrieb mir, die ganze Familie hätte einen Ausflug ins Gebirge gemacht.
> *She wrote me that the whole family had taken a trip to the mountains.*
>
> Die Zeitung berichtete, daß ein berühmter europäischer Schauspieler angekommen wäre.
> *The newspaper reported that a famous European actor had arrived.*

F. Change of pronouns and possessives from direct to indirect statement. In changing sentences from the direct to the indirect form, care must be taken to change not only the verb but also pronouns and possessives. Note particularly changes in reflexive forms:

	Karl sagte: „**Ich** habe **mein** Buch verloren.“
INDIR.:	Karl sagte, **er** hätte **sein** Buch verloren.
	Carl said (that) he had lost his book.
	Sie schrieb mir: „**Ich** bin bei **meiner** Tante.“
INDIR.:	Sie schrieb mir, **sie** wäre bei **ihrer** Tante.
	She wrote me that she was at her aunt's house.
	Er sagte zu mir: „**Ich** kann es **mir** nicht leisten.“
INDIR.:	Er sagte mir, **er** könnte es **sich** nicht leisten.
	He told me that he could not afford it.

Zu after **sagen** is dropped in an indirect statement.

G. Subjunctives in the direct statement. If the direct statement contains a subjunctive, it is retained in the indirect statement:

> Er meinte: „Wenn ich die Universität besuchte, würde ich eine bessere Stelle finden können.“
> *He thought, "If I were to go to college I would be able to find a better job."*
>
> Er meinte, wenn er die Universität besuchte, würde er eine bessere Stelle finden können.
> *He thought that if he went to college he would be able to find a better job.*

H. Dependent clauses in the direct statement. If the direct statement contains a dependent clause, it too becomes subjunctive in the indirect statement:

> Er berichtete: „Karl, der jeden Tag spät ankommt, gewinnt den Preis.“
> Er berichtete, daß Karl, der jeden Tag spät ankäme, den Preis gewänne.
> *He reported that Karl, who came late every day, won the prize.*

§77. INDIRECT QUESTIONS

The sentences in **A** and **B** below show that indirect questions are formulated in the same way as indirect statements. Note that:

1. Indirect questions always begin with an interrogative; if the direct question had no interrogative, the subordinating conjunction **ob** must be supplied:

   Er fragte: „War sie krank?"
   Er fragte, ob sie krank gewesen wäre.

2. Indirect questions are always dependent clauses, with verb-last word order.

A. *Direct question:*	**B.** *Indirect question:*
(1) Ich fragte ihn: „Was **haben Sie** in der Hand?" *I asked him: "What have you got in your hand?"*	(1) Ich fragte ihn, was **er** in der Hand **habe** (or **hätte**). *I asked him what he had in his hand.*
(2) Ich fragte sie: „Wo **waren Sie** heute morgen?" *I asked her: "Where were you this morning?"*	(2) Ich fragte sie, wo **sie** heute morgen **gewesen sei** (or **gewesen wäre**). *I asked her where she had been this morning.*
(3) Ich fragte ihn: „**Haben** die Leute das **verstanden?**" *I asked him: "Did the people understand that?"*	(3) Ich fragte ihn, ob die Leute das **verstanden hätten**. *I asked him whether the people had understood that.*
(4) Ich fragte sie: „**Werden** Ihre Freunde **mitkommen?**" *I asked her: "Will your friends come along?"*	(4) Ich fragte sie, ob ihre Freunde **mitkommen würden**. *I asked her whether her friends would come along.*

C. **The indicative in indirect questions.** After an introductory clause in the present tense, and after an imperative, the indirect question is in the indicative.

Er fragt, ob sie noch **schläft**.
He asks whether she is still asleep.

Erzählen Sie mir, was geschehen **ist!**
Tell me what happened.

§78. INDIRECT COMMANDS

The indirect command in German, as the sentences in **A** and **B** show, is formulated much in the same way as the indirect statement. Note especially that:

1. Direct commands in German have an exclamation mark; indirect commands have a period.

2. An indirect command is customarily expressed by the present Subjunctive I or II of **sollen** and a dependent present infinitive.

3. The English infinitive often represents an indirect command. The German infinitive cannot be used in this way.

*He told me **to come**.*
Er sagte mir, daß ich kommen sollte.

A. Direct command:	*B. Indirect command:*
(1) Er sagte zu mir: „**Stehen Sie auf!**" *He said to me: "Get up."*	(1) Er sagte mir, ich **solle** (or **sollte**) **aufstehen.** Er sagte mir, daß ich **aufstehen solle** (or **sollte**). *He told me to get up (or that I should get up).*
(2) Ich sagte zu ihm: „**Vergessen Sie** das nicht!" *I said to him: "Don't forget that."*	(2) Ich sagte ihm, er **solle** (or **sollte**) das nicht **vergessen.** Ich sagte ihm, daß er das nicht **vergessen solle** (or **sollte**). *I told him not to forget (or that he should not forget) that.*
(3) Wir sagten zu ihr: „**Lesen Sie** das deutsche Buch!" *We said to her: "Read the German book."*	(3) Wir sagten ihr, sie **solle** (or **sollte**) das deutsche Buch **lesen.** Wir sagten ihr, daß sie das deutsche Buch **lesen solle** (or **sollte**). *We told her to read (or that she should read) the German book.*

§79. INDEPENDENT SENTENCES

The subjunctive may also be used in independent sentences to express *wish, command, possibility, doubt,* etc.

A. The subjunctive in wishes.

(1) Es **lebe** die Freiheit!
May freedom live.

Seine Seele **ruhe** in Frieden!
May his soul rest in peace.

Gott **gebe** es!
(May) God grant it.

Möge das neue Jahr Ihnen viel Glück bringen!
May the new year bring you much good fortune.

The present Subjunctive I is used—chiefly in set phrases, prayers, and formal greetings—to express a wish that may be fulfilled. The present Subjunctive I of **mögen** with a dependent infinitive is also used in this construction.

(2) **Wäre** ich nur reich!   **Hätte** er doch Geduld!
Wenn ich nur reich **wäre!**   Wenn er doch Geduld **hätte!**
If only I were rich!   *If only he had patience!*
Would that I were rich.   *Would that he had patience.*

The present Subjunctive II is used to express a wish that is equivalent to a present contrary-to-fact condition of which the conclusion is to be supplied. This form is used both when a wish is incapable and when it is capable of fulfillment, although the idea of unreality may be obvious at the time a wish is expressed:

Wenn ich nur Flügel **hätte!**   Wenn der Zug nur **käme!**
Hätte ich nur Flügel!   **Käme** der Zug nur!
If only I had wings!   *If only the train would come!*

The present Subjunctive II (used in wishes and otherwise) may indicate impatience on the part of the speaker (**Hätte er doch Geduld!**); it may also convey modesty, when the statement concerns the speaker:

Möchte es mir nur bald gelingen!
Gelänge es mir nur bald!
Wenn es mir nur bald **gelänge!**
May I succeed soon!

(3) **Wäre** er nur hier **gewesen!**
Wenn er nur hier **gewesen wäre!**
Would that he had been here.
If he had only been here!

Hätte sie mir doch **geschrieben!**
Wenn sie mir doch **geschrieben hätte!**
Would that she had written me.
If she had only written me!

The past Subjunctive II is used to express a wish that is equivalent to a past contrary-to-fact condition of which the conclusion is to be supplied. The present or past Subjunctive II, when used to express a wish, is usually accompanied by **doch** or **nur**.

B. The subjunctive in commands.

(1) Since the imperative exists only for the second person, singular and plural, the present Subjunctive I is used to express commands for the third

singular and first and third plural. The first person plural is used with inversion:

Lesen wir jetzt weiter!
Let us continue reading.

Fangen wir jetzt **an!**
Let us begin now.

Reden wir nicht mehr davon!
Let us talk no more about it.

Vergessen wir das nicht!
Let us not forget that.

(2) The third person singular may have either normal or inverted word order:

„Edel **sei** der Mensch."
Let man be noble.

Er **komme!** (or **Komme** er!)
Let him come.

Jeder **kehre** vor seiner Tür!
Mind your own business.
lit. *Let each one sweep before his (own) door.*

Man **beachte** die Vorschriften!
Let everybody (lit. *one*) *observe the rules.*

(3) The third person plural is infrequently used:

Alle **setzen** sich!
(Let) all be seated.

(4) The second person singular and plural formal address, identical in form to the third plural, is frequently used. While, strictly speaking, it is present Subjunctive I in form, because of its frequency and because it is always identical to the third plural indicative, it is thought of and listed as an imperative. The exceptional form **seien** betrays its true origin:

Herr Doktor, **seien** Sie ruhig!
Be quiet, doctor.

(5) Far more common than the constructions explained in (1), (2), or (3) is the imperative of **lassen** with a dependent present infinitive. Note that the subject of the subjunctive command becomes the object of **lassen.**

Laß (**laßt** or **lassen Sie**) uns gehen!
Let us go.

Laß (**laßt** or **lassen Sie**) ihn kommen!
Let him come.

C. The subjunctive to express possibility and doubt.

(1) The present Subjunctive II is used to express possibility and doubt, especially in modest, mild, polite, or diplomatic terms.

Wie **wäre** es mit einer Partie Schach?
How would you like to play a game of chess?
How about a game of chess?

Wäre es möglich, daß Rose das Schachbrett **verlegt hätte?**
Is it possible that Rosa misplaced the chessboard?

Nicht daß ich **wüßte.**　　　　　　Das **wäre** schade!
Not that I am aware of.　　　　　*That would be a pity.*

(2) The modal auxiliaries are frequently employed in the same sense.

Wo **könnte** (or **dürfte**) es wohl sein?
Where might it possibly be?

Sie **dürften** sich geirrt haben.
You may possibly have made a mistake.

Das **sollte** ich doch meinen!
I should think so!

Dürfte ich Sie um Ihr Opernglas bitten?
Might I ask you for your opera glasses?

Es **möchte** wohl besser sein, wenn wir es unterließen.
It would probably be better if we did not do it.

§80. CONCESSIVE CLAUSES

Subjunctive I may be used to express concession. The second clause is not inverted because both clauses were originally independent.

A.　　**Sei** die Gefahr auch noch so groß, ich werde mich nicht fürchten.
　　　Die Gefahr **sei** auch noch so groß, ich werde mich nicht fürchten.
　　　Be the danger ever so great, I shall not be afraid.
　　　Although the danger be ever so great, I shall not be afraid.

B.　　**Sei** es früh, **sei** es spät, er ist immer auf seinem Posten.
　　　(Be it) early or (be it) late, he is always at his post.

Concession may be expressed in several ways without the subjunctive. For example, the first clause of **A** above might read:

Mag die Gefahr auch noch so groß sein, . . .
Die Gefahr mag auch noch so groß sein, . . .
Ist die Gefahr auch noch so groß, . . .

E X E R C I S E S

A. Rewrite the following items as indirect statements, questions, or commands. Remember that the tense of the original direct quotation dictates the tense of the derived indirect quotation. Don't forget to adjust pronouns as necessary (review §76F). If an item is followed by a conjunction in parentheses, be sure to use it; otherwise, the choice is up to you.

1. Ursula sagte: "Ich war gestern im Theater. Mein Freund Fritz ist zu Hause geblieben."

2. Sie schrieb mir: "Wir werden morgen abfahren." (daß)

3. Er fragte den Beamten: "Woher haben Sie so viel Geld?"

4. Die Beamtin sagte zu mir: "Kommen Sie morgen wieder!"

5. Die Kunden meinten: "Diese VW-Pritsche gefällt uns."

6. Der Kanzler antwortete: "Ich werde später einen Vortrag über die Gesundheitspflege halten." (daß)

7. Der Arzt sagte zu ihr: "Rauchen Sie nicht so viel!"

8. Ich rief meinen Freunden zu: "Lauft schneller!"

9. Der Gastwirt fragte mich: "Haben Sie schon gegessen?"

10. Der Lehrer hielt uns sofort an und wollte wissen: "Warum antwortet ihr nicht auf die Frage?"

11. Unsre Tochter schrieb uns: "Ich war vorigen Monat sehr beschäftigt." (daß)

12. Karl sagte: "Es ist heute sehr heiß, und es war letzte Woche noch heißer."

13. Die Tageszeitung berichtete: "Ein großes Unglück ist in Marbach geschehen."

14. Annette schrieb uns von ihrem Ferienort: "Das Gewitter war um acht Uhr am heftigsten." (daß)

15. Sie fragte die Eltern: "Freut ihr euch auf meinen Besuch?

16. Die Lehrerin sagte zu dem Schüler: "Setz dich!"

17. Er fragte mich: "In was für einem Haus wohnen Sie?"

18. Wir fragten die Studentin: "Worüber ärgert sich Ihr Kollege so sehr?"

19. Der Prokurist schrie mich an: "Fahr mit dem ersten Schnellzug!"

20. Marie erzählte uns: "Die Mutter hat mir zu Weihnachten einen herrlichen Pelzmantel geschenkt." (daß)

21. Er sagte zu mir: "Ich werde mich vor Montag bestimmt an alles gewöhnt haben."

22. Sie meinte: "Ich hätte gern den chinesischen Film gesehen."

23. Der Abgeordnete berichtete: "Der Plan ist mir noch nicht gelungen." (daß)

24. Der Professor sagte: "Ich werde nächstes Semester eine Studienreise nach Deutschland unternehmen."

25. Der Chef telefonierte: "Ich habe den Bus versäumt. Ich komme erst morgen an."

26. Ein Zollbeamter wollte sogleich wissen: "Haben Sie amerikanisches Geld bei sich?"

27. Der Lehrer sagte dann zu uns: "Lernt Schillers Gedicht auswendig!" Das war nämlich die übliche Strafe.

28. Sie hat uns sogar versprochen: "Es wird Ihnen das nächste Mal gelingen."

29. Ich antwortete auf seine Frage: "Ich habe leider kein Geld bei mir." (daß)

30. Ich sage es Ihnen klar und deutlich, und ich weiß es auch: "Menschen von der Erde sind 1969 auf den Mond gelandet." (daß)

B. One of the advantages of having obvious subjunctive forms is that German scholars can include extensive paraphrases of the work of others in their own texts. As long as they use the subjunctive, they are not claiming the ideas as theirs. Here is a direct quotation from the Amtlicher Führer (official guide) to the Residenz in Munich, published in 1937 by the Bayerische Verwaltung der staatlichen Schlösser. You will probably need a dictionary to follow it. Encapsulate the relevant data in a paraphrase and render your results in the subjunctive. Use the Subjunctive I as much as possible, since this is supposed to sound scholarly.

> Mit König Ludwig I. (regierte 1825/48) beginnt das letzte große Kapitel der Baugeschichte der Münchner Residenz. Die Aufgabe, die sich dieser Herrscher hier gestellt hat, war eine doppelte: Für die Residenz selbst monumentale Raumfluchten als Repräsentation des neuen Königreiches zu schaffen und andererseits städtebaulich eine neue, in sich geschlossene Einheit des gesamten Baukomplexes und damit zusammenhängend eindrucksvolle Schauseiten gegenüber dem neu angelegten Max Josephplatz und dem dem öffentlichen Besuch freigegebenen Hofgarten zu gewinnen. Um dieses Ziel erreichen zu können, mußten zunächst einige bestehende Bauten niedergerissen werden; 1826 werden der Witwenstock an der Residenzstraße und der nach Süden anschließende Bibliotheksflügel, weiterhin von der Grünen Galerie das Südquerstück und Ende 1831 das ehemalige Treppenhaus, außerdem der Arkadenbau am Ostende des Großen Residenzgartens und wenige Jahre später die seit dem Brand von 1750 nur notdürftige wiederhergestellten Teile der Neuveste [die neue Feste] abgetragen. (S. 25)

C. The subjunctive is frequently used in conversation to soften requests. Here are some situations in which you might find yourself. Record polite comments you might make.

1. Sie wissen nicht, wieviel Uhr es ist. Der Polizist an der Ecke hat eine Armbanduhr.

2. Sie sitzen in einem Restaurant und wollen Frühstück bestellen. Hier kommt der Wirt.

3. Sie sind im Zug eingeschlafen. Sie wachen plötzlich auf, und Ihre Akten-

tasche ist verschwunden. Neben Ihnen sitzt ein älterer Herr, vielleicht ein Pfarrer.

4. Sie müssen aus Ihrer Studentenbude ausziehen, und Sie wollen einen Wagen oder einen Kleintransporter mieten. Aber Sie wissen nicht einmal, wieviel das kostet. Die Tankstelle beim Bahnhof soll Kraftfahrzeuge vermieten.

D. Translate into German, paying close attention to tenses and moods. Remember that the present subjunctive in English sounds like the past indicative.

1. My friend wrote me that he had visited every church and cathedral in Germany, but I didn't believe him.
2. She told him not to bother about it.
3. We asked the visitors whether they were hungry.
4. We know for sure that the world is round.
5. We didn't know whether she would visit us if she had the time.
6. Her younger brother said that he preferred to read books.
7. But she said that she took a long walk every day.
8. Sigurd thought that his car must have already been repaired.
9. They said they would answer the easy questions, but not the hard ones.
10. She asked me where I had seen the movie before.
11. They told me not to hurry.
12. The museum official asked us what we were interested in.
13. He said that it reminded him of old times.
14. The hotelkeeper said that he had sold a lot of beer because of the warm weather, and that he only had two bottles left.
15. She wrote us that she was recovering from a severe illness, but that she would soon be better.
16. Although the book might be very long and boring, I'll read it carefully.
17. Could you please tell me where the bus stops?
18. I would like a new coat for Christmas.
19. It would probably be better if you called them first.
20. Might you perhaps have the time?

Conditional Sentences

23

§81. CONDITIONAL SENTENCES WITH THE INDICATIVE

The indicative mood is used in both clauses of a conditional sentence, *provided nothing in the if-clause is contrary to fact.*

A. Wenn er Zeit **hat,** (so) **wird** er mich **besuchen.**
Hat er Zeit, so **wird** er mich **besuchen.**
Er **wird** mich **besuchen,** wenn er Zeit **hat.**
If he has time, he will visit me.
He will visit me if he has time.

B. Wenn es stark **regnet,** (so) **wird** er zu Hause **bleiben.**
Regnet es stark, so **wird** er zu Hause **bleiben.**
Er **wird** zu Hause **bleiben,** wenn es stark **regnet.**
If it rains hard, he will stay at home.
He will stay at home if it rains hard.

(1) The use of **so** (not to be translated but felt as a weak suppressed *then*) may introduce a main clause, provided an *if*-clause precedes; **so** is usually used if **wenn** is omitted in the preceding clause. **So** in such sentences serves to sum up the thought of a preceding clause. It is required in short sentences having the inverted word order in both main and dependent clauses, provided the meaning is not clear otherwise:

Muß er, so kommt er.
If he has to, he will come.

(2) **So** as connective is used chiefly after clauses of *condition* (see first sentences under **A** and **B** above) or *concession*:

Wenn er auch viel geleistet hat, so ist er doch nicht zufrieden.
Even though he has accomplished much, he is nevertheless not satisfied.

§82. CONTRARY-TO-FACT CONDITIONS

Conditions that are contrary to fact (i.e., not true) may refer both to the *present* and to the *past*.

A. Present contrary-to-fact conditions. In the sentences below, the *if*-clauses (the condition clauses) are contrary to fact; thus it follows that the *then*-clauses are incapable of fulfillment. In (1), for example, he does not have the money, so cannot give it away.

(1) Wenn er das Geld **hätte**, (so) **würde** er es mir **geben**.
Wenn er das Geld **hätte**, (so) **gäbe** er es mir.
Hätte er das Geld, so **würde** er es mir **geben**.
Hätte er das Geld, so **gäbe** er es mir.
If he had the money, he would give it to me.

(2) Wenn sie hier **wäre**, (so) **würde** sie ins Theater **gehen**.
Wenn sie hier **wäre**, (so) **ginge** sie ins Theater.
Wäre sie hier, so **würde** sie ins Theater **gehen**.
Wäre sie hier, so **ginge** sie ins Theater.
If she were here, she would go to the theater.

These *if*-clauses refer to present time, and both English and German use a present subjunctive verb; in English, this form is largely identical to the simple past indicative; German employs the Subjunctive II. Note that:

1. If a condition is contrary to fact in present time, the present Subjunctive II must be used in the *if*-clause.

2. In the same case, the main (*then-* or conclusion clause) may have its verb in either the present Subjunctive II or the present Conditional (this latter is much more common in everyday German).

B. Past contrary-to-fact conditions. Sentences expressing conditions contrary to fact in the past time use past Subjunctive II in the *if*-clause and either past Subjunctive II or, more commonly, past Conditional in the main clause.

(1) Wenn er das Geld **gehabt hätte,** (so) **hätte** er es mir **gegeben.**
Wenn er das Geld **gehabt hätte,** (so) **würde** er es mir **gegeben haben.**
Hätte er das Geld **gehabt,** so **hätte** er es mir **gegeben.**
Hätte er das Geld **gehabt,** so **würde** er es mir **gegeben haben.**
If he had had the money, he would have given it to me.

(2) Wenn sie hier **gewesen wäre,** (so) **wäre** sie ins Theater **gegangen.**
Wenn sie hier **gewesen wäre,** (so) **würde** sie ins Theater **gegangen sein.**
Wäre sie hier **gewesen,** so **wäre** sie ins Theater **gegangen.**
Wäre sie hier **gewesen,** so **würde** sie ins Theater **gegangen sein.**
If she had been here, she would have gone to the theater.

C. Mixed contrary-to-fact conditions.

Wenn Sie die Tür nicht **zugemacht hätten,** (so) **wäre** es jetzt nicht so warm im Zimmer.
If you had not closed the door, it would not be so warm in the room now.

The tenses of the two clauses in a contrary-to-fact condition do not always have to agree. Here, **zugemacht hätten** is past because it refers to the past, while **wäre,** speaking of the present, is present.

D. *Als ob* clauses with implied contrary-to-fact ideas. The Subjunctive II is often used in clauses introduced by **als ob.** If **als ob** is shortened to **als,** inverted word order is required.

(1) Sie kleidet sich, **als ob** sie reich **wäre.**
Sie kleidet sich, **als wäre** sie reich.
She dresses as if she were rich.

(2) Sie taten, **als ob** sie es nicht **verstanden hätten.**
Sie taten, **als hätten** sie es nicht **verstanden.**
They acted as if they had not understood it.

E. *Hätte können* and *hätte sollen* indicating past contrary-to-fact conditions and conclusions. Constructions with *could have* and *should have* plus the past participle in English are rendered with the past subjunctive plus dependent infinitive in German. Since the past participles of modals look like infinitives also, the so-called "double infinitive construction" results. See also §83, note 5, §87A(6), and §86D(8).

Er **hätte** es **tun können,** wenn er die Zeit dazu gehabt hätte.
*He **could have done** it if he had had the time for it.*

Ich **hätte** eigentlich nach Hause **gehen sollen.**
*I really **should have gone** home.*

Wenn sie es **hätte tun können,** würde sie es mir gesagt haben.
*If she **could have done** it, she would have told me so.*

E X E R C I S E S

A. Complete the following sentences by supplying the proper forms of the verbs suggested in parentheses.

1. Wenn er _____ (*kommen*), werden wir ihn freundlich empfangen.

2. Wenn der Arzt hier _____ (*sein*), hätten wir ihn nicht anrufen müssen.

3. Wenn das Wetter schön _____ (*sein*), werde ich eine Wanderung durch den Wald machen.

4. Er hätte das Flugzeug gemietet, wenn er genug Geld dafür _____ (*haben*).

5. Wenn sie früher einfacher _____ (*leben*), wäre sie jetzt reicher als sie ist.

6. Wenn die Preise dort nicht so hoch wären, _____ er den Rheinwein _____ (*bestellen*).

7. Ich _____ dorthin _____ (*fahren*), wenn es nicht so weit wäre.

8. Wenn es nicht geregnet hätte, _____ ich nicht so lange zu Hause _____ (*bleiben*).

9. Wäre er da gewesen, so _____ er das _____ (*wissen*).

10. Wäre ich ein Vogel, so _____ ich aus diesem Gefängnis _____ (*fliegen*).

11. Ich würde den Arzt nicht kommen lassen, wenn ich gesund _____ (*sein*).

12. Wenn er _____ _____ (*kommen*), hätte ich ihn bestimmt gesehen.

13. Ich _____ meinen alten Freund _____ (*besuchen*), wenn er hier in Dortmund wäre.

14. _____ (*Haben*) wir Raum und Zeit genug, müßten wir uns nicht beeilen.

15. Sie tut, als ob sie es nicht _____ (*hören*).

B. Complete the sentences by supplying the German forms for the verbs in parentheses. Some blanks need more than one verb.

1. Mein Kollege _____ die Hand in die Tasche _____ (*could have stuck*).

2. Sie hatte die Führerscheinprüfung schon einmal fast bestanden, und sie _____ das zweite Mal keine Fehler _____ (*should have made*).

3. Wir wußten nicht, daß du uns besuchen wolltest. Wir _____ zu Hause _____ (*should have stayed*).

4. Du _____ bessere Fotos von der Familie _____ (*could have sent*).

5. Ihr _____ das Fenster nicht _____ (*should have broken*).

6. Wenn du den Kaffee feiner _____ (*could have ground*), hätte er uns besser geschmeckt.

7. Wenn wir das Liederbuch von Biermann in Berlin _____ (*could have bought*), hätten wir es euch geschenkt.

8. Sie sah dann aus, als _____ sie es nicht _____ (*had understood*).

C. We frequently use single subjunctive clauses to react to a situation, either expressing an obviously unfulfillable condition or a clearly unreal conclusion. Many situations invite both kinds of reactions. Follow the example.

0. Der neue Porsche kostet zweihunderttausend Mark.
   —*Wenn ich nur genug Geld hätte!*
   —*Ich würde sowieso nie soviel Geld für ein Auto verschwenden.*

1. Der Rockstar da drüben scheint Hunger zu haben.

2. Nur Eltern dürfen Eintrittskarten für ihre Kinder kaufen.

3. Das Wasser in Wiesbaden soll gut für die Gesundheit sein.

4. Jeder dritte Besucher des Tierparks bekommt ein freies Foto mit dem Löwen, dem König der Tiere!

5. Alle, die am letzten Tage des Semesters einen roten Pullover trugen, bekamen eine Einladung zum Fest.

D. Translate the following sentences into German. Be very careful to keep your tenses and moods straight.

1. If I had phoned him, he would have met me at the station.

2. I will only change my shirt if I have the time.

3. If the movie were interesting, he would have recommended it to us.

4. If it hadn't rained, my father could have worked in his garden.

5. If it does not snow tonight, we will not be able to go skiing tomorrow.

6. If I don't find her new address I won't be able to visit her.

7. If we had had a larger family, we would have bought that big house in the capital.

8. She would speak German better if she had conversed with more German students during the trip.

9. If the train had been punctual, we would not have arrived so late.

10. You should have visited us last summer. The weather was much better.

11. If I had only known that!

12. I could have rented a more expensive apartment.

13. If she only played golf!

14. They look as if they're really sleepy.

15. You shouldn't have worried so much about that.

16. My customers acted as if they hadn't understood the offer.

17. And then you ate as if you hadn't eaten anything at all since Monday.

18. We really should have found ourselves a bigger hotel room.

19. My mother would have lent me the money if she had earned more last year.

20. If you had sold more paintings in your youth, you would be much better known now.

21. If Heidi only had more patience!

22. I would have thanked you if you had helped me.

23. If I have a toothache I go to the dentist.

24. If I had difficulties with my assignment, I would ask my classmate for help.

25. If she had only paid attention, her notebook would be more complete.

Modal Auxiliaries and the Dependent Infinitive

24

The "modal-plus-infinitive" construction is arguably the most productive verb format in German. In it, the topic comes first as usual, and the lexical (meaningful) verb comes last as the ultimate comment on the topic. The finite verb, meanwhile, provides an attitude against which the whole is understood—a way or mode of understanding, hence "modal" auxiliary.

§83. THE MODALS WITH AND WITHOUT A DEPENDENT INFINITIVE

The six modal auxiliaries are:

können, konnte, hat gekonnt, sie kann	*to be able, can, could, etc.*
müssen, mußte, hat gemußt, er muß	*to have to, must, etc.*
dürfen, durfte, hat gedurft, es darf	*to be allowed*
mögen, mochte, hat gemocht, er mag	*to like to, care for*
wollen, wollte, hat gewollt, sie will	*to want, desire*
sollen, sollte, hat gesollt, es soll	*to be (required) to*

The development of the modals in German has yet to be completely explained. At an older stage, strong verbs in German had different roots for the singular and plural in the past. The past tense of these verbs came to be used as presents. Then a new past, analogous to the weak verb past, was derived.

Sometime later a past participle identical to the infinitive came into use (perhaps on the model of **lassen, ließ, lassen**—the **ge-** prefix was not always added in the older language). And finally another past participle, a projection of the new simple past form, was devised.

This brief survey explains away much of the anomalous nature of the modals. Their important features are:

1. The present singular and the present plural (except **sollen**) have different roots; and the present singular is inflected like the simple past of strong verbs.

2. The modals have two past participles:

   (*a*) The weak form (e.g., **gekonnt**) is employed when there is no dependent infinitive.

   (*b*) The form similar to the infinitive (e.g., **können**) appears in conjunction with a dependent infinitive; its similarity to the present infinitive is reflected in the term *double infinitive*.

   Several other verbs (e.g., **lassen, sehen, hören**) share this characteristic with the modals (see §84).

3. Whereas English modals are defective, German modals have acquired complete paradigms over the years. This results in problems of translation: **Ich muß gehen** = *I must go.* But: **Ich mußte gehen** = *I had to go.* **Ich kann schreiben** = *I can write.* But: **Ich hatte schreiben können** = *I had been able to write.*

The following sentences illustrate the use of the modals absolutely (in column **A**) and with dependent infinitives (in column **B**).

A. *Modals without an infinitive:*	**B.** *Modals with an infinitive:*
(1) **können:**	(1) **können:**
Er kann es.	Er kann es tun.
He can.	*He can do it.*
Er konnte es.	Er konnte es tun.
He could.	*He could do it.*
Er hat es **gekonnt.**	Er hat es tun **können.**
He has been able to.	*He has been able to do it.*
Er hatte es **gekonnt.**	Er hatte es tun **können.**
He had been able to.	*He had been able to do it.*
Er wird es können.	Er wird es tun können.
He will be able to.	*He will be able to do it.*
Er wird es **gekonnt** haben.	Er wird es haben tun **können.**
He will have been able to.	*He will have been able to do it.*

(2) **müssen:**

Wir müssen es.
We must.

Wir mußten es.
We had to.

Wir haben es **gemußt.**
We have had to.

Wir hatten es **gemußt.**
We had had (or been obliged) to.

Wir werden es müssen.
We shall have to.

Wir werden es **gemußt** haben.
We shall have had (or been obliged) to.

(3) **dürfen:**

Er darf es.
He may.

Er hat es **gedurft.**
He has been allowed to.

(4) **mögen:**

Er mag es.
He likes to.

Er hat es **gemocht.**
He has liked to.

(5) **wollen:**

Ich will es.
I want to.

Ich habe es **gewollt.**
I have wanted to.

(6) **sollen:**

Ich soll es.
I am supposed to.

Ich habe es **gesollt.**
I have been required (or called upon) to.

(2) **müssen:**

Wir müssen es tun.
We must do it.

Wir mußten es tun.
We had to do it.

Wir haben es tun **müssen.**
We have had to do it.

Wir hatten es tun **müssen.**
We had had (or been obliged) to do it.

Wir werden es tun müssen.
We shall have to do it.

Wir werden es haben tun **müssen.**
We shall have had (or been obliged) to do it.

(3) **dürfen:**

Er darf es tun.
He may do it.

Er hat es tun **dürfen.**
He has been allowed to do it.

(4) **mögen:**

Er mag es tun.
He likes to do it.

Er hat es tun **mögen.**
He has liked to do it.

(5) **wollen:**

Ich will es tun.
I want to do it.

Ich habe es tun **wollen.**
I have wanted to do it.

(6) **sollen:**

Ich soll es tun.
I am supposed to do it.

Ich habe es tun **sollen.**
I have been required (or called upon) to do it.

From the foregoing it may be observed that:

1. All modal auxiliaries are conjugated with **haben.**

2. As independent transitive verbs, German modals may take their own direct objects.

3. Contrary to English usage, German may retain a direct object (particularly **es** or **das**) with a modal used as an independent transitive verb.

Kann er das beweisen?   Er kann **es.** (or: **Das** kann er.)
Can he prove that?   *He can.*

Here **es** and **das** are direct objects of the verb **beweisen,** which is understood.

4. Modal auxiliaries take dependent infinitives without the infinitive marker **zu.**

5. When used with a dependent infinitive the weak past participles (**gekonnt,** etc.) are replaced by the strong forms (**können,** etc.). The past participle comes at the end of the clause, directly *preceded by the dependent infinitive.*

6. In the future perfect tense, the auxiliary **haben** precedes the double infinitive. Similarly, in a subordinate clause, the auxiliary is displaced from final position by the double infinitive:

Er glaubte, daß er die Hausarbeit nicht hätte schreiben müssen.
He believed that he hadn't been obliged to do the homework.

§84. DOUBLE INFINITIVE CONSTRUCTION WITH VERBS OTHER THAN MODALS

The sentences below illustrate some of the more common verbs which, like modal auxiliaries, take dependent infinitives without **zu** and which may be used in double infinitive constructions.

A. lassen:

(1) Er läßt den Arzt holen.   Er hat den Arzt holen **lassen.**
He sends for the doctor.   *He sent for the doctor.*

(2) Ich lasse mir das Haar schneiden.
I am having my hair cut.

Ich habe mir das Haar schneiden **lassen.**
I had my hair cut.

(3) Sie läßt sich ein neues Kleid machen.
She is having a new dress made.

Sie hat sich ein neues Kleid machen **lassen.**
She had a new dress made.

B. sehen:

Ich sehe ihn kommen.   Ich habe ihn kommen **sehen.**
I see him coming.   *I saw him coming.*

C. heißen:

Er heißt mich gehen.   Er hat mich gehen **heißen.**
He orders me to go.   *He ordered me to go.*

D. helfen:

Ich helfe das Geschäft begründen.
I am helping to establish the business.

Ich habe das Geschäft begründen **helfen.**
Ich habe geholfen, das Geschaft zu begründen.
I helped to establish the business.

E. hören:

Hören Sie die Dame singen?
Do you hear the lady singing?

Haben Sie die Dame singen **hören?**
Did you hear the lady sing?

F. lernen:

Er lernt fliegen.
He is learning to fly.

Ich habe ihn gestern kennen**gelernt** (or kennen**lernen**)
I made his acquaintance yesterday.

G. lehren:

Ich lehre ihn schreiben.
I am teaching him to write.

Ich habe ihn schreiben **lehren** (or **gelehrt**).
I taught him to write.

§85. VERBS OTHER THAN MODALS WHICH APPEAR TO TAKE A DEPENDENT INFINITIVE WITHOUT *ZU*

The sentences below illustrate verbs which appear to take a dependent infinitive without the infinitive marker **zu**. In fact, the complement is not an infinitive but rather a separable prefix. Other examples are **einkaufen•gehen** and **kennen•lernen.** Since the prefix resides in the verbal complement position and was originally a verb, it looks like an infinitive.

A.　(1) **gehen:**

Er **geht** spazieren.
He goes for a walk.

(2) **reiten** (or **fahren**):

Wir **reiten** (or **fahren**) spazieren.
We are going riding (or *for a drive*).

B.　(1) **stehenbleiben:**

Sie **bleibt** stehen.
She stops.

Sie **blieb** stehen.
She stopped.

(2) **sich schlafen legen:**

Er **legt sich** schlafen.
He lies down to sleep.

After a verb of motion German sometimes employs the *past participle* (instead of the present infinitive as in the above sentences) *with present sense,* where the English idiom requires the present participle:

Er kam **gelaufen.**
*He came **running.***

Sie kommt **gesprungen.**
*She comes **jumping** along.*

§86. MODAL AUXILIARIES WITH PASSIVE FORMS

Modal auxiliaries have no passive voice, but may be followed by a *passive infinitive.*

Das kann **gemacht werden.**
That can be done.

Eine Brücke soll **gebaut werden.**
A bridge is to be built.

Das muß **gesagt werden.**
That must be said.

Das Radarsignal konnte sofort **identifiziert werden.**
The radar signal could be identified at once.

An alternative construction with the active infinitive would be:

Man muß das sagen.
That must be said.

Cannot be is often rendered by **sein** followed by **nicht zu** and an active infinitive:

Es **ist nicht zu** leugnen.
*It **cannot be** denied.*

Er **ist** telefonisch **nicht zu** erreichen.
*He **cannot be** reached by telephone.*

§87. IDIOMATIC USES OF MODAL AUXILIARIES

The idiomatic uses of modal auxiliaries are illustrated in **A–F.** Some of the literal meanings of modals have been included for comparison. It is important to study the explanatory notes following each section.

A. sollen:

(1) Was **soll** ich tun?
*What **am** I **to** (or **shall** I) do?*

(2) Sie **sollen** arbeiten.
*You **are supposed to** work.*

(3) Sie **sollten** arbeiten.
*You **should** (or **ought to**) work.*

(4) Er **soll** sehr arm sein.
*He **is said** to be very poor.*

(5) Du **sollst** nicht stehlen.
*Thou **shalt** not steal.*

(6) Er **hätte** zu Hause **bleiben sollen.**
*He **should have stayed** at home.*

Note:

(a) **Sollen** may not be used for English *shall* to denote future time; **werden** is the auxiliary for the future in German.

(b) English *should* (or *ought to*) is rendered by the present Subjunctive II of **sollen,** denoting unaccomplished possibility.

(c) The past indicative, identical in form to the present Subjunctive II, may be illustrated by such a sentence as:

Gestern **sollte** ich abfahren, aber leider mußte ich in der Stadt bleiben.
*Yesterday I **was** (supposed) **to** leave, but unfortunately I had to stay in the city.*

B. wollen:

(1) Er **will** morgen abfahren.
   *He **intends** to leave tomorrow.*

(2) Er **will** es getan haben.
   *He **claims** to have done it.*

(3) Sie **will** einen reichen Onkel haben.
   *She **professes** to have a rich uncle.*

(4) Was **wollen** Sie damit **sagen**?
   *What do you **mean** by that?*

(5) **Wir wollen** (or **Wollen wir**) nicht mehr davon **sprechen**.
   ***Let's** not **talk** any more about it.*

(6) **Wollen Sie** Tee oder Kaffee?
   ***Will you take** tea or coffee?*

Note:

(*a*) German **will** is not to be used for English *will* to denote future time.

(*b*) **Wollen,** in present Subjunctive I but with normal word order permitted, is commonly used in conversation with the force of an imperative (see sentence 5 above).

C. mögen:

(1) Er **mag** das Essen nicht.
   *He does not **like** the food* (or *meal*).

(2) Das **mag** (*or* kann) sein.
   *That **may** be.*

(3) Er **möchte** (gern) ins Theater gehen.
   *He **would like** to go to the theater.*

(4) **Möchten Sie** mit?
   ***Would you like** to go along?*

(5) Er **mochte wohl** dreißig Jahre alt sein.
   *He **was probably** thirty years old.*

(6) Das Buch **mag** auch noch so schwer sein, er wird es lesen.
   Mag das Buch auch noch so schwer sein, er wird es lesen.
   Although the book be ever so difficult, he will read it.

(7) **Möge** Gott dir helfen!
   ***May** God help you.*

Note:

(*a*) English *would* (or *should*) *like* is commonly rendered by the present Subjunctive II of **mögen.**

(*b*) **Mögen** is frequently used to express *probability* (sentence 5) and *concession* (sentence 6).

D. können:

(1) Letzten Monat **konnte** ich ihn nicht besuchen.
   *I **could** not (i.e., was unable to) visit him last month.*

(2) Ich **könnte** ihn jetzt besuchen, wenn ich Zeit **hätte.**
   *I **could** (i.e., would be able to) visit him now if I had time.*

(3) Er **kann** nichts dafür.   Was **kann** ich dafür?
   It is not his fault.   *How can I help it?*
   He can't help it.

(4) Ich **konnte nicht umhin,** ihm die Wahrheit zu sagen.
   *I **couldn't help** telling him the truth.*

(5) Er **kann** Deutsch.
   *He **knows** German.*

The obvious complementary infinitive is left out here, creating the false impression that **können** means *to know.* A similar instance of deleting the obvious complement is in **ich muß nach Berlin,** where the verb of motion implied by the preposition **nach** is left out.

(6) Das **kann** (or mag) sein.
   *That **may** be.*

(7) Es **könnte** nützlich sein.
   *It **might** be useful.*

(8) Sie **hätten** ein deutsches Buch lesen **können.**
   *You **could have** read a German book.*

Note:

(*a*) If English *could* is the equivalent of *was able,* it is rendered by the past indicative **konnte.** If it is the equivalent of *should be able* or *would be able,* it is rendered by the present Subjunctive II **könnte.**

(*b*) Such a sentence as *He could have written it* must *not* be translated by: **Er könnte es geschrieben haben** (i.e., *It might be that he wrote it*). Rather use: **Er hätte es schreiben können.**

(*c*) The phrase **nicht umhin können** takes a dependent infinitive with **zu** (see example 4).

E. dürfen:

(1) Das **dürfen** Sie **nicht** tun.
   *You **must not** do that.*

(2) **Dürfte** ich Sie um das Buch bitten?
Might I ask you for the book?

Darf ich Sie um das Brot bitten?
May I ask you for the bread?

(3) Es **dürfte** (*or* könnte) sein.
It might (possibly) be.

(4) Er **durfte** es tun.
He was allowed to do it.

(5) Sie **dürften** ihn mißverstanden haben.
You may possibly have misunderstood him.

Note:

Used negatively, **dürfen** is far more forceful than **müssen**. In common usage, **nicht dürfen** is the opposite of **müssen**, and **nicht müssen** simply means that one is *not obliged to* do something.

F. müssen:

(1) Ich **muß** gleich an die Arbeit (gehen).
I must go to work at once.

(2) Er **mußte** die Miete bezahlen.
He had to pay the rent.

(3) Wir **haben** es tun müssen.
We were compelled to do it.

(4) Er **hatte** es tun müssen.
He had been obliged to do it.

(5) Er **hätte** es tun müssen.
He would have been obliged to do it.

(6) Er **muß** es **getan haben.**
He must have done it.

Note:

(a) When the inference is that the action implied in a sentence took place, **muß** with the past infinitive is required.

(b) *Not to have to* in the sense of *not to need to* is rendered by **brauchen** with **nicht zu** and a dependent infinitive:

Ich **brauche** es **nicht zu** tun.
I don't have (i.e., *need*) *to do it.*

In conversational German, **brauchen** often appears with a dependent infinitive without the marker **zu:**

Du brauchst nicht gehen.
You don't have to go.

E X E R C I S E S

A. After each sentence below are two parenthetical notes. The first is a modal concept you are to add to the sentence. The second is a tense. It would be best to do each sentence twice, once in the present and once in the tense stipulated. An example is provided.

0. Ich arbeite den ganzen Tag. (obligation) (simple past)
   —*Ich muß den ganzen Tag arbeiten.*
   —*Ich mußte den ganzen Tag arbeiten.*

1. Ich lese das ganze Buch. (obligation) (simple past)

2. Das Kind spielt nicht auf der Straße. (permission) (simple past)

3. Uwe schläft im Hotel *Zum Adler.* (wish) (future)

4. Der Botschafter spricht gutes Deutsch. (supposition) (simple past)

5. Sie hört die Vögel singen. (ability) (simple past)

6. Wir gehen gleich an die Arbeit. (obligation) (compound past)

7. Ich leiste es mir nicht. (ability) (future perfect)

8. Die Studentin mietet sich einen VW-Pritschenwagen. (wish) (past perfect, add *schon*)

9. Sie lädt mich zum Fest ein. (permission) (compound past)

10. Sie arbeiten bis in die Nacht. (supposition) (compound past)

11. Die Taxifahrerin verdient täglich zweihundert Dollar. (wish) (future)

12. Der große Hund übernachtet nicht im Hotel. (permission) (compound past)

13. Jede Schülerin lernt Mathematik. (ability) (future)

14. Du bist sehr müde. (obligation) (simple past)

15. Ariadne schenkt dem Fremden etwas Wein ein. (supposition) (compound past)

B. Following each sentence below are an auxiliary, or another verb, and a tense. As above, it is best to do these in two stages. See the example.

0. Er fährt den ganzen Tag. (müssen) (simple past)
   —*Er muß den ganzen Tag fahren.*
   —*Er mußte den ganzen Tag fahren.*

1. Die Krankenschwester holt den Arzt. (lassen) (simple past)

2. Er kommt. (ich sehe) (simple past)

3. Die Maus kriecht unter die Badewanne. (er hört) (compound past)

4. Man ißt vor der Reise. (brauchen) (simple past)

5. Der König macht sich einen wunderschönen Mantel. (lassen) (future)

6. Der bekannte Tenor singt. (wir hören) (past perfect, add *schon*)

7. Beckenbauer spielt Fußball in New York. (siehst du?) (compound past)

8. Wir bestellen das Wiener Schnitzel mit Salat. (wollen) (compound past)

9. Der Bundeskanzler besucht den amerikanischen Präsidenten. (Ursula sieht) (future)

10. Das Motorrad startet beim zweiten Versuch. (ich höre) (simple past)

C. Rewrite the following sentences with **hätte. . .können** and **hätte. . . sollen,** and translate the results into English. A model is provided.

0. Er geht aufs Land.
   —*Er hätte aufs Land gehen können.*
   He could have gone to the country.
   —*Er hätte aufs Land gehen sollen.*
   He should have gone to the country.

1. Der pensionierte Lehrer macht eine lange Reise.

2. Fritz steht früher als sein Bruder Max auf.

3. Alois liest immer die Heiratsanzeigen in der Zeitung.

4. Sie lernt den neuen Kollegen kennen.

5. Wir gehen im Supermarkt einkaufen.

D. Continue the observations started below with a sentence using a modal auxiliary complemented by a present or past passive infinitive (see §108E). You will need to add characters. Follow the example.

0. Die Gäste sind schon da und der Kaffee ist noch nicht gekocht.
   —*Er muß sofort gekocht werden.*

1. Ich spiele Gitarre und du spielst Banjo. Aber wer spielt die Baßgeige?

2. Die alte Hexe hält einen giftigen Apfel bereit. Wer soll ihn denn essen?

3. Nun, du trägst die Einkaufstasche, ich trage die Aktenmappe, Bärbel trägt die Blumen und den Wein. Der Koffer ist uns zu schwer. Wer trägt denn ihn?

4. Gestern ließ ich die Tür auf, damit die Katze frei hinein- und herauslaufen durfte. Jetzt aber bleibt die Katze im Zimmer und kann nicht heraus. Was ist geschehen?

5. Letzte Woche ging der Wagen nicht, und ich brachte ihn in die Werkstätte. Jetzt geht er sehr gut. Was ist geschehen?

E. Translate into German.

1. We had to go to school, but Ingrid couldn't go to school with us.

2. Mother said that Ingrid ought to stay at home.

3. She should have stayed home yesterday too.

4. It's good that you know German, since you have to go to Berlin.

5. Jakob and Wilhelm were afraid of elephants and never wanted to go to the zoo.

6. We could have gone home on the last train, and now it's too late.

7. Might I ask you for a plan of the city?

8. She was on the point of calling me up when the phone rang.

9. She claims to have seen him at the movies.

10. The ambassador is said to be very rich.

11. You should have seen his official car.

12. Yesterday I could go. Today I could go if I had the time.

13. I don't like eggs for breakfast.

14. If he could have done it, he would have written me.

15. You shouldn't smoke so much.

16. She says that she intends to go to Darmstadt today. That may well be.

17. Why can't you understand these simple announcements?

18. You look very modern. When did you have your hair cut?

19. What are we to do this afternoon?

20. Is anyone sick? Why did you send for the doctor?

21. Then we heard the birds singing in the forest.

22. Brecht wished that people (*use* **man**) were allowed to smoke in the theater.

23. Would you like tea or coffee with the cake?

24. They would have been obliged to buy three tickets instead of two, if you were older.

25. That might be dangerous.

25

Idioms
and
Other Collocations

§88. GERMAN IDIOMS
AND THEIR ENGLISH EQUIVALENTS

Those whose job it is to describe languages start by trying to reduce as much as possible of the target language to a dictionary and a set of grammatical rules. The learner should be able to create sentences simply by combining the words in the dictionary according to the rules of the grammar.

Almost at once, however, collocations are encountered. Certain words require certain other words, frequently prepositions, before they can be combined to make a sentence. These collocations, or word clusters, defy literal translation into another language. Most desk-sized dictionaries draw attention to them in usage notes, as (for example) under **denken:**

> *an einen* or *an eine S. -en,* remember (*or* think
> of) a p. *or* a th., call a p. *or* a th. to mind.

That is, *to think of or about a person or a thing* requires that **denken** be followed by the preposition **an,** which in turn requires the accusative case in this particular usage. The first 85 idioms in the list below are really collocations more often than not. Many have appeared elsewhere in this grammar, and should be familiar to you.

Beyond collocations are true idioms, in which the literal meaning of the words yields to a transferred, metaphorical, or allusive sense. The origin of the transferred meaning is often obscure. A technology may become obsolete, for example, leaving idioms based on it without a context. The remaining few idioms in the list are of this sort, chosen from many hundreds to show the range of possibilities.

1. Sie denkt an ihn. *She thinks of him.*

2. Wir warten auf den Bus. *We wait for the bus.*

3. Seid ihr stolz auf die Tochter? *Are you proud of your daughter?*

4. Er geht in die Schule. *He goes to school.*

5. Er ist in der Schule. *He is in school.*

6. Nach der Schule geht sie skilaufen. *After school she goes skiing.*

7. Hat er recht oder unrecht? *Is he right or wrong?*

8. Wie geht es dir? *How are you?*

9. (a) Ich lese gern. *I like to read.*
   (b) Ich habe es gern. *I like it.*

10. (a) Sie liest lieber. *She prefers to read.*
    (b) Sie hat es lieber. *She prefers it.*

11. (a) Wir lesen am liebsten. *We like to read best.*
    (b) Wir haben es am liebsten. *We like it best.*

12. Er ist auf dem Land. *He's in the country.*

13. Er geht aufs Land. *He's going to the country.*

14. Wir sind zu Hause. *We're home.*

15. Sie gehen nach Hause. *They're going home.*

16. Es wird immer heißer. *It's getting hotter and hotter.*

17. Was fehlt dir? *What's the matter with you?*

18. Es tut mir leid. *I'm sorry.*

19. Sie bittet mich um meine Eintrittskarte. *She asks me for my ticket.*

20. Je öfter ich den Film sehe, desto trauriger finde ich ihn. *The more often I see that film, the sadder I find it.*

21. Er pfiff vor sich [*acc. refl.*] hin. *He whistled to himself.*

22. Er kommt, nicht wahr? *He's coming, isn't he?*

23. Mein Ellenbogen tut mir weh. *My elbow hurts.*

24. Das geht Sie nichts an. *That doesn't concern you.*

25. Erinnerst du dich an unsre erste Tanzstunde? *Do you remember our first dancing class?*

26. Sie hat ein Paar Schuhe. *She has a pair of shoes.*

27. Sie hat ein paar Weingläser. *She has several wine glasses.*

28. Gib mir noch ein Buch! *Give me another [i.e., an additional] book.*

29. Gib mir ein anderes Buch! *Give me another [i.e., a different] book.*

30. Frau O. soll sehr reich sein.   *Mrs. O. is said to be very rich.*

31. Sie denkt sich [*dat. refl.*] das.   *She imagines that.*

32. Ich bin es endlich los.   *I'm finally rid of it.*

33. Kümmern Sie sich nicht um ihn!   *Don't worry about him.*

34. Ich fürchte mich nicht vor dem Löwen.   *I'm not afraid of the lion.*

35. Er ist toll vor Schmerz.   *He's frantic with pain.*

36. Sie ist außer sich vor Zorn.   *She's beside herself with anger.*

37. Alfred ging auf und ab.   *Alfred walked up and down.*

38. Fahren Sie mit dem Wagen oder mit dem Motorrad?   *Are you going by car or motorcycle?*

39. Heute über acht Tage wird er kommen.   *He'll come a week from today.*

40. Nimm dich in acht!   *Be careful. Take care.*

41. Es geschah vor acht Tagen.   *It happened a week ago.*

42. Ich freue mich auf den Besuch.   *I'm looking forward to the visit.*

43. Ich freue mich über deinen Erfolg.   *I'm happy about your success.*

44. Es kommt darauf an.   *That depends.*

45. Um so besser.   *All the better. So much the better.*

46. Sie wohnt bei mir.   *She lives at my house.*

47. Er hat kein Geld bei sich [*dat. refl.*].   *He has no money on him.*

48. Jemand klopft an die Tür.   *Someone knocks at the door.*

49. Ich wollte gerade gehen.   *I was just about to go.*

50. Er tat es auf diese Weise.   *He did it this way.*

51. Eine Türklinke besteht aus zwei Teilen.   *A doorknob consists of two parts.*

52. Man machte ihn zum Torwart.   *They made him goalie.*

53. Man gewöhnt sich an alles.   *You get used to everything.*

54. Es macht ihr Freude.   *It gives her pleasure.*

55. Sie lachten ihn aus.   *They laughed at him.*

56. Sie verliebte sich in den Jungen.   *She fell in love with the boy.*

57. Er antwortet auf meine Frage.   *He answers my question.*

58. Was wird aus ihr werden?   *What will become of her?*

59. (a) Ich bin es. Ich bin's.   *It's me.*
    (b) Ist er es?   *Is it him?*   Er ist es. Er ist's.   *It's him.*

60. Der wievielte ist heute?   *What's the date today?*

61. Um wieviel Uhr kommt er?   *What time is he coming?*

62. Es geschieht ihm recht.   *It serves him right.*

63. Ich bin an der Reihe. Ich bin dran.   *It's my turn.*

64. Auf einmal begann es zu regnen.   *Suddenly it began to rain.*

65. Nicht einmal der Lehrer versteht alles.   *Not even the teacher understands everything.*

66. Diese Uhr geht vor, und jene Uhr geht nach.   *This clock is fast and that clock is slow.*

67. Das macht nichts aus.   *That doesn't matter.*

68. Er geht auf einen Monat aufs Land.   *He goes to the country for a month.*

69. Was iβt du zum Frühstück?   *What do you eat for breakfast?*

70. Hagen sieht zum Fenster hinaus.   *Hagen looks out the window.*

71. Du gehst an dem Hotel vorbei.   *You walk past the hotel.*

72. Er steckt (sich) die Hand in die Tasche.   *He puts his hand in his pocket.*

73. Sie ist Studentin auf der Universität.   *She's a student at the university.*

74. Sie ist Professorin an der Universität.   *She's a professor at the university.*

75. Es ist nicht der Mühe wert. Es ist nicht der Rede Wert.   *It's not worth the trouble. It's not worth mentioning.*

76. Ich bin derselben Meinung [*gen.*].   *I'm of the same opinion.*

77. Sie fährt lieber erster Klasse.   *She prefers to travel first class.*

78. Seien Sie gegen jeden Menschen freundlich!   *Be friendly to every person.*

79. Süditalien ist arm an Wäldern.   *Southern Italy has few forests.*

80. Köln soll durch den Dom berühmt sein.   *Cologne is said to be famous for its cathedral.*

81. Sie wird den Brief auf die Post bringen.   *She'll mail the letter.*

82. Auf beiden Augen ist die Kuh blind.   *The cow is blind in both eyes.*

83. (a) Das schmeckt nach saurer Milch.   *That tastes of sour milk.*
    (b) Das riecht nach Kühen.   *That smells of cows.*

84. Er wird es nicht tun, es sei denn, daβ sie ihn darum bitten.   *He won't do it unless they ask him to.*

85. Wir besuchen entweder die Kirche oder das Schloβ. Dieses ist in der Nähe, während jene in der Nachbarstadt ist.   *We'll visit either the church or the castle. The latter is nearby, while the former is in the next town.*

86. Auf dem Weg nach Prag machte Mozart einen Abstecher durch den Wald.   *On the way to Prague Mozart made a detour* [an "offshoot"] *through the forest.*

87. Als ich die Musik endlich richtig spielte, machte sie groβe Augen.   *When I finally played the music right, she was very surprised.*

88. Wir sind nicht im Bilde.   *We're not in the picture. We don't know what's going on.*

89. Los, Kinder! Ich halte euch [*dat.*] den Daumen.   *Off you go, kids! I wish you good luck. (I'll cross my fingers for you.)*

90. Ich muß mit dem Polizisten deutsch reden.   *I'll have to speak quite candidly with the policeman.*

91. Ich brachte den Aufsatz erst um halb drei unter Dach und Fach.   *I only finished the essay at two-thirty.*

92. Deine Fragen brachten mich aus der Fassung.   *Your questions made me lose my composure.*

93. Ich bin schon fix und fertig.   *I'm all set.* or: *I'm pooped.*

94. Der Berg ist mir zu hoch. Ich bin nicht in Form.   *The mountain is too high for me. I'm not in shape.*

95. Das läßt sich machen.   *It's possible. It can be done.*

96. Das Radio ist zu laut; ich habe die Nase voll davon.   *The radio is too loud; I'm fed up with it.*

97. Das kommt nicht in Frage.   *No. Not a chance.*

98. Er dachte an das Gefängnis und bekam kalte Füße.   *He thought about jail and got cold feet. He chickened out.*

99. Das Kind schrie furchtbar laut, aber die Mutter hatte sich in der Gewalt.   *The child screamed terrifically loudly, but mother had herself under control.*

100. Um Gottes willen!   *For God's sake.*

101. Irgendwo muß man eine Grenze ziehen.   *You've got to draw the line somewhere.*

102. Hals- und Beinbruch!   *Good luck! Break a leg!*

103. Du liegst mir am Herzen.   *You're very important and dear to me.*

104. Um dich zu sehen, werde ich Himmel und Hölle in Bewegung setzen.   *To see you I'll move heaven and earth.*

105. Vorsicht, daß du die Katze nicht aus dem Sack läßt.   *Be careful not to let the cat out of the bag. Be discreet.*

106. Ich weiß nicht, ob es klappt oder nicht.   *I don't know whether it'll work or not.*

107. Sie hatte einen Krach mit ihrem Chef.   *She had a fight.* [lit. *a crash, a noisy din*] *with her boss.*

108. Komm schnell her, sonst kriegst du was!   *Come here at once, or you'll get it!*

109. Du gehst mir auf die Nerven.   *You get on my nerves.*

110. Ich arbeitete im Garten wie ein Pferd.   *I worked like a dog in the garden.*

111. Jetzt kaufe ich dir ein Bier, und dann sind wir miteinander quitt.   *Now I'll buy you a beer, and then we're quits.*

112. Wir sind in eine Sackgasse geraten.   *We're up the creek.* [lit. *We're caught in a blind alley.*]

113. Warum hast du die Deutschstunde geschwänzt? *Why did you cut German class?*

114. Du hast mit deiner Frage wirklich ins Schwarze getroffen. *Your question really hit the bull's eye.*

115. Halt den Mund! Halt die Schnauze! *Shut up!*

116. Schon wieder meinen Geburtstag vergessen? Du hast ein Gedächtnis wie ein Sieb. *You forgot my birthday again? You have a memory like a sieve.*

117. Warum habt ihr mich im Stich gelassen? *Why did you leave me in the lurch?*

118. Sie ist total verrückt nach ihm. *She's totally crazy about him.*

119. Das sage ich dir unter vier Augen. *I'm telling you this in strictest confidence.*

120. Mir ist das alles Wurst. *I couldn't care less.*

E X E R C I S E S

The only way to learn idioms is to practice them in plausible contexts. Here are some questions which could be answered using idioms from the list above, and in parentheses are numbers suggestive of which expressions you might want to modify and use. Once you understand the technique, you can pair up with a friend and take turns asking provocative questions.

1. Was machte er, während er nachts am Friedhof vorbeiging?
   (21) (33) (54) (40) (89)

2. Können Sie eine Kaffeemühle beschreiben?
   (51) (1) (18) (47)

3. Wer steht draußen vor der Tür?
   (59) (67) (70)

4. Ist es dir nicht zu kalt hier?
   (53) (72) (76) (109)

5. Warum siehst du so verwirrt aus?
   (88) (34) (35) (63) (107)

6. Was hielt Ulrich von deinem neuen Rennrad?
   (87) (75) (118) (120) (96) (106)

7. Warum wartet ihr da an der Ecke?
   (2) (4) (6) (13) (24) (44) (63)

8. Da kommt der Polizeibeamte. Was sollen wir tun?
   (90) (98) (108) (117) (115) (105)

9. Wer kann mir das erklären?
   (65) (74) (73) (95) (104) (33)

10. Jetzt, wo die Deutschklasse zu Ende ist, sag mir, was hältst du davon?
    (111) (120) (106) (110) (112)

APPENDIX I
Word Formation
and
Cognates

§89. COMPOUND NOUNS

The German language has a relatively small basic vocabulary and a correspondingly large percentage of words made up by compounding the basic items with each other or with prefixes and suffixes. These abound not only in technical and scientific, but also in everyday parlance: **das Ferngespräch** (*long distance telephone call*), **der Lastkraftwagen** (lit. *the burden-power-vehicle,* that is, *the truck,* usually abbreviated to **Lkw.**), or **die Unterstraßenbahn** (*the subway*). German has also had periods of linguistic xenophobia in which "ethnically pure" coinages were preferred to foreign borrowings: Richard Wagner, for example, called himself **ein Tondichter** and not **ein Komponist.** The first appendix sets forth the various suffixes and prefixes which, together with a modest basic vocabulary and a bit of imagination, will help you figure out many long compounded words without the help of a dictionary.

Remember that German words originally were mostly monosyllabic and had no umlauting: polysyllables with or without umlauting got that way by derivation. For example, **das Gebüsch** can be stripped of its derivational additives to show **Busch,** *bush.* A study of similar words suggests that the **ge-** prefix with umlaut creates collective nouns. The original example means *shrubbery.* Collectives based on **Land, Holz,** and **Berg** are **Gelände** *terrain,* **Gehölz** *woodland* or *copse,* and **Gebirge** *mountain range* (the change of **e > i** is a form of umlaut).

A. Formation of compound nouns. German forms compounds chiefly from simpler German words rather than coining words with Latin and Greek roots, as English so frequently does: **das Bindewort** (*conjunction*), **die Ausnahme** (*exception*), **der Wasserstoff** (*hydrogen*), **die Rolltreppe** (*escalator*).

B. Gender of compound nouns. Compound nouns have the gender of their *last* component:

> der Hausschlüssel (= das Haus + der Schlüssel), *housekey*
>
> die Eisenbahn (= das Eisen + die Bahn), *railroad*
>
> der Birnbaum (= die Birne + der Baum), *pear tree*
>
> das Vaterland (= der Vater + das Land), *native land*
>
> die Raumkapsel (= der Raum + die Kapsel), *space capsule*
>
> die Kernenergie (= der Kern + die Energie), *nuclear energy*
>
> die Feuerversicherungsgesellschaft (= das Feuer + die Versicherung + die Gesellschaft), *fire insurance company*

Note:

(1) A connective **-(e)s-** often appears in the compound, irrespective of the gender of a noun:

> der Geburt**s**tag (= die Geburt + der Tag), *birthday*
>
> das Hochzeit**s**kleid (= die Hochzeit + das Kleid), *wedding dress*
>
> die Jahre**s**zeit (= das Jahr + die Zeit), *season*

(2) A connective **-(e)n-** is also common in compounds: der Hirt**en**knabe (= der Hirt + der Knabe), *shepherd boy*. This connective sometimes shows the old genitive form of certain feminine nouns, which otherwise rarely occurs in modern German:

> der Sonn**en**strahl (= die Sonne + der Strahl), *sunbeam*

(3) Certain compounds betray a change of gender in the history of the final element. Given **der Teil,** one can infer that **der Vorteil** (*the advantage*) is a modern coinage while **das Urteil** (*the judgment*) dates from a time when the German word for *part* was neuter.

§90. SUFFIXES

Originally most suffixes and prefixes were independent words; in modern German, however, they have lost their independent identity and become affixed to other words.

A. Noun suffixes. Noun suffixes occur in all three genders; some of the more common ones are listed below.

(1) Feminine noun suffixes: **-e, -ei, -heit, -keit, -kunft, -in, -schaft, -ung, -ion,** and **-tät.**

(a) **-e:** This suffix forms from adjectives abstract nouns denoting *quality, state,* or *condition.* Note the umlaut on the root vowel:

die Güte, *goodness* or *kindness* (from gut, *good*)

die Kürze, *shortness* or *brevity* (from kurz, *short*)

(b) **-ei:** This suffix forms from nouns of occupation nouns denoting *(place of) business* or *trade:*

die Bäckerei, *bakery* (from der Bäcker, *baker*)

die Druckerei, *printing office* (from der Drucker, *printer*)

die Brauerei, *brewery* (from der Brauer, *brewer*)

(c) **-heit** and **-keit:** These suffixes convert adjectives into abstract nouns denoting *state, condition, quality,* or *character:*

die Schönheit, *beauty* (from schön, *beautiful*)

die Fruchtbarkeit, *fruitfulness* or *fertility* (from fruchtbar, *fertile*)

die Folgsamkeit, *obedience* (from folgsam, *obedient*)

die Leitfähigkeit, *conductivity* (from leitfähig, *conductive*)

Note: The suffix **-heit** is often equivalent to the English suffix **-hood:** die Kindheit, *childhood.*

The suffix **-keit** (rather than **-heit**) is usually appended to adjectives ending in **-bar, -lich, -sam, -er,** and **-ig.**

(d) **-kunft:** This suffix forms from prepositions and adverbs of motion nouns denoting *coming:*

die Ankunft, *arrival* (from an, *at* or *to*)

die Zukunft, *future* (from zu, *to* or *towards*)

Note: The suffix **-kunft** was formerly a noun meaning *coming* and is etymologically related to the verb **kommen,** as its modern German compounds indicate.

(e) **-in:** This suffix forms feminine nouns—usually with umlaut—from masculine nouns[1]:

die Gräfin, *countess* (from der Graf, *count*)

---

[1]Modern German appears to be no less vigilant in the search for gender-neutral terms than American English is. One way to remove gender specificity is to use *-kraft* as a suffix instead of *-er* and *-erin;* thus, instead of *Lehrer* and *Lehrerin,* one has *eine Lehrkraft, drei Lehrkräfte.* Another way is simply to use the masculine form for both men and women, hoping eventually to weaken its restriction to males.

die Lehrerin, *woman teacher* (from der Lehrer, *teacher*)

die Amerikanerin, *American woman* (from der Amerikaner)

die Königin, *queen* (from der König, *king*)

(f) **-schaft:** This suffix forms from nouns abstract and collective nouns denoting *state, condition,* or *quality; office, dignity,* or *profession.* It is often equivalent to the English suffix **-ship.**

die Freundschaft, *friendship* (from der Freund, *friend*)

die Feindschaft, *enmity* (from der Feind, *enemy*)

die Mannschaft, *crew* or *team* (from der Mann, *man*)

die Herrschaft, *dominion* (from der Herr, *master* or *ruler*)

(g) **-ung:** This suffix forms from verbal roots nouns denoting an *action* or the *result of an action:*

die Erfindung, *discovery* (from erfinden, *to discover*)

die Erziehung, *education* (from erziehen, *to educate*)

die Spaltung, *cleavage, splitting* (from spalten, *to cleave* or *split up*); *cf.* Kernspaltung, *nuclear fission.*

Note: The suffix **-ung** is often equivalent to the English suffix *-ing:* die Warnung, *warning;* die Endung, *ending.*

(h) **-ion:** This suffix occurs with nouns of foreign origin, many of which occur in English in about the same form: die Million, *million;* die Religion, *religion;* die Nation, *nation;* die Lektion, *lesson;* die Erdrotation, *rotation of the earth.*

(i) **-tät:** This suffix occurs with nouns of foreign origin and is often equivalent to English **-ty:** die Universität, *university;* die Elektrizität, *electricity;* die Qualität, *quality;* die Quantität, *quantity;* die Relativität, *relativity;* die Radioaktivität, *radioactivity.*

(2) Neuter noun suffixes: **-chen, -lein, -nis, -sal,** and **-tum.**

(a) **-chen** and **-lein:** These suffixes form from nouns *diminutives* and nouns denoting *endearment,* usually with umlaut:

das Bächlein, *little brook* or *brooklet* (from der Bach, *brook*)

das Bäumchen, *little tree* (from der Baum, *tree*)

das Blümlein, *little flower* (from die Blume, *flower*)

das Fräulein, *girl, Miss* (from die Frau, *woman*)

das Mütterchen, *dear mother* (from die Mutter, *mother*)

das Väterchen, *dear father* (from der Vater, *father*)

das Körperchen, *corpuscle* or *particle* (from der Körper, *body*)

Note: The suffix **-chen** is equivalent to the English suffix *-kin:* das Lämmchen, *lambkin.*

The suffix **-lein** originated in South Germany, where it is still used in preference to **-chen** in ordinary conversation and in various dialects.

(b) **-nis:** This suffix forms from verbal roots neuter (and sometimes feminine) nouns, usually with umlaut, denoting the *result* or *object of an activity* implied in the verbal stem of a compound:

das Ergebnis, *result* (from sich ergeben, *to result*)

das Verständnis, *understanding* (from verstehen, *to understand*)

das Vermächtnis, *testament* or *legacy* (from vermachen, *to bequeath*)

Note: The suffix **-nis** is sometimes equivalent to the English suffix *-ness,* as in *darkness.*

Two common feminines formed with **-nis** are:

die Erlaubnis, *permission* (from erlauben, *to permit*)

die Kenntnis, *knowledge* (from kennen, *to know*)

(c) **-sal:** This suffix forms from verbal roots nouns similar to those ending in **-nis** but often more comprehensive and forceful:

das Schicksal, *fate* (from schicken, *to send*)

das Wirrsal, *confusion* (from wirren, *to entangle*)

(d) **-tum:** This suffix forms from noun, adjective, and verbal roots neuter nouns (with only two exceptions) denoting *dignity* or *rank, condition* or *state,* or *a collective idea:*

das Königtum, *royalty* or *kingship* (from der König, *king*)

das Siechtum, *state of poor health* (from siech, *sickly*)

das Bürgertum, *citizenry* (from der Bürger, *citizen*)

Note: The suffix **-tum** is often equivalent to the English suffix *-dom,* as in *martyrdom* (Märtyrtum).

Two *masculine* nouns are formed with **-tum:**

der Reichtum, *riches* (from reich, *rich*)

der Irrtum, *error* (from irr(e), *in error*)

(3) Masculine nouns suffixes: **-er, -el,** and **-ling.**

(a) **-er:** This suffix, identical in English, forms from verbal roots masculine nouns denoting *the personal agent;* from noun stems, nouns of *nationality.* The umlaut is often present:

der Räuber, *robber* (from rauben, *to rob*)

der Maler, *painter* (from malen, *to paint*)

der Arbeiter, *worker* or *workman* (from arbeiten, *to work*)

der Diener, *servant* (from dienen, *to serve*)

der Engländer, *Englishman* (from England, *England*)

der Spanier, *Spaniard* (from Spanien, *Spain*)

der Sender, *sender, transmitter, broadcasting station* (from senden, *to send*)

Note: Nouns denoting the personal agent are sometimes formed with the suffixes **-ler** or **-ner:**

der Künstler, *artist* (from die Kunst, *art*)

der Kellner, *waiter* (from der Keller, *cellar*)

(b) **-el:** This suffix forms from verbal roots nouns—usually masculine—denoting *instrument:*

der Schlüssel, *key* (from schließen, *to close* or *lock*)

der Deckel, *lid* (from decken, *to cover*)

der Zügel, *rein* (from ziehen, *to draw*)

(c) **-ling:** This suffix forms, from adjective, noun, and verbal roots, masculine nouns denoting people or animals who appear *young, small,* or *contemptible.* Umlaut is usual:

der Jüngling, *yoiung man* or *youth* (from jung, *young*)

der Feigling, *coward* (from feig, *cowardly*)

der Emporkömmling, *upstart* (from empor, *up* + kommen, *to come*)

der Sprößling, *scion* or *descendant* (from der Sproß, *sprout*)

Note: Compare the English suffix **-ling,** as in *duckling, foundling,* etc.

B. **Adjective suffixes.** Some of the more common adjective suffixes are: **-er, -(e)n** and **-ern, -haft, -bar, -isch, -lich, -ig, -los, -sam, -reich,** and **-voll.**

(1) **-er:** This suffix forms indeclinable adjectives from names of cities:

eine Münch(e)ner Zeutung, *a Munich newspaper* (from München)

das Heidelberger Schloß, *Heidelberg Castle* (from Heidelberg)

(2) **-(e)n** and **-ern:** These suffixes form from nouns adjectives of *material,* sometimes with umlaut. The English suffix **-en** is often equivalent:

hölzern, *wooden* (from das Holz, *wood*)

ledern, *of leather* (from das Leder, *leather*)

bleiern, *of lead* or *leaden* (from das Blei, *lead*)

stählern, *of steel* (from der Stahl, *steel*)

(3) **-haft:** This suffix (related linguistically to **haben**) forms from nouns adjectives that denote *having the nature of:*

knabenhaft, *boyish* (from der Knabe, *boy*)

schmerzhaft, *painful* (from der Schmerz, *pain*)

meisterhaft, *masterly* (from der Meister, *master*)

fabelhaft, *fabulous* (from die Fabel, *fable*)

vorteilhaft, *advantageous, profitable* (from der Vorteil, *advantage, profit*)

(4) **-bar:** This suffix, equivalent to English *-able* or *-ible,* forms from verbal and noun roots adjectives denoting *ability, fitness,* or *worthiness:*

lesbar, *legible* (from lesen, *to read*)

eßbar, *edible* (from essen, *to eat*)

denkbar, *thinkable* or *conceivable* (from denken, *to think*)

sichtbar, *visible* (from sehen, *to see*)

Note: The negative prefix **un-** is frequently used with adjectives ending in **-bar;** unlesbar (*illegible*), undenkbar (*unthinkable*), unauflösbar (*insoluble*).

(5) **-isch:** This suffix, comparable to English, *-ish,* forms from nouns and proper names adjectives that denote *belonging to* or *of the nature of:*

kindisch, *childish* (from das Kind, *child*)

teuflisch, *devilish* (from der Teufel, *devil*)

himmlisch, *heavenly* (from der Himmel, *heaven*)

regnerisch, *rainy* (from der Regen, *rain*)

englisch, *English* (from England, *England*)

römisch, *Roman* (from Rom, *Rome*)

französisch, *French* (from der Franzose, *Frenchman*)

Do not confuse the following forms: **kindisch,** *childish* and **kindlich,** *childlike;* **weibisch,** *womanish* (i.e., *unmanly* or *effeminate*) and **weiblich,** *womanly.*

(6) **-lich:** This suffix forms from nouns adjectives denoting *full of* or *like in appearance, manner,* or *nature:*

göttlich, *godly* or *divine* (from der Gott, *God*)

gefährlich, *dangerous* (from die Gefahr, *danger*)

schädlich, *harmful* (from der Schaden, *harm*)

Note: The suffix **-lich** is usually equivalent to the English suffixes *-ly, -ous,* and *-ful.*

(7) **-ig:** This suffix forms from nouns adjectives denoting *full of, characterized by,* or *pertaining to.* English equivalents are *-y, -ful,* and *-ous.* There are many cognates in **-ig** equivalent to English final *-y:*

schmutzig, *dirty* (from der Schmutz, *dirt*)

hungrig, *hungry* (from der Hunger, *hunger*)

blutig, *bloody* (from das Blut, *blood*)

mutig, *courageous* (from der Mut, *courage*)

freudig, *joyful* (from die Freude, *joy*)

(8) **-los:** This suffix, usually equivalent to the English suffix *-less,* forms from nouns adjectives denoting *lack of:*

endlos, *endless* (from das Ende, *end*)

grundlos, *groundless* or *bottomless* (from der Grund, *ground* or *bottom*)

zahllos, *countless* (from die Zahl, *number*)

hilflos, *helpless* (from die Hilfe, *help*)

(9) **-sam**: This suffix (sometimes equivalent to the English suffix *-some*) forms adjectives that denote *causing,* or *a considerable degree of:*

mühsam, *troublesome* or *toilsome* (from die Mühe, *trouble* or *toil*)

langsam, *slow* (from lang, *long*)

biegsam, *flexible* (from biegen, *to bend*)

wirksam, *effective, operative* (from wirken, *to effect, to operate*)

(10) **-reich**: This suffix forms from nouns adjectives denoting *full of, rich* (or *abounding*) *in:*

silberreich, *rich in silver* (from das Silber, *silver*)

liebreich, *loving* or *affectionate* (from die Liebe, *love*)

ideenreich, *rich in ideas* (from die Ideen, *ideas*)

Note: There is a difference in meaning, depending on stress, between **stein**reich (accented on the first syllable) = *stony* and steinreich (stressed equally on both syllables) = *very rich.*

Similarly, when **-arm** is used as a suffix, **blut**arm = *anemic;* blutarm = *very poor.*

(11) **-voll**: This suffix forms from nouns adjectives denoting *full of:*

gefahrvoll, *full of danger* or *risky* (from die Gefahr, *danger*)

liebevoll, *loving* or *affectionate* (from die Liebe, *love*)

C. Verbal suffixes. Some of the more common verbal suffixes are: **-eln, -igen, -en, -ern, -ieren,** and **-zen.**

(1) **-eln**: This suffix forms from adjectives, nouns, and other verbs, verbs denoting a *diminutive idea* or the *repetition* of an activity:

säuseln, *to rustle* (from sausen, *to roar,* as wind)

handeln, *to trade* (from die Hand, *hand*)

Note: Sometimes the verb combines both senses of diminution and iteration: kränkeln, *to be sickly* (from krank, *sick*).

In the case of verbs derived from nouns ending in **-el**, the verbal suffix **-eln** can hardly be said to have any meaning other than to convert the noun into a verb:

gurgeln, *to gargle* (from die Gurgel, *throat*)

prügeln, *to fight* or *thrash* (from der Prügel, *cudgel* or *stick*)

(2) **-igen**: This suffix forms verbs from adjectives and nouns:

steinigen, *to stone* (from der Stein, *stone*)

befestigen, *to fasten* or *make secure* (from fest, *firm*)

(3) **-en**: This suffix forms factitive verbs from the positive or comparative of adjectives to which it is affixed. A factitive verb indicates accomplishment of the state denoted by the adjective:

zähmen, *to tame* (from zahm, *tame*)

heizen, *to heat* (from heiß, *hot*)

wärmen, *to warm* (from warm, *warm*)

A number of weak verbs ending in **-nen** are derived from nouns or adjectives in **-en**:

regnen, *to rain* (from der Regen, *rain*)

trocknen, *to dry* (from trocken, *dry*)

zeichnen, *to draw* or *sketch* (from das Zeichen, *sign, mark*)

(4) **-ern**: This suffix forms from verbs and nouns intensives, iteratives, and factitives:

klappern, *to rattle* (from klappen, *to clap* or *clatter*)

räuchern, *to (expose to) smoke* (from der Rauch, *smoke*)

steigern, *to raise, strengthen,* or *enhance* (from steigen, *to mount*)

(5) **-ieren**: This very productive suffix forms derivatives which are usually of foreign origin. They are always weak and do not form their past participle in **ge-**:

ich amüsiere mich, *I enjoy myself*

ich habe mich amüsiert, *I enjoyed myself*

(6) -**zen**: This suffix forms verbs that mean *to utter the word or sound* of the root word:

duzen, *to address with* du (from du, *you*)

§91. PREFIXES

A. Noun and adjective prefixes. A few of the more common noun and adjective prefixes are: **ge-**, **ur-**, **un-**, and .**erz-**.

(1) **ge-**: This prefix forms from noun stems nouns denoting *collectivity;* from verbal roots, nouns denoting the *action of the verb*:

das Gebirge, *mountain range* or *mountainous region* (from der Berg, *mountain*)

das Gebüsch, *bushes, shrubbery* (from der Busch, *bush*)

der Geschmack, *taste* (from schmecken, *to taste*)

der Geruch, *smell* (from riechen, *to smell*)

Note: The prefix **ge-** is often equivalent to the English prefix *com-*:

der Gefährte, *comrade* or *fellow traveler* (from fahren, *to travel*)

der Geselle, *companion,* lit. *roommate* (from der Saal, *room*)

Observe the plural forms **Gebrüder** = *brothers,* and **Geschwister** = *brothers and sisters.*

(2) **ur-**: This prefix forms from nouns and adjectives nouns and adjectives denoting *primitive, original,* or *very ancient:*

uralt, *very old, ancient* (from alt, *old*)

der Urgroßvater, *great-grandfather* (from der Großvater, *grandfather*)

die Ururgroßmutter, *great-great-grandmother* (from die Großmutter, *grandmother*)

der Urwald, *primeval forest* (from der Wald, *forest*)

die Ursache, *the (first) cause* (from die Sache, *thing* or *cause*)

der Urzustand, *original condition* (from der Zustand, *condition*)

das Urgestein, *primitive rock, mother* or *igneous rock* (from das Gestein, *rock*)

(3) **un-**: This prefix *negates* the meaning of the original noun or adjective. English equivalents are *un-*, *in-*, and *im-*.

unmöglich, *impossible* (from möglich, *possible*)

unverständlich, *unintelligible* or *incomprehensible* (from verständlich, *comprehensible*)

der Undank, *ingratitude* (from der Dank, *thanks*)

eine Unzahl, *a great* (i.e., *uncountable*) *number* (from die Zahl, *number*)

umbemannt, *unmanned* (from bemannt, *manned*)

unverdünnt, *undiluted* (from verdünnt, *diluted, thinned*)

Note: Sometimes the prefix **un-** may negate or intensify the original meaning: **die Untiefe** (from die Tiefe, *depth*) may mean either *shallowness* or *great depth.*

(4) **erz-:** This prefix forms from nouns, nouns denoting *chief, principal,* or *master;* from adjectives, adjectives in which the meaning of the original has been intensified. The English equivalent is ***arch-.***

der Erzengel, *archangel* (from der Engel, *angel*)

der Erzbischof, *archbishop* (from der Bischof, *bishop*)

erzfaul, *extremely lazy* (from faul, *lazy*)

B. Verbal prefixes. Verbal prefixes may be either *separable* or *inseparable.* For separable verbal prefixes, see §70. For sentences with inseparable prefixes. see §69.

Inseparable verbal prefixes originally had certain fundamental meanings which are still preserved in some verbs although lost in many others. Only the meaning of **zer-** has remained constant. The inseparable prefixes are: **be-, ent-** (or **emp-**), **er-, ge-, ver-,** and **zer-.**

(1) **be-:** This prefix serves to make a verb transitive (i.e., a verb formed with it may take a direct object): bedienen, *to serve;* bekommen, *to receive;* beantworten, *to answer.*

(2) **ent-** (or **emp-**): This prefix denotes the *beginning of an action* or *separation*: entstehen, *to arise* (or *come into existence*); entzünden, *to inflame;* entlassen, *to dismiss;* entgehen, *to escape;* entlaufen, *to run away;* entsäuern, *to deacidify, to neutralize.*

(3) **er-:** This prefix denotes *origin* or *accomplishment*: erblühen, *to blossom;* erwachen, *to wake;* erleben, *to experience;* erreichen, *to attain;* erraten, *to guess correctly.*

(4) **ge-:** This prefix (which is used to form the past participle) denotes *result* or *completeness* and often *successful action*: gelangen, *to arrive at;* genesen, *to get well;* gewinnen, *to gain.*

The prefix **ge-** originally denoted *with* or *together* (*cf.* noun prefix **ge-** in **A** (1) above) and had perfective force equivalent to the Latin prefix **con-,** as in "*conficers,*" *to accomplish.*

(5) **ver-:** This prefix often denotes that the action of a verb *miscarried*: verführen, *to lead astray;* verspielen, *to lose money in playing;* verkennen, *to misjudge;* verlegen, *to misplace;* sich verschlafen, *to oversleep;* verdrehen, *to distort.*

(6) **zer**-: This prefix is the most constant in meaning of any of the inseparable prefixes. It regularly denotes *going asunder, apart,* or *in pieces;* or *destruction* or *damage* resulting from the action of the original verb: zer**reißen,** *to tear to pieces (damage by tearing)*; zer**brechen,** *to break to pieces*; zer**schneiden,** *to cut to pieces*; zer**fallen,** *to fall to pieces*; zer**legen,** *to take apart*; zer**streuen,** *to scatter;* zer**knallen,** *to explode.*

§92. COGNATES

The ability to recognize English-German cognates (i.e., words etymological-ly related) enables students to understand words which might otherwise be unintelligible to them without the aid of a dictionary.

A. Changes in form and meaning of cognates. Since English and German both belong to the Indo-European language family, there are, as one might expect, many cognate words. Certain cognates are identical in both form and mean-ing (Arm, *arm;* Hand, *hand*), others differ slightly in form but have the same meaning (Distel, *thistle*), and some differ in both form and meaning (Stube, *stove*). Orthographic changes follow definite laws of phonology; thus if the English cognates of **D**istel and **D**urst are *thistle* and *thirst,* we may look for a similar cor-respondence in many other words—e.g., **L**eder and *leather.*

B. Common cognates. A full study of cognates is beyond the scope of this book. The following are merely some of the more common English-German cognates classified according to *consonant* changes. The symbol **>** meaning *becomes* is used because the English consonant system is older than the German.

(1) English *p* **>** German **f, ff,** or **pf**:

sharp, scharf	*open,* offen
up, auf	*ship,* Schiff
leap, laufen	*plant,* Pflanze
deep, tief	*penny,* Pfennig

(2) English *t* **>** German **z** or **ß**:

twig, Zweig	*ten,* zehn
to, zu	*curt,* kurz
timber, Zimmer	*foot,* Fuß

(3) English *k* **>** German **ch**:

week, Woche	*make,* machen
lark, Lerche	*sake,* Sache
token, Zeichen	*book,* Buch

(4) English *d* > German **t**:

day, Tag	*word,* Wort
deal, Teil	*God,* Gott
wide, weit	*blade,* Blatt
side, Seite	*deer,* Tier
old, alt	*fodder,* Futter

(5) English *th* > German **d**:

thou, du	*earth,* Erde
three, drei	*brother,* Bruder
thine, dein	*seethe,* sieden

(6) English *v* or *f* > German **b**:

silver, Silber	*evil,* übel
harvest, Herbst	*deaf,* taub

(7) English *y* > German **g**:

day, Tag	*holy,* heilig
way, Weg	*yester(day),* gestern
fly, fliegen	*yawn,* gähnen

APPENDIX II
Paradigms, Verb Lists, Pitfalls, Punctuation, and Writing Conventions

§93. THE DEFINITE ARTICLE

	SINGULAR			PLURAL
	MASCULINE	FEMININE	NEUTER	ALL GENDERS
Nom.	der	die	das	die
Gen.	des	der	des	der
Dat.	dem	der	dem	den
Acc.	den	die	das	die

§94. THE DEMONSTRATIVE *DIESER*

	SINGULAR			PLURAL
	MASCULINE	FEMININE	NEUTER	ALL GENDERS
Nom.	dieser	diese	dieses	diese
Gen.	dieses	dieser	dieses	dieser
Dat.	diesem	dieser	diesem	diesen
Acc.	diesen	diese	dieses	diese

Note: All **der**-words are declined like **dieser** (see §8).

234

§95. THE INDEFINITE ARTICLE

| | SINGULAR | | |
	MASCULINE	FEMININE	NEUTER
Nom.	ein	eine	ein
Gen.	eines	einer	eines
Dat.	einem	einer	einem
Acc.	einen	eine	ein

Note: **Ein** has no plural forms.

§96. THE POSSESSIVE *MEIN*

| | SINGULAR | | | PLURAL |
	MASCULINE	FEMININE	NEUTER	ALL GENDERS
Nom.	mein	meine	mein	meine
Gen.	meines	meiner	meines	meiner
Dat.	meinem	meiner	meinem	meinen
Acc.	meinen	meine	mein	meine

Note: All **ein**-words are declined like **mein** (see §10).

§97. THE DEMONSTRATIVE *DERSELBE*

| | SINGULAR | | | PLURAL |
	MASCULINE	FEMININE	NEUTER	ALL GENDERS
Nom.	derselbe	dieselbe	dasselbe	dieselben
Gen.	desselben	derselben	desselben	derselben
Dat.	demselben	derselben	demselben	denselben
Acc.	denselben	dieselbe	dasselbe	dieselben

Note: **Derjenige** is declined like **derselbe**.

§98. NOUN DECLENSION

A. The strong declension:

Class I: Plural in -, with frequent umlaut.

	SINGULAR			
Nom.	der Vater	der Onkel	die Mutter	das Mädchen
Gen.	des Vaters	des Onkels	der Mutter	des Mädchens
Dat.	dem Vater	dem Onkel	der Mutter	dem Mädchen
Acc.	den Vater	den Onkel	die Mutter	das Mädchen
	PLURAL			
Nom.	die Väter	die Onkel	die Mütter	die Mädchen
Gen.	der Väter	der Onkel	der Mütter	der Mädchen
Dat.	den Vätern	den Onkeln	den Müttern	den Mädchen
Acc.	die Väter	die Onkel	die Mütter	die Mädchen

Class I comprises:

(1) Masculine and neuter nouns ending in **-el, -en,** and **-er,** except mixed nouns such as der Bauer, and der Vetter, (see **C** below).

(2) Two feminine nouns: die Mutter (pl. Mütter), *mother* and die Tochter (pl. Töchter), *daughter.*

(3) Neuter diminutives in **-chen** and **-lein.**

(4) Neuter nouns with the prefix **ge-** and ending in **-e**: das Gebäude, *building;* das Gebirge, *mountain range* (or *mountainous region*).

Class II: Plural in **-e,** with frequent umlaut.

	SINGULAR				
Nom.	der Baum	der Arm	die Hand	der König	das Ereignis
Gen.	des Baumes	des Armes	der Hand	des Königs	des Ereignisses
Dat.	dem Baum	dem Arm	der Hand	dem König	dem Ereignis
Acc.	den Baum	den Arm	die Hand	den König	das Ereignis
	PLURAL				
Nom.	die Bäume	Arme	Hände	Könige	Ereignisse
Gen.	der Bäume	Arme	Hände	Könige	Ereignisse
Dat.	den Bäumen	Armen	Händen	Königen	Ereignissen
Acc.	die Bäume	Arme	Hände	Könige	Ereignisse

Class II comprises:
(1) Monosyllables:

(*a*)   Many masculines, which usually take umlaut: der Sohn (pl. Söhne).

Exceptions: The following common nouns do *not* take umlaut: der Arm, der Dom, der Hund, der Laut, der Mond, der Park, der Schuh, der Tag.

(*b*)   Some feminines, which always take umlaut: die Wand (pl. Wände).

(*c*)   Some neuters, which do not take umlaut: das Jahr (pl. Jahre).

Exceptions: das Floß (pl. Flöße), *raft;* das Chor (pl. Chöre), *choirloft.*

(2) Polysyllables (usually without umlaut):

(*a*)   Masculine nouns ending in **-ig** and **-ling**: der Honig (pl. Honige), *honey;* der Frühling, *spring.*

(*b*)   Nouns ending in **-nis** and **-sal** (usually neuter but sometimes feminine): das Erlebnis, *experience;* die Erlaubnis, *permission;* das Schicksal, *fate;* die (*or* das) Trübsal, *affliction.*

Note: Nouns in **-nis** double the final **s** before an ending: das Ereignis (die Ereignisse), *event.*

(*c*)   Neuters with the prefix **ge-**: das Gedicht, *poem;* das Gesetz, *law.*

(*d*)   Words of foreign origin accented on the last syllable: der Vokal, *vowel:* das Papier, *paper.*

Class III: Plural in **-er,** with umlaut wherever possible.

	SINGULAR		
Nom.	der	Mann	das Haus	das Eigentum
Gen.	des	Mannes	des Hauses	des Eigentums
Dat.	dem	Mann	dem Haus	dem Eigentum
Acc.	den	Mann	das Haus	das Eigentum
	PLURAL		
Nom.	die	Männer	die Häuser	die Eigentümer
Gen.	der	Männer	der Häuser	der Eigentümer
Dat.	den	Männern	den Häusern	den Eigentümern
Acc.	die	Männer	die Häuser	die Eigentümer

Note: There are no feminine nouns in Class III.

Class III comprises:

(1) Many neuter nouns of one syllable, and some polysyllabic neuters with the prefix **ge**-: das Gesicht, *face;* das Gespenst, *ghost.*

(2) A few masculines of one syllable.

(3) Neuters ending in -**tum,** and two masculines: der Reich**tum,** *riches* and der Ir**tum,** *error.*

B. The weak declension:

	SINGULAR							
Nom.	der	Junge	die	Frau	der	Student	die	Feder
Gen.	des	Jungen	der	Frau	des	Studenten	der	Feder
Dat.	dem	Jungen	der	Frau	dem	Studenten	der	Feder
Acc.	den	Jungen	die	Frau	den	Studenten	die	Feder
	PLURAL							
Nom.	die	Jungen	die	Frauen	die	Studenten	die	Federn
Gen.	der	Jungen	der	Frauen	der	Studenten	der	Federn
Dat.	den	Jungen	den	Frauen	den	Studenten	den	Federn
Acc.	die	Jungen	die	Frauen	die	Studenten	die	Federn

Note: There are no weak neuter nouns. In the weak declension there is never an umlaut in the plural.

The weak declension comprises:

(1) All feminine nouns of more than one syllable except: die Mutter (pl. Mütter), die Tochter (pl. Töchter), and a few feminine nouns ending in -**nis** and -**sal**.

(2) Many feminines of one syllable.

(3) Masculine nouns of one syllable denoting living beings: der Herr, *gentleman, master, Mr.,* or *lord;* der Bär, *bear;* der Mensch, *man.*

(4) Masculine nouns of more than one syllable ending in -**e** and denoting living beings: der Junge, *boy;* der Neffe, *nephew;* der Ochse, *ox;* der Affe, *ape* or *monkey.*

(5) Masculine nouns of foreign origin accented on the last syllable: der Soldat, *soldier;* der Elefant, *elephant;* der Präsident, *president;* der Student, *student.*

C. The mixed (or irregular) declension:

				SINGULAR				
Nom.	der	Staat	der	Professor		das	Auge	
Gen.	des	Staates	des	Professors		des	Auges	
Dat.	dem	Staat	dem	Professor		dem	Auge	
Acc.	den	Staat	den	Professor		das	Auge	
				PLURAL				
Nom.	die	Staaten	die	Professoren		die	Augen	
Gen.	der	Staaten	der	Professoren		der	Augen	
Dat.	den	Staaten	den	Professoren		den	Augen	
Acc.	die	Staaten	die	Professoren		die	Augen	

The mixed (or irregular) declension comprises:

(1) A few native German or naturalized nouns: der Schmerz, *pain;* der Staat, *state;* das Auge, *eye;* das Bett, *bed;* das Ende, *end;* das Hemd, *shirt;* das Ohr, *ear;* der Vetter, *male cousin;* der Bauer,[1] *peasant* (or *farmer*).

(2) Masculine nouns of foreign origin ending in **-or**, in which the short **o** becomes long in the plural by a shift in syllabic stress, e.g., der Proféssor, pl. die Professóren.

(3) Neuter nouns in **-um** of foreign (mostly Latin) origin, with the plural in **-en**:

		SINGULAR	PLURAL
Nom.	das	Gymnasium	die Gymnasien
Den.	des	Gymnasiums	der Gymnasien
Dat.	dem	Gymnasium	den Gymnasien
Acc.	das	Gymnasium	die Gymnasien

Other neuter nouns of this type are: Datum (pl. Daten), *date;* Museum, *museum;* Observatorium, *observatory;* Partizipium, *participle;* Territorium, *territory.*

(4) Foreign neuters in -il and **-al** with the plural in **-ien**: das Fossil (des Fossils, die Fossilien), *fossil;* das Mineral (des Minerals, die Mineralien), *mineral.*

---

[1]Der **Bauer** often has weak endings (**-n**) in the singular.

(5) Foreign nouns with plural forms in **-s** in all cases: das Hotel (des Hotels, die Hotels), *hotel;* das Sofa (des Sofas, die Sofas), *sofa;* das Auto (des Autos, die Autos), *auto;* das Kino, (des Kinos, die Kinos), *cinema;* das Radio (des Radios, die Radios), *radio;* der Tee (des Tees, die Tees), *tea;* das Echo (des Echos), *echo.*

(6) A few foreign nouns ending in **-s** have the same form throughout the singular and plural, e.g., das Relais (*relay*), a word now common in technical vocabulary, especially in compounded forms: der Funk-Relais-Satellit (*radio-relay satellite*).

(7) Several previously weak musculine nouns now appear with or without a new nominative **-n** and with genitive **-(e)ns,** dative and accusative **-(e)n,** and plural **-(e)n.** Such nounts are **der Friede(n), des Friedens,** *peace,* **der Name, des Namens,** *name,* **der Gedanke(n), des Gedankens,** *thought,* and **der Gefallen, des Gefallens,** *favor.* One neuter noun, **das Herz,** is also mixed, but without an accusative singular ending (see § 13.D).

(8) The proper name *Christ* has either no endings or retains its Latin declension: Nom. **Christus,** Gen. **Christi,** Dat. **Christo,** Acc. **Christum.**

§99. ADJECTIVE DECLENSION

A. The strong declension:

	SINGULAR					
Nom.	gut**er**	Tee	rot**e**	Seide	kalt**es**	Bier
Gen.	gut**en**	Tees	rot**er**	Seide	kalt**en**	Bieres
Dat.	gut**em**	Tee	rot**er**	Seide	kalt**em**	Bier
Acc.	gut**en**	Tee	rot**e**	Seide	kalt**es**	Bier
	PLURAL					
Nom.	treu**e**	Freunde	schön**e**	Freuen	reich**e**	Länder
Gen.	treu**er**	Freunde	schön**er**	Frauen	reich**er**	Länder
Dat.	treu**en**	Freunden	schön**en**	Frauen	reich**en**	Ländern
Acc.	treu**e**	Freunde	schön**e**	Frauen	reich**e**	Länder

B. The weak declension:

	SINGULAR							
Nom.	der	gut**e**	Freund	die	lieb**e**	Tochter	das	groß**e**	Haus
Gen.	des	gut**en**	Freundes	der	lieb**en**	Tochter	des	groß**en**	Hauses
Dat.	dem	gut**en**	Freund	der	lieb**en**	Tochter	dem	groß**en**	Haus
Acc.	den	gut**en**	Freund	die	lieb**e**	Tochter	das	groß**e**	Haus
	PLURAL							
Nom.	die	gut**en**	Freunde	die	lieb**en**	Töchter	die	groß**en**	Häuser
Gen.	der	gut**en**	Freunde	der	lieb**en**	Töchter	der	groß**en**	Häuser
Dat.	den	gut**en**	Freunden	den	lien**en**	Töchtern	den	groß**en**	Häusern
Acc.	die	gut**en**	Freunde	die	lieb**en**	Töchter	die	groß**en**	Häuser

Note: The weak adjective declension occurs after any **der**-word (see §8).

C. The mixed declension:

	SINGULAR					
Nom.	ein	klein**er** Stuhl	eine	rote	Rose	ein	klein**es** Zimmer
Gen.	eines	klein**en** Stuhles	einer	rot**en**	Rose	eines	klein**en** Zimmers
Dat.	einem	klein**en** Stuhl	einer	rot**en**	Rose	einem	klein**en** Zimmer
Acc.	einen	klein**en** Stuhl	eine	rote	Rose	ein	klein**es** Zimmer

Note:

(1) The mixed declension uses the masculine and neuter nominative singular and the neuter accusative singular of the strong declension; it takes all other forms, singular and plural, from the weak declension.

(2) The mixed declension occurs after **ein**-words.

§100. DECLENSION OF PROPER NAMES

Nom.	Goethe	Amerika	Karl der Große
Gen.	Goethes	Amerikas	Karls des Großen
Dat.	Goethe	Amerika	Karl dem Großen
Acc.	Goethe	Amerika	Karl den Großen

Nom.	König Friedrich	der König Friedrich
Gen.	König Friedrichs	des Königs Friedrich
Dat.	König Friedrich	dem König Friedrich
Acc.	König Friedrich	den König Friedrich

§101. DECLENSION OF PRONOUNS

A. Personal pronouns:

	SINGULAR					
Nom.	ich (*I*)	du (*you*)	er (*he*)	sie (*she*)	es (*it*)	Sie (*you*)
Gen.	(meiner)	(deiner)	(seiner)	(ihrer)	(seiner)	(Ihrer)
Dat.	mir	dir	ihm	ihr	ihm	Ihnen
Acc.	mich	dich	ihn	sie	es	Sie
	PLURAL					
Nom.	wir (*we*)	ihr (*you*)	sie (*they* [all genders])			Sie (*you*)
Gen.	(unser)	(euer)	(ihrer)			(Ihrer)
Dat.	uns	euch	ihnen			Ihnen
Acc.	uns	euch	sie			Sie

Note: The genitive forms are given in parentheses because they are rare.

B. Interrogative pronouns:

	MASCULINE AND FEMININE	NEUTER
Nom.	wer	was
Gen.	wessen	(wes, wessen)
Dat.	wem	——
Acc.	wen	was

C. Demonstrative pronouns:

(1) **Dieser** and **jener** are declined like the definite article (see paradigm in §94).

(2) For the declension of **derselbe** and **derjenige,** see §97.

(3) **Der** as demonstrative pronoun is declined like the relative pronoun **der** (see **D** below).

  (*a*) **Dieser, jener, derselbe, derjenige,** and **der** are also demonstrative adjectives.

  (*b*) As demonstrative adjective, **der** is declined like the definite article.

D. Relative pronouns:

	SINGULAR			PLURAL
	MASCULINE	FEMININE	NEUTER	ALL GENDERS
Nom.	der, welcher	die, welche	das, welches	die, welche
Gen.	dessen	deren	dessen	deren
Dat.	dem, welchem	der, welcher	dem, welchem	denen, welchen
Acc.	den, welchen	die, welche	das, welches	die, welche

Note: As relative pronouns, **wer** and **was** are declined like the interrogatives **wer** and **was** (see §101 B, § 46, and § 48).

§102. THE AUXILIARY VERBS: *HABEN, SEIN, WERDEN*

A. The indicative mood:

(1) PRESENT (*I have; I am; I become*)

ich habe	ich bin	ich werde
du hast	du bist	du wirst
es hat	es ist	es wird
wir haben	wir sind	wir werden
ihr habt	ihr seid	ihr werdet
sie haben	sie sind	sie werden

(2) SIMPLE PAST (*I had* or *have had; I was* or *have been; I became* or *have become*)

ich hatte	ich war	ich wurde
du hattest	du warst	du wurdest
es hatte	es war	es wurde
wir hatten	wir waren	wir wurden
ihr hattet	ihr wart	ihr wurdet
sie hatten	sie waren	sie wurden

(3) COMPOUND PAST (*same as* SIMPLE PAST)

ich habe	gehabt		ich bin	gewesen		ich bin	geworden
du hast	gehabt		du bist	gewesen		du bist	geworden
es hat	gehabt		es ist	gewesen		es ist	geworden
wir haben	gehabt		wir sind	gewesen		wir sind	geworden
ihr habt	gehabt		ihr seid	gewesen		ihr seid	geworden
sie haben	gehabt		sie sind	gewesen		sie sind	geworden

(4) PAST PERFECT (*I had had; I had been; I had become*)

ich hatte	gehabt		ich war	gewesen		ich war	geworden
du hattest	gehabt		du warst	gewesen		du warst	geworden
es hatte	gehabt		es war	gewesen		es war	geworden
wir hatten	gehabt		wir waren	gewesen		wir waren	geworden
ihr hattet	gehabt		ihr wart	gewesen		ihr wart	geworden
sie hatten	gehabt		sie waren	gewesen		sie waren	geworden

(5) FUTURE (*I shall have; I shall be; I shall become*)

ich werde	haben		ich werde	sein		ich werde	werden
du wirst	haben		du wirst	sein		du wirst	werden
es wird	haben		es wird	sein		es wird	werden
wir werden	haben		wir werden	sein		wir werden	werden
ihr werdet	haben		ihr werdet	sein		ihr werdet	werden
sie werden	haben		sie werden	sein		sie werden	werden

(6) FUTURE PERFECT (*I shall have had; I shall have been; I shall have become*)

ich werde			
du wirst			
es wird			
wir werden	gehabt haben	gewesen sein	geworden sein
ihr werdet			
sie werden			

B. The subjunctive mood:

(1) PRESENT SUBJUNCTIVE I

ich habe		ich sei		ich werde
du habest		du seiest		du werdest
er habe		er sei		er werde
wir haben		wir seien		wir werden
ihr habet		ihr seiet		ihr werdet
sie haben		sie seien		sie werden

(2) PRESENT SUBJUNCTIVE II

ich hätte	ich wäre	ich würde
du hättest	du wärest	du würdest
er hätte	er wäre	er würde
wir hätten	wir wären	wir würden
ihr hättet	ihr wäret	ihr würdet
sie hätten	sie wären	sie würden

(3) PAST SUBJUNCTIVE I

ich habe gehabt	ich sei gewesen	ich sei geworden
du habest gehabt	du seiest gewesen	du seiest geworden
er habe gehabt	er sei gewesen	er sei geworden
wir haben gehabt	wir seien gewesen	wir seien geworden
ihr habet gehabt	ihr seiet gewesen	ihr seiet geworden
sie haben gehabt	sie seien gewesen	sie seien geworden

(4) PAST SUBJUNCTIVE II

ich hätte gehabt	ich wäre gewesen	ich wäre geworden
du hättest gehabt	du wärest gewesen	du wärest geworden
er hätte gehabt	er wäre gewesen	er wäre geworden
wir hätten gehabt	wir wären gewesen	wir wären geworden
ihr hättet gehabt	ihr wäret gewesen	ihr wäret geworden
sie hätten gehabt	sie wären gewesen	sie wären geworden

(5) FUTURE SUBJUNCTIVE I

ich werde haben	ich werde sein	ich werde werden
du werdest haben	du werdest sein	du werdest werden
er werde haben	er werde sein	er werde werden
wir werden haben	wir werden sein	wir werden werden
ihr werdet haben	ihr werdet sein	ihr werdet werden
sie werden haben	sie werden sein	sie werden werden

(6) FUTURE PERFECT SUBJUNCTIVE I

ich werde			
du werdest			
sie werde	gehabt haben	gewesen sein	geworden sein
wir werden			
ihr werdet			
sie werden			

C. The conditional mood:

(1) PRESENT

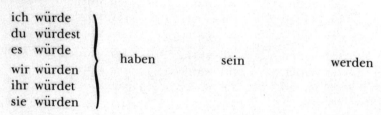

ich würde
du würdest
es würde
wir würden
ihr würdet
sie würden
}   haben   sein   werden

(2) PAST

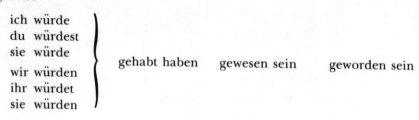

ich würde
du würdest
sie würde
wir würden
ihr würdet
sie würden
}   gehabt haben   gewesen sein   geworden sein

D. The imperative mood:

	SINGULAR	
habe!	sei!	werde!
haben Sie!	seien Sie!	werden Sie!
	PLURAL	
habt!	seid!	werdet!
haben Sie!	seien Sie!	werden Sie!

E. Infinitives:

(1) PRESENT: haben, sein, werden.

(2) PAST: gehabt haben, gewesen sein, geworden sein.

F. Participles:

(1) PRESENT: habend, seiend, werdend. (These forms are rarely used.)

(2) PAST: gehabt, gewesen, geworden.

§103. THE WEAK CONJUGATION

The weak verb **lernen (lernte, hat gelernt)** is conjugated as follows:

A. The indicative mood:

(1) PRESENT (*I learn, am learning, do learn*)

ich lerne
du lernst
er lernt

wir lernen
ihr lernt
sie lernen

(2) SIMPLE PAST (*I learned, have learned*)

ich lernte
du lerntest
sie lernte

wir lernten
ihr lerntet
sie lernten

(3) COMPOUND PAST (*same as* SIMPLE PAST)

ich habe   gelernt
du hast   gelernt
es   hat   gelernt

wir haben gelernt
ihr habt   gelernt
sie haben gelernt

(4) PAST PERFECT (*I had learned*)

ich hatte   gelernt
du hattest gelernt
sie hatte   gelernt

wir hatten gelernt
ihr hattet gelernt
sie hatten gelernt

(5) FUTURE (*I shall learn*)

ich werde   lernen
du wirst   lernen
er   wird   lernen

wir werden lernen
ihr werdet lernen
sie werden lernen

B. The subjunctive mood:

(1) PRESENT SUBJ. I

ich lerne
du lernest
er lerne

wir lernen
ihr lernet
sie lernen

(2) PRESENT SUBJ. II

ich lernte
du lerntest
sie lernte

wir lernten
ihr lerntet
sie lernten

(3) PAST SUBJ. I

ich habe   gelernt
du habest gelernt
es   habe   gelernt

wir haben gelernt
ihr habet gelernt
sie haben gelernt

(4) PAST SUBJ. II

ich hätte   gelernt
du hättest gelernt
sie hätte   gelernt

wir hätten gelernt
ihr hättet gelernt
sie hätten gelernt

(5) FUTURE SUBJ. I

ich werde   lernen
du werdest lernen
er   werde   lernen

wir werden lernen
ihr werdet lernen
sie werden lernen

(6) FUTURE PERFECT (*I shall have learned*)

ich werde	gelernt haben
du wirst	gelernt haben
sie wird	gelernt haben
wir werden	gelernt haben
ihr werdet	gelernt haben
sie werden	gelernt haben

(6) FUTURE PERF. SUBJ. I

ich werde	gelernt haben
du werdest	gelernt haben
sie werde	gelernt haben
wir werden	gelernt haben
ihr werdet	gelernt haben
sie werden	gelernt haben

C. The conditional mood:

(1) PRESENT

ich würde	lernen
du würdest	lernen
er würde	lernen
wir würden	lernen
ihr würdet	lernen
sie würden	lernen

(2) PAST

ich würde	gelernt haben
du würdest	gelernt haben
er würde	gelernt haben
wir würden	gelernt haben
ihr würdet	gelernt haben
sie würden	gelernt haben

D. The imperative mood:

SINGULAR	PLURAL
lerne!	lernt!
lernen Sie!	lernen Sie!

E. Infinitives:

(1) PRESENT: lernen

(2) PAST: gelernt haben

F. Participles:

(1) PRESENT: lernend

(2) PAST: gelernt

Note: For passive forms (of the verb **sehen**) see §108.

§104. THE STRONG CONJUNGATION

A. Sehen. The strong verb **sehen** (**sah, hat gesehen**) is conjugated as follows:

(1) **The indicative mood:**

   (*a*) PRESENT (*I see, I am seeing, I do see*)

ich sehe
du siehst
es sieht

wir sehen
ihr seht
sie sehen

   (b) SIMPLE PAST (*I saw, I have seen*)

ich sah
du sahst
sie sah

wir sahen
ihr saht
sie sahen

   (*c*) COMPOUND PAST (*same as* SIMPLE PAST)

ich habe   gesehen
du hast   gesehen
er hat   gesehen

wir haben gesehen
ihr habt   gesehen
sie haben gesehen

   (*d*) PAST PERFECT (*I had seen*)

ich hatte   gesehen
du hattest gesehen
sie hatte   gesehen

wir hatten gesehen
ihr hattet gesehen
sie hatten gesehen

   (*e*) FUTURE (*I shall see*)

ich werde   sehen
du wirst   sehen
er wird   sehen

wir werden sehen
ihr werdet sehen
sie werden sehen

(2) **The subjunctive mood:**

   (*a*) PRESENT SUBJ. I

ich sehe
du sehest
es sehe

wir sehen
ihr sehet
sie sehen

   (*b*) PRESENT SUBJ. II

ich sähe
du sähest
sie sähe

wir sähen
ihr sähet
sie sähen

   (*c*) PAST SUBJ. I

ich habe   gesehen
du habest gesehen
er habe   gesehen

wir haben gesehen
ihr habet gesehen
sie haben gesehen

   (*d*) PAST SUBJ. II

ich hätte   gesehen
du hättest gesehen
sie hätte   gesehen

wir hätten gesehen
ihr hättet gesehen
sie hätten gesehen

   (*e*) FUTURE SUBJ. I

ich werde   sehen
du werdest sehen
er werde   sehen

wir werden sehen
ihr werdet sehen
sie werden sehen

(*f*) FUTURE PERFECT (*I shall have seen*)

ich werde   gesehen haben
du wirst   gesehen haben
sie wird   gesehen haben

wir werden gesehen haben
ihr werdet gesehen haben
sie werden gesehen haben

(*f*) FUTURE PERF. SUBJ. I

ich werde   gesehen haben
du werdest gesehen haben
sie werde   gesehen haben

wir werden gesehen haben
ihr werdet gesehen haben
sie werden gesehen haben

(3) **The conditional mood:**

(*a*) PRESENT

ich würde   sehen
du würdest sehen
er würde   sehen

wir würden sehen
ihr würdet sehen
sie würden sehen

(*b*) PAST

ich würde   gesehen haben
du würdest gesehen haben
er würde   gesehen haben

wir würden gesehen haben
ihr würdet gesehen haben
sie würden gesehen haben

(4) **The imperative mood:**

SINGULAR	PLURAL
sieh!	seht!
sehen Sie!	sehen Sie!

(5) **Infinitives:**

(*a*) PRESENT: sehen
(*b*) PAST: gesehen haben

(6) **Participles:**

(*a*) PRESENT: sehend
(*b*) PAST: gesehen

Note: Passive forms of the verb **sehen** are given in §108.

B. Kommen. The strong verb **kommen** (**kam, ist gekommen**) is conjugated as follows:

(1) The indicative mood:

(a) PRESENT (*I come, etc.*)

ich komme
du kommst
es kommt

wir kommen
ihr kommt
sie kommen

(b) SIMPLE PAST (*I came, have come*)

ich kam
du kamst
sie kam

wir kamen
ihr kamt
sie kamen

(c) COMPOUND PAST (*same as* SIMPLE PAST)

ich bin gekommen
du bist gekommen
er ist gekommen

wir sind gekommen
ihr seid gekommen
sie sind gekommen

(d) PAST PERFECT (*I had come*)

ich war gekommen
du warst gekommen
sie war gekommen

wir waren gekommen
ihr wart gekommen
sie waren gekommen

(e) FUTURE (*I shall come*)

ich werde kommen
du wirst   kommen
es wird   kommen

wir werden kommen
ihr werdet kommen
sie werden kommen

(2) The subjunctive mood:

(a) PRESENT SUBJ. I

ich komme
du kommest
es komme

wir kommen
ihr kommet
sie kommen

(b) PRESENT SUBJ. II

ich käme
du kämest
sie käme

wir kämen
ihr kämet
sie kämen

(c) PAST SUBJ. I

ich sei   gekommen
du seiest gekommen
er sei   gekommen

wir seien gekommen
ihr seiet gekommen
sie seien gekommen

(d) PAST SUBJ. II

ich wäre gekommen
du wärest gekommen
sie wäre gekommen

wir wären gekommen
ihr wäret gekommen
sie wären gekommen

(e) FUTURE SUBJ. I

ich werde kommen
du werdest kommen
es werde kommen

wir werden kommen
ihr werdet kommen
sie werden kommen

(*f*) FUTURE PERFECT
(*I shall have come*)

ich werde   gekommen sein
du wirst   gekommen sein
er wird   gekommen sein

wir werden gekommen sein
ihr werdet gekommen sein
sie werden gekommen sein

(*f*) FUTURE PERF. SUBJ. I

ich werde   gekommen sein
du werdest gekommen sein
er werde   gekommen sein

wir werden gekommen sein
ihr werdet gekommen sein
sie werden gekommen sein

(3) The conditional mood:

(*a*) PRESENT

ich würde   kommen
du würdest kommen
sie würde   kommen

wir würden kommen
ihr würdet kommen
sie würden kommen

(*b*) PAST

ich würde   gekommen sein
du würdest gekommen sein
sie würde   gekommen sein

wir würden gekommen sein
ihr würdet gekommen sein
sie würden gekommen sein

(4) The imperative mood:

SINGULAR	PLURAL
komme!	kommt!
kommen Sie!	kommen Sie!

(5) Infinitives:

(*a*) PRESENT: kommen
(*b*) PAST: gekommen sein

(6) Participles:

(*a*) PRESENT: kommend
(*b*) PAST: gekommen

§105. SEPARABLE VERBS

The separable verb **anfangen (fing an, hat angefangen)** is conjugated as follows:

A. The indicative mood:

(1) PRESENT (*I begin, etc.*)

ich fange an
du fängst an, *etc.*

(2) SIMPLE PAST (*I began, etc.*)

ich fing an, *etc.*

B. The subjunctive mood:

(1) PRESENT SUBJ. I

ich fange an
du fangest an, *etc.*

(2) PRESENT SUBJ. II

ich finge an, *etc.*

(3) COMPOUND PAST (*same as* SIMPLE PAST)

ich habe angefangen
du hast angefangen, *etc.*

(4) PAST PERFECT (*I had begun*)

ich hatte angefangen, *etc.*

(5) FUTURE (*I shall begin*)

ich werde anfangen
du wirst anfangen, *etc.*

(6) FUTURE PERFECT (*I shall have begun*)

ich werde angefangen haben
du wirst angefangen haben
etc.

(3) PAST SUBJ. I

ich habe angefangen
du habest angefangen, *etc.*

(4) PAST SUBJ. II

ich hätte angefangen, *etc.*

(5) FUTURE SUBJ. I

ich werde anfangen
du werdest anfangen, *etc.*

(6) FUTURE PERFECT SUBJ. I

ich werde angefangen haben
du werdest angefangen haben, *etc.*

C. The conditional mood:

(1) PRESENT: ich würde anfangen, *etc.*

(2) PAST: ich würde angefangen haben, *etc.*

D. Imperatives:

SINGULAR	PLURAL
fange an!	fangt an!
fangen Sie an!	fangen Sie an!

E. Infinitives:

(1) PRESENT: anfangen
(2) PAST: angefangen haben

F. Participles:

(1) PRESENT: anfangend
(2) PAST: angefangen

§106. INSEPARABLE VERBS

The inseparable verb **beginnen** (**begann, hat begonnen**) is conjugated as follows:

A. The indicative mood:

(1) PRESENT (*I begin, etc.*)

ich beginne
du beginnst, *etc.*

B. The subjunctive mood:

(1) PRESENT SUBJ. I

ich beginne
du beginnest, *etc.*

(2) SIMPLE PAST (*I began, etc.*)

ich begann, *etc.*

(3) COMPOUND PAST

ich habe begonnen
du hast begonnen, *etc.*

(4) PAST PERFECT (*I had begun*)

ich hatte begonnen, *etc.*

(5) FUTURE (*I shall begin*)

ich werde beginnen
du wirst   beginnen, *etc.*

(6) FUTURE PERFECT (*I shall have begun*)

ich werde begonnen haben
du wirst   begonnen haben
etc.

(2) PRESENT SUBJ. II

ich begönne (*or* begänne), *etc.*

(3) PAST SUBJ. I

ich habe   begonnen
du habest begonnen, *etc.*

(4) PAST SUBJ. II

ich hätte begonnen, *etc.*

(5) FUTURE SUBJ. I

ich werde   beginnen,
du werdest beginnen, *etc.*

(6) FUTURE PERFECT SUBJ. I

ich werde   begonnen haben
du werdest begonnen haben
etc.

C. The conditional mood:

(1) PRESENT: ich würde beginnen, *etc.*

(2) PAST: ich würde begonnen haben, *etc.*

D. The imperative mood:

SINGULAR	PLURAL
beginne!	beginnt!
beginnen Sie!	beginnen Sie!

E. Infinitives:

(1) PRESENT: beginnen
(2) PAST: begonnen haben

F. Participles:

(1) PRESENT: beginnend
(2) PAST: begonnen

§107. REFLEXIVE VERBS

A. Direct reflexives. The direct reflexive verb **sich setzen (setzte sich, hat sich gesetzt)** is conjugated as follows:

(1) **The indicative mood:**

(a) PRESENT (*I sit down, etc.*)

ich setze mich
du setzt dich
er setzt sich

wir setzen uns
ihr setzt euch
sie setzen sich

(b) SIMPLE PAST (*I sat* or *have sat down*)

ich setzte mich
du setztest dich
sie setzte sich

wir setzten uns
ihr setztet euch
sie setzten sich

(c) COMPOUND PAST (*same as* SIMPLE PAST)

ich habe mich gesetzt
du hast dich gesetzt, *etc.*

(d) PAST PERFECT (*I had sat down*)

ich hatte mich gesetzt, *etc.*

(e) FUTURE (*I shall sit down*)

ich werde mich setzen
du wirst dich setzen, *etc.*

(f) FUTURE PERFECT (*I shall have sat down*)

ich werde mich gesetzt haben
du wirst dich gesetzt haben
etc.

(2) **The subjuntive mood:**

(a) PRESENT SUBJ. I

ich setze mich
du setzest dich
er setze sich

wir setzen uns
ihr setzet euch
sie setzen sich

(b) PRESENT SUBJ. II

ich setzte mich
du setztest dich
sie setzte sich

wir setzten uns
ihr setztet euch
sie setzten sich

(c) PAST SUBJ. I

ich habe   mich gesetzt
du habest dich gesetzt, *etc.*

(d) PAST SUBJ. II

ich hätte mich gesetzt, *etc.*

(e) FUTURE SUBJ. I

ich werde   mich setzen
du werdest dich setzen, *etc.*

(f) FUTURE PERF. SUBJ. I

ich werde   mich gesetzt
haben
du werdest dich gesetzt
haben, *etc.*

(3) **The conditional mood:**

(*a*) PRESENT: ich würde mich setzen, *etc.*

(*b*) PAST: ich würde mich gesetzt haben, *etc.*

(4) **The imperative mood:**

SINGULAR	PLURAL
setze dich!	setzt euch!
setzen Sie sich!	setzen Sie sich!

(5) **Infinitives:**

(*a*) PRESENT: sich setzen
(*b*) PAST: sich gesetzt haben

(6) **Participles:**

(*a*) PRESENT: sich setzend
(*b*) PAST: sich gesetzt

B. **Reflexives that take the dative.** The reflexive verb **sich schaden (schadete sich, hat sich geschadet)** is conjugated as follows:

(1) **The indicative mood:**

(*a*) PRESENT (*I hurt myself*)

ich schade mir
du schadest dir
er schadet sich

wir schaden uns
ihr schadet euch
sie schaden sich

(*b*) SIMPLE PAST: (*I hurt* or *have hurt myself*)

ich schadete mir, *etc.*

(*c*) COMPOUND PAST: (*same as* SIMPLE PAST)

ich habe mir geschadet
du hast dir geschadet, *etc.*

(*d*) PAST PERFECT: (*I had hurt myself*)

ich hatte mir geschadet, *etc.*

(2) **The subjunctive mood:**

(*a*) PRESENT SUBJ. I

ich schade mir
du schadest dir
er schade sich

wir schaden uns
ihr schadet euch
sie schaden sich

(*b*) PRESENT SUBJ. II

ich schadete mir, *etc.*

(*c*) PAST SUBJ. I

ich habe mir geschadet
du habest dir geschadet, *etc.*

(*d*) PAST SUBJ. II

ich hätte mir geschadet, *etc.*

(*e*) FUTURE (*I shall hurt myself*)

ich werde mir schaden
du wirst dir schaden, *etc.*

(*f*) FUTURE PERFECT (*I shall have hurt myself*)

ich werde mir geschadet haben
du wirst dir geschadet haben
etc.

(*e*) FUTURE SUBJ. I

ich werde   mir schaden
du werdest dir schaden, *etc.*

(*f*) FUTURE PERF. SUBJ. I

ich werde   mir geschadet haben
du werdest dir geschadet haben, *etc.*

(3) **The conditional mood:**

    (*a*) PRESENT: ich würde mir schaden, *etc.*

    (*b*) PAST: ich würde mir geschadet haben, *etc.*

(4) **The imperative mood** (*of* sich denken, *to imagine*):

SINGULAR	PLURAL
denke dir!	denkt euch!
denken Sie sich!	denken Sie sich!

(5) **Infinitives:**

    (*a*) PRESENT: sich schaden

    (*b*) PAST: sich geschadet haben

(6) **Participles:**

    (*a*) PRESENT: sich schadend

    (*b*) PAST: sich geschadet

§108. THE PASSIVE VOICE

The passive of **sehen** (**sah, hat gesehen**) is conjugated as follows:

A. The indicative mood:

(1) PRESENT [*I am (being) seen, etc.*]:

ich werde   gesehen
du wirst   gesehen
sie wird   gesehen

wir werden gesehen
ihr werdet gesehen
sie werden gesehen

B. The subjunctive mood:

(1) PRESENT SUBJ. I

ich werde   gesehen
du werdest gesehen
sie werde   gesehen

wir werden gesehen
ihr werdet gesehen
sie werden gesehen

(2) SIMPLE PAST [*I was (being) seen*]

ich wurde   gesehen
du wurdest gesehen
es wurde   gesehen

wir wurden gesehen
ihr wurdet gesehen
sie wurden gesehen

(3) COMPOUND PAST (*same as SIMPLE PAST*)

ich bin gesehen worden
du bist gesehen worden
er ist   gesehen worden

wir sind gesehen worden
ihr seid gesehen worden
sie sind gesehen worden

(4) PAST PERFECT (*I had been seen*)

ich war   gesehen worden
du warst gesehen worden
es war   gesehen worden

wir waren gesehen worden
ihr wart   gesehen worden
sie waren gesehen worden

(5) FUTURE (*I shall be seen*)

ich werde   gesehen werden
du wirst   gesehen werden
sie wird   gesehen werden

wir werden gesehen werden
ihr werdet gesehen werden
sie werden gesehen werden

(6) FUTURE PERFECT (*I shall have been seen*)

ich werde
du wirst
er wird
wir werden
ihr werdet
sie werden
} gesehen worden sein

(2) PRESENT SUBJ. II

ich würde   gesehen
du würdest gesehen
es würde   gesehen

wir würden gesehen
ihr würdet gesehen
sie würden gesehen

(3) PAST SUBJ. I

ich sei   gesehen worden
du seiest gesehen worden
er sei   gesehen worden

wir seien gesehen worden
ihr seiet gesehen worden
sie seien gesehen worden

(4) PAST SUBJ. II

ich wäre   gesehen worden
du wärest gesehen worden
es wäre   gesehen worden

wir wären gesehen worden
ihr wäret gesehen worden
sie wären gesehen worden

(5) FUTURE SUBJ. I

ich werde   gesehen werden
du werdest gesehen werden
sie werde   gesehen werden

wir werden gesehen werden
ihr werdet gesehen werden
sie werden gesehen werden

(6) FUTURE PERFECT SUBJ. I

ich werde
du werdest
er werde
wir werden
ihr werdet
sie werden
} gesehen worden sein

C. The conditional mood:

(1) PRESENT

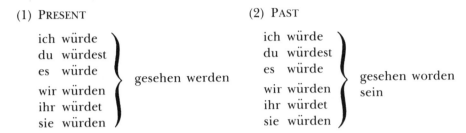

ich würde
du würdest
es würde
wir würden
ihr würdet
sie würden
⎫ gesehen werden

(2) PAST

ich würde
du würdest
es würde
wir würden
ihr würdet
sie würden
⎫ gesehen worden sein

D. The imperative mood:

SINGULAR	PLURAL
sei (*or* werde) gesehen!	seid (*or* werdet) gesehen!
seien (*or* werden) Sie gesehen!	seien (*or* werden) Sie gesehen!

Note: The passive imperative is quite rare. See §74 E for examples.

E. Infinitives:

(1) PRESENT: gesehen werden

(2) PAST: gesehen worden sein

F. Participles:

(1) PRESENT: — (present participles are naturally active)

(2) PAST: gesehen

§109. THE MODAL AUXILIARIES

The modals **können, wollen, müssen, mögen, dürfen,** and **sollen** are conjugated as follows:

A. The indicative mood:

(1) PRESENT:

	KÖNNEN	WOLLEN	MÜSSEN	MÖGEN	DÜRFEN	SOLLEN
ich	kann	will	muß	mag	darf	soll
du	kannst	willst	mußt	magst	darfst	sollst
er	kann	will	muß	mag	darf	soll

wir	können	wollen	müssen	mögen	dürfen	sollen
ihr	könnt	wollt	müßt	mögt	dürft	sollt
sie	können	wollen	müssen	mögen	dürfen	sollen

(2) SIMPLE PAST: ich konnte, wollte, mußte, mochte, durfte, sollte

(3) COMPOUND PAST: ich habe gekonnt, gewollt, gemußt, gemocht, gedurft, gesollt

Note: Participles assume the form of an infinitive when used with dependent infinitives.

(4) PAST PERFECT: ich hatte gekonnt, gewollt, gemußt, gemocht, gedurft, gesollt

(5) FUTURE: ich werde können, wollen, müssen, mögen, dürfen, sollen

(6) FUTURE PERFECT: ich werde gekonnt haben, gewollt haben, gemußt haben, gemocht haben, gedurft haben, gesollt haben

B. The subjunctive mood:

(1) PRESENT I: ich könne, wolle, müsse, möge, dürfe, solle

(2) PRESENT II: ich könnte, wollte, müßte, möchte, dürfte, sollte

(3) PAST I: ich habe gekonnt, gewollt, gemußt, *etc.*

(4) PAST II: ich hätte gekonnt, gewollt, *etc.*

(5) FUTURE I: ich werde können, wollen, müssen, *etc.*

(6) FUTURE PERFECT I: ich werde gekonnt haben, gewollt haben, gemußt haben, *etc.*

C. The conditional mood. The conditional of modals is quite rare and should be avoided.

D. The imperative mood:

SINGULAR	PLURAL
wolle!	wollt!
wollen Sie!	wollen Sie!

Note: **Wollen** is the only modal having imperative forms.

E. Infinitives:

(1) PRESENT: können, wollen, müssen, mögen, dürfen, sollen.

(2) PAST: gekonnt haben, gewollt haben, gemußt haben, gemocht haben, gedurft haben, gesollt haben.

F. Participles:

PAST: without complementary infinitive—gekonnt, *etc.*

PAST: with complementary infinitive—können, *etc.*

Note: The present participle of modals no longer exist.

§110. IRREGULAR WEAK VERBS AND THE PRESENT INDICATIVE OF *WISSEN*

A. Irregular weak verbs:

INFINITIVE	PAST INDICATIVE	COMP. PAST INDICATIVE	PRESENT INDICATIVE	PRESENT SUBJ. II	IMPERATIVE	
brennen	brannte	hat gebrannt	er brennt	brennte	brenn(e)	*to burn*
rennen	rannte	ist gerannt	er rennt	rennte	renn(e)	*to run*
kennen	kannte	hat gekannt	er kennt	kennte	kenn(e)	*to know*
nennen	nannte	hat genanant	er nennt	nennte	nenn(e)	*to name*
senden	sandte (sendete)	hat gesandt (gesendet)	er sendet	sendete	send(e)	*to send*
wenden	wandte (wendete)	hat gewandt (gewendet)	er wendet	wendete	wend(e)	*to turn*
denken	dachte	hat gedacht	er denkt	dächte	denk(e)	*to think*
bringen	brachte	hat gebracht	er bringt	brächte	bring(e)	*to bring*
wissen	wußte	hat gewußt	er weiß	wüßte	wisse	*to know*

B. Present indicative of *wissen*. Although not a modal auxiliary, **wissen** resembles modals in the conjugation of its present indicative:

SINGULAR	PLURAL
ich weiß	wir wissen
du weißt	ihr wißt
es weiß	sie wissen

§111. PRINCIPAL PARTS OF STRONG AND IRREGULAR VERBS

INFINITIVE	PAST INDICATIVE	COMP. PAST INDICATIVE	PRESENT INDICATIVE	PRESENT SUBJ. II	IMPERATIVE	
backen	buk	hat gebacken	er bäckt	büke	back(e)	to bake
befehlen	befahl	hat befohlen	sie befiehlt	beföhle	befiehl	to command
beginnen	begann	hat begonnen	er beginnt	begönne (begänne)	beginn(e)	to begin
beißen	biß	hat gebissen	er beißt	bisse	beiß(e)	to bite
bergen	barg	hat geborgen	er birgt	bürge (bärge)	birg	to hide
bersten	barst	ist geborsten	sie birst	börste (bärste)	birst	to burst
betrügen	betrog	hat betrogen	er betrügt	betröge	betrüg(e)	to deceive
bewegen	bewog	hat bewogen	sie bewegt	bewöge	beweg(e)	to induce (= to move, is weak)
biegen	bog	hat gebogen	sie biegt	böge	bieg(e)	to bend
bieten	bot	hat geboten	er bietet	böte	biet(e)	to offer
binden	band	hat gebunden	er bindet	bände	bind(e)	to bind
bitten	bat	hat gebeten	sie bittet	bäte	bitte	to ask
blasen	blies	hat geblasen	er bläst	bliese	blas(e)	to blow
bleiben	blieb	ist geblieben	sie bleibt	bliebe	bleib(e)	to remain
braten	briet	hat gebraten	er brät	briete	brat(e)	to roast
brechen	brach	hat gebrochen	sie bricht	bräche	brich	to break
dringen	drang	hat gedrungen	er dringt	dränge	dring(e)	to press
dürfen	durfte	hat gedurft	er darf	dürfte	—	to be allowed

cinladen (*see* laden)

INFINITIVE	PAST INDICATIVE	COMP. PAST INDICATIVE	PRESENT INDICATIVE	PRESENT SUBJ. II	IMPERATIVE	
empfehlen	empfahl	hat empfohlen	sie empfiehlt	empföhle (empfähle)	empfiehl	*to recommend*
erlöschen	erlosch	ist erloschen	es erlischt	erlösche	erlisch	*to go out, become extinguished*
erschrecken	erschrak	ist erschrocken	er erschrickt	erschräke	erschrick	*to be frightened (= to frighten, trans., is weak)*
essen	aß	hat gegessen	sie ißt	äße	iß	*to eat*
fahren	fuhr	ist gefahren	er fährt	führe	fahr(e)	*to drive, ride, go*
fallen	fiel	ist gefallen	sie fällt	fiele	fall(e)	*to fall*
fangen	fing	hat gefangen	sie fängt	finge	fang(e)	*to catch*
fechten	focht	hat gefochten	er ficht	föchte	ficht	*to fight, duel*
finden	fand	hat gefunden	er findet	fände	find(e)	*to find*
flechten	flocht	hat geflochten	er flicht	flöchte	flicht	*to braid*
fliegen	flog	ist geflogen	sie fliegt	flöge	flieg(e)	*to fly*
fliehen	floh	ist geflohen	er flieht	flöhe	flieh(e)	*to flee*
fließen	floß	ist geflossen	es fließt	flösse	fließ(e)	*to flow*
fressen	fraß	hat gefressen	es frißt	fräße	friß	*to eat (of animals)*
frieren	fror	hat gefroren	er friert	fröre	frier(e)	*to freeze*
gebären	gebar	hat geboren	sie gebiert	gebäre	gebier	*to bear, give birth to*

Infinitive	Simple past	Subjunctive II	Present	Perfect	Imperative	Meaning
geben	gab	gäbe	er gibt	hat gegeben	gib	to give
gedeihen	gedieh	gediehe	sie gedeiht	ist gediehen	gedeih(e)	to thrive
gehen	ging	ginge	er geht	ist gegangen	geh(e)	to go
gelingen	gelang	gelänge	es gelingt	ist gelungen	—	to succeed
gelten	galt	gölte (gälte)	es gilt	hat gegolten	gilt	to be worth
genesen	genas	genäse	er genest	ist genesen	genese	to recover
genießen	genoß	genösse	sie genießt	hat genossen	genieß(e)	to enjoy
geschehen	geschah	geschähe	es geschieht	ist geschehen	—	to happen
gewinnen	gewann	gewönne (gewänne)	sie gewinnt	hat gewonnen	gewinn(e)	to win, gain
gießen	goß	gösse	es gießt	hat gegossen	gieß(e)	to pour
gleichen	glich	gliche	es gleicht	hat geglichen	gleich(e)	to be like, resemble
gleiten	glitt	glitte	er gleitet	ist geglitten	gleit(e)	to glide
graben	grub	grübe	er gräbt	hat gegraben	grab(e)	to dig
greifen	griff	griffe	er greift	hat gegriffen	greif(e)	to seize
haben	hatte	hätte	sie hat	hat gehabt	hab(e)	to have
halten	hielt	hielte	er hält	hat gehalten	halt(e)	to hold
hangen	hing	hinge	er hängt	hat gehangen	hang(e)	to hang (intr.)
hauen	hieb	hiebe	sie haut	hat gehauen	hau(e)	to hew, chop
heben	hob	höbe (hübe)	sie hebt	hat gehoben	heb(e)	to lift
heißen	hieß	hieße	es heißt	hat geheißen	heiß(e)	to be called
helfen	half	hülfe (hälfe)	er hilft	hat geholfen	hilf	to help
kennen	kannte	kennte	er kennt	hat gekannt	kenne	to know
klingen	klang	klänge	es klingt	hat geklungen	kling(e)	to sound
kommen	kam	käme	er kommt	ist gekommen	komm(e)	to come
können	konnte	könnte	er kann	hat gekonnt	—	to be able

INFINITIVE	PAST INDICATIVE	COMP. PAST INDICATIVE	PRESENT INDICATIVE	PRESENT SUBJ. II	IMPERATIVE	
kriechen	kroch	ist gekrochen	er kriecht	kröche	kriech(e)	to creep
laden	lud (ladete)	hat geladen	sie ladet (lädt)	lüde (ladete)	lad(e)	to invite (usually **einladen**)
lassen	ließ	hat gelassen	er läßt	ließe	laß	to let
laufen	lief	ist gelaufen	sie läuft	liefe	lauf(e)	to run
leiden	litt	hat gelitten	er leidet	litte	leid(e)	to suffer
leihen	lieh	hat geliehen	er leiht	liehe	leih(e)	to lend
lesen	las	hat gelesen	er liest	läse	lies	to read
liegen	lag	hat gelegen	es liegt	läge	lieg(e)	to lie
lügen	log	hat gelogen	er lügt	löge	lüg(e)	to (tell a) lie
meiden	mied	hat gemieden	er meidet	miede	meid(e)	to avoid
messen	maß	hat gemessen	sie mißt	mäße	miß	to measure
mögen	mochte	hat gemocht	er mag	möchte	—	to like; may
müssen	mußte	hat gemußt	er muß	müßte	—	to have, to must
nehmen	nahm	hat genommen	sie nimmt	nähme	nimm	to take
pfeifen	pfiff	hat gepfiffen	sie pfeift	pfiffe	pfeif(e)	to whistle
preisen	pries	hat gepriesen	er preist	priese	preis(e)	to praise
quellen	quoll	ist gequollen	es quillt	quölle	quill	to gush forth
raten	riet	hat geraten	sie rät	riete	rat(e)	to advise; guess
reiben	rieb	hat gerieben	er reibt	riebe	reib(e)	to rub
reißen	riß	hat gerissen	er reißt	risse	reiß(e)	to tear
reiten	ritt	ist geritten	sie reitet	ritte	reit(e)	to ride
riechen	roch	hat gerochen	es riecht	röche	riech(e)	to smell

Infinitive	Simple past	Subjunctive	3rd pers. sing.	Perfect	Imperative	Meaning
rufen	rief	riefe	er ruft	hat gerufen	ruf(e)	to call
saufen	soff	söffe	er säuft	hat gesoffen	sauf(e)	to guzzle
schaffen	schuf	schüfe	sie schafft	hat geschaffen	schaff(e)	to create (= to work, is weak)
scheiden	schied	schiede	er scheidet	ist geschieden	scheid(e)	to part
scheinen	schien	schiene	er scheint	hat geschienen	schein(e)	to seem; shine
scheißen	schiß	schisse	er scheißt	hat geschissen	scheiß(e)	to defecate
schelten	schalt	schölte (schälte)	er schilt	hat gescholten	schilt	to scold
schieben	schob	schöbe	sie schiebt	hat geschoben	schieb(e)	to shove
schießen	schoß	schösse	er schießt	hat geschossen	schieß(e)	to shoot
schlafen	schlief	schliefe	sie schläft	hat geschlafen	schlaf(e)	to sleep
schlagen	schlug	schlüge	er schlägt	hat geschlagen	schlag(e)	to strike
schleichen	schlich	schliche	es schleicht	ist geschlichen	schleich(e)	to creep
schließen	schloß	schlösse	er schließt	hat geschlossen	schließ(e)	to shut
schleifen	schliff	schliffe	er schleift	hat geschliffen	schleif(e)	to whet
schmelzen	schmolz	schmölze	es schmilzt	ist geschmolzen	schmilz	to melt
schneiden	schnitt	schnitte	er schneidet	hat geschnitten	schneid(e)	to cut
schreiben	schrieb	schriebe	sie schreibt	hat geschrieben	schreib(e)	to write
schreien	schrie	schriee	er schrei*	hat geschrie(e)n	schrei(e)	to cry
schreiten	schritt	schritte	sie schreitet	ist geschritten	schreit(e)	to stride
schweigen	schwieg	schwiege	sie schweigt	hat geschwiegen	schweig(e)	to be silent
schwellen	schwoll	schwölle	es schwillt	ist geschwollen	schwill	to swell
schwimmen	schwamm	schwömme (schwämme)	er schwimmt	ist geschwommen	schwimm(e)	to swim

INFINITIVE	PAST INDICATIVE	COMP. PAST INDICATIVE	PRESENT INDICATIVE	PRESENT SUBJ. II	IMPERATIVE	
schwinden	schwand	ist geschwunden	sie schwindet	schwände	schwind(e)	*to vanish (usually* **versch-winden***)*
schwingen	schwang	hat geschwungen	es schwingt	schwänge	schwing(e)	*to swing*
schwören	schwur (schwor)	hat geschworen	sie schwört	schwüre	schwör(e)	*to swear*
sehen	sah	hat gesehen	er sieht	sähe	sieh	*to see*
sein	war	ist gewesen	er ist	wäre	sei	*to be*
sieden	sott (siedete)[1]	hat gesotten	es siedet	sötte	sied(e)	*to boil*
singen	sang	hat gesungen	er singt	sänge	sing(e)	*to sing*
sinken	sank	ist gesunken	es sinkt	sänke	sink(e)	*to sink*
sinnen	sann	hat gesonnen	sie sinnt	sönne (sänne)	sinn(e)	*to think*
sitzen	saß	hat gesessen	er sitzt	säße	sitz(e)	*to sit*
sollen	sollte	hat gesollt	er soll	sollte	—	*to be (required) to; should, ought to*
speien	spie	hat gespie(e)n	er speit	spiee	spei(e)	*to spit*
spinnen	spann	hat gesponnen	er spinnt	spönne (spänne)	spinn(e)	*to spin*
sprechen	sprach	hat gesprochen	sie spricht	spräche	sprich	*to speak*
sprießen	sproß	ist gesprossen	es sprießt	sprösse	spriß(e)	*to sprout*
springen	sprang	ist gesprungen	er springt	spränge	spring(e)	*to jump*
stechen	stach	hat gestochen	es sticht	stäche	stich	*to prick*

Infinitive	Past	Perfect	Present	Past Subjunctive	Imperative	English
stehen	stand	hat gestanden	er steht	stände (stünde)	steh(e)	to stand
stehlen	stahl	hat gestohlen	er stiehlt	stöle (stähle)	stiehl	to steal
steigen	stieg	ist gestiegen	sie steigt	stiege	steig(e)	to climb
sterben	starb	ist gestorben	er stirbt	stürbe	stirb	to die
stieben	stob	ist gestoben	sie stiebt	stöbe	stieb(e)	to scatter
stoßen	stieß	hat gestoßen	er stößt	stieße	stoß(e)	to push
streichen	strich	hat gestrichen	er streicht	striche	streich(e)	to stroke
streiten	stritt	hat gestritten	sie streitet	stritte	steit(e)	to contend
tragen	trug	hat getragen	sie trägt	trüge	trag(e)	to carry
treffen	traf	hat getroffen	er trifft	träfe	triff	to meet; hit
treiben	trieb	hat getrieben	sie treibt	triebe	treib(e)	to drive
treten	trat	ist getreten	er tritt	träte	tritt	to step
trinken	trank	hat getrunken	sie trinkt	tränke	trink(e)	to drink
tun	tat	hat getan	er tut	täte	tu(e)	to do
verderben²	verdarb	hat verdorben	es verdirbt	verdürbe	verdirb	to ruin, spoil
vergessen	vergaß	hat vergessen	er vergißt	vergäße	vergiß	to forget
verlieren	velor	hat verloren	sie verliert	verlöre	verlier(e)	to lose
verschwinden	(see schwinden)					
verzeihen	verzieh	hat verziehen	er verzeiht	verziehe	verzeih(e)	to pardon
wachsen	wuchs	ist gewachsen	es wächst	wüchse	wachs(e)	to grow
waschen	wusch	hat gewaschen	er wäscht	wüsche	wasch(e)	to wash
weichen	wich	ist gewichen	es weicht	wiche	weich(e)	to recede
weisen	wies	hat gewiesen	sie weist	wiese	weis(e)	to show

¹The weak form usually occurs in figurative use, e.g., *seethed* with rage.
²As an intransitive verb, **verderben** is conjugated with the auxiliary **sein**.

INFINITIVE	PAST INDICATIVE	COMP. PAST INDICATIVE	PRESENT INDICATIVE	PRESENT SUBJ. II	IMPERATIVE	
werben	warb	hat geworben	er wirbt	würbe	wirb	to recruit
werden	wurde (ward)	ist geworden	es wird	würde	werd(e)	to become
werfen	warf	hat geworfen	sie wirft	würfe	wirf	to throw
wiegen	wog	hat gewogen	er wiegt	wöge	wieg(e)	to weigh
winden	wand	hat gewunden	sie windet	wände	wind(e)	to wind
wollen	wollte	hat gewollt	er will	wollte	wolle	to wish, to want to
ziehen[1]	zog	hat gezogen	sie zieht	zöge	zieh(e)	to pull, tug
zwingen	zwang	hat gezwungen	er zwingt	zwänge	zwing(e)	to force

---

As an intransitive verb, **ziehen** (*to move*) is conjugated with **sein**.

§112. VERBS THAT ARE SIMILAR IN SOUND AND SPELLING

The following verbs are commonly confused because of similarity in sound or spelling:

A. beten, bieten, and bitten:

beten	betete	hat gebetet	*to pray*
bieten	bot	hat geboten	*to offer*
bitten	bat	hat gebeten	*to ask, request*

B. danken and denken:

danken	dankte	hat gedankt	*to thank*
denken	dachte	hat gedacht	*to think*

C. brechen and bringen:

brechen	brach	hat gebrochen	*to break*
bringen	brachte	hat gebracht	*to bring*

D. kennen and können:

kennen	kann	hat gekannt	*to know* (a person or thing)
können	konnte	hat gekonnt	*to know* (by study)

E. legen, liegen, and lügen:

legen	legte	hat gelegt	*to lay*
liegen	lag	hat gelegen	*to lie*
lügen	log	hat gelogen	*to tell a lie*

Note: **sich legen** means *to lie down.*

F. reisen, reißen, and reizen:

reisen	reiste	ist gereist	*to travel*
reißen	riß	hat gerissen	*to tear*
reizen	reizte	hat gereizt	*to stimulate*

G. setzen and sitzen::

setzen	setzte	hat gesetzt	*to set*
sitzen	saß	hat gesessen	*to sit*

Note: **sich setzen** means *to sit down.*

H. lassen and lesen:

lassen	ließ	hat gelassen	*to let, allow*
lesen	las	hat gelesen	*to read*

I. fallen, gefallen, and fällen:

fallen	fiel	ist gefallen	*to fall*
gefallen	gefiel	hat gefallen	*to please*
fällen	fällte	hat gefällt	*to fell*

J. reiten, raten, and retten:

reiten	ritt	ist geritten	*to ride (on horseback)*
raten	riet	hat geraten	*to advise; guess*
retten	rettete	hat gerettet	*to save, rescue*

K. fliegen and fliehen:

fliegen	flog	ist geflogen	*to fly*
fliehen	floh	ist geflohen	*to flee*

L. erschrecken (transitive and intransitive):

erschrecken	erschrak	ist erschrocken	*to be(come) frightened* (intr.)
erschrecken	erschreckte	hat erschreckt	*to frighten* (tr.)

M. schneien and schneiden:

schneien	schneite	hat geschneit	*to snow*
schneiden	schnitt	hat geschnitten	*to cut*

N. fahren and führen:

fahren	fuhr	ist gefahren	*to ride, travel*
führen	führte	hat geführt	*to lead*

O. lernen and lehren:

lernen	lernte	hat gelernt	*to learn, study*
lehren	lehrte	hat gelehrt	*to teach*

P. leiden and leiten:

leiden	litt	hat gelitten	*to suffer*
leiten	leitete	hat geleitet	*to lead*

Q. wachsen and waschen:

wachsen	wuchs	ist gewachsen	*to grow*
waschen	wusch	hat gewaschen	*to wash*

R. ziehen and zeigen:

ziehen	zog	hat gezogen	*to tug, pull*
zeigen	zeigte	hat gezeigt	*to show*

S. reichen, riechen, and rauchen:

reichen	reichte	hat gereicht	*to reach*
riechen	roch	hat gerochen	*to smell*
rauchen	rauchte	hat geraucht	*to smoke*

§113. NOUN PECULIARITIES

A. Nouns used only in the plural. Some of the more common nouns used only in the plural are: Eltern (*parents*), Leute (*people*), Gebrüder (*brothers*), Geschwister (*brothers and sisters*), Ferien (*vacation*), Masern (*measles*), Insignien (*insignia*). Weihnachten (*Christmas*) and Pfingsten (*Whitsuntide*) occur as plurals and also as feminine and neuter singulars. Ostern (*Easter*) may be either plural or neuter singular.

B. Nouns used only in the singular. Some of the more common nouns used only in the singular are:

der Adel, -s, *nobility*	das Publikum, -s, *public*
die Beute, -, *booty*	die Mathematik, -, *mathematics*
das Elend, -(e)s, *misery*	die Musik, -, *music*
der Hafer, -s, *oats*	

C. Nouns having irregular compound plural forms. A number of abstract and collective nouns have compound forms in the plural. These plural forms are often derivatives in which the singular noun functions as a component part. Some of the more common nouns of this type are:

SINGULAR	PLURAL
der Atem, *breath*	Atemzüge
der Dank, *thanks*	Danksagungen, *expressions of gratitude*
der Fachmann	Fachleute
das Glück, *luck*	Glücksfälle, *piece of good fortune*
der Kaufmann	Kaufleute
der Rat, *advice*	Ratschläge, *counsels*
der Regen, *rain*	Regenfälle (*or* Niederschläge)
der Streit, *dispute*	Streitigkeiten
der Tee, *tea*	Teesorten, *kinds of tea*
der Tod, *death*	Todesfälle
das Unglück, *misfortune*	Unglücksfälle
die Vorsicht, *precaution*	Vorsichtsmaßregeln, *precautionary measures*

§114. PUNCTUATION

Rules for punctuation in German differ in many respects from those in English and should be noted carefully.

A. Punctuation marks. The more common punctuation marks used in German are:

,   = das Komma, *comma*

,   = der Punkt, *period*

:   = der Doppelpunkt, *colon*

;   = das Semikolon, *semicolon*

!   = das Ausrufungszeichen, *exclamation mark*

?   = das Fragezeichen, *question mark*

„ "   = Anführungszeichen (pl.), *quotation marks*

—   = der Gedankenstrich, *dash*

-    = der Bindestrich, *hyphen*

( )   = runde Klammern (pl.), *parentheses*

B. The comma. Commas are used:

(1) To set off dependent (*or* subordinate) clauses:

Die Dame, die uns jetzt besucht, ist sehr reich.
The lady who is visiting us now is very rich.

(2) Before **ohne . . . zu, um . . . zu,** and **(an)statt . . . zu** (all of which are followed by an infinitive):

Er ging an mir vorbei, ohne etwas zu sagen.
He passed me without saying anything.

Note: Phrases with **zu** are also preceded by a comma when the following infinitive has modifiers, and when **zu** is the equivalent of **um . . . zu:**

Gewöhne dich daran, immer früh aufzustehen.
Get used to getting up early.

Es lebt ein Gott, zu strafen und zu rächen.
There is (lit. *lives) a God, to punish and take revenge.*

but: Es fing an zu regnen.
It began to rain.

(3) Before the coordinating conjunctions **und** and **oder,** provided the following clause contains both subject and verb:

Die Luft ist blau, und die Felder sind grün.
The air is blue and the fields are green.

but: Er legte sich hin und schlief sogleich ein.
He lay down and fell asleep at once.

(a) Contrary to English usage, **aber** meaning *however* is not set off by commas:

Der alte Mann aber verlor den Mut nicht.
The old man, however, did not lose courage.

(b) Contrary to English usage, no comma is used before **und** or **oder** in a series:

Karl, Fritz und Johann sind meine besten Freunde.
Carl, Fred, and John are my best friends.

(4) Where English uses a period as a decimal point:

Fünf geteilt durch zwei ist 2,5. . . .*two point five.*

C. The period. Periods are used:

(1) Where English uses commas to set off thousands:

4.500 *four thousand, five hundred*

(2) When the endings of the ordinals have been omitted:

den 4. (= 4ten *or* vierten) März, *March 4.*

Friedrich II. (= der Zweite), *Frederick II*

D. Exclamation marks are used:

(1) Usually after the salutation in letters:
Lieber Vater! *Dear Father*

(2) Regularly after emphatic commands:
Folgen Sie mir! *Follow me.*

E. Question marks are used at the end of interrogative sentences, as in English:

Haben Sie ihn gesehen?
Did you see him?

Indirect questions, however, end with a period:

Er fragte mich, ob ich den Mann gesehen hätte.
He asked me whether I had seen the man.

F. Quotation marks are used to enclose a direct quotation, as in English:

Der Fuchs sprach: „Die Trauben sind mir zu sauer."
The fox said, "The grapes are too sour for me."

(1) In printed German, opening quotation marks are written *below* the line; close quotes, *above* the line. Computer keyboards and typewriters do not have the lower marks and must place both above the line.

(2) The opening quotation mark is preceded in German by a colon.

G. Hyphens are used:

(1) To divide words at the end of a line. In words hyphenated in the middle of **-ck-**, the **c** becomes a **k—schmek-ken**—so as not to mislead pronunciation.

(2) To indicate the omission of the last component common to two or more compounds in a series:

Haupt- und Nebensatz, *main and dependent clause*

Feld- und Gartenfrüchte, *field and garden fruits*

(3) Rarely, to form compound nouns.

§115. CAPITALIZATION

Capitalization is far more frequent in German than in English, and has important grammatical significance. The conditions under which it occurs should therefore be noted very carefully.

A. Words that *must* be capitalized. Capitalization is required by:

(1) Neuter adjectives used as nouns after **etwas** *(something),* **viel** *(much),* **nichts** *(nothing),* **alles** *(all),* **allerlei** *(all kinds* or *sorts of),* and **wenig** *(little, not much):*

etwas **Sch**önes, *something beautiful*

viel **W**ichtiges, *much of importance*

nichts **S**chlechtes, *nothing bad*

alles **G**ute, *all good things* (or *all that is good*)

allerlei **U**nverständliches, *all kinds of unintelligible things*

wenig **N**ützliches, *little of use*

(2) Words of all kinds used as nouns:

der **A**rme, *the poor man*

Gutes und **B**öses, *good and evil*

jedem das **S**eine, *to each his own*

Das **L**esen fällt ihm schwer.
Reading is difficult for him.

eine **F**ünf, *a (figure) five*

Altes und **N**eues, *old and new*

Die **A**rmen haben nichts zu essen.
The poor have nothing to eat.

(3) The pronoun of formal address **Sie** *(you),* and its corresponding adjective **Ihr** *(your):*

Haben Sie Ihr Buch?
Do you have your book?

(a) The reflexive **sich** is *not* capitalized:

Setzen Sie sich! *Sit down.*

(b) **Du, dein, ihr,** and **euer** are *not* capitalized unless used in direct address in letters:

Karl, hast du dein Buch?
Carl, do you have your book?

Kinder, was tut ihr?
Children, what are you doing?

but: Lieber Karl!
Hoffentlich hast **D**u **D**ich nicht erkältet.
Dein **D**ich liebender Fritz.

(4) The first word of a direct quotation (following a quotation mark preceded by a colon):

Der Schüler sagte: „Jetzt verstehe ich diesen Satz."
The pupil said, "Now I understand this sentence."

(a) If a direct quotation is interrupted, the word resuming the quotation is *not* capitalized:

„Die Trauben," sprach der Fuchs, „sind mir zu sauer."

(b) The word directly after a question mark or an exclamation mark is *not* capitalized if what follows completes the sentence:

„Was wollen Sie?" fragte der Mann.
"What do you wish?" asked the man.

„Karl, mache deine Aufgabe!" sagte der Lehrer.
"Carl, do your lesson!" said the teacher.

B. Words that are *not* capitalized. Capitalization does *not* occur in:

(1) Combinations with **heute, morgen,** and **gestern** (because they are adverbs of time derived from nouns):

heute **m**orgen, *this morning*

gestern **m**orgen, *yesterday morning*

gestern **a**bend, *yesterday evening* (or *last night*)

(2) Proper adjectives such as *German, English, French*—unless they are used in titles:

Wo ist Ihr **d**eutsches (**e**nglisches, **f**ranzösisches) Buch?
Where is your German (English, French) book?

but: das **D**eutsche Reich, *the German empire*

(a) Observe the absence of capitalization in the phrase **auf deutsch,** *in German.* Similarly:

auf **e**nglisch, *in English*   auf **f**ranzösisch, *in French*

(b) Observe the use of **Deutsch** as noun:

Studieren Sie **D**eutsch?
Are you studying German? (= *the German language*)

(3) The following common pronouns and numerals are not capitalized:
beide (die beiden or **alle beide),** *both;* **der eine. . .der andere,** *the one. . .the other;*

alle drei, *all three;* **das andere,** *the other, the second;* **die anderen,** *the others;* **alle anderen,** *all others;* **nichts anderes,** *nothing else;* **das übrige,** *the rest;* **alles übrige,** *all else;* **die übrigen,** *the others;* **alle übrigen,** *all others;* **der erste. . .der letzte,** *the first. . .the last;* **das meiste,** *the most;* **das mindeste,** *the least;* **der einzelne,** *the individual;* **einzelne,** *individuals;* **alles mögliche,** *everything possible.*

(4) The following boldfaced words in verbal idioms are not capitalized:

Er ist **schuld** daren.
He is to blame for that.

Es tut mir **leid.**
I am sorry.

Tut es Ihnen **weh?**
Does it hurt you?

(Das ist) **schade!**
That is too bad.

Nehmen Sie sich in **acht!**
Take care (or be careful).

Er nimmt daran **teil.**
He takes part (in it).

Sind Sie **imstande,** das zu tun?
Can you do that?

Jetzt geht er **heim.**
He is going home now.

Wann findet die Vorstellung **statt?**
When will the performance take place?

§116. HANDWRITING

Contemporary German handwriting, while of course different from American script, is quite easy. Even beginning students do not have trouble when the numeral **eins** looks like a **sieben,** and the **sieben** is crossed to keep it from looking like an **eins.** Lower case **n** and **e** looked so much like **u** in older script (see below), that writers surmounted **u** with a disambiguating miniature **u,** and many people still do. The umlaut dots are usually parallel slashes, betraying their heritage from the old-fashioned **e** with the diagional removed. But in general, the *Deutsche Normalschrift* is a generic European style of penmanship.

This was not always so. Until the first World War, cursive writing in German-speaking countries was an idiosyncratic outgrowth of a late mediaeval convention often called *gothisch,* shown below as "the old script". The printed version, characterized by broken strokes, angles, and spikes, is called *Fraktur.* In 1915 a rationalized cursive style designed by the Berliner graphic artist Sütterlin was introduced in many German schools, where it was taught until 1941. It too is shown below. Older handwriting is still encountered, and is of course preserved in heirloom documents.

The Old Script (before 1915)

The Sütterlin Script (1915–1941)

Sample of Sütterlin Script. Here are the opening lines of Schiller's play *Wilhelm Tell*, first in the Sütterlin style, then in *Fraktur*, and finally in standard Latin type (known in the 19th century as *Antiqua*).

Es lächelt der See, er ladet zum Bade,
Der Knabe schlief ein am grünen Gestade,
Da hört er ein Klingen,
Wie Flöten so süß,
Wie Stimmen der Engel
Im Paradies.

Es lächelt der See, er ladet zum Bade,
Der Knabe schlief ein am grünen Gestade,
Da hört er ein Klingen,
Wie Flöten so süß,
Sie Stimmen der Engel
Im Paradies.

GLOSSARIES
German-English
and
English-German

A glossary, unlike a dictionary, is a text-specific word list. The two glossaries which follow are meant to help you with the exercises that accompany each chapter. They are not exhaustive in their treatment of words or usage.

Students who are advanced enough in their study of German to use this book should acquire a decent German-English/English-German dictionary. In selecting a dictionary, be sure that it is well-bound, for such books are meant to be opened and closed repeatedly. The number of entries advertised is less important than the amount of information included under each entry. The word **knapp,** for example, should have a dozen lines of illustrative usage and not simply the English equivalents *scarce* and *scanty.* Check for British spellings like *colour* to make sure that you will be dealing with American English. Finally, always run a word through both ways to be certain you have the one you want: *reins* yields both **Zügel** and **Nieren,** and you will have to look them up if you want to avoid saying **General Haig griff die Nieren der Macht**—*General Haig seized the kidneys of power.*

LIST OF ABBREVIATIONS

abbr.	=	abbreviation	*colloq.*	=	colloquial
acc.	=	accusative	*comp.*	=	comparative
adj.	=	adjective	*conj.*	=	conjunction
adv.	=	adverb(ial)	*correl.*	=	correlative
art.	=	article	*dat.*	=	dative
aux.	=	auxiliary	*decl.*	=	declension

def.	= definite	*obj.*	= object
dem.	= demonstrative	*part.*	= particle
dep.	= dependent	*pers.*	= person
dir.	= direct	*p.p.*	= past participle
emph.	= emphatic	*pl.*	= plural
excl.	= exclamation	*poss.*	= possessive
fem.	= feminine	*prep.*	= preposition(al)
fig.	= figurative(ly)	*pres.*	= present
fut.	= future	*pres. p.*	= present participle
gen.	= genitive	*pret.*	= preterit
imperf.	= imperfect	*prin.*	= principal
impers.	= impersonal	*pron.*	= pronoun
indecl.	= indeclinable	*ques.*	= question
indef.	= indefinite	*ref.*	= referring
indir.	= indirect	*refl.*	= reflexive
inf.	= infinitive	*rel.*	= relative
insep.	= inseparable	*sep.*	= separable
intens.	= intensive	*sing.*	= singular
inter.	= interrogative	*str.*	= strong
interj.	= interjection	*sub.*	= subordinating
intr.	= intransitive	*subj.*	= subjunctive
invar.	= invariable	*superl.*	= superlative
lit.	= literally	*temp.*	= temporal
masc.	= masculine	*th.*	= thing
neg.	= negative	*tr.*	= transitive
neut.	= neuter	*vb.*	= verb
nom.	= nominative	*w.*	= with
num.	= numeral	*wk.*	= weak

GERMAN-ENGLISH VOCABULARY

Genitive singular and nominative plural endings are given for all nouns.

Principal parts are given only for strong or irregular verbs. The auxiliary is indicated only for verbs conjugated with **sein,** e.g., **abfahren, fuhr ab, ist abgefahren, fährt ab;** if no auxiliary is given, the verb is conjugated with **haben.** Reflexive verbs show **sich** with the infinitive only: *sich ausziehen, zog aus, ausgezogen.* Separable verbs show an accent on the prefix when their principal parts are not given: **ánklagen;** inseparable verbs indicate the stress only when it is doubtful: **überráschen.**

A

der **Abend, -s, -e,** evening; **eines—s,** one evening; **gestern abend,** last night; **heute abend,** this evening, tonight

das **Abendessen, -s, -,** supper, evening meal
aber, but, however

abfahren, fuhr ab, ist abgefahren, fährt ab, to depart, leave

der **Abgeordnete(r),** *adj. used as noun,* delegate

die **Abgeordnete,** *adj. used as noun, (female)* delegate
abholen, holte ab, abgeholt, to call (*or* come) for

abnehmen, nahm ab, abgenommen, nimmt ab, to take off; **er nimmt den Hut ab,** he takes off his hat

die **Abreise, -, -n,** departure

abreisen, reiste ab, ist abgereist, to depart, leave

abschaffen, schaffte ab, abgeschafft, to do away with, abolish

der **Abschied, -(e)s, -e,** departure

abschreiben, schrieb ab, abgeschrieben, to copy

die **Absicht, -, -en,** intention

abspielen, spielte ab, abgespielt, to play back

absteigen, stieg ab, ist abgestiegen, to come down from; **er steigt vom Pferde ab,** he dismounts

abwesend, absent

acht, eight

der **Acker, -s, -̈,** field

der **Adler, -s, -,** eagle

die **Adresse, -, -n,** address

der **Advokat, -en, -en,** lawyer

der **Affe, -n, -n,** monkey, ape

ähnlich (*w. dat.*), similar (to), **er ist dem Vater—,** he resembles his father

alle (*pl.*), all; **auf—n vieren,** on all fours

allein (*adv.*), alone; (*conj.*), but

allerlei, all kinds of

allerschönst-, most beautiful of all

alles, everything, all; **—, was,** all that

allmählich, gradually

als (*after a comp.*) than; (*conj. ref. def. past action*) when;**—ob,** as if

also, so, consequently, therefore

alt, old

das **Alter, -s, -,** age

altmodisch, old fashioned

amerikanisch, American

sich **amüsieren,** to have a good time

an (*prep. w. dat. or acc.*), at, on, to, **Professor an der Universität,** professor at the university

anbieten, bot an, angeboten, to offer

ander-, other

ändern, to change

anders, differently, otherwise

anderthalb, one and a half

der **Anfang, -(e)s, -̈e,** beginning

anfangen, fing an, angefangen, fängt an, to begin

das **Angebot, -es, -e,** offer, bid

angehen, ging an, hat (or ist) angegangen, to concern; **das geht ihn nichts an,** that does not concern him

angenehm (*w. dat.*), pleasant, agreeable

die **Angst, -, -̈e,** fear

anhalten, hielt an, angehalten, hält an, to stop, check, restrain

ánklagen (*w. acc. of the pers. & gen. of the th.*), to accuse of

ankommen, kam an, ist angekommen, to arrive

die **Ankunft, -, -̈e,** arrival

annehmen, nahm an, angenommen, nimmt an, to accept

der **Ansager, -s, -,** announcer (*male*)

die **Ansagerin, -, -nen,** announcer (*female*)

ansehen, sah an, angesehen, sieht an, to look at

der **Anspruch, -(e)s, -̈e** (*w. auf and acc.*), claim

anständig, decent, proper

(an)statt (*prep. w. gen.*), instead of

anstrengend, exhausting

die **Antwort, -, -en,** answer

antworten, to answer; **man antwortet einer Person** (*dat.*), **man antwortet auf eine Frage** (*acc.*)

die **Anweisung, -, -en,** order, instruction

anwesend, present

die **Anzeige, -, -n,** announcement, advertisement

anziehen, zog an, angezogen, to put on; (*refl*) **sie zieht sich an,** she dresses (herself); (*w. dat.*) **du solltest dir ein neues Kleid—,** you should put on a new dress

der **Anzug, -(e)s, -̈e,** suit of clothes

der **Apfel, -s, -̈,** apple

der **Apfelbaum, -(e)s, -̈e,** apple tree

der **Appetit, -s, -e** appetite

die **Arbeit, -, -en,** work

arbeiten, to work; **fleißig (schwer or tüchtig)—,** to work hard

der **Arbeiter, -s, -,** laborer

ärgerlich, vexed, provoked

sich **ärgern über** (*w. acc.*), to be provoked at

arm, poor

der **Arm, -(e)s, -e,** arm

die **Armbanduhr, -, -en,** wrist watch

die **Armut, -,** poverty

die **Art, -, -en,** kind

der **Arzt, -es, -̈e,** physician, doctor; **den—holen (or kommen) lassen,** to send for the doctor

der **Ast, -es, -̈e,** branch

der **Atem, -s, -züge,** breath

der **Athlet, -en, -en,** athlete

die **Athletin, -, -nen,** (*female*) athlete

athletisch, athletic

atmen, to breathe

die **Atmosphäre, -, -n,** atmosphere

atomisch, atomic; **das atomische Zeitalter,** the Atomic Age

auch, also, too

auf (*prep. w. dat. or acc.*), on, to;—**dem Lande,** in the country; **Student auf der Universität,** student at the university;—**einmal,** suddenly;—**s Land,** to the country

der **Aufenthalt, -(e)s, -e,** stay, residence, sojourn

die **Aufgabe, -, -n,** lesson, assignment, task, exercise, homework; **er macht seine—n,** he does his lessons

aufgeben, gab auf, aufgegeben, gibt auf, to give up

aufhalten, hielt auf, aufgehalten, hält auf, to stop, check

aufheben, hob auf, aufgehoben, hebt auf, to pick up

aufhören, hörte auf, aufgehört, to stop, cease

aufmachen, machte auf, aufgemacht, to open

aufmerksam, attentive

die **Aufnahme, -, -n,** photograph

aufräumen, to tidy up, pick up

der **Aufsatz, -es, -e,** composition, essay

aufsetzen, setzte auf, aufgesetzt, to put on (*as hat or glasses*); **setz (dir) den Hut auf!** put on your hat

aufstehen, stand auf, ist aufgestanden, to (a)rise, get up

aufsteigen, stieg auf, ist aufgestiegen, to rise, ascend

der **Aufstieg, -s, -e,** ascent

das **Auge, -s, -n,** eye

der **Augenblick, -(e)s, -e,** moment

aus (*prep. w. dat.*) out (of), from;—**welchem Grunde?** for what reason?

ausbessern, besserte aus, ausgebessert, to repair, mend

der **Ausdruck, -(e)s, -e,** expression

ausführen, führte aus, ausgeführt, to execute, carry out

die **Auskunft, -, -e,** information, intelligence, particulars

der **Ausländer, -s, -,** foreigner

ausländisch, foreign, from another country

sich **ausruhen, ruhte aus, ausgeruht,** to rest

aussehen, sah aus, ausgesehen, sieht aus, to look, appear

außen, outside; outwardly

außer (*prep. w. dat.*), besides; except; **ich bin—**

mir vor Freude, I am beside myself with joy

außerdem, besides, moreover

außerhalb (*prep. w. gen.*)., outside of

aussetzen, setzte aus, ausgesetzt, to expose

aussprechen, sprach aus, ausgesprochen, spricht aus, to pronounce

auswendig, by heart;—**lernen,** to learn by heart

sich **ausziehen, zog aus, ausgezogen,** to undress

das **Auto, -s, -s,** auto, car

automatisch, automatic, self-acting

B

der **Bach, -(e)s, -e,** brook

backen, buk, gebacken, bäckt, to bake

der **Bäcker, -s, -,** baker

die **Bäckerei, -, en,** bakery

das **Bad, -(e)s, -er,** bath

baden, to bathe

die **Badewanne, -, -n,** bath tub

der **Bagger, -s, -,** (steam-)shovel, excavator

die **Bahn, -, -en,** road, track

der **Bahnhof, -(e)s, -e** station

der **Ball, -(e)s, -e,** ball

der **Ballon, -s, -e** (*or* **-s**), balloon

der **Band, -(e)s, -e,** volume

das **Band, -(e)s, -er,** ribbon

die **Bank, -, -e,** bench

die **Bank, -, -en,** bank (*monetary*)

der **Bär, -en, -en,** bear

der **Barbier, -s, -e,** barber

der **Bart, -(e)s, -e,** beard

bauen, to build

der **Bauer, -n, -n,** farmer, peasant

der **Bauer, -s, -** birdcage

der **Baum, -(e)s, -e,** tree

Bayern, -s (*neut.*), Bavaria

beachtlich, noteworthy

der **Beamte, -n, -n,** official; **ein—r** (*w. adj. decl.*)

die **Beamtin, -, -nen,** (*female*) official

beantworten (*w. acc.*), to answer

sich **bedanken,** to thank; **sich bei einer Person für etwas—,** to thank a person for something

bedeuten, to mean

bedeutend, important, significant, considerable

bedeutsam, significant

die **Bedeutung, -, -en,** meaning, importance

bedienen, to serve

sich **bedienen** (*w. gen.*), to make use of

die **Bedienung, -, -en,** service, *also* (*sing.*) servants, waiters

bedrohen, to threaten

bedürfen (*w. gen.*), to need

bedürftig (*adj. w. gen.*), in need of

sich **beeilen,** to hurry

sich **befassen mit,** to concern oneself with, occupy oneself with

befehlen, befahl, befohlen, befiehlt (*w. dat.*), to order, command

sich **befinden, befand, befunden,** to be, fare, feel

begegnen, begegnete, ist begegnet (*w. dat.*), to meet

beginnen, begann, begonnen, to begin

begleiten, to accompany

begraben, begrub, begraben, begräbt, to bury

begrüssen, to greet

behalten, behielt, behalten, behält, to retain, keep

behandeln, to treat

behaupten, to maintain, assert

bei (*prep. w. dat.*), next to, with, at (the house of);—**mir** at my house; **das Geld, das ich—mir hatte,** the money I had with me

beibringen, brachte bei, beigebracht, (*w. dat. of person, acc. of thing*) to teach, indoctrinate

beide, both;—(*or* **die—n**) **Brüder,** the two (*or* both) brothers

das **Bein, -(e)s, -e,** leg

das **Beispiel, -(e)s, -e,** example; **zum—** (*abbr.* **z.B.**), for example

beißen, biß, gebissen, to bite

beistehen, stand bei, beigestanden (*w. dat.*), to render aid, assist

bekannt, (well-)known

der **Bekannte, -n, -n,** acquaintance (*adj. used as noun*); **ein —r** (*w. adj. decl.*)

sich **beklagen über** (*w. acc.*), to complain about

bekommen, bekam, bekommen, to receive

belegen, to cover; **belegtes Brot mit Käse,** open-faced cheese sandwich

beliebt, beloved; favorite, popular

bellen, to bark

belohnen, to reward

bemannt, manned

bemerken, to notice

sich **benehmen, benahm, benommen, benimmt,** to behave

benutzen, to use, utilize, employ, take advantage of, avail, profit

beobachten, to observe

die **Beobachtung, -, -en,** observation, study

bequem, comfortable; **mach es dir—!** make yourself at home.

berauben (*w. acc. of the pers. & gen. of the th.*), to rob

der **Bereich, -s, -e,** (*also neuter*) area, range, region

bereit, ready, prepared

bereiten, to prepare

bereithalten, hielt bereit, bereitgehalten, hält bereit, to have ready

bereits, already

der **Berg, -(e)s, -e,** mountain

berichten, to report

der **Beruf, -(e)s, -e,** profession, calling, vocation

berühmt famous; **—durch** (*w. acc.*) [*or* **wegen** (*w. gen.*)] famous for

beschäftigt, busy

beschreiben, beschrieb, beschrieben to describe

beschuldigen (*w. acc. of the pers. & gen. of the th.*), to accuse

der **Besen, -s, -,** broom

besiedeln, to settle

besiegen, to conquer

besitzen, besaß, besessen, to possess

besonders, especially

besser (*comp. of* **gut**), better

bestehen, bestand, bestanden, to pass (*an examination*);**—aus,** to consist of; **-auf** (*w. dat.*), to insist upon

bestellen, to order

bestimmt, certain(ly), sure(ly); determined, destined

bestrafen, to punish

der **Besuch, -(e)s, -e,** visit

besuchen, to visit

beten, to pray

betrachten, to observe

sich **betragen, betrug, betragen, beträgt,** to behave

betrügen, betrog, betrogen, to deceive

das **Bett, -(e)s, -en,** bed

betteln, to beg

bevor (*conj.*), before

die **Bewegung, -, -en,** movement

beweisen, bewies, bewiesen, to prove

sich **bewerben, bewarb, beworben, bewirbt** (*w.* **um** *& acc.*), to apply for

bewundern, to admire

bewußt (*adj. w. gen.*), aware of

bezahlen, to pay

bezug: in— (*or* **Bezug**) **auf** (*w. acc.*), with reference to, with regard to

die **Bibliothek, -, -en,** library

biegen, bog, gebogen, to bend

die **Biene, -, -n,** bee

das **Bier, -(e)s, -e,** beer
bieten, bot, geboten, to offer
das **Bild, -(e)s, -er,** picture
bilden, to form
die **Bildung, -, -en,** education
binden, band, gebunden, to tie
der **Bio-Laden, -s, ∴,** health-food store
die **Birne, -, -n,** pear
bis (*prep. w. acc.*), to, as far as; (*conj.*) until; (*often w. other preps.*)—**an das Fenster,** up to the window
bisher, until now
bitte, (if you) please; you are welcome
bitten, bat, gebeten, to ask; **um etwas** (*acc.*)—, to ask for something
bitter, bitter
blasen, blies, geblasen, bläst, to blow
blaβ, pale
das **Blatt, -(e)s, ∵er,** leaf; sheet
blau, blue
das **Blei, -s, -e,** lead
bleiben, blieb, ist geblieben, to remain, stay; **er bleibt stehen,** he stops
der **Bleistift, -(e)s, -e,** pencil
der **Blick, -(e)s, -e,** glance, look
blicken, to look
blind, blind;—**auf** (*w. dat.*), blind in
blitzen, to glitter, sparkle; **es blitzt,** it is lightning
bloβ, bare; **mit bloβem Auge,** with the naked eye
blühen, to bloom
die **Blume, -, -n,** flower
das **Blut -(e)s,** blood
der **Boden, -s, ∴(or -),** floor
der **Bogen, -s, - (or ∵),** arch; bow; sheet of paper
das **Boot, -(e)s, -e,** boat
die **Börse, -, -n,** purse; stock exchange
böse, angry;—**sein auf** (*w. acc.*), to be angry with
der **Botschafter, -s, -,** ambassador
die **Botschafterin, -, -nen,** (*female*) ambassador
der **Boxer, -s, -,** boxer, pugilist
braten, briet, gebraten, brät, to roast
brauchen, to need
braun, brown
die **Braut, -, ∵e,** fiancée
der **Bräutigam, -s, -e,** fiancé
brechen, brach, gebrochen, bricht, to break
breit, wide, broad; **einen Fuβ—,** a foot wide
brennen, brannte, gebrannt, to burn; **er brennt vor Ungeduld,** he burns with impatience
das **Brett, -(e)s, -er,** board
der **Brief, -(e)s, -e,** letter
der **Briefträger, -s, -,** letter carrier

die **Briefträgerin, -, -nen,** (*female*) letter carrier
die **Briefmarke, -, -n,** stamp
die **Briefmarkensammlung, -, -en,** stamp collection
die **Brille, -, -n,** (eye)glasses, spectacles; **eine—tragen,** to wear glasses
bringen, brachte, gebracht, to bring
die **Broschüre, -, -n,** brochure, pamphlet, booklet
das **Brot, -(e)s, -e,** bread
die **Brücke, -, -n,** bridge
der **Bruder, -s, ∴,** brother
die **Brust, -, ∵e,** breast
das **Buch, -(e)s, ∵er,** book
buchstabieren, to spell
sich **bücken,** to stoop
die **Bude, -, -n,** place, room (*in a rooming house or dormitory*), booth
bunt, variegated, many-colored
die **Burg, -, -en,** castle
der **Bürger, -s, -,** citizen
der **Bürgermeister, -s, -,** mayor
die **Bürgermeisterin, -, -nen,** (*female*) mayor
der **Bursche, -n, -n,** fellow; lad; student
die **Butter, -,** butter

C

der **Charákter, -s, Charaktére,** character
die **Chemie, -,** chemistry
chemisch, chemical

D

da (*adv.*) there; (*conj.*) since, as
dabei, thereby; while doing it
das **Dach, -(e)s, ∵er,** roof
dafür, for it
dagegen, on the other hand; against it
daheim, at home
daher, therefore
damals, at that time, then
die **Dame, -, -n,** lady
damit (*adv.*), with it; (*conj.*) in order that
der **Dampfer, -s, -,** steamer
das **Dampfschiff, -(e)s, -e,** steamship
der **Dank, -(e)s,** thanks
dankbar (*w. dat.*), thankful, grateful
danken (*w. dat*), to thank; **ich danke Ihnen für das Buch,** I thank you for the book
dann, then, at that time;—**und wann,** now and then

darauf, thereupon, after that; upon it (that *or* them)

darauffolgend, following, later

darin, therein; in it (that *or* them)

darum, therefore

daß (*conj.*), that

das **Datum, -s, Daten,** date

dauern, to last, endure

dauernd, continually, constantly

der **Daumen, -s, -,** thumb

davon, of (*or* about) it (*or* them)

dazu, for that; in addition

die **Decke, -, -n,** ceiling; cover

decken, to cover

dein, deine, dein (*poss.*), your

denken, dachte, gedacht, to think; **—an** (*w. acc.*), to think of

denn (*conj.*) for, because, then; **warum hat er es— getan?,** why then did he do it?; (*adv.*) in that case; **es sei denn, daß,** unless, except

derselbe, dieselbe, dasselbe, the same

deshalb, therefore

dessen (*masc. & neut. sing.*), **deren** (*fem. sing.*), **deren** (*pl.*) (*gen. forms of the rel. pron.* **der, die, das**), whose

desto: je. . .desto, the. . .the; **je höher er steigt,— kälter wird es,** the higher he climbs, the colder it gets

deutlich, distinct(ly)

deutsch (*adj.*), German; **auf—,** in German

Deutsch (*noun*), German; **lernen Sie —?** are you studying German?

der **Deutsche, -n, -n** (*w. adj. decl.*), German, native of Germany; **ein—r,** a German (man)

Deutschland, -s (*neut.*), Germany

dicht, dense, compact

der **Dichter, -s, -,** poet

die **Dichterin, -, -nen,** (*female*) poet

dick, thick; **einen Fuß—,** a foot thick

der **Dieb, -(e)s, -e,** thief

dienen (*w. dat.*), to serve

der **Diener, -s, -,** servant

die **Dienerin, -, -nen,** (*female*) servant

der **Dienstag, -(e)s, -e,** Tuesday

das **Dienstmädchen, -s, -,** maid, servant

dieser, -e, -es (*adj.*), this; (*pron.*) this one

diesseits (*prep. w. gen.*), on this side of

die **Diktatur, -, -en,** dictatorship

das **Ding, -(e)s, -e,** thing

direkt, direct

doch, still, however, yet

der **Doktor, -s, en,** doctor, physician

der **Dom, -(e)s, -e,** cathedral

donnern, to thunder

der **Donnerstag, -s, -e,** Thursday

doppelt, double, doubly

das **Dorf, -(e)s, ¨-er,** village

der **Dorn, -(e)s, -en (-e or ¨-er),** thorn

dort, there (*in that place*)

dorthin, there (*to that place*), thither

draußen, outside

drehen (*often refl.*), to turn

drei, three

dreibeinig, three-legged

dreifach, threefold, triple

dreimal, three times

drinnen, inside

dritt (*num. adj.*), third

drohen (*w. dat.*), to threaten

drüben, over there

dumm, stupid

die **Dummheit, -, en,** stupidity

dunkel, dark

dünn, thin

durch (*prep. w. acc.*), through, by

durchführen, führte durch, durchgeführt, to carry out, perform, accomplish

dúrchschauen, to look through

durchscháuen, to see through, not be fooled

dürfen, durfte, gedurft, darf, to be allowed to; **das—Sie nicht tun,** you must not do that; **dürfte ich Sie darum bitten?** might I ask you for that?

der **Durst, -es,** thirst

durstig, thirsty

das **Dutzend, -s, -e,** dozen

E

eben, even; just

ebenso, just as;**—groß wie,** just as large as

das **Echo, -s, -s,** echo

echt, genuine

das **(Deutsche) Eck,** the Rhine Elbow (the confluence of the Mosel and Rhine Rivers at Koblenz); **das Dreieck,** triangle

die **Ecke, -, -n,** corner

edel, noble

ehe (*conj.*), before

das **Ehepaar, -s, -e,** married couple

die **Ehre, -, -n,** honor

ehrlich, honest

das **Ei, -(e)s, -er,** egg

die **Eiche, -, -n,** oak
eigen (*adj.*), own
eigentlich, real(ly)
eilen (*w.* **sein**), to hasten
einander, each other
sich (*dat.*) **einbilden,** to imagine
eindrucksvoll, impressive
einfach, simple
der **Einfall, -(e)s, ̈-e,** idea, notion
einfallen, fiel ein, ist eingefallen, es fällt ein, to occur; **das war mir nie eingefallen,** that had never occurred to me
einladen, lud ein, eingeladen, ladet (*or* **lädt**) **ein,** to invite
einmal, once; once upon a time; **auf—,** suddenly
einschlafen, schlief ein, ist eingeschlafen, schläft ein, to fall asleep
einseitig, one-sided, partial, biased
einsilbig, monosyllabic
einstecken, to put in; **man hat ihn ins Gefängnis eingesteckt,** they put him in prison
éinwandern, to immigrate
der **Einwohner, -s, -,** inhabitant
die **Einwohnerin, -, -nen,** (*female*) inhabitant
das **Eis, -es,** ice
das **Eisen, -s,** iron
die **Eisenbahn, -, -en,** railroad
der **Elefant, -en, -en,** elephant
Elsaß, -es (*neut.*) Alsace
die **Eltern, -** (*pl.*), parents
empfangen, empfing, empfangen, empfängt, to receive
der **Empfangschef, -s, -s,** deskclerk, chief clerk at a reception desk
die **Empfangschefin, -, -nen,** (*female*) desk clerk
empfinden, empfand, empfunden, to feel; **er empfindet es schmerzlich,** it pains him
empfindlich, susceptible, sensitive
emporsteigen, stieg empor, ist emporgestiegen, to climb up
das **Ende, -s, -n,** end; **zu—lesen,** to finish reading, read through
enden, to end
endlich, finally, at last
eng, narrow
der **Engländer, -s, -,** Englishman
die **Engländerin, -, -nen,** English woman
der **Enkel, -s, -,** grandson, grandchild
die **Enkelin, -, -nen,** granddaughter
entdecken, to discover
entfernt, distant, remote
entgegen (*prep. w. dat.*), toward, against, in face of

entlang (*w. acc.*), along
entlassen, entließ, entlassen, entläßt, to dismiss
entscheiden, entschied, entschieden, to decide; (*refl.*) to make up one's mind
sich **entschließen, entschloß, entschlossen,** to decide, make up one's mind
entschuldigen (*w. acc.*), to excuse, pardon
die **Entstehung, -, -en,** origin, formation, genesis
entwickeln, to develop
entzünden, to inflame
entzweibrechen, brach entzwei, entzweigebrochen, bricht entzwei, to break in two
erben, to inherit
die **Erde, -,** earth, world
erfahren, erfuhr, erfahren, erfährt, to learn, experience, discover (knowledge); **—über** (*w. acc.*) to learn about
erfinden, erfand, erfunden, to invent
der **Erfolg, -(e)s, -e,** success
erfolgreich, successful
erforderlich, necessary, required, requisite
das **Ergebnis, -ses, -se,** result
erhalten, erhielt, erhalten, erhält, to receive
sich **erholen von,** to recover (*or* recuperate) from
sich **erinnern** (*w. gen. or an w. acc.*), to remember
sich **erkälten,** to catch cold
erkennen, erkannte, erkannt, to recognize
sich **erkundigen nach,** to make inquiries about
erlauben (*w. dat.*), to permit
die **Erlaubnis, -,** permission
erleben, to experience, live through
das **Erlebnis, -ses, -se,** experience
ernst, serious
die **Ernte, -, -n,** harvest
erreichen, to reach, attain
erscheinen, erschien, ist erschienen, to appear
erschöpfend, exhausting
erschrecken, erschrak, ist erschrocken, erschrickt (*intr.*), to be frightened; (*wk. tr.*), to frighten
erst (*adj.*), first, foremost; (*adv.*), at first, first of all; not until, only
erstaunt, astonished
erwachen, erwachte, ist erwacht (*intr.*), to awake
erwarten, to expect
erweisen, erwies, erwiesen, to show, render (*e.g., honor*)
erwidern, to reply
erzählen, to tell, relate
erziehen, erzog, erzogen, to bring up, rear, educate
der **Esel, -s, -,** donkey
essen, aß, gegessen, ißt, to eat

etliche (*pl.*), some, several
etwa, perhaps
etwas, some, something, somewhat
euer, eure, euer (*poss.*), your
ewig, eternal

F

fabelhaft, fabulous, marvelous
das Fach, -(e)s, ¨er, subject, branch, specialty
fähig (*adj. w. gen.*), capable (of)
fahren, fuhr, ist gefahren, fährt, to ride, travel, drive, go
die Fahrkarte, -, -n, ticket
die Fahrt, -, -en, trip, voyage, ride
das Fahrzeug, -s, -e, vehicle, vessel, craft
der Fall, -(e)s, ¨e, fall; case, instance
fallen, fiel, ist gefallen, fällt, to fall; das Schreiben fällt mir schwer, writing is difficult for me
der Fallschirm, -s, -e, parachute
die Familie, -, -n, family
fangen, fing, gefangen, fängt, to catch
die Farbe, -, -n, color
fassen, to grasp, conceive, comprehend
fast, almost
faul, lazy; rotten
die Feder, -, -n, feather; pen
fehlen, to be absent; lack, miss; be the matter with; was fehlt Ihnen? what is the matter with you?
der Fehler, -s, -, mistake
feiern, to celebrate
der Feiertag, -(e)s, -e, holiday
fein, fine
der Feind, -(e)s, -e enemy
feindlich (*adj. w. dat.*), hostile;—gesinnt, hostile toward
das Feld, -(e)s, -er, field; auf dem—, in the field
der Felsen, -s, -, rock, cliff
das Fenster, -s, -, window
die Ferien (*pl.*), vacation
fern, far, distant, remote
der Fernsehapparat, -s, -e, television set
férnsehen, to watch television
fertig, ready, finished
das Fertighaus, -es, ¨er, prefabricated house
festhalten, hielt fest, festgehalten, hält fest, to hold on, cling, adhere to
fett, fat
das Feuer, -s, -, fire
finden, fand, gefunden, to find

der Finger, -s, -, finger
der Fisch, -es, -e, fish
flach, flat, plain; shallow
die Fläche, -, -n, plane surface, area
die Flamme, -, -n, flame
die Flasche, -, -n, bottle, flask
das Fleisch, -es, meat
der Fleiß, -es, diligence
fleißig, diligent, industrious;—arbeiten, to work hard
fliegen, flog, ist geflogen, to fly
fliehen, floh, ist geflohen, to flee
fließen, floß, ist geflossen, to flow
fließend, fluent(ly)
der Flug, -(e)s, ¨e, flight
der Flügel, -s, -, wing
das Flugzeug, -(e)s, -e, airplane
der Fluß, -(ss)es, -ü(ss)e, river
das Flußpferd, -(e)s, -e, hippopotamus
die Folge, -, -n, consequence, result, Folge leisten, to pay attention
folgen, folgte, ist gefolgt (*w. dat.*), to follow
die Form, -, -en, form, shape
die Forschung, -, -en, investigation, research, inquiry, study
fort, away
fortgehen, ging fort, ist fortgegangen, to go away
fortlaufen, lief fort, ist fortgelaufen, läuft fort, to run away
forttragen, trug fort, fortgetragen, trägt fort, to carry away
fortwährend, continual(ly)
das Foto (or Photo), -s, -s, photograph, snapshot
die Frage, -, -n, question; eine—an eine Person (*acc.*) stellen, to ask a person a question
fragen, to ask, question
Frankreich, -s (*neut.*), France
der Franzose, -n, -n, Frenchman
die Französin, -, -nen, French woman
französisch, French
die Frau, -, -en, woman; wife; Mrs.
das Fräulein, -s, -, young woman, Miss
frei, free
die Freiheit, -, -en, freedom, liberty
der Freitag -(e)s, -e, Friday
fremd, strange, foreign; er ist mir—, he is a stranger to me
die Freude, -, -n, joy, happiness, pleasure; ich bin außer mir vor—, I am beside myself with joy; es macht mir—, it gives me pleasure; ich habe meine—daran, I take pleasure in that

freuen, to make glad; **es freut mich,** I am glad

sich **freuen,** to be glad; **er freut sich,** he is glad; **sich— auf** (*w. acc.*), to look forward with pleasure to; **sich—über** (*w. acc.*), to be happy about, be pleased with, rejoice at

der **Freund, -(e)s, -e,** (*male*) friend

die **Freundin, -, -nen,** (*female*) friend

freundlich, friendly; **seien Sie— zu ihm!** be friendly to him

die **Freundschaft, -, -en,** friendship

der **Friede(n), -ns,** peace

der **Friedhof, -s, -̈e,** cemetery

frieren, fror, gefroren, to freeze; **vorige Nacht hat es stark gefroren,** last night it froze hard

frisch, fresh

der **Friseur, -s, -e,** barber, hairdresser

die **Friseuse, -, -n,** (*female*) barber, hairdresser; Austrian dialect, **Friseurin, -, -nen**

froh, glad, happy; **er wird seines Lebens nicht—,** he leads an unhappy life

fröhlich, happy, cheerful

fromm, pious

die **Frucht, -, -̈e,** fruit

früh, early

früher, earlier; sooner; formerly

der **Frühling, -s, -e,** spring; **im—,** in spring

das **Frühstück, -(e)s, -e,** breakfast; **zum—,** for breakfast

frühstücken, frühstückte, gefrühstückt, to have breakfast

fühlen, to feel

führen, to lead

der **Führer, -s, -,** leader, guide

füllen, to fill

die **Füllfeder, -, -n,** fountain pen

für (*prep. w. acc.*), for; **—fünf Mark Zucker,** five marks worth of sugar

furchtbar, frightful, awful

fürchten, to fear; **sich—vor** (*w. dat.*), to be afraid of

fürchterlich, frightful, horrible

der **Fürst, -en, -en,** prince

die **Fürstin, -, -nen,** princess

der **Fuß, -es, -̈e,** foot

der **Fußboden, -s, -̈,** floor

füttern, to feed

G

die **Gabel, -, -n,** fork

der **Gang, -(e)s, -̈e** course (*of a meal*); corridor

die **Gans, -, -̈e,** goose

ganz, entire(ly), all, whole

gar, quite, very; **—nicht,** not at all; **—nichts,** nothing at all

der **Garten, -s, -̈,** garden

die **Gasse, -, -n,** alley

der **Gast, -es, -̈e,** guest

der **Gastarbeiter, -s, -,** foreign worker

gebären, gebar, geboren, gebiert, to give birth to

das **Gebäude, -s, -,** building

geben, gab, gegeben, gibt, to give: **es gibt** (*impers. w. acc.*), there is (*or* are)

das **Gebiet, -(e)s, -e,** territory, domain; (*fig.*) field

das **Gebirge, -s, -,** mountain range, mountainous region

geboren (*p.p* of **gebären**), born; **wurde—,** was born (*used for the dead*); **ist—,** was born (*used for the living*); **wann sind Sie—?** when were you born?

gebrauchen, to use

gebraucht, used

die **Geburt, -, -en,** birth

der **Geburtstag, -(e)s, -e,** birthday; **zum—,** for one's birthday

das **Gedächtnis, -ses, -se,** memory

der **Gedanke, -ns, -n,** thought

gedenken (*w. gen.*), to remember

das **Gedicht, -(e)s, -e,** poem

die **Geduld, -,** patience

geduldig, patient

die **Gefahr, -, -en,** danger

gefährlich, dangerous

gefallen, gefiel, gefallen, gefällt (*w. dat.*), to please; **es gefällt mir,** I like it

der **Gefallen, -s, -,** favor; **er tut mir den—,** he does me the favor

das **Gefängnis, -ses, -se,** prison

das **Gefühl, -(e)s, -e,** feeling

gegen (*prep. w. acc.*), against; toward; contrary to

die **Gegend, -, -en,** region, neighborhood

der **Gegensatz, -es, -̈e,** contrast, opposite

gegenüber (*prep. w. dat.*), opposite

die **Gegenwart, -,** the present, modern times; presence; **in meiner—,** in my presence

geheim, secret(ly)

das **Geheimnis, -ses, -se,** secret

geheimnisvoll, mysterious

gehen, ging, ist gegangen, to go; **in die Schule—,** to go to school; **wie geht es Ihnen?** how are you?

gehorchen (*w. dat.*), to obey

gehören (*w. dat. & no prep. if ownership is denoted*), to belong to; —**zu,** to be part (*or* member) of

die **Geige, -, -n,** violin, fiddle

der **Geist, -es, -er,** mind, spirit

gelangen, gelangte, ist gelangt, to attain; come to; **endlich ist er zu einem Schluß gelangt,** he finally reached a conclusion

gelb, yellow

das **Geld, -(e)s, -er,** money

gelegen (*adj. w. dat.*), opportune

die **Gelegenheit, -, -en** opportunity, occasion; **bei dieser—,** on this occasion

gelingen, gelang, ist gelungen (*w. dat.*), to succeed; **es ist mir gelungen, Ihre Schrift zu entziffern,** I succeeded in deciphering your writing

gelten, galt, gegolten, gilt, to be worth (*or* of value); be meant for

das **Gemüt, -(e)s, -er,** feeling, soul, heart

gemütlich, cosy, comfortable; sociable

genau, exact(ly)

genesen, genas, ist genesen, genest, to recover (*from illness*)

genießen, genoß, genossen, genießt, to enjoy

genug, enough

genügen (*w. dat.*), to be enough; satisfy

das **Gepäck, -(e)s, -e,** baggage, luggage

der **Gepäckträger, -s, -,** porter

gerade (*adj. & adv.*), straight, direct; (*adv.*) just, exactly

das **Gerät, -s, -e,** tool, implement, utensil

geraten, geriet, ist geraten, gerät (*w. in w. acc.*), to get (*or* stray) into; turn out to be

das **Gericht, -(e)s, -e,** court (of justice); dish, course

gern (lieber, am liebsten), gladly, willingly; **er hat es—,** he likes it; **er tut es—,** he likes to do it

der **Gesangverein, -(e)s, -e,** glee club, choral society

das **Geschäft, -(e)s, -e,** business; occupation

geschehen, geschah, ist geschehen, es geschieht, to happen; **es geschieht ihm recht,** it serves him right

das **Geschenk, -(e)s, -e,** gift, present

die **Geschichte, -, -n,** story; history

das **Geschlecht, -(e)s, -er,** sex, gender, race, stock, species

geschmückt, decorated

die **Geschwindigkeit, -, -en** speed, velocity

der **Geschwindigkeitsmesser, -s, -,** speedometer

der **Geselle, -n, -n,** fellow; journeyman

die **Gesellschaft, -, -en,** society, company

das **Gesetz, -es, -e,** law

das **Gesicht, -(e)s, -er,** face

gesinnt (*adj.*), minded, disposed; **feindlich—,** hostile toward

das **Gespräch, -(e)s, -e,** conversation

die **Gestalt, -, -en,** form, figure, stature

gestern, yesterday

gesund, well, healthy

die **Gesundheit, -, -en,** health

die **Gesundheitspflege,** (public) health, healthcare

das **Getränk, -(e)s, -e,** drink

gewahr werden (*w. gen.*), to become aware of, perceive

die **Gewalt, -, -en,** force

das **Gewehr, -s, -e,** rifle

das **Gewicht, -s, -e,** weight; **Gewichte heben,** to lift weights; —**stemmen,** to lift weights above the head (as in the Olympic Games)

gewinnen, gewann, gewonnen, to win, gain

gewiß (*adj. w. gen.*), sure, certain; (*adv.*) surely, indeed, certainly

das **Gewitter, -s, -,** (thunder)-storm

sich **gewöhnen an** (*w. acc.*), to get used to; **ich bin nicht daran gewöhnt,** I am not used to it

gewohnt, accustomed; **ich bin es** (*acc.*)—, I am used to it

gießen, goß, gegossen, to pour

das **Gift, -(e)s, -e,** poison

der **Gipfel, -s, -,** top, summit

glänzen, to shine, sparkle

das **Glas, -es, -er,** glass

glatt, slippery, slick

der **Glaube, -ns, -n,** belief

glauben, (*w. dat. of the pers. & acc. of the th.*), to believe; **er glaubt mir,** he believes me; **er glaubt es,** he believes it

gleich, equal; like; (=**sogleich**) immediately; **es ist mir ganz—,** it is all the same to me

gleichen, glich, geglichen (*w. dat.*), to resemble

die **Glocke, -, -n,** bell

das **Glück, -(e)s, -sfälle,** (good) luck, fortune, happiness

glücklich, happy

das **Gold -(e)s,** gold

der **Gott, -es, -er,** God

graben, grub, gegraben, gräbt, to dig

der **Graf, -en, -en,** count

die **Gräfin, -, -nen,** countess

sich **grämen über** (*w. acc.*), to grieve at (*or* over)

das **Gras, -es, -er,** grass

grau, gray

grauen (*impers.*), to shudder; **mir graut,** I shudder

greifen, griff, gegriffen, to grasp, seize, take hold of

die **Grenze -, -n,** boundary, limit

grob, rude

groß, (größer, größt-), large, big; tall; great

großartig, grand

die **Großeltern** (*pl.*), grandparents

die **Großmutter, -, -̈,** grandmother

der **Großvater, -s, -̈,** grandfather

grün, green

der **Grund, -(e)s, -̈e,** reason; ground, bottom; **aus welchem—?** for what reason?

gründlich, thoroughly

die **Gruppe, -, -n,** group, troop

der **Gruß, -es, -̈e,** greeting; **besten Gruß an** (*w. acc.*), best regards to

grüßen, to greet

das **Gummiband, -(e)s; -̈er,** rubber band

günstig, favorable

gut (besser, best-), good

das **Gymnasium, -s, Gymnasien,** academic high school

H

das **Haar, -(e)s, -e,** hair

haben, hatte, gehabt, hat, to have

die **Hafenstadt, -, -̈e,** seaport

der **Hahn, -(e)s, -̈e,** cock, rooster; faucet

halb, half

die **Hälfte, -, -n,** half

der **Hals, -es, -̈e,** neck, throat

das **Halsweh, -(e)s,** sore throat

halten, hielt, gehalten, hält, to hold; **eine Rede—,** to deliver a speech; **er hält Wort,** he keeps his word; **ich halte ihn für einen ehrlichen Mann,** I believe he is an honest man

die **Hand, -, -̈e,** hand; **mit der—winken,** to wave, beckon

der **Handel, -s,** trade

sich **handeln um** (*impers.*), to concern, be a question of; **um was handelt es sich?** what is it (all) about?

der **Handschuh, -(e)s, -e,** glove

der **Handschuhkasten, -s, -,** glove compartment (in a car)

hängen, hing, gehangen, hängt (*intr.*), to hang

hängen (*tr.*), to hang

hart, hard

hartnäckig, stubborn

der **Hase, -n, -n,** hare

hassen, to hate

häufig, frequent(ly)

das **Haupt, -(e)s, -̈er,** head; chief

das **Haus, -es, -̈er,** house; **zu Hause,** at home; **nach Hause,** home(ward)

das **Haustier, -(e)s, -e,** domestic animal

die **Haustür, -, -en,** front door

heben, hob, gehoben, hebt, to lift, raise; (*refl.*) to rise

das **Heer, -(e)s, -e,** army

das **Heft, -(e)s, -e,** notebook

heftig, violent

heilig, holy

die **Heimat, -, -en,** home(land)

heimlich, secret(ly)

heiraten, to marry

heiß, hot

heißen, hieß, geheißen, heißt, to be called; mean; command; call; **wie—Sie?** what is your name? **er heißt,** his name is; **das heißt** (*abbr. d.h.*), that is, (i.e.)

helfen, half, geholfen, hilft (*w. dat.*), to help

hell, light, bright(ly)

das **Hemd, -(e)s, -en,** shirt

die **Henne -, -n,** hen

herabsinken, sank herab, ist herabgesunken, to (sink down), drop

der **Herbst, -es, -e,** fall, autumn

herkommen, kam her, ist hergekommen, to come hither, approach

der **Herr, -n, -en,** master, lord, gentleman, sir, Mr.; **meine—en!** gentlemen!

herrlich, glorious, magnificent; **sich—amüsieren,** to have a wonderful time

herrschen, to rule

der **Herrscher, -s, -,** ruler

das **Herz, -ens, (*acc.* Herz), -en,** heart

herzlich, cordial(ly)

der **Herzog, -(e)s, -̈e,** duke

die **Herzogin, -, -nen,** duchess

heute, today; **—morgen,** this morning; **—abend,** this evening, tonight

heutig, today's

die **Hexe, -, -n,** witch

hier, here

die **Hilfe, -, -n,** help

der **Himmel, -s, -,** heaven, sky

hinaufgehen, ging hinauf, ist hinaufgegangen, to go up

das **Hindernis, -ses, -se,** obstacle, hindrance

hingehen, ging hin, ist hingegangen, to go there (*or* to a place)

hinten (*adv.*), in the rear
hinter (*prep. w. dat. or acc.*), behind
der **Hinweis, -es, -e,** indication, hint, allusion
der **Hirt, -en, -en,** shepherd
die **Hitze, -, -n,** heat
hoch, (höher, höchst-), high; **einen Fuß—,** a foot high
die **Hochzeit, -, -en,** wedding
der **Hof, -(e)s, ̈-e,** yard; court; estate
hoffen auf (*w. acc.*), to hope for
die **Hoffnung, -, -en,** hope
höflich, polite
die **Höhe, -, -n,** height, altitude, elevation
hohl, hollow
holen, to get, fetch;**—lassen,** to send for; **er hat den Arzt—lassen,** he sent for the doctor
das **Holz, -es, ̈-er,** wood
der **Honig, -s,** honey
hören, to hear; **ich höre ihn lachen,** I hear him laughing
das **Horn, -(e)s, ̈-er,** horn
das **Hotel, -s, -s,** hotel
der **Hügel, -s, -,** hill
das **Huhn, -(e)s, ̈-er,** chicken
humoristischerweise, in a humorous manner
der **Hund, -(e)s, -e,** dog
hundert (*num. adj.*), a hundred
das **Hundert, -s, -e,** hundred
hundertmal, a hundred times
der **Hunger, -s,** hunger; **ich habe—,** I am hungry
hungrig, hungry
der **Hut, -(e)s, ̈-e,** hat
sich **hüten vor** (*w. dat.*), to guard against

I

idiomatisch, idiomatic
ihr, ihre, ihr (*poss.*), her; their; its
Ihr, Ihre, Ihr (*poss.*), your
immer, always
in (*prep. w. dat. or acc.*), in(to)
indem, while
der **Indianer, -s, -,** Indian
Indien, -s, (*neut.*), India
der **Inhaber, -s, -,** proprietor
die **Inhaberin, -, -nen,** (*female*) proprietor
der **Inhalt, -(e)s, -e,** contents
inner, inner, internal, interior
innerhalb (*prep. w. gen.*), within
die **Insel, -, -n,** island

das **Instrument, -(e)s, -e,** instrument, device, apparatus
interessant, interesting
sich **interessieren für,** to be interested in
inzwischen, in the meantime
irgend (*used in various compounds*), any; some; — **jemand,** anybody
irgendwo, anywhere
sich **irren,** to be mistaken
der **Irrtum, -(e)s, ̈-er,** mistake

J

ja, yes; indeed
jagen, to hunt, chase
das **Jahr, -(e)s, -e,** year
die **Jahreszeit, -, -en,** season
das **Jahrhundert, -(e)s, -e,** century
je, ever; **je. . .desto,** the. . .the
jeder, jede, jedes, each, every
jedermann, everbody
jemals, ever, at any time
jemand, someone; anyone; **irgend—,** anybody
jener, jene, jenes (*dem. adj.*), that; (*dem, prom.*) that one
jenseits (*prep. w. gen.*), on that side of
jetzt, now
der **Job, -s, -s,** job, occupation
der **Juli, -s, -s,** July
jung, young
der **Junge, -n, -n,** boy
der **Jüngling, -s, -e,** young man
der **Juni, -(s), -s,** June

K

der **Kaffee, -s, -s,** coffee
die **Kaffeetasse, -, -n,** coffee cup
der **Kahn, -(e)s, ̈-e,** boat
der **Kaiser, -es, -,** emperor
das **Kalb, -(e)s, ̈-er,** calf
kalt, cold
die **Kälte, -,** cold
der **Kamerad, -en, -en,** comrade, companion, chum
der **Kamm, -(e)s, ̈-e,** comb
der **Kampf, -(e)s, ̈-e,** fight, struggle
kämpfen, to fight, battle
Kanada, -s (*neut.*), Canada
der **Kanal, -s, Kanäle,** canal
der **Kanzler, -s, -,** chancellor

karg, stingy

die **Karte, -, -n,** card; map

die **Katze, -, -n,** cat

kaufen, to buy

der **Kaufmann, -(e)s, Kaufleute,** merchant

kaum, hardly, barely, scarcely

kein, keine, kein, no, not a, not any

keiner, keine, keines *(pron.),* none, not one *(or any)*

keineswegs *(adv.),* by no means

der **Keks, -es, -e,** cookie

der **Keller, -s, -,** cellar

der **Kellner, -s, -,** waiter

die **Kellnerin, -, -nen,** *(female)* bartender

kennen, kannte, gekannt, to know, be acquainted with

kénnenlernen, to get to know, to become acquainted with

das **Kind, -(e)s, -er,** child

der **Kinderpfleger, -s, -,** baby sitter, nurse, nanny

die **Kinderpflegerin, -, -nen,** *(female)* baby sitter, nurse, nanny; also **der Sitter, die Sitterin**

die **Kindheit, -,** childhood

das **Kinn, -(e)s, -e,** chin

das **Kino, -s, -s,** the movies

die **Kirche, -, -n,** church

die **Kirsche, -, -n,** cherry

das **Kissen, -s, -,** pillow, cushion

klagen, to complain

klar, clear(ly)

die **Klärung, -, -en,** clarification

die **Klasse, -, -n,** class; **erster—***(gen.)* **fahren,** to travel first class

das **Klassenzimmer, -s, -,** classroom

klatschen, to clap; **in die Hände—,** to clap one's hands

das **Klavier, -s, -e,** piano;—*(no art.)* **spielen,** to play the piano

das **Kleid, -(e)s, -er,** dress; *(pl.)* clothes

sich **kleiden,** to dress (oneself)

klein, small, little

der **Kleintransporter, -s, -,** light delivery truck

klettern (auf), to come (up)

klingeln, to ring

klingen, klang, geklungen, to ring, chime, sound

die **Klinik, -, -en,** clinic, clinical hospital, nursing home

klopfen, to knock; **an die Tür—,** to knock at the door

der **Klub, -s, -s,** club, club-room

klug, clever, intelligent, wise, bright

der **Knabe, -n, -n,** boy

die **Kneipe, -, -n,** tavern, bar

das **Knie, -s, -,** knee

der **Knopf, -(e)s, ̈-e,** button

kochen, to cook

der **Koffer, -s, -,** trunk

die **Kohle, -, -n,** coal

der **Kollege, -n, -n,** colleague

die **Kollegin, -, -nen,** *(female)* colleague

Köln, -s, *(neut.),* Cologne

kommen, kam, ist gekommen, to come

der **König, -s, -e,** king

die **Königin, -, -nen,** queen

können, konnte, gekonnt, kann, to be able, can; **er hätte es tun—,** he could have done it; **er kann Deutsch,** he knows German; **er kann nichts dafür,** it is not his fault

konstruieren, to construct, design, build

das **Konzert, -(e)s, -e,** concert

der **Kopf, -(e)s, ̈-e,** head

das **Kopfweh, -s,** headache

der **Korb, -(e)s, ̈-e,** basket

der **Körper, -s, -,** body

der **Körperbau, -s,** bodily structure, frame, build

kostbar, expensive, precious

kosten, to cost; **es kostete mich** (or **mir**) **einen Dollar,** it cost me a dollar

kostspielig, expensive, costly

die **Kraft, -, ̈-e,** strength, power

das **Kraftfahrzeug, -s, -e,** vehicle, motor vehicle

krank, sick, ill

die **Krankheit, -, -en,** sickness, illness

das **Kraut, -(e)s, ̈-er,** plant, vegetable, herb, weed; cabbage

die **Krawatte, -, -n,** necktie, cravat

die **Kreide, -,** chalk

der **Kreis, -es, -e,** circle

die **Kreisbahn, -, -en,** orbit

kriechen, kroch, ist gekrochen, to creep

der **Krieg, -(e)s, -e,** war

krumm, crooked

die **Küche, -, -n,** kitchen

die **Kugel, -, -n,** bullet, ball, sphere

der **Kugelschreiber, -s, -,** ballpoint pen

die **Kuh, -, ̈-e,** cow

kühl, cool

der **Kummer, -s,** *(no pl.),* sorrow, grief, worry, trouble

sich **kümmern um,** to worry (care) about

der **Kunde, -n, -n,** customer

die **Kundin, -, -nen,** *(female)* customer

die **Kunst, -, ̈-e,** art

der **Künstler, -s, -,** *(male)* artist

die **Künstlerin, -, -nen** *(female)* artist

künstlerisch, artistic
künstlich, artificial, synthetic
kurz, short

L

lächeln, to smile
lachen, to laugh;**—über** *(w. acc.)*, to laugh at
der **Laden, -s, -̈,** store
lahm, lame
die **Lahn,** a river running through Wetzlar and Marburg in central Germany
das **Lamm, -(e)s, -̈er,** lamb
die **Lampe, —, -n,** lamp
das **Land, -(e)s, -̈er,** land, country; **aufs—,** to the country; **auf dem—,** in the country
lang, long; **einen Fuß —,** a foot long
lange, (for) a long time
langsam, slow(ly)
die **Langstrecke, -, -n,** a long distance; **Langstrecke laufen,** to run a distance race, to run cross-country
langweilig, tedious, boring
der **Lärm, -(e)s,** noise
lassen, ließ, gelassen, läßt, to let, leave; have done; **sich** *(dat.)* **das Haar schneiden—,** to have one's hair cut
laufen, lief, ist gelaufen, läuft, to run; **Schlittschuh—,** to skate
laufend, current(of time); **auf dem laufenden,** up-to-date; running; **mit laufendem Motor,** with engine running
die **Laune, -, -n,** mood, humor; **guter—***(gen.)* **sein,** to be in a good mood
lauschen, to listen
laut, loud(ly), aloud
der **Laut, -(e)s, -e,** sound
das **Leben, -s, -,** life
leben, to live
das **Leder, -s, -,** leather
leer, empty
legen, to lay, place, put
sich **lehnen an** *(w. acc.)*, to lean on
lehren, to teach; **sie lehrte ihn das Lied,** she taught him the song
der **Lehrer, -s, -,** *(male)* teacher
die **Lehrerin, -, -nen,** *(female)* teacher
der **Lehrling, -s, -e,** apprentice
leicht, easy; light;**—en Herzens,** with a light heart
leiden, litt, gelitten, to suffer
leider *(adv.)*, unfortunately; *(interj.)*, alas

leid tun *(impers.)*, to be sorry; **es tut mir leid,** I am sorry
leihen, lieh, geliehen, to lend
leisten, to perform, accomplish; **sich** *(dat.)***—,** to afford
leiten, to lead, guide
lenken, to steer, direct
die **Lerche, -, -n,** lark
lernen, to learn, study
lesen, las, gelesen, liest, to read
letzt-, last
die **Leute** *(pl.)*, people
das **Licht, -(e)s, -er,** light
lieb, dear
die **Liebe, -, -n,** love
lieben, to love
lieber *(comp. of* **lieb***)*, dearer; *(comp. of* **gern***)*, rather
lieblich, lovely, sweet
der **Liebling, -s, -e,** favorite; darling
das **Lied, -(e)s, -er,** song
liefern, to supply, furnish, deliver, render, yield
liegen, lag, gelegen, to lie; be situated
die **Limonade, -, -n,** soda, lemonade
die **Linde, -, -n,** linden
der **Lindenbaum, -(e)s, -̈e,** linden tree
die **Linie, -, -n,** line, streetcar or bus route; **in gerader Linie,** in a straight line, as the crow flies
link, left
links, on the left; **nach—,** to the left
die **Lippe, -, -n,** lip
die **Literatur, -, -en,** literature
loben, to praise
das **Loch, -(e)s, -̈er,** hole
der **Löffel, -s, -,** spoon
los, rid of; **ich bin es—,** I am rid of it; **was ist—?** what is the matter?
das **Los, -es, -e,** lottery ticket, share, lot (in life)
das **Löschblatt, -(e)s, -̈er,** (sheet of) blotting paper
löschen, to blot; quench
lösen, to loosen; solve *(a puzzle)*; buy *(a ticket)*; **sich—***(refl.)*, to loosen, become detached, be released
loslassen, ließ los, losgelassen, läßt los, to release, let go
der **Löwe, -n, -n,** lion
die **Luft, -, -̈e,** air
die **Luftdichte, -,** air density
das **Luftschiff, -(e)s, -e,** airship
der **Luftverkehr, -s,** air traffic
die **Lüge, -, -n,** lie, falsehood
lügen, log, gelogen, to (tell a) lie
die **Lust, -, -̈e,** joy, pleasure; **Lust haben zu,** to be in the mood for

lustig, merry, gay

M

machen, to make, do; **eine Reise (einen Spaziergang, eine Prüfung)—,** to take a trip (walk, examination); **sich** *(dat.)* **Sorgen—um,** to worry about; **man machte ihn zum Präsidenten,** he was made president

die **Macht, -, ¨-e,** might, power

mächtig, mighty; *(w. gen.)* master (*or* in control) of

das **Mädchen, -s, -,** girl

mähen, to mow

mahlen, mahlte, gemahlen (!), to grind

die **Mahlzeit, -, -en,** meal

der **Mai, -s, -e,** May

das **Mal, -(e)s, -e,** time; **das erste—,** the first time

malen, to paint

der **Maler, -s, -,** painter; artist

die **Malerin, -, -nen,** *(female)* artist

malerisch, artistic, picturesque

man *(indef. pron.),* one, they, people

mancher, manche, manches, many a; *(pl.)* some

manchmal, sometimes, many a time

der **Mann, -(e)s, ¨-er,** man

der **Mantel, -s, ¨-,** cloak; overcoat

die **Mark, -,** mark *(monetary)*

der **Markt, -(e)s, , ¨-e,** market

marschieren, to march

das **Maß, -es, -e,** measure

das **Material, -s, -ien,** material, substance, matter

der **Mathematiker, -s, —,** mathematician

die **Mauer, -, -n,** *(outside)* wall

die **Maus, -, ¨-e,** mouse

das **Meer, -(e)s, -e,** sea, ocean

mehr *(comp. of* **viel**), more

mehrere *(pl.),* several, a number of

die **Meile, -, -n,** mile

mein, meine, mein *(poss.),* my

meinen, to mean *(only of people),* think, believe

die **Meinung, -, -en,** opinion

meist- *(superl. of* **viel**), most

der **Meister, -s, -,** master; expert; master tradesman

die **Meldung, -, -en,** message, report

der **Mensch, -en, -en,** man, human being

das **Merkmal, -s, -e,** characteristic, feature, symptom

merkwürdig, peculiar

die **Messe, -, -n,** fair, market

messen, maß, gemessen, mißt, to measure

das **Messer, -s, -,** knife

das **Metall, -s, -e,** metal

das **Meter, -s, -e,** meter (39.37 inches)

mieten, to rent (as a tenant)

die **Milch, -,** milk

die **Miliarde, -, -n,** billion

die **Million, -, -en,** million

der **Ministerpräsident, -en, -en,** prime minister

die **Ministerpräsidentin, -, -nen,** *(female)* prime minister

die **Minute, -, -n,** minute

mischen, to mix

mißverstehen, mißverstand, mißverstanden, to misunderstand

mit *(prep. w. dat.),* with

mitbringen, brachte mit, mitgebracht, to bring along

das **Mitglied, -(e)s, -er,** member

mithelfen, half mit, mitgeholfen, hilft mit, cooperate with, help, collaborate, assist

der **Mittag, -(e)s, -e,** noon; **am—,** at noon

die **Mitte, -,** middle

mitten in, in the middle of

der **Mittwoch, -s, -e,** Wednesday

mögen, mochte, gemocht, mag, to like to, care for; **er möchte (gern) mitgehen,** he would like to go along; **er mochte wohl dreißig Jahre alt sein,** he was probably thirty years old; **das mag sein,** that may be

möglich, possible

der **Monat, -(e)s, -e,** month

monatelang, for months

der **Mond, -(e)s, -e,** moon

der **Montag, -(e)s, -e,** Monday

morgen *(adv.),* tomorrow

der **Morgen, -s, -,** morning; **am —** *(des* **—s** *or* **mort-gens),** in the morning; **eines —s,** one morning; **heute morgen,** this morning

müde *(adj. w. gen. or acc.),* tired; **ich bin des Lebens —,** I am tired of life; **ich bin es —,** I am tired of it

die **Mühe, -, -n,** trouble; **der —** *(gen.)* **wert sein,** to be worth the trouble

die **Mühle, -, -n,** mill

der **Müller, -s, -,** miller

der **Mund, -(e)s, ¨-er,** mouth

das **Museum, -s, Museen,** museum

die **Musik, -,** music

müssen, mußte, gemußt, muß, to be obliged, have to, must

das **Muster, -s, -,** model, sample, pattern

der **Mut, -(e)s,** courage

mutig, courageous

die **Mutter, -, ¨-,** mother

N

nach *(prep. w. dat.)*, after; toward, according to; — **Hause**, home, homeward

der **Nachbar, -s** (*or* **-n**), **-n**, *(male)* neighbor

die **Nachbarin, -, -nen,** *(female)* neighbor

die **Nachbarschaft, -, -en,** neighborhood

nachdem *(conj.)*, after

nachher *(adv.)*, afterwards

nachlassen, ließ nach, nachgelassen, läßt nach, to cease, quit

nachlässig, negligent

nachlaufen, lief nach, ist nachgelaufen, läuft nach, to run after

der **Nachmittag, -(e)s, -e,** afternoon; **am —** (**des —s** *or* **nachmittags**), in the afternoon; **eines —s** *(indef. time)*, one afternoon; **heute nachmittag,** this afternoon

die **Nachricht, -, -en,** news, information

nächst- (*superl. of* **nach**), next, nearest; **—es Jahr,** next year

die **Nacht, -, ⁻e,** night; **in der —,** at night

nackt, naked, bare

die **Nadel, -, -n,** needle

der **Nagel, -s, ⁻,** nail

nah(e) (näher, nächst-) *(w. dat.)*, near

die **Nähe, -, -n,** vicinity, neighborhood; **in seiner —,** near him

sich **nähern** *(w. dat.)*, to approach

nähren, to nourish

der **Name, -ns, -n,** name; **beim Namen nennen,** to call by name

namens, named, by the name of; **ein Mann — Schmidt,** a man named Smith

nämlich, namely

der **Narr, -en, -en,** fool

die **Nase, -, -n,** nose

naß, wet

die **Natur, -, -en,** nature

natürlich, natural(ly)

der **Nebel, -s, -,** fog

neben *(prep. w. dat. or acc.)*, beside, by the side of, next to

das **Nebenzimmer, -s, -,** adjoining room

necken, to tease

der **Neffe, -n, -n,** nephew

nehmen, nahm, genommen, nimmt, to take

nein, no

nennen, nannte, genannt, to name, call; **er nannte ihn beim Namen,** he called him by name

das **Nest, -es, -er,** nest; small town

nett, pleasant; pretty; tidy; nice; **ein —es Mädchen,** a nice girl

das **Netz, -es, -e,** net; network

neu, new

neulich, recently

neutral, neutral

nicht, not; **gar —,** not at all; **noch —,** not yet; **— einmal,** not even; **— nur. . . sondern auch,** not only. . .but also; **— wahr?** right? not so?

die **Nichte, -, -n,** niece

nichts, nothing; **gar —,** nothing at all; **das geht ihn — an,** that does not concern him

die **Niederlande** *(pl.)*, Netherlands

sich **niederlegen, legte nieder, niedergelegt,** to lie down

niedrig, low

nie(mals), never

niemand, -(e)s, nobody

nirgend *(neg. of* **irgend**; *used in various compounds)*, no-

nirgends, nowhere

noch, still, yet; **— einmal,** again; **— ein,** another; **— immer** (*or* **immer —**), still; **— nicht,** not yet; **weder . . . —,** neither. . .nor; **was —?** what else?

der **Norden, -s,** north

die **Not, -, ⁻e,** need, necessity; trouble

nötig, necessary; **ich habe es —,** I need it

die **Nummer, -, -n,** number

nun *(adv.)*, now; *(part.)* now, well

nur, only

die **Nuß, -, Nüsse,** nut

nützlich, useful

O

ob *(conj.)*, whether, if; **als —,** as if

oben *(adv.)*, above, at the top of, up; upstairs

oberflächlich, superficial

oberhalb *(prep. w. gen.)*, above

die **Oberfläche, -, -n,** surface

obgleich *(conj.)*, although

das **Obst, -(e)s,** fruit

der **Obstbaum, -(e)s, ⁻e,** fruit tree

obwohl *(conj.)*, although

der **Ochse, -n, -n,** ox

oder *(conj.)*, or

der **Ofen, -s, ⁻,** stove

offen *(adj.)*, open

öffnen, to open

oft, often

ohne *(prep. w. acc.),* without

das **Ohr.** -(e)s, -en, ear

der **Oktober,** -(s), -, October

das **Öl,** -(e)s, -e, oil

der **Onkel,** -s, -, uncle

die **Oper,** -, -n, opera

das **Opfer,** -s, -, victim, sacrifice

opfern, to sacrifice

organisch, organic

die **Orgel,** -, -n, organ

der **Ort,** -(e)s, -e, place

der **Osten,** -s, east

das **Ostern** (-, -), Easter

der **Ozean,** -s, -e, ocean

P

das **Paar,** -(e)s, -e, pair; **ein paar,** several, a few

packen, to pack; to seize

die **Packung,** -, -en, package

das **Papier,** -s, -e, paper

der **Park,** -(e)s, -e, park

passen *(w. dat.),* to fit; be convenient, suit

der **Pelz,** -es, -e, fur, pelt, hide, skin

pensioniert, retired

die **Perle,** -, -n, pearl

die **Person,** -, -en, person

die **Persönlichkeit,** -, -en, personality, personage

die **Pfalz,** the Palatinate

der **Pfarrer,** -s, -, pastor, clergyman

die **Pfeife,** -, -n, pipe; whistle

pfeifen, pfiff, gepfiffen, to whistle

der **Pfennig,** -s, -e, pfennig (1/100 *mark*)

das **Pferd,** -(e)s, -e, horse

die **Pflanze,** -, -n, plant

pflanzen, to plant

pflastern, to pave

pflegen, to take care of; be accustomed; **wie er zu sagen pflegt,** as he usually says

pflichtmäßig, dutiful

das **Pfund,** -(e)s, -e, pound

der **Physiker,** -s, -, physicist

physiologisch, physiological

der **Plan,** -(e)s, -e, plan

planen, to plan

der **Planet,** -en, -en, planet

der **Platz,** -es, -e, place; seat; square; **nehmen Sie —!** be seated

plötzlich, sudden(ly)

der **Polizist,** -en, -en, policeman

die **Polizistin,** -, -nen, policewoman

das **Porträt,** -s, -s, portrait, likeness

die **Post,** -, -en, mail; post office; **auf die — bringen,** to mail

der **Postbote,** -n, -n, letter carrier, mailman

die **Postbotin,** -, -nen, *(female)* letter carrier

die **Postkarte,** -, -en, postal card

der **Präsident,** -en, -en, president

der **Preis,** -es, -e, price; prize

preiswert, worth the price, a good value

Preußen, -s, *(neut.),* Prussia

der **Prinz,** -en, -en, prince

die **Pritsche,** -, -n, pick-up truck

der **Pritschenwagen,** -s, -, pick-up truck

der **Professor,** -s, -en, professor; *(Austr.)* secondary school teacher

die **Professorin,** -, -nen, *(female)* professor

der **Prokurist,** -en, -en, clerk, office supervisor

die **Prokuristin,** -, -nen, *(female)* clerk, office supervisor

die **Prüfung,** -, -en, examination

das **Pult,** -(e)s, -e, desk

der **Punkt,** -(e)s, -e, point, dot, period; **— zwei Uhr,** at two o'clock sharp, on the dot of two

pünktlich, punctual(ly)

putzen, to clean, shine; *(refl.),* to dress up

Q

die **Quelle,** -, -n, spring; source

die **Quittung,** -, -en, receipt

R

die **Rache,** -, revenge

sich **rächen an** *(w. dat.),* to take revenge on

das **Rad,** -(e)s, -er, wheel; bicycle

radikal, *(politically)* radical

der **Rand,** -(e)s, -er, edge

rasch, quick(ly)

der **Rasen,** -s, -, lawn, turf

rasieren, to shave *(often refl.)*

die **Rasierklinge,** -, -n, razor blade

der **Rat,** -(e)s, -schläge, (piece of) advice

der **Rat,** -(e)s, -e, councilor, adviser

raten, riet, geraten, rät *(w. dat.),* to advise; *(w. acc.),* to guess

das **Rathaus,** -es, /häuser, city hall

die **Rätin,** -, -nen, *(female)* city councilor

das **Rätsel,** -s, -, riddle, puzzle

die **Ratte, -, -n,** rat
der **Räuber, -s, -,** robber
　rauchen, to smoke
der **Raum, -(e)s, ̈-e,** room, space
　rauschen, to rustle
die **Rechnung, -, -en,** bill
　recht, right; **er hat —,** he is right; **es gerschieht ihm —,** it serves him right
　rechts, on the right; **nach —,** to the right
der **Rechtsanwalt, -s, ̈-e,** attorney, lawyer
die **Rechtsanwältin, -, -nen,** *(female)* attorney, lawyer
die **Rede, -, -n,** speech, discourse
　reden, to speak, talk
der **Redner, -s, -,** speaker, orator
die **Regel, -, -n,** rule; **in der —,** as a rule
　regelmäßig, regular(ly)
der **Regen, -s, -fälle** (*or* **Niederschläge**), rain
der **Regenschirm, -(e)s, -e,** umbrella
　regieren, to rule, govern
die **Regierung, -, -en,** government
　regnen, to rain; **stark —,** to rain hard
　regulieren, to regulate, govern, control
　reiben, rieb, gerieben, to rub
　reich, rich; **— an** *(w. dat.),* rich in
das **Reich, -(e)s, -e,** empire, realm, state;
　reichen, to reach, pass, hand over
　reif, ripe; mature
die **Reihe, -, -n,** row; **ich bin an der —** (*or* **die — ist an mir**), it is my turn
　rein, pure, clean, clear
　reinigen, to clean
die **Reise, -, -n,** trip, journey; **eine — machen,** to take a trip
　reisen, reiste, ist gereist, to travel
das **Reiseziel, -(e)s, -e,** destination of a trip
　reißen, riß, gerissen, to tear
　reiten, ritt, ist geritten, to ride (horseback)
der **Reiter, -s, -e,** rider, horseman
　reizen, to excite, irritate
　reizend *(pres. p. used as adj.),* charming
die **Rennbahn, -, -en,** racetrack
　rennen, rannte, ist gerannt, to run
das **Rennen, -s, -,** race
der **Rennwagenfahrer, -s, -,** race-car driver
die **Rennwagenfahrerin, -, -nen,** *(female)* race-car driver
　reparieren, to repair
die **Republik, -, -en,** republic
　retten, to save, rescue
der **Rhein, -(e)s,** Rhine
der **Richter, -s, -,** judge
　richtig, correct

　riechen, roch, gerochen, to smell — **nach,** to smell of
der **Riese, -n, -n,** giant
　riesig, gigantic
der **Ring, -(e)s, -e,** ring
　ringen, rang, gerungen, to wrestle
der **Ritter, -s, -,** knight
der **Rock, -(e)s, ̈-e,** coat
　roh, raw
　rollen, rollte, ist gerollt, to roll
die **Rose, -, -n,** rose
　rot, red
der **Rücken, -s, -,** back
　rücken, to move
die **Rücksicht, -, -en,** consideration
　rufen, rief, gerufen, to call
die **Ruhe, -,** peace, quiet, rest
　ruhig, quiet(ly)
der **Ruhm, -(e)s,** fame
sich **rühmen** *(w. gen.),* to boast of
　rühren, to stir, move; *(often refl.)* — **Sie sich nicht von der Stelle!** don't move from the spot
　rund, round

　　　　S

der **Saal, -(e)s, Säle,** hall
die **Sache, -, -n,** thing; matter; **er ist seiner — gewiß,** he knows what it's all about
der **Sack, -(e)s, ̈-e,** sack
die **Sage, -, -n,** legend, tradition; **der — nach,** according to legend
　sagen, to say, tell; **— wollen,** to mean
das **Salz, -es, -e,** salt
　sammeln, to collect
der **Samstag, -s, -e,** Saturday
　sanft, mild(ly), gentle, gently
der **Sänger, -es, -,** *(male)* singer
die **Sängerin, -, -nen,** *(female)* singer
der **Satellit, -en, -en,** satellite
der **Satz, -es, ̈-e,** sentence
　sauber, clean
　sauer, sour
　schade *(interj.),* too bad, (what) a pity
　schaden *(w. dat.),* to hurt, injure
die **Schadenfreude, -, -n,** malicious joy at another's discomfort
das **Schaf, -(e)s, -e,** sheep
der **Schaffner, -s, -,** conductor (on a train)
die **Schaffnerin, -, -nen,** *(female)* conductor (on a train)

sich **schämen,** *(w. gen. or* **über** *w. acc.),* to be ashamed of

scharf, sharp

der **Schatten, -s, -,** shade, shadow

der **Schatz, -es, ˮe,** treasure; sweetheart

schätzen, to appreciate

schauen, to look

der **Scheck, -s, -e,** check (as a form of money)

scheiden, schied, geschieden, *(tr.)* to separate; *(intr. w.* **sein***)* to take leave

der **Schein, -(e)s, -e,** light, brilliancy

scheinen, schien, geschienen, to shine; appear, seem

schelten, schalt, gescholten, schilt, to scold; call names

schenken, to give, present *(as a gift)*

die **Schicht, -, -en,** layer, stratum

schicken, to send

das **Schicksal, -s, -e,** fate, destiny

schieben, schob, geschoben, to shove

schief, uneven, crooked, wry

schießen, schoß, geschossen, to shoot

das **Schiff, -(e)s, -e,** ship

der **Schild, -(e)s, -e,** shield

das **Schild, -(e)s, -er,** sign(board); door plate

der **Schimpanse, -n, -n,** chimpanzee

der **Schirm, -(e)s, -e,** shelter; shade, screen

die **Schlacht, -, -en,** battle

der **Schlaf, -(e)s,** sleep

schlafen, schlief, geschlafen, schläft, to sleep

schläfern *(impers.),* to be sleepy; **mich schläfert,** I am sleepy

schläfrig, sleepy

der **Schlag, -(e)s, ˮe,** blow; stroke

schlagen, schlug, geschlagen, schlägt, to strike, hit

schlank, slender, slim

schlau, sly, cunning

schlecht, bad

schleifen, schliff, geschliffen, to whet, sharpen

schließen, schloß, geschlossen, to close, lock

das **Schließfach, -s, ˮer,** locker, safe deposit box

schlimm, bad(ly)

der **Schlittschuh, -(e)s, -e,** skate; — **laufen,** to skate

das **Schloß, Schlosses, Schlösser,** castle

der **Schluß, Schlusses, Schlüsse,** end

der **Schlüssel, -s, -,** key

schmal, narrow; thin, slender

schmecken, to taste

schmeicheln *(w. dat.),* to flatter; *(refl.),* to flatter oneself; **du schmeichelst dir,** you flatter yourself

schmelzen, schmolz, ist geschmolzen, schmilzt, to melt

der **Schmerz, -es, -en,** pain; **toll vor —,** frantic with pain

schmerzlich, painful(ly); **er empfindet es —,** it pains him

schmücken, to adorn

schmutzig, dirty

der **Schnee, -s,** snow

schneiden, schnitt, geschnitten, to cut

der **Schneider, -s, -,** tailor

schneien, to snow

schnell, quick(ly)

der **Schnellimbiß, -(ss)es, -(ss)e,** fast-food restaurant, snack bar

der **Schnellzug, -(e)s, ˮe,** express train

schon, already

schön, beautiful(ly)

die **Schönheit, -, -en,** beauty

der **Schrank, -(e)s, ˮe,** cupboard, cabinet

schreiben, schrieb, geschrieben, to write; **ich schreibe meinem Freund einen Brief (***or* **ich schreibe einen Brief an meinen Freund),** I write my friend a letter

schreien, schrie, geschrien, to scream

die **Schrift, -, -en,** writing

schriftlich, in writing, written

der **Schuh, -(e)s, -e,** shoe

der **Schulabschluß, -(ss)es, ˮ(ss)e,** graduation from school

die **Schuld, -, -en,** guilt; debt

schuldig, guilty; indebted; **ich bin ihm nichts —,** I owe him nothing

die **Schule, -, -n,** school; **in der —,** in school; **nach der —,** after school; **in die (***or* **zur) — gehen,** to go to school

der **Schüler, -s, -,** *(male)* pupil

die **Schülerin, -, -nen,** *(female)* pupil

die **Schulter, -, -n,** shoulder

die **Schüssel, -, -n,** dish; platter; bowl

schütteln, to shake

schützen, to protect

schwach, weak

der **Schwager, -s, ˮ,** brother-in-law

die **Schwägerin, -, -nen,** sister-in-law

schwarz, black

der **Schwarzwald, -(e)s,** Black Forest

schwätzen (*or* **schwatzen),** to gossip, chatter, babble

schweben, to hover, float, hang, be suspended

schweigen, schwieg, geschwiegen, to be silent

die **Schweiz, -,** Switzerland

schwer, heavy; difficult; — **arbeiten,** to work hard
die **Schwester, -, -n,** sister
schwierig, hard, difficult
schwimmen, schwamm, ist **geschwommen,** to swim
der **See, -s, -n,** lake
die **See, -, -n,** ocean, sea
die **Seele, -, -n,** soul
segeln, to sail
sehen, sah, gesehen, sieht, to see; **haben Sie ihn kommen —?** did you see him coming?
sich **sehnen nach,** to long for
sehr, very (much)
die **Seide, -, -n,** silk
sein, war, ist gewesen, ist, to be; **mir ist,** it seems to me; **mir ist schlecht zumute,** I am in a bad mood
sein, seine, sein *(poss.),* his, its
seiner, seine, seines *(poss. pron.),* his, its
seit *(prep. w. dat.),* since, for; — **wann?** since when?
seitdem *(adv. & conj.),* since
die **Seite, -, -n,** side; page
seither *(adv.),* since then
die **Sekunde, -, -n,** second
selbst *(indecl. adj. and pron.),* self; *(adv.)* even
selig, blessed; blissful(ly)
selten, seldom, rare(ly)
seltsam, peculiar
senden, sandte, gesandt, to send
die **Sendung, -, -en,** program, (radio or TV) transmission
setzen, to set, place; *(refl),* to sit down; **er setzt sich an den Tisch,** he sits down at the table
sicher *(adj. w. gen.)* sure; *(adv.),* surely, safe(ly)
der **Sieg, -(e)s, -e,** victory
siegen, to conquer
das **Signal, -s, -e,** signal, sign
das **Silber, -s,** silver
silbern *(adj.),* (of) silver
singen, sang, gesungen, to sing
sinken, sank, ist gesunken *(intr.),* to sink
der **Sinn, -(e)s, -e,** mind; sense
die **Sitte, -, -n,** custom, habit, practice
sitzen, saß, gesessen *(intr.),* to sit; **er sitzt am Tisch,** he sits at the table
der **Skat -(e)s, -e,** skat, a German card game involving three players, 32 cards, contracts, and tricks
so, so, thus, as
sobald, as soon as
sofort, at once

sogar, even
sogleich, at once, immediately
der **Sohn, -(e)s, ̈-e,** son
solcher, solche, solches, such
der **Soldat, -en, -en,** soldier
sollen, sollte, gesollt, soll, to be (required) to; be said; **er hätte arbeiten —,** he should have worked; **er soll reich sein,** he is said to be rich; **er sollte** *(subj.)* **arbeiten,** he should (or ought to) work
der **Sommer, -s, -,** summer
der **Sommermonat, -(e)s, -e,** summer month
sonderbar, unusual, peculiar
sondern, but; **nicht nur. . .—auch,** not only. . .but also
der **Sonnabend, -s, -e,** Saturday
die **Sonne, -, -n,** sun
die **Sonnenfinsternis, -, -se,** solar eclipse
der **Sonnenschein, -(e)s,** sunshine
das **Sonnensystem, -s, -e,** solar system
sonnig, sunny
der **Sonntag, -(e)s, -e,** Sunday
sonst, otherwise
die **Sorge, -, -n,** care, worry; **sich** *(dat.)* **—n machen um,** to worry about
sorgen für, to care for, take care of
sorgfältig, careful(ly)
die **Spalte, -, -n,** crack, cleft, fissure, split, gap
sparen, to save, economize
der **Spaß, -es, ̈-e,** joke
spät, late
spazierengehen *(conjugated like* **gehen***),* to go for a walk; **ich bin spazierengegangen,** I went for a walk
der **Spaziergang, -(s), ̈-e,** walk; **einen — machen,** to take a walk
die **Speise, -, -n,** food, dish
der **Spiegel, -s, -,** mirror
das **Spiel, -(e)s, -e,** play, game
spielen, to play
die **Spitze, -, -n,** tip, head, point; lace
spitzen, to sharpen
die **Sprache, -, -n,** language
sprechen, sprach, gesprochen, spricht, to speak; — **über** *(w. acc.)* or **von** *(w. dat.)* to talk about
das **Sprichwort, -(e)s, ̈-er,** proverb
springen, sprang, ist gesprungen, to jump
spüren, to detect
der **Staat, -(e)s, -en,** state
der **Stab, -(e)s, ̈-e,** staff, stick
die **Stadt, -, ̈-e,** city
der **Stadtplan, -s, ̈-e,** city plan, map of the city

der **Stall** -(e)s, ¨-e, stable
der **Stand,** -(e)s, ¨-e, standing; class
   stark, strong; — **regnen,** to rain hard
   starr, fixed; stiff
   statt (= **anstatt**) *(prep. w. gen.),* instead of
   stattfinden, fand statt, stattgefunden, to take
      place
   stattlich, stately
der **Staub,** -(e)s, -e, dust
   stechen, stach, gestochen, sticht, to prick, sting
   stecken, to stick; put; — **Sie das in die Tasche!**
      put that in your pocket
   stehen, stand, gestanden, to stand
   stehlen, stahl, gestohlen, stiehlt, to steal; **er hat**
      mir die Uhr gestohlen, he stole my watch
   steigen, stieg, ist gestiegen, to climb, mount, rise,
      ascend
   steil, steep
der **Stein,** -(e)s, -e, stone
die **Stelle,** -, -n, spot, place; position
   stellen, to place, put; **eine Frage an eine Person**
      (acc.)—, to ask a person a question
die **Stellung,** -, -en, position; rank
der **Stempel,** -s, -, rubber stamp
   sterben, starb, ist gestorben, stirbt, to die
der **Stern,** -(e)s, -e, star
die **Sternwarte,** -, -n, observatory
   stets, always
   still, quiet, still
die **Stimme,** -, -n, voice
der **Stock,** -(e)s, ¨-e, cane, stick
der **Stoff,** -(e)s, -e, material; matter
   stolz, proud; — **sein auf** *(w. acc.),* to be proud of
   stören, to disturb
   stoßen, stieß, gestoßen, stößt, to push
   strafen, to punish
   strahlen, to shine, be radiant
der **Strand,** -(e)s, -e, shore
die **Straße,** -, -n, street
die **Straßenbahn,** -, -en, streetcar
die **Stratosphäre,** -, stratosphere
der **Streit,** -(e)s, -e, (or —**igkeiten**), quarrel, fight,
      strife
   streng, strict, severe
der **Strom** -(e)s, ¨-e, river, stream
die **Stube,** -, -n, room
das **Stück** -(e)s, -e, piece
der **Student,** -en, -en, student
die **Studentenbude,** -, -n, student room
die **Studentin,** -, -nen, *(female)* student
   studieren, to study
die **Stufe,** -, -n, step

der **Stuhl,** -(e)s, ¨-e, chair
   stumm, dumb, mute, silent
   stumpf, blunt, without a point
die **Stunde,** -, -n, hour; **ich nehme —n,** I take lessons
der **Sturm,** -(e)s, ¨e, storm
   stürmisch, stormy
   stützen, to support; *(refl. w. auf & acc.),* to lean on
   suchen, to look for, seek
der **Süden,** -s, south
die **Summe,** -, -n, amount, sum
der **Supermarkt,** -(e)s, ¨-e, supermarket
die **Suppe,** -, -n, soup
   süß, sweet
die **Szene,** -, -n, scene

T

   tadeln, to criticize, rebuke
die **Tafel,** -, -n, blackboard
der **Tag,** -(e)s, -e, day; — **für —,** day after day; **einen**
      — um den anderen, every other day; **am**
      —, in the daytime; **eines —es** *(indef. time),*
      one day; **heute über acht —e,** a week from
      today; **vor acht —en,** a week ago
   täglich, daily
das **Tal,** -(e)s, ¨-er, valley
die **Tanne,** -, -n, fir (tree)
die **Tante,** -, -n, aunt
der **Tante-Emma-Laden,** -s, ¨-, mom and pop store,
      neighborhood store
der **Tanz,** -es, ¨-e, dance
   tapfer, brave(ly)
die **Tapferkeit,** -, bravery
die **Tasche,** -, -n, pocket
das **Taschentuch,** -(e)s, ¨-er, handkerchief
die **Taschenuhr,** -, -en, (pocket) watch
die **Tasse,** -, -n, cup
die **Tat,** -, -en, deed; **in der —,** indeed, in fact
   tätig, active
die **Tätigkeit,** -, -en, activity, action
   tauchen, tauchte, ist getaucht, to dive
   taugen, to be fit (good, useful)
   tauschen, to exchange
   täuschen, to deceive
   tausend *(num. adj.),* thousand
das **Tausend,** -(e)s, -e, thousand
   tausendmal, a thousand times
der **Taxifahrer,** -s, -, taxicab driver
die **Taxifahrerin,** -, -nen, *(female)* taxicab driver
der **Techniker,** -s, -, technician
   technisch, technical

der **Tee, -s,-sorten,** tea *(plural:* kinds of tea; *otherwise:* **Tees)**

der **Teil, -(e)s, -e,** part

die **Teilung, -, -en,** division

das **Telefon, -s, -e,** telephone

telefonieren to telephone

telefonisch, by phone; **— erreichen,** to reach by phone

telegrafieren, to telegraph

das **Teleskop, -s, -e,** telescope

der **Teller, -s, —,** plate

das **Temperament, -s, -e,** temperament

die **Temperatur, -, -en,** temperature

das **Tennis,** tennis

der **Tenor, -s, ̈e** (*or* **-e**) tenor

teuer, dear; expensive

der **Teufel, -s, -,** devil

das **Theater, -s, -,** theater; **ins — gehen,** to go to the theater

tief, deep

die **Tiefe, -, -n,** depth

das **Tier, -(e)s, -e,** animal

der **Tierpark, -(e)s, -e,** zoo

die **Tinte, -, -n,** ink

der **Tisch, -es, -e,** table; **den — decken,** to set the table

das **Tischtuch, -(e)s, ̈er,** tablecloth

die **Tochter, -, ̈,** daughter

der **Tod, -es, -esfälle,** death

toll, mad crazy; **— vor Schmerz,** frantic with pain

der **Ton, -(e)s, ̈e,** tone, sound

das **Tonbandgerät, -s, -e,** tape recorder

die **Torte, -, -n,** flat cake, tart, flan

tot, dead

töten, to kill

der **Tourist, -en, -en,** tourist

die **Touristin, -, -nen,** *(female)* tourist

tragen, trug, getragen, trägt, to carry; wear

die **Träne, -, -n,** tear

der **Trank, -(e)s, ̈e,** drink, beverage

der **Traum, -(e)s, ̈e,** dream

träumen, to dream

traurig, sad

treffen, traf, getroffen, trifft, to meet; hit

treiben, trieb, getrieben, to drive; be engaged in

trennen, to separate

die **Treppe, -, -n,** stairs

treten, trat, ist getreten, tritt, to step

treu, faithful(ly), true

trinken, trank, getrunken, to drink

das **Trinkgeld, -(e)s, -er,** tip

der **Tritt, -(e)s, -e,** kick, step, pace

trocken *(adj.),* dry

trocknen, to dry

trösten, to comfort, console

trotz *(prep. w. gen.),* in spite of

trotzdem, nevertheless, in spite of it

die (*or* das) **Trübsal, -,** (*or* **-s**)**, -e,** affliction, trouble

der **Trunk, -(e)s, ̈e,** drink, draught

die **Tschechoslowakei,** Czechoslovakia

das **Tuch, -(e)s, ̈er,** cloth

tüchtig, capable; strong; **— studieren,** to study hard

tun, tat, getan, tut, to do; act, pretend; **er tut als ob,** he acts as if

die **Tür, -, -en,** door

die **Türkei, -,** Turkey

der **Turm, -(e)s, ̈e,** tower

U

üben, to practice

über *(prep. w. dat. or acc.),* over, above

überall, everywhere

überhaupt, on the whole, altogether; **— nicht,** not at all

überholen, to pass (another car), overtake

übermorgen, day after tomorrow

überraschen, to surprise

der **Überrock, -(e)s, ̈e,** overcoat

überschwémmen, to flood

übersétzen, to translate

überwinden, überwand, überwunden, to overcome

üblich, usual

die **Übung, -, -en,** exercise

das **Ufer, -s, -,** shore, river bank

die **Uhr, -, -en,** watch; clock; o'clock; **um zwei —,** at two o'clock; **wieviel — ist es?** what time is it?

um *(prep. w. acc.)* around, about; **— drei Uhr,** at three o'clock; **—. . .willen,** for. . .sake; **— . . .zu** *(w. pres. inf.)* in order to

umsonst, in vain

der **Umstand, -(e)s, ̈e,** circumstance; **unter Umständen,** under certain circumstances

umständlich, involved, troublesome, fussy, intricate

umsteigen, stieg um, ist umgestiegen, to change (trains, streetcars, busses)

unaufhörlich, constantly, without stopping

unbefriedigend, unsatisfactory, a failing grade in school

unbemannt, unmanned, pilotless

und, and

unehrlich, dishonest

der **Unfall, -s, ⸚e,** accident (with injury)

ungefähr, about, approximately

das **Unglück, -(e)s, -sfälle,** misfortune

unglücklich, unhappy, unlucky

die **Universität, -, -en,** university; *(student)* **auf der —,** *(professor)* **an der —,** at the university

unmöglich, impossible

unser, uns(e)re, unser *(poss.),* our

uns(e)rer, uns(e)re, uns(e)res *(poss. pron.)* our

unten *(adv.),* below; downstairs

unter *(prep. w. dat. or acc.),* under, below, beneath; among

die **Untergrundbahn, -, -en,** subway

unterhalb *(prep. w. gen.),* below

unterhálten, unterhielt, unterhalten, unterhält, to entertain; *(refl.)* to converse

der **Unterschied, -(e)s, -e,** difference

unterscheiden, unterschied, unterschieden, to distinguish

untersúchen, untersuchte, untersucht, to examine, test, investigate

die **Untersuchung, -, -en,** investigation, test

unzufrieden, dissatisfied

die **Urgroßmutter, -, ⸚,** great-grandmother

der **Urgroßvater, -s, ⸚,** great-grandfather

der **Urlaub, -(e)s, -e,** vacation, leave

die **Ursache, -, -n,** cause

urteilen, urteilte, geurteilt, to judge

V

der **Vater, -s, ⸚,** father

das **Vaterland, -(e)s, ⸚er,** fatherland, native land

die **Vaterstadt, -, ⸚e,** native city

verändern, to change, alter, transform

verbergen, verbarg, verborgen, verbirgt, to hide, conceal

verbessern, to correct

sich **verbeugen vor** *(w. dat.),* to bow to (*or* before)

verbieten, verbot, verboten *(w. dat. of the pers.),* to forbid

verbinden, verband, verbunden, to unite

der **Verbrauchermarkt, -(e)s, ⸚e,** discount store

verbrennen, verbrannte, verbrannt *(tr.)* to burn up; *(intr. w.* **sein***)* to burn up

verbringen, verbrachte, verbracht, to pass, spend time

verdanken *(w.dat. of the pers.),* to owe

verdienen, to earn; deserve

der **Verein, -(e)s, -e,** club

die **Vereinigten Staaten** *(pl.),* United States

die **Verfassung, -, -en,** constitution, system of government; state of mind

verfolgen *(w. acc.),* to pursue

die **Vergangenheit, -, -en,** past, time gone by

vergeben, vergab, vergeben, vergibt *(w. dat. of the pers.),* to forgive

vergebens, in vain

vergehen, verging, ist vergangen, to pass; elapse; disappear

vergessen, vergaß, vergessen, vergißt, to forget

vergleichen, verglich, verglichen, to compare

das **Vergnügen, -s, -,** pleasure

das **Verhältnis, -ses, -se,** relation, relationship

verkaufen, to sell

das **Verkehrsamt, -(e)s, ⸚er,** travel bureau, tourist information bureau

verlangen, to demand

verlassen, verließ, verlassen, verläßt, to leave, forsake; leave behind; **sich — auf** *(w. acc.),* to depend (*or* rely) on

verlegen, to misplace

verleihen, verlieh, verliehen, lend, loan, bestow

sich **verlieben,** to fall in love; **sich in jmdn verlieben,** to fall in love with someone

verlieren, verlor, verloren, to lose

sich **verloben mit,** to become engaged to

der **Verlust -(e)s, -e,** loss, damage

vermieten, to rent out

vermissen, to miss

das **Vermögen, -s, -,** fortune

verpassen, to miss *(as a train)*

der **Verrat, -(e)s,** treason

sich **versammeln,** to gather, assemble

versäumen, to miss *(as a train)*

verschieden *(adj.)* different; *(pl.)* several, various

verschlingen, verschlang, verschlungen, to devour

verschwenden, to squander

verschwinden, verschwand, ist verschwunden, to disappear

die **Versicherungsgesellschaft, -, -en,** insurance company

versprechen, versprach, versprochen, verspricht, to promise

verstehen, verstand, verstanden, to understand; **das versteht sich,** that is obvious

versteigern, to auction off

der **Versuch, -(e)s, -e,** attempt

versuchen, to try, experiment

verteidigen, to defend

der **Vertrag, -(e)s, ⸚e,** contract

vertreten, vertrat, vertreten, vertritt, to represent

verwandt *(adj.),* related

der **Verwandte, -n, -n** *(w. adj. decl.)*, relative; **ein —r,** a relative; **meine —n,** my relatives

verwenden, verwandte, verwandt to utilize, apply

die **Verwendung, -, -en,** use, application

verwirrt, confused

verwöhnen, to spoil, pamper

verzeihen, verzieh, verziehen *(w. dat.)*, to pardon

der **Vetter, -s, -n,** *(male)* cousin

das **Vieh, -(e)s,** cattle

viel (mehr, meist-), much, a great deal; *(pl.)* many; **—es,** many things

vielleicht, perhaps

vielmehr, rather

vier, four; **auf allen —en,** on all fours

viert-, fourth

das **Viertel, -s, -,** quarter, one-fourth

die **Viertelstunde, -, -n,** quarter of an hour

der **Vogel, -s, ⸚,** bird

das **Volk, -(e)s, ⸚er,** people, nation

das **Volkslied, -(e)s, -er,** folksong

die **Volkswirtschaft, -,** economics

voll, full

vollständig, complete(ly)

von *(prep. w. dat.)*, of, from

vor *(prep. w. dat. or acc.)*, before, in front of; *(w. dat. only)*, ago; **—einem Monat,** a month ago; **ich bin außer mir — Freude,** I am beside myself with joy; **er brennt — Ungeduld,** he burns with impatience

vorbei, past, over

vorbeifliegen, flog vorbei, ist vorbeigeflogen, to fly past *(w. an & dat.)*

vorbeigehen, ging vorbei, ist vorbeigegangen, to walk past; **an etwas** *(dative)* **vorbeigehen,** to walk past something

vorbeikommen, kam vorbei, ist vorbeigekommen, to pass by; **bei einer Person vorbeikommen,** to drop in on a person

vorbereiten, to prepare; *(refl. w. auf & acc.)*, to prepare for

vorgehen, ging vor, ist vorgegangen, to precede; **die Uhr geht vor,** the clock is fast

vorgestern, day before yesterday

vorig, last, previous; **—e Nacht,** last night

vorkommen, kam vor, ist vorgekommen, to happen; occur; appear

vorlesen, las vor, vorgelesen, liest vor, to read aloud to *(w. dat. pers. & acc. th.)*

die **Vorlesung; -, -en,** lecture

vorletzt-, before (the) last; **—es Jahr,** year before last

der **Vormittag, -(e)s, -e,** forenoon

vorn *(adv.)*, in front

vorsingen, sang vor, vorgesungen, to sing to *(w. dat. pers. & acc. th.)*

die **Vorstadt, -, ⸚e,** suburb

die **Vorstellung, -, -en,** performance

der **Vortrag, -(e)s, ⸚e,** lecture; **einen Vortrag halten,** to give a lecture

vorüber, past, over with

vorwärts, forward

W

wach, awake; **— sein,** to be awake

wachsen, wuchs, ist gewachsen, wächst, to grow

die **Waffe, -, -n,** weapon

der **Wagen, -s, -,** wagon, carriage; car *(of a train);* auto

wagen, to dare

die **Wahl, -, -en,** choice, selection; election

wählen, to choose; elect

wahr, true; **nicht —?** right? not so?

während *(prep. w. gen.)*, during; *(conj.)*, while

die **Wahrheit, -, -en,** truth

wahrscheinlich, probable, probably

der **Wald, -(e)s, ⸚er,** forest

die **Wand, -, ⸚e,** wall

wandern *(w. sein)*, to walk, travel *(on foot)*, go; wander

die **Wanderung, -, -en,** hike

die **Wandkarte, -, -n,** wall map

die **Wange, -, -n,** cheek

wann *(inter. adv.)*, when; **seit —?** since when?

die **Ware, -, -n,** ware; *(pl.)* merchandise

warnen, to warm

warten, to wait; **— auf** *(w. acc.)*, to wait for

warum, why

was *(inter. pron.)*, what; *(rel. pron.)*, what, that which; **alles, was ich habe,** all (that) I have; **— für ein,** what kind of

waschen, wusch, gewaschen, wäscht, to wash; **ich wasche mir die Hände,** I wash my hands; *(dir. refl.)*, **ich wasche mich,** I wash (myself)

das **Wasser, -s, -,** water

der **Wasserfall, -(e)s, ⸚e,** waterfall

weder. . .noch, neither. . .nor

der **Weg, -(e)s, -e,** way; **gehe deines —es!** go your way

wegen *(prep. w. gen.)*, on account of; **meinet—,** on my account

weggehen, ging weg, ist weggegangen, to go away

weh tun, to hurt; **es tut mir weh,** it hurts me

das **Weib, -(e)s, -er,** woman *(usually contemptuous)*

weich, soft

die **Weihnachten** *(pl. w. sing, vb.)*, Christmas
weil, because
der **Wein, -(e)s, -e**, wine
weinen, to weep
die **Weise, -, -n**, way, manner; **auf diese —**, in this manner
weise, wise
die **Weisheit, -, -en**, wisdom
weiß, white
weit, wide; far
welcher, welche, welches *(rel. & inter. adj. & pron.)*, which (one), what (one), who; *(in excls.)* what
die **Welle, -, -n**, wave
die **Welt, -, -en**, world
weltbekannt, known worldwide
der **Weltmeister, -s, -**, world champion
der **Weltraum, -(e)s**, (outer) space
wenden, wandte, gewandt, to turn
wenig, little, not much
wenige *(pl.)*, few
wenigstens, at least
wenn, if, whenever
wer *(inter. pron.)*, who; *(indef. rel. pron.)* he who, whoever
werden, wurde, ist geworden, wird, to become; **aus**, to become of
werfen, warf, geworfen, wirft, to throw
das **Werk, -(e)s, -e**, work, deed, opus
die **Werkstatt, -, ̈-e**, workshop
die **Werkstätte, -, -n**, workshop
das **Werkzeug, -s, -e**, tool
wert, worth; **einen Dollar —**, worth a dollar; **der Mühe** *(gen.)* **—**, worth the trouble; **der Rede —**, worth mentioning
der **Wert, -(e)s, -e**, worth
wesentlich, essential, intrinsic
weshalb, why
wessen *(gen. of **wer**)*, whose
der **Westen, -s**, west
wetten, to bet, wager
das **Wetter, -s, -**, weather
wichtig, important
wider *(prep. w. acc.)*, against
widersprechen, widersprach, widersprochen, widerspricht *(w. dat.)*, to contradict
wie, how; as
wieder, again
wiederhólen, wiederholte, wiederholt, to repeat
das **Wiedersehen, -s**, reunion; **auf —!** goodbye, see you!
die **Wiege, -, -n**, cradle
die **Wiese, -, -n**, meadow

wieviel, how much; **der wievielte ist heute?** what is today's date?
willkommen *(adj.)*, welcome
der **Wind, -(e)s, -e**, wind
windig, windy
winken, to wink, beckon; **einem mit den Augen —**, to wink at a person; **mit der Hand —**, to beckon, wave
der **Winter, -s, -**, winter
der **Wipfel, -s, -**, tree top
wirken, to be effective, make an impression
wirklich, real(ly)
die **Wirklichkeit, -, -en**, reality
der **Wirt, -(e)s, -e**, host, innkeeper
wissen, wußte, gewußt, weiß, to know *(a fact)*
das **Wissen, -s**, knowledge, learning; **meines —s**, as far as I know
die **Wissenschaft, -, -en**, science; knowledge
der **Wissenschaftler, -s, -**, scientist
die **Wissenschaftlerin, -, -nen**, *(female)* scientist
wissenschaftlich, scientific
der **Witz, -es, -e**, joke
wo, where
die **Woche,-, -n**, week
wöchentlich, weekly
wofür, for what *(or which)*
woher, from where, whence; **— wissen Sie das?** how do you know that?
wohin, whither, to what place
wohl, well; indeed; probably
wohnen, to live, dwell
die **Wohnung, -, -en**, residence
der **Wolf, -(e)s, ̈-e**, wolf
die **Wolke, -, -n**, cloud
wolkenerfüllt, cloud-filled
wollen, wollte, gewollt, will, to want, wish; **er will morgen abfahren**, he intends to leave tomorrow; **er will eine reiche Tante haben**, he professes to have a rich aunt; **er will es getan haben**, he claims to have done it; **er wollte eben ausgehen**, he was (just) on the point of going out
womit, with what *(or which)*
das **Wort, -(e)s, -e** *(in connected discourse)*, **̈-er** *(disconnected words)*, word; **er hält —**, he keeps his word
das **Wörterbuch, -(e)s, ̈-er**, dictionary
wörtlich, literally
das **Wunder, -s, -**, wonder, miracle
sich **wundern über** *(w. acc.)*, to be surprised at
wunderschön, exceedingly beautiful
der **Wunsch, -es, ̈-e**, wish, desire
wünschen, to wish

die **Würde, -, -n,** dignity
würdig, worthy; *(w. gen.)* worthy of
die **Wurst, -, ̈-e,** sausage
die **Wut, -,** rage
wüten, to rage
wütend, raging, very angry

Z

die **Zahl, -, -en,** number
zahlen, to pay
zählen, to count
zahllos, countless, innumerable
zahlreich, numerous
zahm, tame
der **Zahn, -(e)s, ̈-e,** tooth
der **Zahnarzt, -es, ̈-e,** dentist
das **Zahnweh, -(e)s,** toothache
zart, tender, delicate
der **Zauber, -s, -,** charm, magic
der **Zaun, -(e)s, ̈-e,** fence
z.B. (= **zum Beispiel**), for example
zehn, ten
die **Zehnerpackung, -, -en,** a package of ten
das **Zeichen, -s, -,** sign, signal
zeichnen, to draw
zeigen, to show
die **Zeile, -, -n,** line
die **Zeit, -, -en,** time; **zur —, als (da** *or* **wo),** at the time when
das **Zeitalter, -s, -,** age; era; **das atomische —,** atomic age
die **Zeitschrift, -, -en,** magazine
die **Zeitung, -, -en,** newspaper
zerbrechen, zerbrach, zerbrochen, zerbricht, to break (to pieces)
zerfleischen, to mangle
zerreißen, zerriß, zerrissen, to tear (to pieces)
der **Zeuge, -n, -n,** witness
die **Ziege, -, -n,** goat
ziehen, zog, gezogen, to pull; *(intr.w. sein),* to go, move
das **Ziel, -(e)s, -e,** aim, goal
ziemlich, rather
zig, *indefinite numeral,* umpteen
das **Zimmer, -s, -,** room
der **Zimmerkollege, -n, -n,** roommate
die **Zimmerkollegin, -, -nen,** *(female)* roommate
der **Zimmermann, -(e)s, Zimmerleute,** carpenter

zittern, to tremble
der **Zoll, -s, ̈-e,** customs, duty, tariff
zornig, angry
zu *(prep. w. dat.),* to; at; for; *(adv.)* too; **— Hause,** at home; **— Weihnachten,** for (*or* at) Christmas
der **Zucker, -s,** sugar
zuerst, at first
der **Zufall, -s, ̈-e,** accident (fortuitous)
zufällig, accidental(ly); **er war — zu Hause,** he happened to be at home
zufälligerweise *(adv.),* by chance; **— war ich auch da,** I happened to be there too
zufrieden, satisfied
zufriedenstellend, satisfactory
der **Zug, -es, ̈-e,** train, parade, draught (of wind), (facial) feature
zugleich, at the same time
zuhören, hörte zu, zugehört *(w. dat.),* to listen to
die **Zukunft, -,** future
zuletzt, finally, at the end
zum (= **zu dem**), to (at *or* for) the; **— Geburtstag,** for one's birthday
zumachen, machte zu, zugemacht, to close
zunächst, first of all
die **Zunge, -, -n,** tongue
zur (= **zu der**), to (at *or* for) the; **— Zeit als (da** *or* **wo),** at the time when
zurückkehren, kehrte zurück, ist zurückgekehrt, to turn (*or* come) back, return
zusammen, together
zusammenbringen, brachte zusammen, zusammengebracht, to bring together; gather
der **Zustand, -(e)s, ̈-e,** condition
zuverlässig, reliable, dependable
zuvor, before
zuweilen, occasionally
zuwenden, wandte zu, zugewandt, to turn to(ward); **er wandte mir den Rücken zu,** he turned his back on me
zwanzig, twenty
zwar, to be sure, I admit
der **Zweck, -(e)s, -e,** purpose
zweierlei, of two kinds
der **Zweifel, -s, -,** doubt
der **Zweig, -(e)s, -e,** twig
zweimal, twice
der **Zwerg, -(e)s, -e,** dwarf
zwingen, zwang, gezwungen, to force
zwischen *(prep. w. dat. or acc.),* between

ENGLISH-GERMAN VOCABULARY

A

a, an, ein; **not—,** kein

able: to be—, können, konnte, gekonnt, kann

about (= *approximately*), ungefähr; **to talk—,** sprechen von (*w. dat.*) or über (*w. acc.*) **what was it (all)—?** um was handelte es sich?: **do you know what you are—?,** sind Sie Ihrer Sache gewiß? **he was—to leave,** er wollte eben abfahren (*or* er war im Begriff abzufahren)

above, über (*w. dat. or acc.*); oberhalb (*w. gen.*)

absent, abwesend; **to be—,** fehlen; **he is—,** er fehlt

accident (*with injury*), der Unfall, -s, -̈e; (*by chance*), der Zufall, -s, -̈e, **by accident,** zufällig

accompany, begleiten

accomplishment, die Leistung, -, -en

according to, nach (*w. dat.*)

account: on—of, wegen (*w. gen.*); **on—of the weather,** wegen des Wetters (*or* des Wetters wegen); **on my—,** meinetwegen; **on your—,** Ihretwegen

accuse of, ánklagen *or* beschuldigen (*w. acc. of the pers. & gen. of the th.*)

accustomed: become—to, such gewöhnen an (*w. acc.*); **I am—to it,** ich bin daran gewöhnt; *or* ich bin es gewohnt

acquaintance, der Bekannte, -n, -n (*w. adj. decl*); ein Bekannter; **I made his—,** ich lernte ihn kennen, *or* ich machte seine Bekanntschaft

acquainted: to be—with, kennen, kannte, gekannt

acquire (*knowledge or information*), Kenntnisse erlangen

across, durch (*w. acc.*)

act (= *pretend*), tun, tat, getan, tut; **he acts as if,** er tut, als ob

actually (= *really*), wirklich; (= *indeed*) in der Tat

add, hinzufügen, fügte hinzu, hinzugefügt

address, die Adresse, -, -n

admire, bewundern

advance, der Fortschritt, -(e)s, -e

advice, der Rat, -(e)s, -schläge

advise, raten, riet, geraten, rät (*w. dat.*)

afford, sich (*dat.*) leisten

afraid: to be—of, sich fürchten vor (*w. dat.*); **to be— that,** fürchten, daß

Africa, (das) Afrika, -s

after, nach (*w. dat.*); **—school,** nach der Schule; (*conj.*), nachdem

afternoon, der Nachmittag, -(e)s, -e; **this—,** heute nachmittag; **tomorrow—,** morgen nachmittag; **yesterday—,** gestern nachmittag; **the whole—,** den ganzen Nachmittag (*duration of time*); **one—,** eines Nachmittags (*indef. time*); **in the—,** am Nachmittag (nachmittags)

afterwards, nachher, darauf, danach

again, wieder, noch einmal

against, gegen (*w. acc.*); wider (*w. acc.*)

age, das Alter, -s, -; (= *period of time*) das Zeitalter; **atomic—,** das atomische Zeitalter; **Middle Ages,** das Mittelalter

ago, vor (*w. dat.*), her; **two years—,** vor zwei Jahren; **a week—,** vor acht Tagen; **that was long—,** das ist schon lange her

agreeable, angenehm

air, die Luft, -, -̈e

air density, die Luftdichte, -

air layer, die Luftschicht, -, -en

airplane, das Flugzeug, -(e)s, -e

airship, das Luftschiff, -(e)s, -e

air traffic, der Luftverkehr, -s

all, alle; ganz; **—Europe,** ganz Europa; **for—I care,** meinetwegen; **it was—the same to me,** es war mir ganz gleich; **almost—week,** fast die ganze Woche; **—I have,** alles, was ich habe:—**good things,** alles Gute; **—else,** alles andere; **not at—,** gar nicht; **nothing at—,** gar nichts

alley, die Gasse, -, -n

allow, erlauben (*w. dat.*)

allowed: to be—, dürfen, durfte, gedurft, darf

almost, fast, beinah(e)

alone, allein

along (*prep.*), entlang (*usually w. acc.*); **he is going— the river,** er geht den Fluß entlang; (*adv.*), mit; **come—,** kommen Sie mit!

aloud, laut; **to read—,** vorlesen

alphabet, das Alphabet, -(e)s, -e

alphabetically, nach dem Alphabet

Alps, die Alpen (*pl.*)

already, schon

also, auch

although, obgleich

altitude, die Höhe, -, -n

always, immer, stets

ambassador (*male*), der Botschafter, -s, -; (*female*), die Botschafterin, -, -nen

America, (das) Amerika, -s

American, amerikanisch (*adj.*)

among unter (*w. dat. or acc.*); **—other things,** unter ander(e)m

and, und; **colder—colder,** immer kälter

anger, der Zorn, -(e)s

angry, zornig, böse;**—with,** böse auf (*w. acc.*); **he is— with me,** er ist mir böse; *or* er ist böse auf mich

animal, das Tier, -(e)s, -e; **domestic—,** das Haustier

announcement, die Anzeige, -, -n

announcer (*male*), der Ansager, -s, -; (*female*), die Ansagerin, -, -nen

another, noch ein; (= *a different one*) ein anderer; **one after—,** einer nach dem anderen

answer die Antwort, -, -en; **an—to,** eine Antwort auf (*w. acc.*)

answer, antworten (*w. dat. of the pers.*); **—a question,** auf eine Frage (*acc.*) antworten, *or* eine Frage (*dir. obj.*) beantworten; **I—him,** ich antworte ihm

any, etwas (*indecl. w. sing. noun or alone as pron.*); irgend- (*in various combinations*); (irgend) welche (*w. a pl. noun*); **not—,** kein; **I haven't—money,** ich habe kein Geld; **not—longer,** nicht mehr

anybody, (irgend) jemand

anyhow (= *somehow*), irgendwie, auf irgendeine Weise; (= *in any case*), jedenfalls

anyone, (irgend) jemand; **—else,** jemand anders, sonst jemand

anything, (irgend) etwas

appear, erscheinen, erschien, ist erschienen

appetite, der Appetit, -(e)s, -e

apple, der Apfel, -s, ¨

apply for, sich bewerben um (*w. acc.*)

approach, sich nähern (*w. dat.*)

April, der April -s, -e

arm, der Arm, -(e)s, -e

army, das Heer, -(e)s, -e; die Armee, -, -n

around, um (*w. acc.*)

arrest, verhaften

arrival, die Ankunft, -, ¨e

arrive, ankommen, kam an, ist angekommen

art, die Kunst, -, ¨e

article, der Artikel, -s, -

artificial, künstlich

artist, der Künstler, -s, -; (*female*) die Künstlerin, -, -nen

artistic, künstlerisch, artistisch

as wie: (*causal*) da; (*temp.*) indem; **white—snow,** weiß wie Schnee; **he was famous—an orator,** als Redner war er berühmt; **—if** als ob; **—far—,** bis; **—soon—,** sobald; **—long—,** solange; **—often—,** sooft; **—well—,** so gut wie; **just—,** ebenso

ascend, steigen, stieg, ist gestiegen; aufsteigen

ashamed: to be—(of), sich schämen (*w. gen. or* über *& acc.*)

Asia, (das) Asien, -s

ask, fragen; **—a person a question,** eine Frage an eine Person (*acc.*) stellen; **—for something,** um etwas (*acc.*) bitten; **—about,** fragen nach (*w. dat.*)

asleep: fall—, einschlafen, schlief ein, ist eingeschlafen, schläft ein

assert, behaupten

associated with, verbunden mit

assume, annehmen, nahm an, angenommen, nimmt an

astonished, erstaunt; **—at,** erstaunt über (*w. acc.*)

at, an, auf, in, bei zu (*w. dat.*); **—eight o'clock,** um acht Uhr; **—the top of,** oben auf; **—his house,** bei ihm; **—home,** zu Hause; **—once,** gleich, sogleich, sofort; **—the time when,** zur Zeit, als (da *or* wo); (*student*)**—the university,** auf der Universität; (*professor*) **—the university,** an der Universität; **—night,** in der Nacht, nachts

athlete (*male*), der Athlet, -en, -en; (*female*), die Athletin, -, -nen

atmosphere, die Atmosphäre, -, -en

atomic, atomisch; **—Age,** das atomische Zeitalter

attain, erreichen

attempt, versuchen

attend (*a school*), besuchen; (*a performance*), beiwohnen (*w. dat.*); (*a lecture*), einem Vortrag beiwohnen, eine Vorlesung hören (*or* besuchen)

attention, die Aufmerksamkeit, -, -en; **to pay—,** aufpassen, paßte auf, aufgepaßt; **I paid no—to it** (*didn't care*), ich kümmerte mich nicht darum

attentive, aufmerksam

August, der August, -(e)s, -e

aunt, die Tante, -, -n; **at my—'s,** bei meiner Tante

auto, das Auto, -s, -s

autumn, der Herbst, -es, -e

avail oneself of, sich bedienen (*w. gen.*); von etwas (*dat.*) Gebrauch machen

awake, wach: **to be—,** wach sein

awaken (*tr.*), aufwecken; (*intr.*) aufwachen, wachte auf, ist aufgewacht

aware of, bewußt (*adj. w. gen.*); **not that I am aware,** nicht daß ich wüßte

away, fort, weg

B

babysitter (*male*), der Kinderpfleger, -s, -; (*female*), die Kinderpflegerin, -, -nen; *also,* der Sitter, -s, -; die Sitterin, -, -nen

back (*adv.*), zurück

back, der Rücken, -s, -

bad, schlecht, böse, übel; schlimm; **—times,** schlechte Zeiten; **that is not a—idea,** das ist kein übler Einfall; **that is too—,** schade! **that is not a bad idea,** das ist (gar) nicht schlecht

bake, backen, buk, gebacken, bäckt

bakery, die Bäckerei, -, -en

ball, der Ball, -(e)s, ¨e

balloon, der Ballon, -s, -e *or* -s

ballpoint (*pen*), der Kugelschreiber, -s, -
bank (*of a river*), das Ufer, -s, -; (*for money*) die Bank, -, -en
barber, der Barbier, -s, -e
bark, bellen
bathe, baden
bathroom, das Badezimmer, -s, -
bathtub, die Badewanne, -, -n
Bavaria, (das) Bayern, -s
be (= *exist*), sein, war, ist gewesen, ist; (= *be situated*) liegen, lag, hat gelegen; Köln liegt am Rhein;—**it early or late**, sei es früh, sei es spät; **how are you?** wie geht es Ihnen?; **that is** (= *i.e.*) das heißt (*abbr.* d.h.); **there is** (**are**), es gibt (*w. acc.*); **he is right,** er hat recht
beach, der Strand, -(e)s, -e; **to go to the—,** an den Strand gehen
beard, der Bart, -(e)s, ¨e
beautiful, schön; **most—of all,** allerschönst-
because (*conj.*), weil, denn; **—of** (*prep.*), wegen (*w. gen.*)
become, werden, wurde, ist geworden, wird; **what will—of him?** was wird aus ihm werden?
bed, das Bett, -(e)s, -en; **to go to—,** zu Bett gehen; **in—,** im Bett
bedroom, das Schlafzimmer, -s, -
beer, das Bier, -(e)s, -e; **dark (light)—,** dunkles (helles) Bier
before, vor (*w. dat. or acc.*); **day—yesterday,** vorgestern; **year—last,** vorletztes Jahr; (*conj.*), ehe, bevor; (*adv.*), vorher, früher; **the day—,** den Tag vorher
begin, beginnen, begann, begonnen, beginnt; anfangen, fing an, angefangen, fängt an; **—at the beginning,** fangen Sie von vorn an!
beginning, der Anfang, -(e)s, ¨e
behave, sich betragen (*or* benehmen) (*str.*)
behind (*prep.*), hinter (*w. dat. or acc.*); (*adv.*), hinten
believe, glauben (*w. dat. of the pers. & acc. of the th.*); **—in,** glauben an (*w. acc.*); **he believes me (it),** er glaubt mir (es); **he believes in me (in it),** er glaubt an mich (daran); meinen (*to have an opinion*)
bell, die Glocke, -, -n; die Klingel, -, -n; **the—rings,** es klingelt
belong to, gehören (*w. dat. = ownership*); gehören zu (= *to be part or member of*)
beloved (*adj.*), geliebt; (*a person*), der Geliebte (*adj. used as noun*)
below, unter (*w. dat. or acc.*), unterhalb (*w. gen.*)
bench, die Bank, -, ¨e
beside, bei (*w. dat.*), neben (*w. dat. or acc.*): **I am—myself with joy,** ich bin außer mir vor Freude
best, best-; **—of all,** allerbest-; **I like it—,** es gefällt mir am besten; *or* ich habe es am liebsten; **the—I have,** das Beste, was ich habe

betray, verraten, verriet, verraten, verrät
better, besser (*comp. of* gut)
between, zwischen (*w. dat. or acc.*)
Bible, die Bibel, -, -n
bicycle, das Fahrrad, -(e)s, ¨er; das Rad, -(e)s, ¨er
big, groß
biological, biologisch
biology, die Biologie, -
bird, der Vogel, -s, ¨
birthday, der Geburtstag, -(e)s, -e; **for one's—,** zum Geburtstag
bite, beißen, biß, gebissen
black, schwarz
(black)board, die Tafel, -, -n
blame, die Schuld, -, -en; **he is to—for that,** er ist schuld daran
blind, blind; **—in,** blind auf (*w. dat.*)
blond, blond
blue, blau
board, das Brett, -(e)s, -er
boast of, prahlen mit (*w. dat.*); sich rühmen (*w. gen.*)
body, der Körper, -s, -; **celestial—,** der Himmelskörper
bold, kühn; frech (*impudent*)
book, das Buch, -(e)s, ¨er
bored: to be—, sich langweilen, langweilte, gelangweilt
born, geboren (*p.p of* gebären); **was— (of the dead),** wurde geboren; (*of the living*), ist geboren; **when were you—?** wann sind Sie geboren?
both, beide; **—brothers,** beide (*or* die belden) Brüder
bother about, sich kümmern um (*w. acc.*)
bottle, die Flasche, -, -n
box, der Kasten, -s, -; die Kiste, -, -n
boy, der Junge, -n, -n; der Knabe, -n, -n
brave, tapfer
bread, das Brot -(e)s, -e
break, brechen, brach, gebrochen, bricht; **—one's arm,** sich (*dat.*) den Arm brechen; **—to pieces,** zerbrechen
breakfast, das Frühstück, -(e)s, -e; **for—,** zum Frühstück; **after—,** nach dem Frühstück; **to eat—,** frühstücken, frühstückte, gefrühstückt
breath, der Atem, -s, -züge; **to take—,** Atem holen
breathe, atmen
breathless, atemlos
bridge, die Brücke, -, -n
bright, hell
bring, bringen, brachte, gebracht; **—along,** mitbringen
broad, breit
brochure, die Broschüre, -, -n
brook, der Bach, -(e)s, ¨e
brother, der Bruder, -s, ¨
brown, braun

brush, (sich) bürsten; **—one's teeth,** sich (*dat.*) die Zähne putzen

build, bauen

building, das Gebäude, -s, -

bundle, das (*or* der) Bündel, -s, -

burn, brennen, brannte, gebrannt: **—with** (*fig.*) brennen vor

business, das Geschäft, -(e)s, -e **to go into—,** ein Geschäft eröffnen (*or* gründen)

busy, beschäftigt

but, aber; sondern

butcher, der Fleischer, -s, -; der Metzger, -s, -

butter, die Butter, -

buy, kaufen

by, von (*pers. agent*), mit, bei (*all w. dat.*); durch (*means or instrument; w. acc.*); an, neben (*both w. dat. or acc.*); **—heart,** auswendig; **—steamer,** mit dem Dampfer; **—rail,** mit der Eisenbahn

C

cake, der Kuchen, -s, -; (*flat cake, torte, flan*) die Torte, -, -n

call, rufen, rief, gerufen; (= *to name*), nennen, nannte, genannt; (= *to be called*), heißen, hieß, geheißen; (= *to call names*) schimpfen (*wk.*); schelten, schalt, gescholten, schilt: **—on** (= *to visit*), besuchen;**—up** (*on the phone*), ánrufen; **—for** (= *to pick up*), ábholen

Canada, (das) Kanada, -s

canal, der Kanal, -s, ¨e

candle, die Kerze, -, -n

cane, der Stock, -(e)s, ¨e

cap, die Mütze, -, -n

capable (of), fähig (*w. gen.*)

capital, die Haupstadt, -, ¨e

capitalize, großschreiben

car, das Auto, -s, -s; der Wagen, -s, -; **streetcar,** die Straßenbahn, -, -en

care, die Sorge, -, -n; **for all I—,** meinetwegen; **to take—,** sich in acht nehmen; **to take—of,** sorgen für (*w. acc.*)

care (for) (= *to like*), mögen, gern haben

careful, sorgfältig; (= *cautious*) vorsichtig; **to be—,** sich in acht nehmen

carpenter, der Zimmermann, -(e)s, Zimmerleute

carry, tragen, trug, getragen, trägt; **to—away,** fórttragen

carry out, ausführen, führte aus, ausgeführt; durchführen, führte durch, durchgeführt

case (= *circumstance or grammatical*), der Fall, -(e)s, ¨e; **in—**(*sub. conj.*), falls; in **any—,** jedenfalls

cash, das Bargeld, -(e)s

cask, das Faß, Fasses, Fässer

castle, das Schloß, Schlosses, Schlösser; die Burg, -, -en

cat, die Katze, -, -n

catch, fangen, fing, gefangen, fängt; **—(a) cold,** sich erkälten; **—sight of,** erblicken

cathedral, der Dom, -(e)s, -e

cause, die Ursache, -, -n; der Grund, -(e)s, ¨e

celebrate, feiern

cellar, der Keller, -s, -

cemetary, der Friedhof, -s, ¨e

cent, der Cent, -(s), -(s); **fifty—s' worth of stamps,** für fünfzig Cent Briefmarken

century, das Jahrhundert, -(e)s, -e

certain(ly), gewiß

chain, die Kette, -, -n

chair, der Stuhl, -(e)s, ¨e

chalk, die Kreide, -

chancellor (*male*), der Kanzler, -s, -; (*female*), die Kanzlerin, -, -nen

change, die Abwechs(e)lung, -, -en; **for a—,** zur Abwechs(e)lung

change (= *to alter*), ändern; (*for better or worse*) (sich), verändern; (= *to exchange*) wechseln; **—money,** Geld wechseln; **—cars,** umsteigen (*w. sein*); **—clothes,** sich umziehen (*or* umkleiden); **—one's mind,** sich anders besinnen; **you have changed very much,** Sie haben sich sehr verändert; **I have changed my place of residence,** ich habe meine Wohnung gewechselt (*or* ich bin umgezogen) **change one's mind,** es sich wieder überlegen

Charlemagne, Karl der Große

charm, bezaubern

charming, reizend

cheap, billig

check (*for money*), der Scheck, -s, -e *or* -s

cheek, die Wange, -, -n

cheese, der Käse, -s, -

chess, das Schach, -(e)s; **a game of—,** eine Partie Schach

child, das Kind, -(e)s, -er

chimpanzee, der Schimpanse, -n, -n

choose, wählen

Christmas, (die) Weihnachten, -; **for** (*or* at)**—,** zu Weihnachten

church, die Kirche, -, -n

cigar, die Zigarre, -, -n

cigarette, die Zigarette, -, -n

circle, der Kreis, -es, -e

circumstance, der Umstand, -(e)s, ¨e

circus, der Zirkus, -, -se

citizen, der Bürger, -s, -

city, die Stadt, -, ⸚e; **the—of Hamburg,** die Stadt Hamburg

city hall, das Rathaus, -es, / häuser

city plan, der Stadtplan, -s, ⸚e

claim (= *assert*), behaupten; wollen, wollte, gewollt, will; **he claims to have done it,** er will es getan haben

clap, klatschen; **—one's hands,** in die Hände klatschen

class, die Klasse, -, -n; **to travel second—,** zweiter Klasse (*gen.*) fahren

classroom, das Klassenzimmer, -s, -

clean (*adj.*) rein

clean, reinigen; **—up,** aúfräumen

clear(ly) (= *bright*), hell; klar; (= *distinct*) deutlich

cleft, die Spalte, -, -n

clever, klug

cliff, der Felsen, -s, -

climb (up), klettern (*w.* sein) auf (*w. acc.*)

clinic, die Klinik, -, -en

clock, die (Wand)uhr, -, -en

close, zumachen, machte zu, zugemacht; schließen, schloß, geschlossen

cloth, das Tuch, -(e)s, ⸚er

clothes, Kleider (*pl. of* das Kleid)

club, der Verein, -s, -e; der Klub, -s, -s

coal, die Kohle, -, -n; **rich in—,** reich an Kohlen

coast, die Küste, -, -n

coat, der Rock, -(e)s, ⸚e

coat of ice, die Eisdecke, -, -n

coffee, der Kaffee, -s, -sorten

coffee cup, die Kaffeetasse, -, -n

cold (*adj.*), kalt; **I am—,** mir ist kalt

cold (*weather*), die Kälte, -; (*respiratory*) die Erkältung, -, -en; **to catch (a)—,** sich erkälten; **I caught a bad—,** ich habe mich stark erkältet

collar, der Kragen, -s, -

colleague (*male*), der Kollege, -n, -n, (*female*), die Kollegin, -, -nen

collect, sammeln

Cologne, (das) Köln, -s

color, die Farbe, -n, -n

comb, der Kamm, -(e)s, ⸚e

comb, kämmen

come, kommen, kam, ist gekommen; **—back,** zurückkommen; **—up,** heraúfkommen; **—in** (= *enter*), hereinkommen; **—in** (*of money*), einkommen; **—late,** zu spät kommen; **he came running,** er kam gelaufen; **come along,** kommen Sie mit!

comfortable, bequem

command, befehlen, befahl, befohlen, befiehlt (*w. dat.*)

company (= *society*), die Gesellschaft, -; -en; (= *visitors*) der Besuch, -(e)s, -e, **we had—,** wir hatten Besuch (*or* Gäste)

comparatively, verhältnismäßig

compare, vergleichen, verglich, verglichen

compel, zwingen, zwang, gezwungen

complain about, klagen über (*w. acc.*)

complete (*adj.*), ganz, vollständig, fertig, vollendet

complete, vollenden

composition (= *essay*), der Aufsatz, -es, ⸚e

conductor (*on a train or bus, male*), der Schaffner, -s, -; (*female*), die Schaffnerin, -, -nen

confirm, bestätigen

confused, verwirrt

congratulate, gratulieren (*w. dat.*); **I—you on your great success,** ich gratuliere Ihnen zu Ihrem großen Erfolg

conquer (*intr.*), siegen; (*tr.*) besiegen

consequence, die Folge, -, -n; **as a—,** zur Folge

consequently, infolgedessen

consist of, bestehen aus (*w. dat.*)

constant, unaufhörlich

construct, konstruieren, bauen

contain, enthalten, enthielt, enthalten, enthält

continually, fortwährend

continue, fortfahren, fuhr fort, hat fortgefahren, fährt fort; **—reading,** lesen Sie weiter!: **he continued reading,** er hat fortgefahren zu lesen

contract, der Vertrag, -s, ⸚e

contradict, widerspréchen (*w. dat.*)

contrary to, gegen (*w. acc.*)

control: in—of, mächtig (*w. gen.*)

conversation, das Gespräch, -(e)s, -e

converse, sich unterhálten

convince, überzeugen

cook, kochen

cookie, der *or* das Keks, - *or* -es, -e

cool, kühl

cooperate, mithelfen, half mit, mitgeholfen, hilft mit; **he—with the housework,** er hilft im Haushalt mit

copy, abschreiben, schrieb ab, abgeschrieben

corner, die Ecke, -, -n

correct (*adj.*), richtig

correct, verbessern, korrigieren

cosmic, kosmisch

cost, kosten; **it—me a dollar,** es kostete mich (*or* mir) einen Dollar

could (= *was able*), konnte (*refers to a fact*); (= *would be able*) könnte (*contrary to fact*); **he—have done it,** er hätte es tun können

countless, zahllos

country, das Land, -(e)s, ⸚er; **in the—,** auf dem Lande; **to the—,** aufs Land

couple, das Paar, -(e)s, -e

course (*of a meal*), der Gang, -(e)s, ⸚e; (*of time*) der Lauf, -(e)s, ⸚e; **in the—of time,** im Laufe der Zeit

court, der Hof, -(e)s, ⸚e; (*of justice*) das Gericht, -(e)s, -e; **at—,** am Hofe

cousin (*male*), der Vetter, -s, -n; (*female*), die Kusine, -, -n

cover, bedecken; belegen

covered, bedeckt

cow, die Kuh, -, ⸚e

cowardly, feige

crazy, verrückt

crooked, krumm

cross-country run, die Langstrecke, -, -n; **to run cross-country, distance races,** Langstrecke laufen, rennen

crowd, die Menge, -, -n

cruel, grausam; **—to,** grausam gegen (*w. acc.*)

cup, die Tasse, -, -n

curious, neugierig

cushion, das Kissen, -s, -

custom, die Sitte, -, -n

customer (*male*), der Kunde, -n, -n; (*female*), die Kundin, -, -nen

customs, der Zoll, -(e)s, ⸚e

cut, schneiden, schnitt, geschnitten; **to—class,** schwänzen

Czechoslovakia, die Tschechoslowakei

D

dance, der Tanz, -es, ⸚e

dance, tanzen

dangerous, gefährlich

Danube, die Donau, -

dare, wagen

dark, dunkel

darkness, die Finsternis, -, -se

date, das Datum, -s, Daten; **what is today's—?** der wievielte ist (*or* den wievielten haben wir) heute?

daughter, die Tochter, -, ⸚

day, der Tag, -(e)s, -e; **—before yesterday,** vorgestern; **—after tomorrow,** übermorgen; **one—**(*indef. time*), eines Tages; **all—**(*duration of time*), den ganzen Tag; **—after—,** Tag für Tag; **every other—,** einen Tag um den anderen; **the—before,** den Tag vorher

daytime: in the—, bei Tag(e)

dead, tot

deaf, taub

deal: a great—(of), viel

dear (*beloved*), lieb, teuer; (*expensive*) teuer

death, der Tod, -(e)s, -esfälle

debt, die Schuld, -, -en

December, der Dezember, -(s), -

decide, sich entschließen; **I have decided upon a trip,** ich habe mich zur Reise entschlossen; **I have decided to work hard,** ich habe mich entschlossen, schwer zu arbeiten

decorate, schmücken

deed, die Tat, -, -en

deep, tief; **a foot—,** einen Fuß tief

defend, verteidigen

delegate, der Abgeordnete (*adj. used as noun*)

deliver (*a speech*), halten, hielt, gehalten, hält; **he delivered a long speech,** er hat eine lange Rede gehalten

dentist, der Zahnarzt, -es, ⸚e

deny, leugnen; (= *refuse*) verweigern

depend, darauf ankommen; **that depends,** es kommt darauf an; **it all depends on the weather,** alles hängt vom Wetter ab

dependent, abhängig

describe, beschreiben, beschrieb, beschrieben

desk, das Pult, -(e)s, -e

dessert, der Nachtisch, -es, -e; **for—,** zum Nachtisch

destroy, zerstören

detect, spüren, entdecken

devil, der Teufel, -s, -

dictatorship, die Diktatur, -, -en

dictionary, das Wörterbuch, -(e)s, ⸚er

die, sterben, starb, ist gestorben, stirbt; **—of,** sterben an (*w. dat.*)

difference, der Unterschied, -(e)s, -e; **that makes no—,** das macht nichts aus

different, ander-; verschieden

difficult, schwer, schwierig

difficulty, die Schwierigkeit, -, -en; (*obstacle*), das Hindernis, -ses, -se

diligent(ly), fleißig

dining room, das Eßzimmer, -s, -

dinner, das Mittagessen, -s, -; **is—ready?** ist das Mittagessen fertig? **after—,** nach dem Mittagessen

direct (*vb.*), richten; **—toward** (*aim at*), richten auf (*w. acc.*)

direction, die Richtung, -, -en: **in all—s,** nach allen Richtungen

dirty, schmutzig

disappear, verschwinden, verschwand, ist verschwunden

disappointed, enttäuscht

discharge, entlassen, entließ, entlassen, entläßt

discount store, der Verbrauchermarkt, -(e)s, ⸚e

discover, entdecken

discoverer, der Entdecker, -s, -; der Erfinder, -s, - (*inventor*)

discovery, die Entdeckung, -, -en; die Erfindung, -, -en (*invention*)

discuss, besprechen (*str.*)

dish, die Schüssel, -, -n; **to wash dishes,** Geschirr (*neut. sing.*) ábwaschen

dishonest, unehrlich

dissatisfied, unzufrieden

distance, die Ferne, -, -n; die Entfernung, -, -en; **from a—,** aus der Ferne; **at a—,** in der Ferne

disturb, stören

divide, teilen

dizzy, schwind(e) lig; **she is—,** ihr ist schwind(e)lig (*or* ihr schwindelt)

do, tun, tat, getan, tut; machen; **what are we to—?** was sollen wir tun? **he does me a favor,** er tut mir einen Gefallen; **he does his lessons,** er macht seine Aufgaben

doctor, der Arzt, -es, ¨e; der Doktor, -s, -en; (*female*) die Ärztin, -, -nen; (*rarely used*) die Doktorin

dog, der Hund -(e)s, -e

doll, die Puppe, -, -n

dollar, der Dollar, -s, -(s); **a thousand—s,** tausend Dollar; **a—'s worth of sugar,** für einen Dollar Zucker

domesticated, zahm

donate, verleihen, verlieh, verliehen, verleiht

door, die Tür, -, -en; **front—,** Haustür

doubt, der Zweifel, -s, -

doubt, bezweifeln (*tr.*)

doubtless, wohl (*often w. fut.*); ohne Zweifel

down, nieder; hinab, hinunter; **to lie—,** sich níederlegen; **to settle—,** sich níederlassen; **to go—,** hinúntergehen, hinábsteigen (*substitute prefix* her- *if denoting motion toward the observer*)

downstairs, (nach) unten; **to go—,** nach unten gehen (*or* die Treppe hinutergehen)

dozen, das Dutzend, -s, -e; **half a—,** ein halbes Dutzend

dragon, der Drache, -n, -n

drama, das Drama, -s, Dramen

draught, der Zug, -(e)s, ¨e

draw (*pull*), ziehen, zog, gezogen; (*sketch*) zeichnen

dream, der Traum, -(e)s, ¨e

dream, träumen

dress, das Kleid, -(e)s, -er

dress (oneself), sich ánziehen (*or* ánkleiden)

drink, trinken, trank, getrunken (*of people*); saufen, soff, gesoffen, säuft (*of animals and inebriates*)

drive, treiben, trieb, getrieben; (*to go driving*), fahren, fuhr, ist gefahren, fährt; **to—a car,** (ein) Auto fahren (*tr.*)

drop, der Tropfen, -s, -

drop, fallen lassen: **he dropped his handkerchief,** er hat das Taschentuch fallen lassen

drop in. vorbeikommen, kam vorbei. ist vorbeigekommen, kommt vorbei, an einer Person

drown (*tr.*) ertränken (*wk.*)

drowned: to be—, ertrinken, ertrank, ist ertrunken

drugstore, die Apotheke, -, -n

dry (*adj.*), trocken

dry, trocknen: **—dishes,** Geschirr (*neut. sing.*) ábtrocknen

duchess, die Herzogin, -, -nen

duke, der Herzog, -(e)s, -e (*or* ¨e)

during, während (*w. gen.*)

dusty, staubig

dutiful, pflichtmäßig

duty, die Pflicht, -, -en

dwarf, der Zwerg, -(e)s, -e

E

each, jeder, **—other,** einander (*or* sich)

ear, das Ohr, -(e)s, -en

early, früh; **—in the morning,** frühmorgens

earn, verdienen

earth, die Erde, -, -n

easily, leicht

east, der Osten, -s; **—of,** östlich von (*w. dat.*)

Easter, (das) Ostern, -, - (*usually used without article; also used in plural with singular verb*)

easy, leicht

eat, essen, aß, gegessen, ißt (*of people*); fressen, fraß, gefressen, frißt (*of animals*); **what does he—for breakfast?** was ißt er zum Frühstück?

eclipse (*lunar*), die Mondfinsternis, -, -se; (*solar*), die Sonnenfinsternis, -, -se

economics, die Volkswirtschaft, -

educated, gebildet

egg, das Ei, -(e)s, -er

eight, acht; die Acht

eighteen, achtzehn

eighty, achtzig

either, (= *both*) beide; (= *each*) jeder, **on—side,** auf jeder Seite (*or* beiden Seiten); **I did not see—of them,** ich habe keinen (keine, *or* keines) von ihnen gesehen

either. . .or (*conj.*), entweder. . .oder

elderly, älter-

eldest, ältest-

elect, wählen

election, die Wahl, -, -en

electric, elektrisch

elevated railroad, die Hochbahn, -, -en

eleven, elf

else (= *otherwise*), sonst; ander-; **no one**—, niemand anders (*or* sonst niemand); **someone** (*or* **anyone**)—, jemand anders (*or* sonst jemand)

embarrassed, verlegen

emperor, der Kaiser, -s, -

empire, das Reich, -(e)s, -e

empty, leer

end, das Ende, -s, -n; **at the**—, am Ende

end, enden

enemy, der Feind, -(e)s, -e

engaged, verlobt: **to become**—**to,** sich verloben mit

England, (das) England, -s

English, englisch; **he is learning**—, er lernt Englisch; **in**—, auf englisch

English-German (*adj.*), englisch-deutsch; **an**—**dictionary,** ein englisch-deutsches Wörterbuch

enjoy, genießen, genoß, genossen; froh werden (*w. gen.*)

enough, genug

enter, eintreten (gehen *or* kommen) in (*w. acc.*) (*often w. the separable prefixes* herein *and* hinein)

entire, ganz

entrance, der Eingang, -(e)s, ̈-e

especially, besonders

Europe, (das) Europa, -s

even (*adj.*), eben, gerade; (*adv.*), sogar, selbst; —**a physician,** selbst ein Arzt; —**if he were here,** wenn er auch hier wäre

evening, der Abend, -s, -e; **this**—, heute abend; **tomorrow**—, morgen abend; **yesterday**—, gestern abend; **one**— (*indef. time*), eines Abends; **all**—(*duration of time*), den ganzen Abend; **in the**—, am Abend (abends *or* des Abends); **good**—, guten Abend!

ever (= *always*), immer; (= *at any time*), je(mals)

every, jeder, jede, jedes

everybody, jedermann, -s

everything, alles, —**he had,** alles, was er hatte; —**possible,** alles mögliche; —**else,** alles andere; —**good,** alles Gute

everywhere, überall

evil, übel

exact(ly), genau

examination, die Prüfung, -, -en; das Examen, -s, Examina; **to take an**—, eine Prüfung machen; **to pass an**—, eine Prüfung bestehen; **to fail an**—, bei einer Prüfung durchfallen (*w. sein*)

example, das Beispiel, -(e)s, -e; **for**—, zum Beispiel (*abbr.* z.B.)

excited, aufgeregt

exercise, die Aufgabe, -, -n; die Übung, -, -en

exercise, üben (*often refl.*)

exhausting, erschöpfend, anstrengend

expect, erwarten

expensive, teuer, kostspielig

experience, das Erlebnis, -ses, -se; die Erfahrung, -, -en

experience, erleben; erfahren

experiment, der Versuch, -s, -e

explain, erklären

expose, aussetzen, setzte aus, ausgestzt

express, ausdrücken

expression, der Ausdruck, -(e)s, ̈-e

express train, der Schnellzug, -(e)s, ̈-e

extremely, höchst; äußerst

eye, das Auge, -s, -n

F

fabulous, fabelhaft

face, das Gesicht, -(e)s, -er

fact, die Tatsache, -, -n; **in**—, in der Tat

fail (*an examination*), (bei einer Prüfung) durchfallen

fair, die Messe, -, -n

fairy tale, das Märchen, -s, -

faithful, treu (*w. dat.*)

fall (*season*), der Herbst, -es, -e

fall, fallen fiel, ist gefallen, fällt; **to**—**asleep,** einschlafen, schlief ein, ist eingeschlafen, schläft ein; **to**—**in love with,** sich verlieben in (*w. acc.*)

family, die Familie, -, -n

famous, berühmt; —**for,** berühmt durch (*w. acc.*) or wegen (*w. gen.*)

far, weit; —**and wide,** weit und breit; **as**—**as I know,** soviel ich weiß (*or* meines Wissens); **as**—**as** (*prep.*), bis

fare, der Fahrpreis, -es, -e

farewell, leben Sie wohl!

farmer, der Bauer, -s (*or* -n), -n; (*female*) die Bäuerin, -, -nen

fast, schnell; **my watch is**—, meine Uhr geht vor

fast food restaurant, der Schnellimbiß, -(ss)es, -(ss)e

father, der Vater, -s, ̈-

fault, die Schuld, -, -en; **it is not his**—, er kann nichts dafür

favor, der Gefallen, -s, -; **he does me a**—, er tut mir einen Gefallen

favorable, günstig

fear, die Furcht, -

fear, fürchten; sich fürchten vor (*w. dat.*); fürchten, daß

February, (der) Februar, -(s), -e

Federal Republic of Germany (FRG), die Bundesrepublik Deutschland (BRD)

feed, füttern

feel, fühlen; sich fühlen (*or* befinden); **how do you**— (= *how are you*)? wie geht es Ihnen?

fell (= *cut down*), fällen
fellow, der Kerl, -(e)s, -e
fense, der Zaun, -(e)s, -̈e
few, wenige; **a—,** ein paar (*indecl.*)
field, das Feld, -(e)s, -er; **in the—,** auf dem Feld
fifteen, fünfzehn
fifty, fünfzig
fight, der Kampf, -(e)s, -̈e
fight, kämpfen; (= *come to blows*) sich prügeln
fill, füllen
finally, endlich, schließlich, zuletzt
find, finden, fand, gefunden
fine, fein; **very—**(*sarcastic*), sehr schön
finger, der Finger, -s, -
finish, vollenden
fire, das Feuer, -s, -
firm (*adj.*), fest
firm, die Firma, -, Firmen
first, erst-; **in the—place,** erstens: **at—,** zuerst
fish, der Fisch, -es, -e
fishing: to go—, fischen gehen; **I went—,** ich bin fischen gegangen
fist, die Faust, -, -̈e
five, fünf
flag, die Fahne, -, -n
flame, die Flamme, -, -n
flat, flach
flat (*simple apartment*), die Bude, -, -n
flatter, schmeicheln (*w. dat.*); **you—yourself,** du schmeichelst dir
flee, fliehen, floh, ist geflohen
flight (*by plane*), der Flug, -es, -̈e; (*escape*), die Flucht, -, -en
floor, der Boden, -s, -̈ (*or* -); **ground—,** das Erdgeschoß; **first—,** der erste Stock; **top—,** der oberste Stock
flour, das Mehl, -(e)s, -e (*or* -arten)
flow, fließen, floß, ist geflossen
flower, die Blume, -, -n
fluent(ly), fließend
fly, fliegen, flog, ist geflogen; (*of time*) vergehen; **how time flies!** wie schnell die Zeit vergeht!
flyer, der Flieger, -s, -
folksong, das Volkslied, -(e)s, -er
follow, folgen, folgte, ist gefolgt (*w. dat.*)
fool, der Narr, -en, -en
foolish, närrisch
foot, der Fuß, -es, -̈e; **on—,** zu Fuß
for, für (*w. acc.*); **—what reason?** aus welchem Grunde?; **—example,** zum Beispiel; **—heaven's sake!** um Himmels willen!**—all I care,** meinetwegen; **—two years,** zwei Jahre lang; **he is going to the country—a month,** er geht auf einen Monat aufs Land; **I have been**

here—a month, ich bin seit einem Monat hier; **to ask—,** bitten um (*w. acc.*); **to long—,** sich sehnen nach
for (*causal conj.*), denn
force, die Gewalt, -, -en
foreign, fremd; **—language,** die Fremdsprache, -, -n
forenoon, der Vormittag, -(e)s, -e (*see* afternoon *phrases*)
forest, der Wald, -(e)s, -̈er,
forget, vergessen, vergaß, vergessen, vergißt
fork, die Gabel, -, -n
form, die Form, -, -en; **—of government,** die Regierungsform
former, jener (*in contrast with dieser*); vorher erwähnt (previously mentioned)
formerly, früher
fortunately, glücklicherweise
fortune (*good luck*), das Glück, -(e)s; (*wealth*), das Vermögen, -s, -
fountain, der Brunnen, -s, -
fountain pen, die Füllfeder, -, -n
four, vier
fourfold, vierfach
fourteenth, vierzehnt-
fourth (*num. adj.*), viert-; (*noun*), das Viertel, -s, -
fox, der Fuchs, -es, Füchse
France, (das) Frankreich, -s
frantic, toll; **—with pain,** toll vor Schmerz
free, frei
freedom, die Freiheit, -, en
freeze, frieren, fror, gefroren; **it froze hard,** es hat stark gefroren
French, französisch; **do you speak—?** sprechen Sie Französisch?
Frenchman, der Franzose, -n, -n
Frenchwoman, die Französin, -, -nen
fresh, frisch
Friday, der Freitag, -(e)s, -e
friend (*male*), der Freund, -(e)s, -e: (*female*) die Freundin, -, -nen; **a—of mine,** ein Freund von mir
friendly, freundlich; **he is—towards me,** er ist zu mir freundlich
friendship, die Freundschaft, -, -en
frighten (*tr.*) erschrecken (*wk.*)
frightened: to be—(*intr.*), erschrecken, erschrak, ist erschrocken, erschrickt
frightful, furchtbar, fürchterlich
from, von, aus (*both w. dat.*)
front: in—of, vor (*w. dat. or acc.*)
fruit, die Frucht, -, -̈e; das Obst. -es
full, voll
fun, der Spaß, -es, -̈e
funny, komisch

fur, der Pelz, -es, -e
furious, wütend
further, weiter
future (*adj.*), (zu)künftig
future, die Zukunft, -; **plans for the—,** die Zukunftspläne

G

game, das Spiel, -(e)s, -e; **football—,** das Fußballspiel; **to play a—of chess,** eine Partie Schach spielen
garden, der Garten, -s, ¨
gas, das Gas, -es, -e
gay, fröhlich, lustig, heiter
generally, gewöhnlich, in der Regel
gentleman, der Herr, -n, -en
German, deutsch; **in—,** auf deutsch; **are you studying—?** lernen Sie Deutsch? (*native of Germany*), der Deutsche, -n, -n (*w. adj. decl.*); ein Deutscher
German Democratic Republic (GDR), die Deutsche Demokratische Republik (DDR)
Germany, (das) Deutschland, -s
get (= *to receive*), erhalten, erhielt, erhalten, erhält; bekommen, bekam, bekommen; **—in,** einsteigen, stieg ein, ist eingestiegen; **—to be** (= *become*), werden, wurde, ist geworden, wird; **—up,** aufstehen, stand auf, ist aufgestanden; **—used to,** sich gewöhnen an (*w. acc.*)
get to know, kénnenlernen
giant, der Riese, -n, -n
giant, gigantic, riesig
gift, das Geschenk, -(e)s, -e
girl, das Mädchen, -s, -
give, geben, gab, gegeben, gibt; **it gives me pleasure,** es macht mir Freude; (*as a gift*), schenken
glad, froh; **I am—of it;** ich freue mich darüber (*or* es freut mich)
glass, das Glas, -es, ¨er; **a—of beer,** ein Glas Bier
glasses (= *spectacles*), die Brille, -, -n
glee club, der Gesangverein, -(e)s, -e
glove, der Handschuh, -(e)s, -e; **a pair of—s,** ein Paar Handschuhe
glove compartment (*in a car*), der Handschuhkasten, -s, -
go, gehen, ging, ist gegangen: (= *to travel*) fahren, fuhr, ist gefahren, fährt; reisen, reiste, ist gereist; **—home,** nach Hause gehen; **—to bed,** zu Bett gehen; **—walking,** spazierengehen (*or* einen Spaziergang machen); **—to school,** in die (*or* zur) Schule gehen; **—to the theater (to the opera),** ins Theater (in die Oper) gehen; **—away,** fortgehen; **—along** mitgehen;

—out (hin)aúsgehen; **—down,** hinúntergehen; **—to sleep,** einschlafen, schlief ein, ist eingeschlafen, schläft ein; **—out of the door,** zur Tür hinausgehen; **he goes second class,** er fährt zweiter Klasse; **the fire is going out,** das Feuer geht aus
God, der Gott, -es, ¨er; (*female*) die Göttin, -, -nen
gold, das Gold, -(e)s
golden, golden
good, gut; **to have a—time,** sich amüsieren
goodbye, auf Wiedersehen!
goods, die Waren (*pl. of* die Ware)
gorgeous, prächtig
gossip, schwätzen *or* schwatzen
govern, regieren
grade (*school mark*), die Zensur, -, -en; die Note, -, -n
gradually, allmählich, nach und nach
grammar, die Grammatik, -, -en
granddaughter, die Enkelin, -, -nen
grandfather, der Großvater, -s, ¨
grandmother, die Großmutter, -, ¨
grandparents, die Großeltern, -, (*pl.*)
grandson, der Enkel, -s, -
grape, die Traube, -, -n
grasp, fassen
grass, das Gras, -es, ¨er
grateful, dankbar (*w. dat.*)
grave, das Grab -(e)s, ¨er
gray, grau
great, groß
green, grün
greet, grüßen *or* begrüßen
grind, mahlen
groan, stöhnen
ground, der Boden, -s, ¨ (*or* -); der Grund, -(e)s, ¨e
group, die Gruppe, -, -n
grow, wachsen, wuchs, ist gewachsen, wächst
guard, bewachen
guess (= *guess right, solve*), erraten, erriet, erraten, errät; **to—at,** raten, riet, geraten, rät
guest, der Gast, -es, ¨e
guilty, schuldig
gymnasium, (*physical education*) die Turnhalle, -, -n; (*German high school*) das Gymnasium, -s, Gymnasien
gymnastic, gymnastisch

H

hail, hageln
hair, das Haar, -(e)s, -e; **I had my—cut,** ich habe mir das Haar schneiden lassen; **my—stood on end,** mir standen die Haare zu Berge

half (*adj.*), halb; **one and a—,** anderthalb; **at—past nine,** um halb zehn; **—a pound,** ein halbes Pfund

half, die Hälfte, -, -n

hall, der Saal, -(e)s, Säle

halt, halten, hielt, gehalten, hält; anhalten

hammer, der Hammer, -s, ̈

hand, die Hand, -, ̈e; **on the other—,** dagegen

handful, die Handvoll, -, -

handkerchief, das Taschentuch, -(e)s, ̈er

happen, geschehen, geschah, ist geschehen, geschieht; vorkommen, kam vor, ist vorgekommen; passieren (*w. sein*): **he happened to be at home,** er war zufällig *or* (zufälligerweise war er) zu Hause

happiness, das Glück, -(e)s

happy, glücklich, fröhlich; **I am—about it.** ich freue mich darüber (*or* es freut mich)

harbor, der Hafen, -s, ̈

hard, hart; schwer: **to study (work)—,** fleißig (tüchtig *or* schwer) studieren (arbeiten): **to rain—,** stark regnen

hardly, kaum

harm, schaden (*w. dat.*)

harmful, schädlich (*w. dat.*)

harvest, die Ernte, -, -n

hat, der Hut, -(e)s, ̈e

hate, hassen

hatred, der Haß, Hasses

have, haben, hatte, gehabt, hat; **to—a good time,** sich amüsieren; **to—something done,** etwas tun lassen: **to—to,** müssen, mußte, gemußt, muß: **I have to go,** ich muß gehen; **you don't have** (= **need) to do that,** das brauchen Sie nicht zu tun; **I had a new suit made,** ich habe mir einen neuen Anzug machen lassen

he, er

head, der Kopf, -(e)s, ̈e; das Haupt, -(e)s, ̈er

headache, das Kopfweh, -(e)s; **I have a—,** ich habe Kopfweh

health, die Gesundheit, -, -en

healthy, gesund

heap, der Haufe(n), -ns, -n

hear, hören: **I heard him sing,** ich habe ihn singen hören

heart, das Herz, -ens, -en; **by—,** auswendig

hearty, herzlich

heat, die Hitze, -, -n

heaven, der Himmel, -s, -; **for—'s sake,** um Himmels (*or* Gottes) willen!

heavy, schwer

height, die Höhe, -, -n

help, helfen, half, geholfen, hilft (*w. dat.*); **I couldn't— it,** ich konnte nichts dafür; **I couldn't—telling him**

the truth, ich konnte nicht umhin, ihm die Wahrheit zu sagen; **to—out,** aushelfen

help, die Hilfe, -, -n

her (*pers. pron.*), ihr (*dat.*); sie (*acc.*); (*poss.*), ihr, ihre, ihr

here, hier: **spring is—,** der Frühling ist gekommen; **come—!** kommen Sie her!

hero, der Held, -en, -en; (*female*) die Heldin, -, -nen

hers (*poss. pron.*), ihrer, ihre, ihres; der (die *or* das) ihre (*or* ihrige)

herself (*refl. pron.*), sich; (*intens.*) selbst; **she—,** sie selbst (*or* selber)

hesitate, zögern

high, hoch; **a foot—,** einen Fuß hoch

hike (*verb*), wandern; (*noun*) die Wanderung, -, -en

hill, der Hügel, -s, -

him (*pers. pron.*), ihm (*dat.*); ihn (*acc.*)

himself (*refl. pron.*), sich; (*intens.*) selbst: **he—,** er selbst (*or* selber)

hippopotamus, das Flußpferd, -(e)s, -e

his (*poss.*), sein, seine, sein: (*poss. pron.*), seiner, seine, seines: der (die *or* das) seine (*or* seinige)

historic, historisch

history, die Geschichte, -, -n

hit, treffen, traf, getroffen, trifft; schlagen, schlug, geschlagen, schlägt

hold, halten, hielt, gehalten, hält; fassen; **—together,** zusammenhalten

holidays, die Ferien (*pl.*)

holy, heilig

home, das Heim, -(e)s, -e; (= *dwelling*), das Haus, -es, Häuser; (= *native place*) die Heimat, -, -en; **at—,** zu Hause (*or* daheim); **make yourself at—,** machen Sie es sich (*dat.*) bequem!

homeland, die Heimat, -, -en

homeward, heim(wärts), nach Hause

honest, ehrlich

honesty, die Ehrlichkeit, -

honor, die Ehre, -, -n

hope, hoffen: **—for,** hoffen auf (*w. acc.*)

hope, die Hoffnung, -, -en

horn, das Horn, -(e)s, ̈er

horse, das Pferd, -(e)s, -e

horseback: on—, zu Pferde

hostile, feindlich (gesinnt) (*w. dat.*)

hot, heiß

hotel, das Gasthaus, -es, / häuser; das Hotel, -s, -s

hotelkeeper, der Wirt, -(e)s, -e; (*female*) die Wirtin, -, -nen

hour, die Stunde, -, -n; **half an—,** eine halbe Stunde: **an—and a half,** anderthalb Stunden

house, das Haus, -es, Häuser; **at his—,** bei ihm; **at whose—?** bei wem?

how, wie; **—much?** wieviel?; **—many?** wie viele? — **long?** wie lange?; **—are you?** wie geht es Ihnen?; **—do you know that?** woher wissen Sie das?; **—much does it cost?** was kostet es?

however, aber; doch

huge, ungeheuer; riesig (*gigantic*)

humor (= *mood*), die Laune, -, -n; **he is in a good—,** er ist guter Laune (*gen.*)

hundred, (*num. adj.*): **a—,** hundert (*no art.*)

hundred, das Hundert, -(e)s, -e

hungry, hungrig; **I am—,** ich bin hungrig (*or* ich habe Hunger)

hunt, (*noun*), die Jagd, -, -en

hunt, jagen, auf die Jagd gehen

hunter, der Jäger, -s, -

hurry, eilen (*w.* sein); sich beeilen

hurt, schaden (*w. dat.*); **—oneself,** sich (*dat.*) weh tun [*or* sich (*acc.*) verletzen]; **that will—your health,** das wird Ihrer Gesundheit schaden; **it hurts me,** es tut mir weh

husband, der Gatte, -n, -n; der Mann, -(e)s, ̈-er

hydrogen, der Wasserstoff, -(e)s

I

I, ich: **nor—,** ich auch nicht

idea, der Einfall, -(e)s, ̈-e; die Idee, -n, -n; **that is not a bad—,** das ist kein übler Einfall

idiomatic, idiomatisch

if, wenn, falls; ob (*in indir. ques.*); **as—,** als ob

ill, krank

imagine, sich (*dat.*) denken (einbilden *or* vorstellen)

immediately, sogleich, gleich, sofort

immigrate, éinwandern

impatience, die Ungeduld, -: **he is burning with—** er brennt vor Ungeduld

impatient, ungeduldig

implore, bitten, bat, gebeten

importance, die Wichtigkeit, -; die Bedeutung, - (*significance*)

important, wichtig; bedeutend (*significant*)

impossible, unmöglich

impression, der Eindruck, -(e)s, ̈-e

impressive, eindrucksvoll

in (*prep.*), in, an, auf (*w. dat. or acc.*)**—1989,** im Jahre 1989; **—German,** auf deutsch

inch, der Zoll, -(e)s, -

incombustible, unverbrennbar

income, das Einkommen, -s, -

indeed, wirklich, in der Tat; **they would be stupid—,** sie wären schön dumm!

independent, unabhängig

indication, der Hinweis, -es, -e

individual, (*adj.*), einzeln

individual, das Individuum, -s, Individuen

industrious, fleißig

industry (= *diligence*), der Fleiß, -es

inevitable, unvermeidlich

information, die Nachricht, -, -en; die Auskunft, -, ̈-e

inhabit, bewohnen

inhabitant, der Einwohner, -s, -; (*female*) die Einwohnerin, -, -nen

inherit, erben

injustice, das Unrecht, -(e)s

ink, die Tinte, -, -n

inn, das Gasthaus, -es, / häuser

in order to (*conj.*), damit; (*prep.*), um . . . zu; **—learn,** um zu lernen

inquire about, sich erkundigen nach

insist (up)on, bestehen auf (*usually w. dat.*)

in spite of, trotz (*w. gen.*)

instance, das Beispiel, -(e)s, -e; **for—,** zum Beispiel (*abbr.* z.B.)

instead of, (an)statt (*w. gen.*); **—working,** anstatt zu arbeiten

instruction, die Anweisung, -, -en

intend, beabsichtigen; vórhaben: wollen, wollte, gewollt, will; **he intends to leave tomorrow,** er will morgen abfahren

intentionally, absichtlich

interest, das Interesse, -s, -n; **to bear—** (*on money*), Zinsen tragen; **to take an—in,** sich interessieren für (*w. acc.*)

interested: to be—in, sich interessieren für (*w. acc.*)

interesting, interessant

interrupt, unterbréchen

into, in (*w. acc.*)

intricate, umständlich

introduce, vorstellen; **he introduced her to me,** er hat sie mir vorgestellt

in vain, vergebens, umsonst

invention, die Erfindung, -, -en

investigate, untersuchen

investigation, die Forschung, -, -en; die Untersuchung, -, -en; die Prüfung, -, -en

invite, einladen, lud ein, eingeladen, ladet (*or* lädt) ein; **he invited me for supper,** er hat mich zum Abendessen eingeladen

iron, das Eisen, -s

island, die Insel, -, -n

it, es (*nom. & acc.*); ihm (*dat.*); **is—him?** ist er es?; **—is him,** er ist es; *da-forms:* damit, darauf, *etc.*

Italian, italienisch

Italy, (das) Italien, -s

its, sein (*refers to masc. & neut. nouns*); ihr (*refers to fem. nouns*)

J

January, der Januar, -(s), -e

jet (aircraft), das Düsenflugzeug, -(e)s, -e

job, der Job, -s, -s

joke, der Scherz, -es, -e; der Spaß, -es, ̈-e

joke, scherzen

joy, die Freude, -, -n; (*at another's misfortune*), die Schadenfreude

judge, der Richter, -s, -

July, der Juli, -(s), -s

jump, springen, sprang, ist gesprungen

June, der Juni -(s), -s

just, (*adj.*) gerecht; (*adv.*), gerade; eben; **—try it,** versuchen Sie es nur!; **she is— as industrious as he,** sie ist ebenso fleißig wie er

justice, die Gerechtigkeit, -, -en

K

keep, behalten behielt, behalten, behält; **he keeps his word,** er hält Wort

key, der Schlüssel, -s, -

kick, der Tritt, -es, -e

kill, töten; ermorden (*to murder*)

kilometer, das Kilometer, -s, -

kind (*adj.*), gütig

kind, die Art -, -en; **what—of,** was für; **four kinds of,** viererlei

king, der König, -s, -e

kitchen, die Küche, -, -n

knee, das Knie, -s, -

knife, das Messer, -s, -

knight, der Ritter, -s, -

knighthood, das Rittertum, -s

knock at, klopfen an (*w. acc.*)

know (= *to know a fact*), wissen, wußte, gewußt, weiß; (= *to be acquainted with*) kennen, kannte, gekannt; **how do you—that?** woher wissen Sie das? **do you— what you are about?** sind Sie Ihrer Sache gewiß? **as far as I—,** soviel ich weiß; **but she knows German,** sie kann Deutsch (*w. verbal complement deleted*)

knowledge, die Kenntnis, -, -se; (= *science*) die Wissenschaft, -, -en

known (= *well-known*), bekannt

L

labor, die Arbeit, -, -en

lady, die Dame, -, -n

lamp, die Lampe, -, -n

land, das land, -(e)s, ̈-er; **native—,** das Vaterland

land, landen, landete, ist gelandet; **—on,** landen auf (*w. dat.*)

landscape, die Landschaft, -, -en

language, die Sprache, -, -n; **foreign—,** die Fremdsprache

lap, der Schoß, -es, ̈-e

large, groß

last (*adj.*), letzt-; **next to—,** vorletzt

last, dauern

late, spät; **to come too—,** zu spät kommen

later on, späterhin

latter, der (die, das) letztere; dieser (*in contrast with* jener)

laugh, lachen; **to—at,** auslachen (*tr.*), lachen über (*w. acc.*)

laughter, das Lachen, -s; **there was much—,** es wurde viel gelacht

law, das Gesetz, -es, -e

lawn, der Rasen, -s, -

lawyer, der Advokat, -en, -en; (*more common*) der Rechtsanwalt, -s, ̈-e; (*female*) die Rechtsanwältin, -, -nen

lay, legen

laziness, die Faulheit, -

lazy, faul

lead (*noun*), das Blei -(e)s, -e

lead, führen, leiten

leader, der Führer, -s, -

leaf, das Blatt, -(e)s, ̈-er

leap, spring, sprang, ist gesprungen

leap, der Sprung, -(e)s, ̈-e

learn, lernen; erfahren (über) *w. acc.*

least: at—, wenigstens; **—of all,** am allerwenigsten

leather, das Leder, -s, -

leave, lassen, ließ, gelassen, läßt; (= *to bequeath*) hinterlassen; (= *to depart*) abfahren, fuhr ab, ist abgefahren, fährt ab; **to—behind** (= *to forsake*), verlassen, verließ, verlassen, verläßt

lecture, die Vorlesung, -, -en; der Vortrag, -(e)s, ̈-e

left (*adj.*), link-; (*adv.*), links; **on the—,** links; **to the—,** nach links

left (over), übrig; **I have only three bottles—,** ich habe nur drei Flaschen übrig

leg, das Bein, -(e)s, -e

legend, die Sage, -, -n; **according to—,** der Sage nach

lend, leihen, lieh, geliehen

less, weniger

lesson, die Lektion, -, -en; die Aufgabe, -, -n; **to take— s,** Stunden nehmen

let, lassen, ließ, gelassen, läßt

let know, wissen lassen; **let me know,** lassen Sie mich wissen

letter, der Brief, -(e)s, -e

letter carrier (*male*), der Postbote, -n, -n; (*female*), die Postbotin, -, -nen

library, die Bibliothek, -, -en; **to take books out of the—,** Bücher aus der Bibliothek entnehmen

lie (*falsehood*), die Lüge, -, -n

lie (*tell a lie*) lügen, log, gelogen; (*be situated*), liegen, lag, gelegen; **to—down,** sich (hin)legen

life, das Leben, -s, -; **to lead a simple—,** ein einfaches Leben führen

lift, heben, hob, gehoben; aufheben

light (= *bright*), hell; (= *of small weight*) leicht

light, das Licht, -(e)s, -er

light, anzünden

like (*adj.*), gleich (*w. dat.*); ähnlich (*w. dat.*)

like, gern haben; gefallen (*w. dat.*); mögen; **to be—** (= *to resemble*), gleichen (*w. dat.*), ähnlich sein (*w. dat.*); **I—it,** ich habe es gern (es gefällt mir *or* ich mag es); **I—to read,** ich lese gern; **I—best to read,** ich lese am liebsten; **he would—to go along,** er möchte mitgehen

line (*of print*), die Zeile, -, -n; (*geometric*) die Linie, -, -n; **a straight—,** eine gerade Linie

line (*streetcar or bus route*), die Linie, -, -n

lion, der Löwe, -n, -n

lip, die Lippe, -, -n

listen to, zuhören (*w. dat.*); (*tr.*) anhören

little (*as to size*), klein; (*as to quantity*) wenig; **a—,** ein wenig (*or* bißchen)

live, leben; (= *dwell*) wohnen, bewohnen

locker, das Schließfach, -(e)s, ̈-er

long (*adj.*), lang; **a foot—,** einen Fuß lang; (*adv.*) (= *for a long time*), lange; **how—** (*a time*)? wie lange?

longer, länger; **no—,** nicht mehr

long for, sich sehnen nach

look, aussehen, sah aus, ausgesehen, sieht aus; **to — at,** ánsehen; **—for,** suchen; **—forward with pleasure to,** sich freuen auf (*w. acc.*); **—out of the window,** zum Fenster hinaussehen; **he looks as if he were ill,** er sieht aus, als ob er krank wäre; **I am looking for it,** ich suche es; **she is looking out of the window,** sie sieht zum Fenster hinaus

look through, dúrchschauen

Lord, der Herr, -n

lose, verlieren, verlor, verloren; **—one's way,** sich verirren

loss, der Verlust, -es -e

lottery ticket, das Los, -es, -e

loud, laut

love, lieben: **to fall in—with,** sich verlieben in (*w. acc.*)

love, die Liebe, -, -n

luck: good—, das Glück, -(e)s

lunch (= *snack*), der Imbiß, Imbisses, Imbisse

M

magazine, die Zeitschrift, -, -en

maiden, die Jungfrau, -, -en

mail (*noun*), die Post, -, -en

mail, auf die Post bringen; **he mailed the letter,** er hat den Brief auf die Post gebracht

maintain (= *to assert*), behaupten

make, machen: **—up** (*work, lessons, etc.*), nachholen; **—up one's mind,** sich entschließen; **—money,** Geld verdienen; **—a speech,** eine Rede halten; **that makes no difference,** das macht nichts aus; **he was made king,** man machte ihn zum König; **I made her acquaintance,** ich lernte sie kennen

man, der Mann, -(e)s, ̈-er; (= *human being*) der Mensch, -en, -en

manner, die Weise, -, -n; **in this—,** auf diese Weise

many, viele; **—a,** mancher; **—things,** vieles; **— beautiful things,** viel Schönes; **how—?** wie viele?

March, der März, -(es), -e

march, marschieren

mark (*money*), die Mark, -; (*school grade*), die Zensur, -, -en; die Note, -, -n

market, der Markt, -(e)s, ̈-e

married, verheiratet

married couple, das Ehepaar, -s, -e

marry, heiraten; sich verheiraten

master, der Herr, -n, -en

mathematics, die Mathematik, -

matter, die Sache, -, -n; die Angelegenheit, -, -en; **what is the—?** was ist los?; **what is the—with him?** was fehlt ihm?

May, der Mai, -(e)s, -e

may (= *to be permitted*), dürfen, durfte, gedurft, darf; mögen, mochte, gemocht, mag; **that—be,** das mag (*or* kann) sein; **whoever she—be,** wer sie auch sein mag; **however that—be,** wie das auch sein mag

mayor, der Bürgermeister, -s, -; (*female*) die Bürgermeisterin, -, -nen

me, mir (*dat.*); mich (*acc.*)

meadow, die Wiese, -, -n

meal, das Essen, -s; die Mahlzeit, -, -en

mean, meinen (*of people*); bedeuten (*of things*); **what** (in the world) **do you—?** was fällt Ihnen denn ein?

means: by no—, keineswegs, durchaus nicht

means (= *expedient, contrivance*), das Mittel, -s, -, (*pl. often = resources*)

meantime: in the—, inzwischen, währenddessen

meanwhile, *see* **meantime**

meat, das Fleisch, -es

medicine, die Medizin, -, -en

medieval, mittelalterlich

meet, begegnen, begegnete, ist begegnet (*w. dat.*); treffen, traf, getroffen, trifft (*w. acc.*)

melt, schmelzen, schmolz, ist geschmolzen, schmilzt

member, das Mitglied, -(e)s, -er

mention, erwähnen

merchant, der Kaufmann, -(e)s, Kaufleute

merry, fröhlich, lustig, munter

meter, das Meter, -s, - (39.37 U.S. inches)

middle, die Mitte, -; **in the—of the forest,** mitten (*adv.*) im Walde

midnight, die Mitternacht, -; ̈-e

might, (= *power*), die Macht, -, ̈-e; die Gewalt, -, -en

might, dürfte, könnte; **I ask you for the book?** dürfte ich Sie um das Buch bitten?; **that—be,** das könnte (*or* dürfte) sein

mighty, mächtig, gewaltig

mile, die Meile, -, -n

milk, die Milch, -

miller, der Müller, -s, -

million, die Million, -, -en

millionaire, der Millionär, -s, -e; (*female*) die Millionärin, -, -nen

mind (= *memory*), das Gedächtnis, -ses, -se; der Sinn, -(e)s, -e; **to make up one's—,** sich entschließen

mine (*poss. pron.*), meiner, meine, meines; der (die *or* das) meine (*or* meinige); **a friend of—,** ein Freund von mir

minute, die Minute, -, -n

mirror, der Spiegel, -s, -

misfortune, das Unglück, -(e)s, -sfälle

misplace, verlegen

miss (*a person*), vermissen; (*a train*) versäumen, verpassen

mistake, der Fehler, -s, -

mistaken: to be—, sich irren

misunderstand, mißverstehen, mißverstand, mißverstanden

model, das Muster, -s, - (*pattern, sample*)

model airplane, das Musterflugzeug, -s, -e; das Flugzeugmodell, -s, -e

modern, modern

modest, bescheiden

moment, der Augenblick, -(e)s, -e; **wait a—,** warten Sie einen Augenblick!

monarchy, die Monarchie, -, -n

money, das Geld, -(e)s, -er; **to make—,** Geld verdienen; **to save (spend, squander)—,** Geld sparen (ausgeben, verschwenden)

monkey, der Affe, -n, -n

monosyllabic, einsilbig

month, der Monat, -(e)s, -e; **for months,** monatelang

monthly, monatlich

mood, die Laune, -, -n

moon, der Mond, -(e)s, -e

more, mehr: **—and—,** immer mehr; **—beautiful,** schöner; **the— . . ., the—,** je mehr . . . desto mehr

morning, der Morgen, -s, -; **good—,** guten Morgen! **tomorrow—,** morgen früh; **early in the—,** frühmorgens; **all—,** den ganzen Morgen; **this—,** heute morgen

mortal, sterblich

most (*adj.*), meist-; **—people,** die meisten Leute (*def. art. required*)

most (*adv.*), am meisten; **—interesting,** höchst interessant

mostly, meistens, meistenteils

mother, die Mutter, -, ̈

mother-in-law, die Schwiegermutter, -, ̈-

mountain, der Berg, -(e)s, -e; **we are going to the—s,** wir gehen in die Berge (*or* ins Gebirge)

mouse, die Maus, -, Mäuse

mouth (*of a pers.*), der Mund, -(e)s, Münder *rarely* Munde; (*of an animal*) das Maul, -(e)s, ̈-er: (*of a river*) die Mündung, -, -en

move (*tr.*), bewegen; (*intr.*) ziehen, zog, ist gezogen; (*refl.*) sich bewegen (*or* rühren); (= *to change residence*) umziehen; **I have moved,** ich bin umgezogen; **don't—from the spot!** rühren Sie sich nicht von der Stelle!

movement, die Bewegung, -, -en

movie, der Film, -s, -e; **is there a good movie playing tonight?** gibt's heute abend einen guten Film?

movies, das Kino, -s, -s; **we rarely go to the—,** wir gehen selten ins Kino

mow, mähen

Mr., Herr: **—Wagner's overcoat,** Herrn Wagners Mantel

Mrs., Frau; **—Wagner's gloves,** Frau Wagners Handschuhe

much (*quantity*), viel; (*degree*) sehr; **how—?** wieviel?; **how—does it cost?** was kostet es?; **twice as—,** zweimal soviel; **he suffers—,** er leidet sehr

Munich, (das) München, -s; **of—** (*adj.*), Münchner (*indecl.*)

museum, das Museum, -s, Museen

music, die Musik, -

must, müssen; **you—not do that,** das dürfen Sie nicht tun

my (*poss.*), *mein, meine, mein;* **for—sake,** um meinetwillen

myself (*refl. pron.*), mich (*acc.*); mir (*dat.*); (*intens.*), ich selbst (*or* selber); **I seat—** (*or* sit down), ich setze mich; **I hurt—,** ich habe mir weh getan

N

nail, der Nagel, -s, ¨

naked, nackt; **with the—eye,** mit bloßem Auge

name (*noun*), der Name, -ns, -n; **his—is,** er heißt

name, nennen, nannte, genannt; **to be named** (*or* called), heiß, hieß, geheißen

narrow, eng

nation, das Volk, -(e)s, ¨er; die Nation, -, -en

native land, das Vaterland, -(e)s, ¨er

natural(ly), natürlich

nature, die Natur, -, -en

near, nah(e) (*w. dat.*); **—them,** in ihrer Nähe

necessary, nötig

neck, der Hals, -es, Hälse

need, brauchen, nötig haben, bedürfen (*w. gen.*)

need, die Not, -, ¨e; **in—of repair** (*adj.*), ausbesserungsbedürftig

negligent, nachlässig

neighbor, (*male*) der Nachbar, -s (*or* -n), -n; (*female*) die Nachbarin, -, -nen

neighborhood, die Nachbarschaft, -, -en

neither (*conj.*), weder; **—. . .nor,** weder. . .noch; **—the father nor the mother,** weder der Vater noch die Mutter

nest, das Nest, -es, -er

Netherlands, die Niederlande (*pl.*)

network, das Netz, -es, -e; das Netzwerk -(e)s, -e; **—communication,** der Netzverkehr, -s

never, nie(mals)

nevertheless, trotzdem, dessenungeachtet

new, neu; **the—year,** das neue Jahr; **what's—?** was gibt's Neues?

news, die Nachricht, -, -en; die Neuigkeit, -, -en

newspaper, die Zeitung, -, -en

New Year's Day, das Neujahr, -s, -e

next, nächst-; **the—,** (= *adjoining*) **room,** das Nebenzimmer

night, die Nacht, -, ¨e; **at—,** in der Nacht; **last—,** gestern nacht (*or* abend), vorige Nacht; **one—** (*indef. time*), eines Nachts

nine, neun

ninth, neunt-

no (*adj.*), kein, keine, kein; **—one,** keiner; niemand, -(e)s; **—one else,** niemand anders, sonst niemand; **—such,** kein solch

no (*adv.*), nein; **—more,** nicht mehr

nobility, der Adel, -s

noble, edel; vornehm

nobody, niemand, -s

none (*pron.*), keiner, keine, keines

nonsense, der Unsinn, -(e)s

nor, noch; **neither. . .—,** weder. . .noch; **—I,** ich auch nicht

north, der Norden, -s; **—of,** nördlich von (*w. dat.*)

northeast (*adj.*), nordöstlich; (*noun*), der Nordosten, -s

northwest (*adj.*), nordwestlich; (*noun*), der Nordwesten, -s

nose, die Nase, -, -n

not, nicht; **—a, any,** kein; **—at all,** gar nicht; **—yet,** noch nicht; **—even,** nicht einmal; **—only. . .but also,** nicht nur. . .sondern auch; **—until seven o'clock,** erst um sieben Uhr

notebook, das Heft, -(e)s, -e

nothing, nichts; **—at all,** gar nichts; **— (that) he has,** nichts, was er hat; **—new,** nichts Neues; **—will come of it,** es wird nichts daraus werden

notice, bemerken

November, der November, -(s), -

now, jetzt

nowadays, heutzutage

nowhere, nirgendwo, nirgends

number, die Nummer, -, -n (*cipher; size*); die Zahl, -, -en; **the even—s,** die geraden Zahlen; **a—of,** mehrere

numberless, zahllos

numerous, zahlreich

nurse, die Krankenschwester, -, -n

nurse, pflegen

O

obey, gehorchen (*w. dat.*)

objection: I have no—to that, ich habe nichts degegen

observe (*to look at*), betrachten; bemerken; (*to take note of*), beobachten

obstacle, das Hindernis, -ses, -se

occasionally, dann und wann, gelegentlich

occupy (*live in*), bewohnen (*w. dir. obj.*), wohnen in (*w. dat.*); (*busy oneself*), sich beschäftigen; (*take possession of*), besetzen

occur to, einfallen, fiel ein, ist eingefallen, fällt ein (*w. dat.*)*;* **that never occurred to me,** das ist mir nie eingefallen

ocean, der Ozean, -s, -e; das Meer, -(e)s, -e

o'clock: at two—, um zwei Uhr

of, von (*w. dat.*); **—course,** natürlich, selbstverständlich; **I think—him,** ich denke an ihn; **full—,** voll(er); **the square is full—people,** der Platz ist voll(er) Menschen; (*Often omitted:* **the city—Munich,** die Stadt München; **a pound—butter,** ein Pfund Butter)

offer, bieten, bot, geboten; anbieten

offer (*noun*), das Angebot, -es, -e

office, das Amt, -(e)s, ⸚er; (*place of business*) das Büro, -s, -s

official, der Beamte, -n, -n (*w. adj. decl.*); ein Beamter; *but* (*female*) die Beamtin, -, -nen

official (*adj.*) offiziell, amtlich

official record, der offizielle Rekord, -s

often, oft

old, alt; **—age,** das Alter, -s

old-fashioned, altmodisch

on, auf, an (*w. dat. or acc.*); **—Monday,** am Montag (*or* montags); **—my account,** meinetwegen; **—condition that,** unter der Bedingung, daß

once, einmal; **at—,** sogleich, gleich, sofort; **—upon a time there was,** es war einmal; **—more,** noch einmal

one (*num. adj.*), ein; (= *single*) einzig; **—and a half,** anderthalb

one (*indef. art.*), ein, eine, ein

one (*pron.*), einer, eine, ein(e)s; man (*indef., used only in nominative*); **which—?** welcher?; **—of the pupils,** einer von den Schülern, einer der (*gen.*) Schüler

onion, die Zwiebel, -, -n

only (*adj.*), einzig; (*adv.*), nur, bloß; erst; **not—. . .but also,** nicht nur. . .sondern auch; **it is—two o'clock,** es ist erst zwei Uhr

open (*adj.*), offen

open, öffnen, aufmachen

opinion, die Meinung, -, -en

opportunity, die Gelegenheit, -, -en

opposite, gegenüber (*w. dat.*); **we live—the park,** wir wohnen dem Park gegenüber

or, oder; **either. . .—,** entweder. . .oder

oral, mündlich

orange, die Orange, -, -n, die Apfelsine, -, -n

orator, der Redner, -s, -

order (*command*), der Befehl, -(e)s, -e; (*arrangement*), die Ordnung, -, -en; **to give an—for,** bestellen; **to put something in—,** etwas in Ordnung bringen; **it might perhaps be in—,** es wäre wohl an der Zeit; **in—to** (*conj.*), damit; (*prep.*) um. . .zu (*w. inf.*)

order, befehlen, befahl, befohlen, befiehlt (*w. dat.*); (*to*

give an order for), bestellen; **to—a taxi,** ein Taxi bestellen

originally, ursprünglich

originate, entstehen, entspringen (*both str. & w. sein*)

other (*adj.*), ander-

other (*pron.*), der (die *or* das) andere, (*pl.*) die anderen; **they love each—,** sie lieben einander (*or* sich)

otherwise, sonst; anders, auf andere Weise

ought (= *should*), sollte (*subj. of* sollen); **I—to work,** ich sollte arbeiten

our (*poss. pron.*), uns(e)rer, uns(e)re, uns(e)res; der (die *or* das) unsrige *or* uns(e)re

ourselves (*refl.*), uns (*dat. & acc.*); (*intens.*) **we—,** wir selbst (*or* selber)

out (*w. vbs. of motion*), hinaus, heraus; (= *outside*) draußen; (= *not at home*) nicht zu Hause, ausgegangen

out of, aus (*w. dat.*); **—what?** woraus? **—it,** daraus

outside, draußen; **—of,** außerhalb (*w. gen.*)

over (*prep.*), über (*w. dat. or acc.*)

over (*adv.*), vorüber; (*to this side*) herüber; (*to that side*) hinüber; (*on the other side*) drüben; (= *in excess remaining*) übrig; (= *past*) vorüber; **I have only ten marks left—,** ich habe nur zehn Mark übrig; **winter is—,** der Winter ist vorüber

overcoat, der Überrock, -(e)s, ⸚e; der Mantel, -s, ⸚

overcome, überwinden, überwand, überwunden

own (*adj.*), eigen

own, besitzen, besaß, besessen

P

package, die Packung, -, -en

page, die Seite, -, -n

pain, der Schmerz, -es, -en; **frantic with—,** toll vor Schmerz

paint (*art*), malen; (*as a house*), anstreichen, strich an, angestrichen

painter, der Maler, -s, -; (*female*) die Malerin, -, -nen

painting, das Gemälde, -s, -

pair, das Paar, -(e)s, -e; **a—of gloves,** ein Paar Handschuhe

palace, der Palast, -(e)s, ⸚e

pale, blaß

paper, das Papier, -s, -e; (*newspaper*), die Zeitung, -, -en

parade, der Zug, -es, ⸚e

pardon, die Verzeihung, -; **I beg your—,** (ich bitte um) Verzeihung!

pardon, entschuldigen (*wk, w. acc.*); verzeihen, verzieh, verziehen (*w. dat.*)

parents, die Eltern (*pl.*)

parks, der Park, -(e)s, -e

part, der Teil, -(e)s, -e; **for the most—,** meistens, meistenteils

part (*take leave*), Abschied nehmen, sich verabschieden

party (*social gathering*), die Gesellschaft, -, -en; (*picnic*), die Landpartie, -, -n; (*political party*), die Partei, -, -en

pass (*elapse*), vergehen, verging, ist vergangen; (*spend time*) verbringen, verbrachte, verbracht; **—by,** vorübergehen, ging vorüber, ist vorübergegangen (*w. an & dat.*); vorbeigehen (*w. sein, an & dat.*); **—an examination,** eine Prüfung (*or* ein Examen) bestehen (*str.*); **how do you—your leisure time?** wie verbringen Sie Ihre Muβestunden? *or* Freizeit?; **time passes,** die Zeit vergeht; (*a car on a highway*) überholen (*sep.*)

passenger, der Passagier, -s, -e; der Reisende (*adj. used as noun*)

past (*adv.*), vorüber; **half—twelve,** halb eins

past, die Vergangenheit, -

pastor, der Pfarrer, -s, -; (*female, in Protestant churches*) die Pfarrarin, -, -nen

path, der Pfad, -(e)s, -e

patience, die Geduld, -

patient, geduldig

pave, pflastern

pay, bezahlen; **—attention,** aufpassen, paβte auf, aufgepaβt

pea, die Erbse, -, -n

peace, der Friede(n), -ns

peculiar, sonderbar

pen, die Feder, -, -n; **fountain—,** die Füllfeder, -, -n

pencil, der Bleistift, -(e)s, -e

people, die Leute (*pl.*); die Menschen (*pl.*); (= *nation*) das Volk, -(e)s, ¨-er; man (*indef. pron. w. sing. vb.*)

pepper, der Pfeffer, -s, -

perceive, gewahr werden (*w. gen.*)

perhaps, vielleicht; **that might—be in order,** das wäre wohl an der Zeit

permission, die Erlaubnis, -, -se

permit, erlauben (*w. dat.*)

permitted, erlaubt; **to be—,** dürfen, durfte, gedurft, darf

personality, die Persönlichkeit, -, -en

personified, personifiziert; **kindness—,** die Güte selbst

persuade, überreden, überredete, überredet (*w. acc. of the pers.*)

photo, das Foto (*or* Photo), -s, -s

physician, der Arzt, -es, ¨-e; (*female*) die Ärztin, -, -nen

piano, das Klavier, -s, -e; **to play—,** Klavier (*no art.*) spielen

pick, pflücken; **to—up,** aúfheben; (*receive, record*), aufnehmen, nahm auf, aufgenommen, nimmt auf; **to—up** (*to make neat*), aufräumen

pick-up (*light truck, van*), der Pritschenwagen, -s, -, *abbr.* die Pritsche, -, -n; *also* der Kleintransporter, -s, -

picture, das Bild, -(e)s, -er; **to take—s of,** Aufnahmen machen von (*w. dat.*)

picturesque, malerisch

piece, das Stück -(e)s, -e; **to tear to—s,** zerreiβen, zerriβ, zerrissen

pipe, die Pfeife, -, -n

pity, das Mitleid, -(e)s; **that would be a—,** das wäre schade! **what a—,** schade! **for—'s sake,** um Gottes (*or* Himmels) willen!

pity, sich erbarmen (*w. gen. or* über *& acc.*); Mitleid haben mit (*w. dat.*)

place, der Platz, -es, ¨-e; die Stelle, -, -n; (= *locality*) der Ort, -(e)s, -e; **I would do it if I were in your—,** ich täte es an Ihrer Stelle

place (*in a horizontal position*), legen; (*in an upright position*), stellen; (= *to set*) setzen

plan, der Plan, -(e)s, ¨-e; **to carry out a—,** einen Plan aúsführen

plan, planen

planet, der Planet, -en, -en

plant, die Pflanze, -, -n

plant, pflanzen

plate, der Teller, -s, -

play, spielen; **to—the piano,** Klavier (*no art.*) spielen; **to—ball,** Ball spielen

pleasant, angenehm

please, gefallen, gefiel, gefallen, gefällt (*w. dat.*); (**if you)—,** bitte; **it pleases me** (= *I like it*), es gefällt mir

pleasure, die Freude, -, -n; das Vergnügen, -s, -; **to look forward to with—,** sich freuen auf (*w. acc.*); **I look forward with—to the vacation,** ich freue mich auf die Ferien; **I take—in it,** ich finde meine Freude daran; **it gives me—,** es macht mir Freude

plum, die Pflaume, -, -n

pocket, die Tasche, -, -n

poem, das Gedicht, -(e)s, -e; **a—by Biermann,** ein Gedicht von Biermann

poet, der Dichter, -s, -; (*female*) die Dichterin, -, -nen

poetic, poetisch

point, der Punkt, -(e)s, -e; **he was on the—of going out,** er wollte eben ausgehen (*or* er war im Begriff auszugehen)

point, zeigen

police, die Polizei, -

policeman, der Polizist, -en, -en

policewoman, die Polizistin, -, -nen

polite, höflich; **—to,** höflich zu (*w. dat.*)

poor (*adj.*), arm; **—in,** arm an (*w. dat.*)

poor person, der (*or* die) Arme, (*pl.*) die Armen

popular, beliebt

population, die Bevölkerung, -, -en
porter, der Gepäckträger, -s, -
portrait, das Porträt, -s, -e
position, die Stellung, -, -en; die Stelle, -, -n
possess, besitzen, besaß, besessen
possession, der Besitz, -es; **to take—of,** etwas (*acc.*) in Besitz nehmen
possessor, der Besitzer, -s, -
possible, möglich; (*Possibility is often expressed by the subjunctive*)
post office, das Postamt, -(e)s, ¨er; die Post, -, -en
postpone, aufschieben, schob auf, aufgeschoben; — **to,** verschieben auf (*w. acc.*)
potato, die Kartoffel, -, -n
pound, das Pfund, -(e)s, -e; **half a—,** ein halbes Pfund; **a—and a half,** anderthalb Pfund; **two marks a—,** zwei Mark das Pfund
pour, gießen, goß, gegossen
powder (*for the face*), der Puder, -s, -
power, die Macht, -, ¨e; die Gewalt, -, -en; die Kraft, -, ¨e
powerful, mächtig, gewaltig
practice, üben (*often refl.*); **he practices fencing (swimming),** er übt sich im Fechten (Schwimmen)
praise, das Lob, -(e)s
praise, loben
pray, beten
prayer, das Gebet, -(e)s, -e
prefer, vorziehen, zog vor, vorgezogen; lieber haben; **I—it,** ich habe es lieber; **I—to do it,** ich tue es lieber
prepare, bereiten; vórbereiten; (*often refl.*) **to—for,** sich vórbereiten auf (*w. acc.*); **I was preparing for the examination,** ich bereitete mich auf die Prüfung vor
prepared, bereit; vorbereitet; **he is—for the worst,** er ist auf das Schlimmste gefaßt
present (*in attendance*), anwesend; (= *at present*) gegenwärtig
present (= *gift*), das Geschenk, -(e)s, -e; (*time*) die Gegenwart; **for the—,** vorläufig (*adv.*)
present (*as a gift*), schenken
preserve, erhalten, erhielt, erhalten, erhält
president, der Präsident, -en, -en; (*female*) die Präsidentin, -, -nen
press (*clothes*), bügeln
pretty, hübsch, schön
pride, der Stolz, -es
prime minister (*male*), der Ministerpräsident, -en, -en; (*female*), die Ministerpräsidentin, -, -nen
prince, der Fürst, -en, -en; der Prinz, -en, -en
princess, die Prinzessin, -, -nen
print, drucken
prison, das Gefängnis, -ses, -se

prisoner, der Gefangene (*w. adj. decl.*); ein Gefangener
prize, der Preis, -es, -e
probability, die Wahrscheinlichkeit, -, -en
probably, wahrscheinlich; wohl (*often w. fut. tenses*); **he was—twenty years old,** er mochte wohl zwanzig Jahre alt sein
procession, der Zug, -(e)s, ¨e
profess, wollen, wollte, gewollt, will; **he professes to have a rich uncle,** er will einen reichen Onkel haben
profession, der Beruf, -(e)s, -e
professor (*male*), der Professor, -s, -en; (*female*), die Professorin, -, -nen; **he is a—at the university,** er ist Professor an der Universität
program (*radio or TV*), die Sendung, -, -en
prominent, hervorragend
promise, das Versprechen, -s, -
promise, versprechen, versprach, versprochen, verspricht
pronounce, aússprechen; **he always pronounces the word wrong,** er spricht das Wort immer falsch aus
proof, der Beweis, -es, -e
property, das Eigentum, -(e)s, ¨er
proprietor (*male*), der Inhaber, -s, -; (*female*), die Inhaberin, -, -nen
protect, (be)schützen
proud, stolz; **—of,** stolz auf (*w. acc.*)
prove, beweisen, bewies, bewiesen
proverb, das Sprichwort, -(e)s, ¨er
provoked: to be—at, sich ärgern über (*w. acc.*)
Prussia, (das) Preußen, -s
public(ly), öffentlich; **—library,** die Volksbibliothek, -, -en
punctual(ly), pünktlich
punish, strafen, bestrafen
pupil, (*male*) der Schüler, -s, -; (*female*) die Schülerin, -, -nen
pure, rein
pursue, verfolgen (*w. acc.*)
put (*in a horizontal position*), legen; (*in an upright position*) stellen; (= *to set*) setzen; hintun; **to—a question,** eine Frage stellen; **—it there,** tun Sie es hin!
put on (*clothes, shoes*) [sich (*dat.*) *w. dir. obj.*] anziehen, zog an, angezogen; (*hat, glasses*) aufsetzen, setzte auf, aufgesetzt

Q

quarrel, der (Wort)streit, -(e)s, -e (*or* Streitigkeiten)
quarrel, streiten, stritt, gestritten
quarter, das Viertel, -s, -; **a—to nine,** ein Viertel vor

neun; **a—after three,** ein Viertel nach drei; **a—of an hour,** eine Viertelstunde

queen, die Königin, -, -nen

quench, löschen

question, die Frage, -, -n; **to ask a—,** eine Frage stellen; **to answer a—,** eine Frage beantworten (*or* auf eine Frage antworten)

quick(ly), schnell

quiet(ly), ruhig

quiet, die Ruhe, -, -n

quite, ganz

R

rabbit, das Kaninchen, -s, -

race, rennen; das Rennen, -s, -; **racecar,** der Rennwagen, -s, -; **racetrack,** die Rennbahn, -, -en

radiation, die Strahlung, -; **cosmic—,** die kosmische Strahlung, die Weltraumstrahlung

radical (*politically*), radikal, sehr progressiv oder konservativ

radio, das Radio, -s, -s; der Rundfunk, -s; **to listen to (turn on, turn off) the—,** das Radio ánhören (ánstellen, ábstellen); **—set,** der Radioapparat, -(e)s, -e

rage, die Wut, -

railway, die Eisenbahn, -, -en; **by—,** mit der Eisenbahn; **—station,** der Bahnhof, -(e)s, ¨e; **elevated—,** die Hochbahn, -, -en

rain (*noun*), der Regen, -s, -fälle (*or* Niederschläge)

rain, regnen; **to—hard,** stark regnen

raincoat, der Regenmantel, -s, ¨

raise, heben, hob, gehoben, hebt; áufheben

rapid(ly), schnell

rare, selten

rat, die Ratte, -, -n

rather, ziemlich

razorblade, die Rasierklinge, -, -n

reach, reichen; erreichen (*attain*); **he cannot be reached by phone,** er ist telefonisch nicht zu erreichen

read, lesen, las, gelesen, liest; **to—aloud to,** vórlesen (*w. dat. of the pers.*); **to—through,** zu Ende lesen

reading, das Lesen, -s

ready (= *finished*), fertig; (= *prepared*) bereit; **he is—for everything,** er ist zu allem bereit

real(ly), wirklich

realize, einsehen, sah ein, eingesehen, sieht ein; sich (*dat.*) etwas vórstellen

rear (= *to bring up*), erziehen, erzog, erzogen

reason, der Grund, -(e)s, ¨e; **for what—?** aus welchem Grund?

receive, erhalten, erhielt, erhalten, erhält; bekommen, bekam, bekommen; (= *to welcome*), freundlich empfangen, empfing, empfangen, empfängt; (*messages, etc.*), aufnehmen, nahm auf. aufgenommen, nimmt auf

recently, neulich, kürzlich, vor kurzem

recognize, erkennen, erkannte, erkannt

recommend, empfehlen, empfahl, empfohlen, empfiehlt

recover (= *recuperate*) **from,** sich erholen von (*w. dat.*)

red, rot

reference: with—to, in bezug (*or* Bezug) auf (*w. acc.*)

refuse, verweigern (*w. dat. of the pers. & acc. of the th.*)

regard: with—to, hinsichtlich (*w. gen.*); in bezug auf (*w. acc.*)

regards, der Gruß, -es, ¨e; **best—to your father,** besten Gruß an Ihren Vater

region, die Gegend, -, -en

regret, bedauern

regulate, regulieren

rejoice at, sich freuen über (*w. acc.*)

relate, erzählen

relatively, relativ; **in a—short time,** in relativ kurzer Zeit

reliable, zuverlässig

religion, die Religion, -, -en

rely on, sich verlassen auf (*w. acc.*)

remain, bleiben, blieb, ist geblieben; verbleiben

remark, die Bemerkung, -, -en

remark, bemerken

remarkable, merkwürdig

remember, sich erinnern [*w. gen. or an & acc. (more modern)*]; gedenken (*w. gen.*)

remind, erinnern; **—me of that,** erinnern Sie mich daran!

remove (*as hat, glasses*), abnehmen, nahm ab, abgenommen, nimmt ab; (*as clothes, shoes*) ausziehen, zog aus, ausgezogen

rent, die Miete, -, -n

rent (*from a pers.*), mieten; (*to a pers.*) vermieten

repair, ausbessern, besserte aus, ausgebessert; reparieren

repeat, widerhólen, wiederholte, wiederholt

reply, antworten (*w. dat. of the pers.*); erwidern

reply, die Antwort, -, -en

report, der Bericht, -(e)s, -e

report, berichten

represent, vertreten, vertrat, vertreten, vertritt

representative, der Vertreter, -s, -

republic, die Republik, -, -en

request, die Bitte, -, -n

require, verlangen, fordern
research, die Forschung, -, -en
resemble, gleichen (*w. dat.*), ähnlich sein (*w. dat.*)
reside, wohnen
respect, die Hinsicht, -, -en; **in this—,** in dieser Hinsicht
responsible, verantwortlich; **—for,** verantwortlich für
rest, die Ruhe, -
rest, sich aúsruhen
restaurant, das Restaurant, -s, -s
result, die Folge, -, -n; **as a—,** zur Folge; **as a—of that,** infolgedessen
retired, pensioniert
return (= *to go back*), zurückkehren, kehrte zurück, ist zurückgekehrt; (= *to give back*) zurückgeben, gab zurück, zurückgegeben
revolution, die Revolution, -, -en
Rhine, der Rhein, -(e)s
ribbon, das Band, -(e)s, ̈-er
rich, reich; **—in,** reich an (*w. dat.*)
riches, der Reichtum, -(e)s, ̈-er
rid of, los; **he is—it,** er ist es los
riddle, das Rätsel, -s, -
ride (= *journey*), die Fahrt, -, -en
ride (*on horseback*), reiten, ritt, ist geritten; (*travel*) fahren, fuhr, ist gefahren, fährt
rider, der Reiter, -s, -; (*female*) die Reiterin, -, -nen
rifle, das Gewehr, -s, -e
right, recht; **he is—,** er hat recht; **it serves him—,** es geschieht ihm recht; **to the—,** nach rechts; **on the—,** rechts; **I shall be there—away,** ich bin gleich da
ring, der Ring, -(e)s, -e
ring, läuten; klingeln; **the bell is ringing,** es klingelt
ripe, reif
rise (*of persons*), aufstehen, stand auf, ist aufgestanden; (*of the sun and moon*) aufgehen, ging auf, ist aufgegangen; (*of a river*) entspringen, entsprang, ist entsprungen; steigen, stieg, ist gestiegen *or* aufsteigen (*esp. of a rocket*)
river, der Fluß, Flusses, Flüsse
road, der Weg, -(e)s, -e
roar (*as a lion*), brüllen
roast, braten, briet, gebraten, brät
rob, rauben (*w. dat. of the pers. & acc. of the th.*), berauben (*w. acc. of the pers. & gen. of the th.*); **they robbed him of everything,** man hat ihm alles geraubt; **they robbed him of all his money,** man hat ihn seines ganzen Geldes beraubt
robber, der Räuber, -s, -
rock, der Felsen, -s, -
rocket, die Rakete, -, -n

roof, das Dach, -(e)s, ̈-er
room, das Zimmer, -s, -; die Stube, -, -n; (= *hall*) der Saal, -(e)s, Säle; (= *space*) der Raum, -(e)s, ̈-e
roommate (*male*), der Zimmerkollege, -n, -n; (*female*), die Zimmerkollegin, -, -nen
rope, der Strick, -(e)s, -e
rose, die Rose, -, -n
rouge, die Schminke, -, -n
round, rund
row, die Reihe, -, -n
row, rudern
royal, königlich
rubber stamp, der Stempel, -s, -
rubberband, das Gummiband, -(e)s, ̈-er
ruin, die Ruine, -, -n; **castle—s,** Schloßruinen
rule, die Regel, -, -n; (= *rulership*) die Herrschaft, -, -en; **as a—,** in der Regel
run, laufen, lief, ist gelaufen, läuft; rennen, rannte, ist gerannt

S

sad, traurig
safe, sicher
said, gesagt; **to be—,** sollen; **he is—to be rich,** er soll reich sein
sake: for the—of. . .um. . .willen; for my—, um meinetwillen; **for heaven's—,** um Himmels willen!
same: the—, derselbe, dieselbe, dasselbe; **it is all the— to me,** es ist mir ganz gleich (*or* einerlei)
satellite, der Satellt, -en, -en
satisfied, zufrieden
Saturday, der Samstag, -(e)s, -e; der Sonnabend, -s, -e; **on—(s),** am Samstag (*or* samstags)
save (*by economizing*), sparen; (= *to rescue*), retten; **— me the trouble,** ersparen Sie mir die Mühe!
say, sagen
saying, der Spruch, -(e)s, ̈-e
scarcely, kaum
school, die Schule, -, -n; **in—,** in der Schule; **to—,** in die (*or* zur) Schule; **after—,** nach der Schule
schoolmate, der Schulkamerad, -en, -en
science, die Wissenschaft, -, -en
scientific, wissenschaftlich
scientist, der Wissenschaftler, -s, -; (*female*) die Wissenschaftlerin, -, -nen; der Forscher, -s, -; (*female*) die Forscherin, -, -nen
scold, schelten, schalt, gescholten, schilt
scratch, kratzen
sea, die See, -, -n; das Meer, -(e)s, -e

seasick, seekrank

seasickness, die Seekrankheit, -, -en

season, die Jahreszeit, -, -en

seat, der Sitz, -es, -e; der Platz, -es, ¨-e

seated: be—, setzen Sie sich (*or* nehmen Sie Platz)!

second (*adj.*), zweit-; **in the—place,** zweitens

second, die Sekunde, -, -n

secret, das Geheimnis, -ses, -se

secretly, heimlich

see, sehen, sah, gesehen, sieht; **—to it,** sorgen Sie dafür; **have you seen him working?,** haben Sie ihn arbeiten sehen?

seek, suchen

seem, scheinen, schien, geschienen

see through (*not be fooled*), durchscháuen

seize (*= to grasp*), fassen; (*= to take possession of*) sich bemächtigen (*w. gen.*)

seldom, selten

self, selbst, selber

sell, verkaufen

semester, das Semester, -s, -

send, senden, sandte, gesandt; schicken; **to—by mail,** mit der Post schicken; **to—for,** holen (*or* kommen) lassen; **did you—for the doctor,** haben Sie den Arzt holen (*or* kommen) lassen?

sense, der Sinn, -(e)s, -e; **there is no—in doing such a thing,** es hat keinen Sinn, so etwas zu tun; **he is not in his—s,** er ist nicht bei Sinnen

sentence, der Satz, -es, ¨-e

separate, trennen

September, der September, -s, -

serious, ernst(haft)

servant, der Diener, -s, -; **—girl,** das Dienstmädchen, -s, -; (*gender-neutral*) die Bedienung

serve, dienen (*w. dat.*); **that serves him right,** das geschieht ihm recht

service, die Bedienung, -, -en

set (*= to place, put*), setzen; (*of the sun and moon*) untergehen, ging unter, ist untergegangen; **—the table,** den Tisch decken

seven, sieben

seventeen, siebzehn

seventeenth, siebzehnt-

seventh, siebt-

several, mehrere, ein paar (*indecl.*)

severe (*as sickness*), schwer; (*= strict*) streng

shade, der Schatten, -s, -

shadow, der Schatten, -s, -

shady, schattig

shall (*aux. of fut. tenses*), werden; (*to denote moral obligation*) sollen

shape, die Gestalt, -, -en; die Form, -, -en

sharp, scharf; **we left at ten o'clock—,** Punkt zehn Uhr sind wir abgefahren

sharpen (*as a pencil*), spitzen; (*as a knife*), schleifen, schliff, geschliffen, schleift

shave (**oneself**), sich rasieren; **to get shaved,** sich rasieren lassen

she, sie

shine, scheinen, schien, geschienen

ship, das Schiff, -(e)s, -e

shirt, das Hemd, (-e)s, -en

shoe, der Schuh, -(e)s, -e

shoot, schießen, schoß, geschossen

shore, das Ufer, -s, -

short, kurz

shot, der Schuß, Schusses, Schüsse

should (*= ought*), sollte (*subj. of* sollen); **he—go,** er sollte gehen; **he—have gone,** er hätte gehen sollen; **I—like to travel,** ich möchte (*subj. of* mögen) (gern) reisen

shout, schreien, schrie, geschrien

show, zeigen; **—honor to,** Ehre erweisen (*w. dat.*)

shudder, grauen (*impers.*); **I—,** mir graut

sick, krank

side, die Seite, -, -n; **on this—of,** diesseits (*w. gen.*); **on that—of,** jenseits (*w. gen.*)

sight (*= something worth seeing*) die Sehenswürdigkeit, -, -en; (*= aspect*) der Anblick, -(e)s, -e

sign, das Zeichen, -s, -

sign, unterschreiben, unterschrieb, unterschrieben; unterzeichnen

signature, die Unterschrift, -, -en

significance, die Bedeutung, -; die Wichtigkeit,

significant, bedeutend

silent (*adj.*), still, schweigsam; **to be—,** schweigen, schwieg, geschwiegen

silk, die Seide, -, -n; (*adj.*), seiden

silver, das Silber, -s; (*adj.*) silbern

similar, ähnlich (*w. dat.*)

simple, simply, einfach

since (*prep.*), seit (*w. dat.*); **—when?,** seit wann?

since (*conj.*), seitdem (*temp.*); da (*causal*)

since (*adv.*), seitdem; **—then,** seitdem

sincere(ly) aufrichtig; **—ly yours,** Ihr (ganz) ergebener *or* Ihre (ganz) ergebene

sing, singen, sang, gesungen

singer (*male*), der Sänger, -s, -; (*female*) die Sängerin, -, -nen

single (*= only, sole*), einzig; (*= individual*), einzeln; (*= unmarried*), ledig

sink (*intr.*), sinken, sank, ist gesunken; versinken (*w. sein*); (*tr.*) versenken (*wk.*)

sister, die Schwester, -, -n

sit, sitzen, saß, gesessen; **—down,** sich setzen
situated: to be—on, liegen (*str.*) an (*w. dat.*)
six, sechs
sixteen, sechzehn-
sixteenth, sechzehnt-
sixth, sechst
sixty, sechzig
size, die Größe, -, -n
skate (*noun*), der Schlittschuh, -(e)s, -e
skate, Schlittschuh laufen; **I went skating,** ich bin Schlittschuh gelaufen
skip, überspringen, übersprang, übersprungen; **he skipped a grade,** er hat eine Klasse übersprungen
slave, der Sklave, -n, -n
sleep, schlafen, schlief, geschlafen, schläft; **go to—** (= *to fall asleep*), einschlafen (*w. sein*)
sleepy, schläfrig
sleeve, der Ärmel, -s, -
slide (= *slip*), gleiten, glitt, ist geglitten
slippery, glatt
slow(ly), langsam
small, klein
smell, riechen, roch, gerochen; **—of,** riechen nach (*w. dat.*)
smoke, der Rauch, -(e)s
smoke, rauchen
smoking, das Rauchen, -s; **—is forbidden,** das Rauchen ist verboten
snore, schnarchen
snow, der Schnee, -s
snow, schneien
so (*adv.*), so; **and—forth,** und so weiter (*abbr.* usw.)
sob, schluchzen
so-called, sogenannt
sofa, das Sofa, -s, -s
soft(ly) (= *not hard*), weich; (= *not loud*) leise
soldier, der Soldat, -en, -en
solve, lösen; **—a puzzle,** ein Rätsel lösen
some, etwas (*indecl.; w. sing. noun*); einige (*w. pl. noun*); **—. . .or other,** irgendein (*adj.*)
somebody, someone, jemand, -(e)s; irgend jemand; **—else,** jemand anders (*or* sonst jemand)
something, etwas (*indecl.*); **—he likes,** etwas, was er gern hat; **—good,** etwas Gutes; **—else,** etwas anderes
sometimes, dann und wann, zuweilen, gelegentlich, manchmal
somewhat, etwas; **—sour,** etwas sauer
somewhere, irgendwo(hin)
son, der Sohn -(e)s, -̈e
song, das Lied, -(e)s, -er
soon, bald; **as—as,** sobald
sooner (= *earlier*), früher; (= *rather*) lieber

sorrow, der Kummer, -s,
sorry: to be—, leid tun; **I am—for him,** er tut mir leid (*or* es tut mir leid um ihn)
sort, die Art, -, -en; **what—of (a),** was für ein; **what—of** (*pl.*), was für; **all—s of,** allerlei (*indecl.*)
so that, damit; um. . .zu (*w. pres. inf.*)
soul, die Seele, -, -n
sound (*adj.*) (= *well*), gesund; (= *stout or strong*), stark; (= *firm*) fest
sound, der Laut, -(e)s, -e
soup, die Suppe, -, -n
sour, sauer
source, die Quelle, -, -n
south, der Süden, -s; **—of,** südlich von (*w. dat.*)
southeast (*adj.*), südöstlich; (*noun*), der Südosten, -s
southwest (*adj.*), südwestlich; (*noun*), der Südwesten, -s
space, der Raum, -(e)s, -̈e; der Weltraum (*outer space*)
space flight, der Raumflug, -(e)s, -̈e
space ship, das Raumschiff, -(e)s, -e
Spain, (das) Spanien, -s
Spanish, spanisch
spare (= *unoccupied*), frei; **—time,** die Mußestunden, die Freizeit (*leisure*)
speak, sprechen, sprach, gesprochen, spricht; **—about,** sprechen über (*w. acc.*) *or* von (*w. dat.*)
speech, die Rede, -, -n; **to make a—,** eine Rede halten
spend (*time*), verbringen, verbrachte, verbracht; (*money*) ausgeben, gab aus, ausgegeben, gibt aus
spit, speien, spie, gespie(e)n
spite: in—of (*prep.*), trotz (*w. gen.*): **in—of that,** trotzdem, dessenungeachtet
spoil (= *pamper*), verwöhnen
spring (*of water*), die Quelle, -, -n; (*the season*) der Frühling, -s, -e; **in—,** im Frühling; **—is here,** der Frühling ist gekommen
squander, verschwenden, vergeuden
stamp, die Briefmarke, -, -n
stand, stehen, stand, gestanden
star, der Stern -(e)s, -e
start, ánfangen (*str.*), beginnen (*str.*); (*on a journey*) ábreisen (*wk. intr. w.* sein), sich auf den Weg machen; starten (*to take off*)
starve, verhungern, verhungerte, ist verhungert
state, der Staat, -(e)s, -en
station (= *rank*), der Stand, -es, -̈e; (= *situation*) die Stelle, -, -n; (= *position*) die Stellung, -, -en; (= *railroad depot*) der Bahnlof, -(e)s, -̈e; (= *stopping place*) die Station, -, -en; die Haltestelle, -, -n; **at the—,** auf dem Bahnhof; **to call for someone at the—,** jemand vom Bahnhof abholen; **radio—,** die Funkenstation, die Sendestation, der Sender

stay, bleiben, blieb, ist geblieben; **—at home,** zu Hause bleiben

stay (*as in a residence or a visit*), der Aufenthalt, -(e)s, -e

steamer, der Dampfer, -s, -; **by—,** mit dem Dampfer

steel, der Stahl, -(e)s, ̈e

steep, steil

steer, lenken

stem, der Stamm, -(e)s, ̈e; der Stengel, -s, -

step, der Schritt, -(e)s, -e; **to keep—** Schritt halten

step, treten, trat, ist getreten, tritt

stick, stecken

stiff, steif

still (*adj.*), still, ruhig

still (= *yet*), noch, immer noch; (= *nevertheless*), doch

stingy, geizig

stocking, der Strumpf, -(e)s, ̈e

stomach, der Magen, -s,

stone, der Stein, -(e)s, -e

stop, halten, hielt, gehalten, hält; ánhalten; **it has stopped snowing,** es hat aufgehört zu schneien; **suddenly he stopped,** plötzlich blieb er stehen; **my watch has stopped,** meine Uhr ist stehengeblieben

store, der Laden, -s, ̈

stork, der Storch -(e)s, ̈e

storm, das Gewitter, -s, -

story, die Geschichte, -n, -n; (*of a house*) das Stockwerk, -(e)s, -e

stove, der Ofen, -s, ̈

straight: a—line, eine gerade Linie; **—ahead,** geradeaus (*adv.*)

straighten (oneself) up, sich aúfrichten

strange, fremd (*w. dat.*)

stranger, der Fremde, -n, -n (*w. adj. decl.*); ein Fremder; **he is a—to me,** er ist mir fremd

stratosphere, die Stratosphäre, -

stream, der Strom, -(e)s, ̈e

street, die Straße, -, -n; **in** (*or* **on**) **the—** auf der Straße

streetcar, die Straßenbahn, -, -en; **by—,** mit der Straßenbahn

strict, streng

strike, schlagen, schlug, geschlagen, schlägt

strive for, streben nach (*w. dat.*)

strong, stark

stubborn, hartnäckig

student, der Student, -en, -en; **to be a—at a university,** auf einer Universität Student sein

study, das Studium, -s, Studien; (*subject in school*) das Fach, -(e)s, ̈er

study (*of students*), studieren; (*of pupils*) lernen; **to—hard,** fleißig (schwer, tüchtig) studieren (*or* lernen)

stumble, stolpern

stupid, dumm; **that would be—indeed,** das wäre schön dumm!

stupidity, die Dummheit, -, -en

style, die Mode, -, -n; **it is in—,** es ist (in der) Mode

subject (*in school*), das Fach, -(e)s, ̈er

suburb, die Vorstadt, -, ̈e

subway, die Untergrundbahn, -, -en

succeed, gelingen, gelang, ist gelungen (*impers. w. dat.*); **I have not succeeded in deciphering your handwriting,** es ist mir nicht gelungen, Ihre Handschrift zu entzifern

success, der Erfolg, -(e)s, -e

successful, erfolgreich

such, solcher, solche, solches; **—a storm,** solch ein (*or* ein solches) Gewitter; **he is no—fool,** er ist kein solcher Narr

suddenly, plötzlich, auf einmal

suffer, leiden, litt, gelitten

sugar, der Zucker, -s

suit (*of clothes*), der Anzug, -(e)s, ̈e

suit, passen (*w. dat.*)

suitcase, der Handkoffer, -s, -

summer, der Sommer, -s, -; **in—,** im Sommer

sun, die Sonne, -, -n; **the—rises (sets),** die Sonne geht auf (unter)

sunburnt, sonnenverbrannt

Sunday, der Sonntag, -(e)s, -e

sunny, sonnig

sunrise, der Sonnenaufgang, -(e)s, ̈e

sunset, der Sonnenuntergang, -(e)s, ̈e

sunshine, der Sonnenchein, -(e)s

superficial, oberflächlich

supermarket, der Supermarkt, -(e)s, ̈e

supper, das Abendessen, -s, -; **after—,** nach dem Abendessen; **for—,** zum Abendessen

sure, sicher; **—of,** sicher (*w. gen.*)

surface, die Oberfläche, -, -n

surprise, die Überraschung, -, -en

surprise, überraschen, übberaschte, überrascht

sweetheart, der Schatz, -es, ̈e

swim, schwimmen, schwamm, ist geschwommen

Switzerland, die Schweiz

sword, das Schwert, -(e)s, -er

sympathetic(ally), mitleidsvoll

sympathy, das Mitleid, -(e)s

system, das System, -s, -e

T

table, der Tisch, -es, -e; **to sit at (the)—,** am Tisch(e) sitzen; **to sit down at (the)—,** sich an den Tisch setzen

tachometer, der Geschwindigkeitsmesser, -s, -

tail, der Schwanz, -es, ¨-e

tailor, der Schneider, -s, -

take, nehmen, nahm, genommen, nimmt; **—a walk (a trip, an examination),** einen Spaziergang (eine Reise, eine Prüfung) machen; **—off** (*as clothes, shoes*), [sich (*dat.*) *w. dir. obj.*] ausziehen; (*as hat, glasses*), abnehmen; **—part in,** teilnehmen an (*w. dat.*); **—leave,** sich empfehlen, empfahl, empfohlen, empfiehlt; **will you—tea or coffee?,** wollen Sie Tee oder Kaffee?

talk, sprechen, sprach, gesprochen, spricht; **—about,** sprechen über (*w. acc.*) *or* von (*w. dat.*); **—to oneself,** vor sich (*acc.*) hinsprechen; **he talks to himself,** er spricht vor sich hin

tall, hoch; von hoher Gestalt; groß; lang

tape recorder, das Tonbandgerät, -s, -e

taste, der Geschmack, -(e)s, ¨-e

taste, schmecken; **—of,** schmecken nach (*w. dat.*); **it tastes of sour milk,** es schmeckt nach saurer Milch

tavern, die Kneipe, -, -n

tax, die Steuer, -, -n

tea, der Tee, -s, -s (*or* Teesorten)

teach, lehren (*w. two accs.*); **she taught him the song,** sie lehrte ihn das Lied

teacher (*male*), der Lehrer, -s -; (*female*) die Lehrerin, -, -nen; (*gender-neutral*) die Lehrkraft, -, ¨-e

team (*in a game*), die Mannschaft, -, -en

tear, reißen, riß, gerissen; **—to pieces,** zerreißen

technical, technisch; **—dictionary,** das Fachwörterbuch, -(e)s, ¨-er, **—term,** der Fachausdruck, -(e)s, ¨-e

technician, der Techniker, -s, -; der Facharbeiter, -s, -

telegraph, telegrafieren

telephone, telefonieren; **he cannot be reached by—,** er ist telefonisch (*adv.*) nicht zu erreichen

telescope, das Teleskop, -s, -e; das Fernrohr, -s, -e

television, das Fernsehen; **—set,** der Fernsehapparat

tell, erzählen, sagen

temperature, die Temperatur, -, -en

temptation, die Versuchung, -, -en

ten, zehn; **—times,** zehnmal

tennis, das Tennis, -

tenor, der Tenor, -s, ¨-e

tent, das Zelt, -(e)s, -e

tenth, zehnt-

terrible, schrecklich

test, die Prüfung, -, -en; der Versuch, -(e)s, -e

test, prüfen

than, als

thank, danken; **—for,** danken (*w. dat. of the pers*) für (*w. acc.*); **—a person for something,** sich bei einer Person für etwas bedanken

thankful, dankbar (*w. dat.*)

that (*conj.*), daß; **so—,** damit; um. . .zu (*w. pres. inf.*)

that (**one**) (*dem. adj. & pron.*), jener, jene, jenes; der, die, das; **that is** (**i.e**), das heißt (d.h.)

that (*rel. pron.* = *which*), der, die, das; welcher, welche, welches

thaw, tauen

theater, das Theater, -s, -; **to go to the—,** ins Theater gehen

theft, der Diebstahl, -s, ¨-e

their (*poss.*), ihr, ihre, ihr

theirs (*poss. pron.*), ihrer, ihre, ihres

them, ihnen (*dat.*); sie (*acc.*)

themselves (*refl. pron.*), sich (*dat. & acc.*); (*intens.*) selbst (*or* selber); **they—,** sie selbst (*or* selber)

then (*adv.*), damals; dann; da; denn; **now and—,** dann und wann; **not till—,** erst dann; **what—?** was dann? **well—,** nun gut denn

there, da, dort; **—is** (**are**), es gibt (*w. acc.*), es ist (sind) (*w. nom.*)

thereafter, danach, nachher

therefore, darum, deshalb, deswegen, daher, also

thereupon, darauf

they, sie

thick, dick; **a foot—,** einen Fuß dick

thief, der Dieb, -(e)s, -e

thin, dünn

thing, die Sache, -, -n; das Ding, -(e)s, -e; **main—,** die Hauptsache; **most beautiful—,** das Schönste (*adj. used as a noun*); **such a—,** so etwas (*indecl.*); **such—s,** dergleichen (*indecl.*); **all good—s,** alles Gute; **among other—s,** unter ander(e)m; **many—s,** vieles

think, denken, dachte, gedacht; **—of,** denken an (*w. acc.*); **he has thought up a good plan,** er hat sich einen guten Plan ausgedacht

third, dritt-; das Drittel, -s, -

thirst, der Durst, -es

thirsty, durstig

thirteenth, dreizehnt-

thirtieth, dreißigst-

thirty, dreißig

this, dieser, diese, dieses; **on—side of** (*prep. w. gen.*) diesseits

thorough(ly), gründlich

thought, der Gedanke, -ns, -n

thousand (*adj.*), tausend

thousand, das Tausend, -(e)s, -e; **two—,** zweitausend; **many—s,** viele Tausende

threaten, drohen (*w. dat.*); bedrohen

three, drei; **—times,** dreimal; **of—kinds,** dreierlei (*invar.*)

threefold, dreifach

three-legged, dreibeinig

three-stage, dreistufig; **—rocket,** die dreistufige Rakete

through (*prep.*), durch (*w. acc.*); **the whole year—,** das ganze Jahr hindurch; (*adj.* = *finished*), fertig

throw, werfen, warf, geworfen, wirft

thumb, der Daumen, -s, -

thunder, der Donner, -s, -

thunder, donnern

Thursday, der Donnerstag, -(e)s, -e

thus, so; auf diese Weise

ticket, die Fahrkarte, -, -n; **—of admission,** die Eintrittskarte, -, -n

tie, die Krawatte, -, -n; der Schlips, -es, -e; die Halsbinde, -n, -n; **bowtie,** die Schleife, -, -n

tie, binden, band, gebunden

tiger, der Tiger, -s, -

time, die Zeit, -, -en; (= *occasion*) das Mal, -(e)s, -e; **at what—?** um wieviel Uhr? **what—is it?** wieviel Uhr ist es? **to have a good—,** sich amüsieren; **at the—when,** zur Zeit, als (da *or* wo); **for the first—,** zum ersten Mal (*or* zum erstenmal); **(for) a long—,** lange; **how long a—?** wie lange? **ten—s,** zehnmal; **old(en)—s,** die alten Zeiten

tip, das Trinkgeld, -(e)s, -er

tired, müde; **he is—of life,** er ist des Lebens müde; **he is—of it,** er ist es müde

title, der Titel, -s, -

to (*prep.*), zu, nach (*both w. dat.*); auf, in, bis (*all w. acc.*); **—my brother's (house),** zu meinem Bruder; **(up)—the window,** bis an das Fenster; **to go—the theater,** ins Theater gehen; **to go—the country,** aufs Land gehen; **to go—school,** in die (*or* zur) Schule gehen; **(in order)—,** um...zu (*w. pres. inf.*) [*or* damit (*sub. conj.*)]

tobacco, der Tabak, -(e)s

today, heute; **a week from—,** heute über acht Tage; **what is—'s date?,** der wievielte ist (*or* den wievielten haben wir) heute?

today's heutig

together, zusammen

tomato, die Tomate, -, -n

tomorrow (*adv.*), morgen; **—morning,** morgen früh; **—afternoon,** morgen nachmittag; **day after—,** übermorgen

tongue, die Zunge, -, -n

tonight, heute abend (*or* nacht)

too, zu; (= *in addition also*) auch

tool, das Werkzeug, -(e)s, -e; Handwerkszeug = (kit of) tools

tooth, der Zahn, -)e)s, ¨-e

toothache, das Zahnweh, -(e)s; **I have a—,** ich habe Zahnweh (*no art.*)

top, die Spitze, -, -n; (*of a mountain*) der Gipfel, -s, -;

at the—of, oben auf; **on the—floor,** im obersten Stock(werk)

tourist (*male*), der Tourist, -en, -en; (*female*), die Touristin, -, -nen

tourist information bureau, das Verkehrsamt, -(e)s, ¨-er

toward (*prep.*), gegen (*w. acc.*); entgegen (*w. dat.*)

tower, der Turm, -(e)s, ¨-e

town, die Stadt, -, ¨-e; **in—,** in der Stadt; **to—,** in die Stadt

toys, die Spielsachen (*pl.*)

train, der Zug, -(e)s, ¨-e

translate, übersétzen, übersetzte, übersetzt; **—into English,** ins Englische übersetzen

translation, die Übersetzung, -, -en

transmit, übertrágen, übertrug, übertragen

transparent, durchsichtig

travel, reisen, reiste, ist gereist; fahren, fuhr, ist gefahren, fährt; **he travels second class,** er fährt zweiter Klasse

traveler, der Reisende, -n, -n; (*w. adj. decl.*) ein Reisender

treason, der Verrat, -(e)s

treasure, der Schatz, -es, ¨-e

treat, behandeln

tree, der Baum, -(e)s, ¨-e

tremble, zittern

trick, (= *prank*), der Streich, -(e)s, -e

trip, die Reise, -, -n; **to take a—,** eine Reise machen

trouble, die Mühe, -, -n; **it is not worth the—,** es ist nicht der Mühe wert

trouble oneself about, sich kümmern um (*w. acc.*)

true, wahr; (= *faithful*) treu

trunk, der Koffer, -s, -

truth, die Wahrheit, -, -en

try, versuchen

Tuesday, der Dienstag, -(e)s, -e

tune, die Melodie, -, -n (*pl. w. four syllables*)

tunnel, der Tunnel, -s, -s (*or*-)

turkey (*cock*), der Truthahn, -(e)s, ¨-e; der Puter, -s, -; (*hen*) die Pute, -, -n

Turkey, die Türkei, -

turn: it is my—, ich bin an der Reihe (*or* die Reihe ist an mir); **his—has come,** er ist an die Reihe gekommen

turn, kehren; wenden, wandte, gewandt; (= *to become*) werden; **—on** (*light, gas, water*), ándrehen, (*radio*) ánstellen; **to—off,** ábdrehen, ábstellen; **—one's back on someone,** jemand (*dat.*) den Rücken zúwenden; **he turned pale with fright,** vor Schreck ist er blaß geworden

twelve, zwölf

twenty, zwanzig
twice, zweimal; **—as much,** zweimal soviel
two, zwei; beide (*or* die beiden); **his—sons,** seine
beiden Söhne

U

umbrella, der Regenschirm, -(e)s, -e
umpteen, *indefinite numeral,* zig
unable: to be—, nicht können; **he is—to go,** er kann
nicht gehen
uncle, der Onkel, -s, -
under (*prep.*), unter (*w. dat. or acc.*)
understand, verstehen, verstand, verstanden; **that is
understood,** das versteht sich (von selbst) (*or* das ist
selbstverständlich)
undertake, unternéhmen, unternahm, unternommen,
unternimmt
undress (oneself), sich aúsziehen (*str.*)
unemployed (*adj.*), arbeitslos
unemployed, der Arbeitslose, -n, -n (*adj. used as noun*)
unexpected, unerwartet
unfinished, unvollendet
unfortunately, leider
unhappy, unglücklich
unite, vereinigen
United States, die Vereinigten Staaten
university, die Universität, -, -en; **to be a student at
the—,** auf der Universität Student sein; **to be a professor at the—,** an der Universität Professor sein
unjust, ungerecht
unknown, unbekannt
unless, wenn. . .nicht; (*after a neg. statement*) es sei denn,
daß. . .
unsatisfactory (*failing grade*), unbefriedigend
until (*prep.*), bis (*w. acc.*) **not—,** erst; **not—seven,** erst
um sieben Uhr
unusual, ungewöhnlich
up, auf; **—and down,** auf und ab
upset, umstürzen (*wk. tr. w.* haben; *intr. w.* sein)
upstairs, oben; **he goes—,** er geht nach oben (*or* die
Treppe hinauf)
urge, treiben, trieb, getrieben
us, uns (*dat. and acc.*)
use (*noun*), der Gebrauch -(e)s, ¨e; **to make—of,** sich
bedienen (*w. gen.*); Gebrauch von etwas (*dat.*) machen;
of what— is that to you? was nützt Ihnen das?
use, gebrauchen; verwenden, verwandte (*or*
verwendete), verwandt (*or* verwendet)
used, gebraucht

used to (= *accustomed*), gewohnt (*w. acc. & no prep.*); **he
is—it,** er ist es gewohnt (*or* daran gewöhnt); **to
become—,** sich gewöhnen an (*w. acc.*); **he used to
smoke,** er pflegte zu rauchen; früher rauchte er
useful, nützlich (*w. dat.*)
usual, gewöhnlich, üblich

V

vacation, die Ferien (*pl.*); der Urlaub, -(e)s, -e
vain: in—, vergebens, umsonst
valuable, wertvoll
value, der Wert, -(e)s, -e
various, verschieden
vast, riesig; unermesslich (*immeasurable*)
vehicle, das Kraftfahrzeug, —(e)s, -e
velocity, die Geschwindigkeit, -, -en
velvet, der Samt, -(e)s, -e
verb, das Zeitwort, -(e)s, ¨er; das Verb(um), -s, Verben
verse, der Vers, -es, -e
very, sehr
vest, die Weste, -, -n
vicinity, die Nähe, -, -n
victim, das Opfer, -s, -
Vienna, (das) Wien, -s
view, die Aussicht, -, -en
view, betrachten
village, das Dorf, -(e)s, ¨er
vinegar, der Essig, -s, -e
violent, heftig
violin, die Geige, -, -n
virtue, die Tugend, -, -en
visit, der Besuch, -(e)s, -e
visit, besuchen
voice, die Stimme, -, -n
volume (*of a book*), der Band, -(e)s, ¨e
vote, die Stimme, -, -n
vote for, stimmen für (*w. acc.*)

W

wait, warten; **—for,** warten auf (*w. acc.*)
waiter, der Kellner, -s, -; (*female*) die Kellnerin, -, -nen;
(*gender-neutral*) die Bedienung
wake, aufwecken (*tr.*); aúfwachen (*intr. w.* sein)
walk, der Spaziergang, -(e)s, ¨e; **to take a—,** einen
Spaziergang machen
walk, gehen, ging, ist gegangen; zu Fuß gehen

walking: to go—, spazierengehen; **he went—,** er ist spazierengegangen

wall, die Wand, -, ¨-e; (*outside*) die Mauer, -, -n

wander, wandern (*w.* sein)

want (*noun*) (= *need*), die Not, -, ¨-

want, (= *desire*), wollen, wollte, gewollt

war, der Krieg, -(e)s, -e

ware, die Ware, -, -n

warm, warm

warn, warnen

wash, waschen, wusch, gewaschen, wäscht; **to—dishes,** Geschirr (*neut. sing.*) ábwaschen; **I—my hands,** ich wasche mir die Hände; **I—(myself),** ich wasche mich

waste (= *squander*), verschwenden

wastepaper basket, der Papierkorb, -(e)s, ¨-e

watch, die Uhr, -, -en; **wristwatch,** die Armbanduhr

watch, bewachen

watch television, fernsehen, sah fern, ferngesehen, sieht fern

water, das Wasser, -s, - (*or* ¨-)

wave, die Welle, -, -n

way, der Weg, -(e)s, -e; **go your—,** geh fort!

we, wir

weak, schwach

wear, tragen, trug, getragen, trägt

wear out, abnutzen, nutzte ab, abgenutzt

wearability, die Abnutzbarkeit, -

weather, das Wetter, -s, -; **—forecast,** die Wettervoraussage, -, -n; **—information,** die Wetternachrichten (*pl.*)

wedding, die Hochzeit, -, -en

Wednesday, der Mittwoch, -s, -e

week, die Woche, -, -n; **once a—,** einmal die Woche; **a—ago,** vor acht Tagen; **a—from today,** heute über acht Tage; **for a—,** auf eine Woche

weekly, wöchentlich

weep, weinen

weight, das Gewicht, -s, -e; **to lift weights,** Gewichte heben (o, o), stemmen

welcome, begrüßen, freundlich empfangen (*str.*)

welfare (= *prosperity*), der Wohlstand, -(e)s

well, gut; wohl (*occurs only in a few set phrases as adv. of* well); **I am very—,** es geht mir sehr gut; **did you sleep—?** haben Sie gut geschlafen? **fare you—,** leben Sie wohl! **sleep—,** schlafen Sie wohl!

well-known, bekannt

well-meant, wohlgemeint

well off, wohlhabend

west, der Westen, -s; **—of,** westlich (*adj.*) von (*w. dat.*)

wet, naß

what (*inter.*), was; **—is today's date?** der wievielte ist heute (*or* den wievielten haben wir heute)?; **out of—?** woraus?; **with—?** womit?; (*inter. adj.*) welcher, welche, welches; (*adj. in excl.*) welch; **—a man!** welch ein Mann! **—time is it?** wieviel Uhr ist es? **—kind of,** was für ein, (*pl.*) was für

whatever, was; was . . . auch; **—he says,** was er auch sagt

wheel, das Rad, -(e)s, ¨-er

when, wann (*inter.*); (= *whenever*) wenn; (*relating to one def. past action*) als; **since—?** seit wann?

whenever, wenn

where, wo (*w. vb. of rest*); wohin (*w. vb. of motion*)

whether, ob

which, der, die, das; welcher, welche, welches; **—one?** welcher? welche? welches?

while (*conj.*), während; indem

while (*noun*), die Weile, —; **for a—,** eine Zeitlang; **a little—ago,** vor kurzer Zeit (*or* vor kurzem)

whisper, flüstern

whistle, pfeifen, pfiff, gepfiffen

white, weiß

who (*inter.*), wer

whoever, wer; wer . . . auch; **—she may be,** wer sie auch sein mag

whole, ganz

whom (*inter.*), wem (*dat.*), wen (*acc.*); (*rel.*) dem, der, dem, (*pl.*) denen (*dat.*); den, die, das, (*pl.*) die (*acc.*); (*or proper forms of* welcher)

whose (*inter.*), wessen; **at—house?** bei wem?

whose (*rel.*), dessen, deren, dessen, (*pl.*) deren

why, warum

wide, weit; breit; **a foot—,** einen Fuß breit

wife, die Frau, -, -en; die Gattin, -, -nen

wild, wild

will (*in fut. tense*), werden

will, der Wille, -ns, -n

win, siegen

wind, der Wind, -(e)s, -e

wind (*a watch*), aúfziehen (*str.*)

window, das Fenster, -s, -; **to the—,** ans Fenster; **at the—,** am Fenster; **to look out of the—,** zum Fenster hinaúsehen

windy, windig

wine, der Wein, -(e)s, -e

wing, der Flügel, -s, -

winter, der Winter, -s, -; **in—,** im Winter

wise, weise, klug

wish, der Wunsch, -es, ¨-e

wish, wollen, wollte, gewollt, will; wünschen (*w. zu & dep. inf.*); (= *to long for*) sich sehnen nach

with (*prep.*), mit, bei (*both w. dat.*); **to fall in love—,** sich verlieben in (*w. acc.*); **have you any money—you?** haben Sie etwas Geld bei sich?; **—what?** womit?; **—it,** damit

within (*prep.*), innerhalb (*w. gen.*); **—a short time,** in kurzer Zeit

without (*prep.*), ohne (*w. acc.*)

witness, der Zeuge, -n, -n; (*female*) die Zeugin, -, -nen

wolf, der Wolf, -(e)s, ̈-e

woman, die Frau, -, -en

wonderful, wunderbar

wood, das Holz, -es, ̈-er

wooden, hölzern

word, das Wort, -(e)s, ̈-er (*disconnected*), -e (*in connected discourse*); **he keeps his—,** er hält Wort

work, die Arbeit, -, -en; das Werk, -(e)s, -e; **Schiller's— s,** Schillers Werke

work, arbeiten; **to—hard,** schwer (fleißig *or* tüchtig) arbeiten; **to go to—,** an die Arbeit gehen

workshop, die Werkstätte, -, -n

world, die Welt, -, -en

worry about (= *be anxious*), sich (*dat.*) Sorgen machen um; (= *bother about*) sich (*acc.*) kümmern um

worth (*adj.*), wert; **it is—a dollar,** es ist einen Dollar (*acc.*) wert; **it is not—the trouble,** es ist nicht der Mühe (*gen.*) wert; **five marks'—of sugar,** für fünf Mark Zucker

worth, der Wert, -(e)s, -e

worthy of, würdig (*w. gen.*)

would:—like, möchte (gern) (*w. inf.*); **he—like to go to the theater,** er möchte (gern) ins Theater gehen

wrap up, einwickeln; **wrap it up in clean paper,** wickeln Sie es in sauberes Papier ein!

wrestle, ringen, rang, gerungen, ringt

write, schreiben, schrieb, geschrieben; **—on the (black)board,** an die Tafel schreiben; **I wrote my friend a letter,** ich habe meinem Freund einen Brief geschrieben (*or* ich habe einen Brief an meinen Freund geschrieben)

writing (*noun*), das Schreiben, -s; **—is difficult for him,** das Schreiben ist (*or* fällt) ihm schwer

written (*adj.*), schriftlich

wrong: he is—, er hat unrecht

Y

yard (*courtyard*), der Hof, -(e)s, ̈-e

year, das Jahr, -(e)s, -e; **leap—,** das Schaltjahr; **she is five—s, old,** sie ist fünf Jahre alt

yell, schreien, schrie, geschrien

yellow, gelb

yes, ja; **—indeed,** jawohl

yesterday, gestern; **day before—,** vorgestern

yet noch; **not—,** noch nicht; (= *nevertheless*) doch

you, du, ihr, Sie (*nom.*); dir, euch, Ihnen (*dat.*); dich, euch, Sie (*acc.*)

young, jung

your (*poss.*), dein, deine, dein (*sing. fam.*); euer, eu(e)re, euer (*pl. fam.*); Ihr, Ihre, Ihr (*formal*)

yours (*poss. pron.*), deiner, deine, deines; eurer, eure, eures; Ihrer, Ihre, Ihres

yourself (*refl. pron.*), dich, euch, sich (*all acc.*); dir, euch, sich (*all dat.*); (*intens.*) du, ihr, Sie selbst (*or* selber)

youth, die Jugend, -

Z

zeal, der Eifer, -s

zealous, eifrig

zero, die Null, -, -en

zero hour, die Angriffzeit, -; die Nullzeit, -

zoölogical, zoologisch; **—garden,** der Tiergarten, -s, ̈-; der zoologische Garten

zoölogy, die Zoologie, -; die Tierkunde, -

Index